W9-ACB-090

THE MEMORY OF CERTAIN PERSONS

THE MEMORY
OF
CERTAIN PERSONS

BY

John Erskine

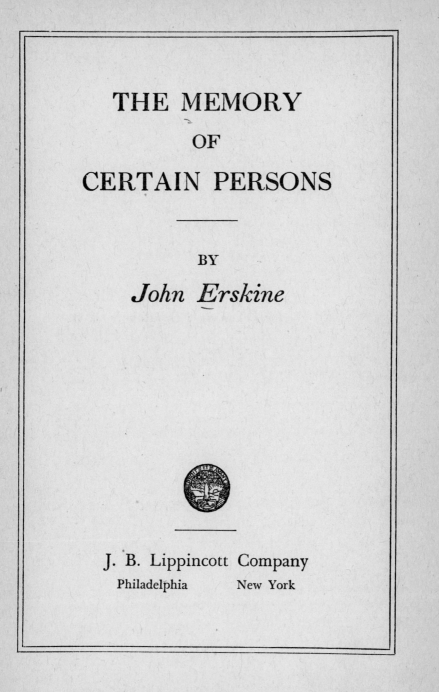

J. B. Lippincott Company
Philadelphia   New York

CONTENTS

Part I: 1879–1903

Part II: 1903–1909

Part III: 1909–1917

PART I

1879–1903

First Visit to New York

I

I WAS born on October 5, 1879, in a brownstone house at 108 East Forty-fifth Street. The house long ago made way for a succession of other buildings, last of all for the Grand Central Annex. The section of this large structure which stands immediately above my birthplace, has an importance to which I in a modest fashion still contribute. It contains the office of the Federal Tax Collector.

My arrival at 108 was expected, but not quite so soon, and Father—it was before telephones—hurried off in the night to wake the doctor. When I say hurried, I mean he urged the cabby to drive faster. When he got back, Mother and I were expressing our thanks to Mrs. O'Reilly, a neighborhood midwife. Nine or ten years later I was troubled to learn I had been helped into this world by a person without a medical degree.

Our household, when I joined it, consisted of my parents, my sister Anna Graham, known to me always as Sister, my senior by a year and ten months—and two aunts, Annabella and Margaret, whom Sister and I renamed Nanna and Memmem. Without these sisters of my mother in it, I cannot remember my father's home. Neither could he.

When I was three years old we moved to 6 West One Hundred Twenty-fourth Street, where on January 30, 1883, was born my second sister, Helen, whose great qualities, at first sight, I underestimated. The truth is, only two memories survive in me from this period, and both are self-centered.

On pleasant evenings in spring or early autumn I walked with Father and Mother to an establishment not unlike a farmhouse, with a yard around it. Entering the yard, which I still see clearly, if perhaps inaccurately, we approached a low window, on the ground level. The window was open, and I could see women in cool clean dresses busy in a kind of cellar. Father reached down and handed one of them a pail, which she promptly returned full of warm milk.

My mother years later assured me that this Harlem memory is essentially correct. In the days before bottles and pasteurizing, the milk wagon on its rounds dipped out any desired quantity from large cans, but I made myself a nuisance by insisting on the produce of one dairy near our home, and I liked to fetch it myself. The rest of the family were content with what the wagon delivered. No doubt we all drank the same milk.

And I remember being taken to Mt. Morris Park on a sled, one winter day, to slide down the incline just inside the entrance. There were, and still are, four entrances, and at each the path slopes for a yard or two. The fall must be as much as six inches. I am uncertain at which entrance I did my coasting, but the excitement was breath taking.

My love for the sea, I am told, showed itself early. When the heat of my first summers pulled me down, Mother and Nanna would take me, with a blanket and a lunch basket, to Coney Island. There for the whole day I slept off and on, absorbed nourishment likewise, and applauded the breaking waves. I dare say I draw on later visits to piece out the first thin recollections. We voyaged to Coney Island, of course, by water, on a gallant vessel of the fleet maintained by the Iron Steamboat Company. I learned to wait for the cool shock of ocean air, as the side-wheeler paddled down the bay. A harp and a violin entertained us on deck, playing pieces which all sounded alike. Never since have I heard music so haunting and wistful. From observation I concluded, far too hastily, that a good violin can be known by the powdered rosin it carries, in a little mound, just in front of the bridge.

As for the Island itself in those days, it was still undeveloped, even a little wild. The warm sand seemed to stretch further than now at Jones' Beach. There were no boardwalks, no hot dogs, I had almost said no people—nothing but sky and ocean and fierce sunlight, and a strong salty breeze.

With an effort I could pretend I remember one more incident from my furthest years, since my parents often spoke of it. Father belonged to a choral group of some thirty or forty amateurs who rehearsed around at each other's homes, and during one of these meetings, at our house in One Hundred Twenty-fourth Street, I made my first appearance in musical society. Arthur Woodruff was conducting. Mother set me in a chair at the door of the room, to listen. At first I was not noticed, but halfway through the piece the singers stopped abruptly, startled by their effect on me. According to Father my eyes were dilated and staring, I was in a trance, hypnotized. Here I should like to give the name of the music that thrilled me, but I fear that what my dear father took for evidence of precocious sensibility was only a concentrated effort to stay awake.

2

In my fifth year Father started to build a home across the Hudson River, in Weehawken, and my earliest and briefest sojourn in my native city came to an end. Before I go on to the better-remembered passages of boyhood and youth, let me sketch in preliminary outline the portraits of both parents, of Nanna and Memmem, of all who belonged to my first New York period, but whose character and whose story I learned in full only as I grew up.

My parents were James Morrison Erskine and Eliza Jane Hollingsworth. My young father, twenty-eight years old at my birth, had a silk factory on Forty-fifth Street, between Tenth Avenue and Eleventh. The business, founded by my grandfather in 1841, under the same name, John Erskine and Company, was carried on by him and by my father after him until 1912. Only a few months before I was born, my grandfather died, leaving a terrific burden for Father. Not only his own growing family but his mother, his brothers, his sisters and some cousins, had their support from his ribbon making. Associated with him at various times and in various degrees were his brothers John, Arthur, William and Charles, and during my youth Uncle Will and Uncle Charlie were his partners.

Father was the wistful kind of Scot, only through moral obligation a businessman. With fewer relatives to care for, he might have followed his bent toward music or history. Mother's temperament came from Yorkshire. There was something of Scotland in her too, and something of Ireland, but she and Father were totally unlike. He was very tall, six-feet-two or more; she was very short. He was gentle, thoughtful, scholarly, affectionate but slightly reserved, always balanced and self-controlled; she had a keenness of mind which could embarrass, and a wit that could be devastating. She was full of headlong admirations and magnificent prejudices. I adored her. She was an explosive reservoir of force—and of fun.

Out of a clear sky, one day, she teased Father about a girl he was engaged to when she met him. It was news to her children.

"Mother!" we exclaimed. "Don't say you had to snitch Dad!"

Father laughed, but she pressed on, apparently forgetting her diminutive stature. "Children, she was short! How ridiculous your father would have been, walking around with an abbreviated wife!"

They were lovers from the day they met till the hour they died.

She was two years younger than he. Aunt Memmem was slightly older. Sister invented her nickname, trying to say Margaret. There was an uncle, William Samuel Hollingsworth, older than Memmem. Sister and I, in our attempts at William, evolved a sound perilously close to Wee-wee. He was a small man, too, but he accepted the label with the best of humor, though it provoked amazement in visitors. Nanna was the one fairly tall person in Mother's family. She was older than Wee-wee.

Memmem like Mother was short, but otherwise there was no resemblance. She was amusingly self-centered, she had no mind to speak of, and she spent her long life in a childish game of make-believe. I would remember her otherwise if I could, for to all of us, in childhood and later, she invariably showed affection in her own way, and she brought to our lives a fantastic color which may have influenced us, for better or for worse. She had a marked flair for style of all kinds, literary as well as sartorial. The sweep and pretension of her speech had no match in my experience, nor had the rhetoric and poetizing of her letters. She said nothing, but how she said it! Essentially an artist, she had as much distinction as can be applied from the outside. The amount of time that woman spent on her hats and gowns!

She was histrionic, to say it most agreeably. When my sister Lois died, in 1892, Memmem wore at the funeral the same mourning as Mother and Nanna, but either because she thought the costume becoming, or because it secured sympathetic attention from strangers, she continued to wear mourning for the rest of her life. Gradually she lengthened the veil until it obviously covered a grief-stricken widow, providing a sort of compensation, perhaps more than compensation, for the husband she never had. But of course, to play the part effectively, a wedding ring was needed. In time the ring appeared on her left hand. From then on she was a full-fledged relict, cherishing intimate memories. Where the ring came from, she never told. One inquirer she disposed of by suggesting that even in a callous epoch, some things should remain sacred.

Nanna had distinction of quite another kind. Whatever she did or said was touched by an inner nobleness. Her speech and her writing were direct and sincere, full of wit and good sense. She had one of the rarest of literary gifts, the ability to read with imagination. She was fond of history, but her favorite books were novels. So long as the story was well told, she could accept the illusion and think of the characters as real persons, with an existence outside the pages. Of *Rob Roy,* in her opinion a superlative masterpiece, I heard her say, "How do you suppose Di Vernon got on with that Osbaldistone boy? He was a pleasant young fellow, but I doubt if he ever amounted to much."

Between her and Memmem collisions were inevitable, and always dramatic. If Memmem had a small ache or twinge, she announced that she was going to die, so that we might have warning, and be adequately thankful when she recovered. I recall one occasion when, having been out in the rain, she sent word to the doctor that pneumonia threatened. Instead of replying in person, the doctor, who knew her well, had a mean-tasting tonic left at our door. Nanna took the concoction up to her.

In the sickroom Memmem was in the midst of her usual build-up: "Something tells me I shall not recover. Yet it may be as well! The hour arrives for us all, and worse things might happen than to be summoned to our rest."

"Perhaps you are right," said Nanna, who disliked humbug. "It would be a waste of good tonic to pour this bottle into you. I will draw the shades and let you die in peace." Then she came down and put the medicine in the icebox, while Memmem had hysterics upstairs. As a family we were not tranquil.

Let me say here, in case I forget it later, that Nanna was a genius in the garden. Anything she planted, just had to grow.

As for Uncle Wee-wee, he deserves a volume to himself. Indeed, he occupies considerable space in my story, *Mrs. Doratt,* where his looks, his manner of speaking, and one episode from his strange life, helped me to fill out the portrait of Maggie Doratt's husband. What impression he made on my infancy, I can guess at; he fascinated all children. He was a short man, high strung and tireless, yet in manner cool and deliberate. He was warmhearted and sensitive, very courtly in an old fashion; his taste was fastidious in books, paintings, music and food, and he liked, really liked, the society of the intelligent, preferably the well-traveled and sophisticated. He spoke slowly, choosing his words, and what he said struck you at once as even more important than the way he said it, and behind the large thought and the precise word you were aware of a furnace or boiler, which might blow up at any minute. The possibility of explosion caught your attention, and the iron self-control inspired awe. No matter what the provocation, he never raised his voice, never swore. When shocked or exasperated, he would go so far as to say "Dear me!" or "I declare!"

As I grew up I learned the range of his accomplishments. Father was an excellent swimmer, but Uncle Wee-wee was prodigious. Father could ride or drive a horse, but it is hardly an exaggeration to say that Uncle Wee-wee could hold his own with any professional jockey or trainer. I admired him for these skills years before I began to wonder how he acquired them. Father and Mother were quite masterly at old-fashioned whist, but Uncle Wee-wee could clean out anyone in a game of cards, or indeed in any game of chance. I was never told how this part of his education came to him, but now I can guess.

Father and he, though poles apart, were fond of each other. Memmem admired him without reservation. Mother and Nanna loved him, but always seemed concerned for his fate. This attitude of theirs impressed my early years, and gave him a somewhat frightening charm.

He succeeded in whatever he undertook, but success bored him, as soon as it was assured. He understood the advantages and admired the virtues of a sane life, but he was drawn to risks as another might be to a drug. I remember no man more brilliant, and none more unhappy. If I introduce him here at length, it is because he influenced me greatly, and in some corners of my heart I need him to explain myself. His knowledge and judgment of books was above anything I encountered until I went among scholars and creators. My natural inclination to literature he encouraged with eye-opening talk whenever we met. His own library was strong in eighteenth century writers.

At the time of my birth he was manufacturing brushes and amassing wealth, but since the brush business was too safe to be interesting, he looked around for a little engrossing danger, and by conscientious search managed to find it.

3

Father's one great hobby was music. Mother's square piano stood in the parlor, but thanks to me and my sisters she was too busy to play it, and I did not know she could, until one Sunday morning when her children were shut in the house with colds, and she was hard put to keep us amused. Aware of the effect she was creating, she sat down at the piano and got her hands ready above the keys. "Children," she announced, "I am in the mood to perform!" We challenged her to go ahead, and wonder of wonders, she did. Had she turned a somersault, we should not have been more astounded.

Even if there had been leisure in her days, I doubt if she would have played much. What she liked best in music was Father's really remarkable singing. He had a fine tenor voice, well trained, and he derived a peculiarly British pleasure from singing in choruses. While I was finishing out my first three years he was a member of the Oratorio Society, under the leadership of Dr. Leopold Damrosch, and on Sundays he sang in the volunteer double quartet of St. Bartholomew's Church, then at Madison Avenue and Forty-fourth Street. In that respectable organ loft I believe he saw as much of Bohemia, of the manners and morals of society's Left Bank, as he was destined to know. And saint though he was, he enjoyed the glimpse, and told me about it later with immense gusto.

The organist who presided over the music in the gallery of old St. Bartholomew's, was a certain General Charles C. Dodge, a reasonably worldly person, drawn into the house of God by the opportunity to play the organ, which he did very well, according to Father. The General was wealthy. Foreseeing the possibility that he might not always care to get out of bed Sunday morning, he had a bright young substitute ready at hand, to serve as librarian when the General was in place, as I believe he usually was, and invariably to play the postludes, since the General, as soon as the congregation started to go home, wanted to go too—or perhaps he needed a word with Mrs. Imogen Brown, his soprano soloist, famed in New York fifty years ago for beauty as well as for a lovely voice. The young librarian and substitute organist was Carl Walter, my father's life-long friend and the best piano teacher I had in my youth.

In addition to the volunteer double quartet, the choir included, for backbone and glory, a professional quartet, very professional indeed. I have named the soprano. Fritz Remmertz was the bass. I suppose the amateurs had whatever is, for choir singers, a normal share of piety, but not an ounce of it could have been detected among the solo quartet. The Rector of St. Bartholomew's at the time was Dr. Samuel Cooke, a gracious gentleman of advancing years, innocent in the twofold sense of blamelessness and ignorance. His four most valuable singers spent Saturday nights giving concerts at the ends of the earth, or having a good time nearer home. Sunday morning, as the service was beginning, they would arrive in the choir loft, just aroused from sleep, or just off a train, usually without breakfast. The General, humane and practical, established a kind of room service to the choir loft from a neighboring hotel in Forty-second Street. During the prelude the quartet fortified themselves with hot coffee, or if their energies were unusually depleted, they would risk an egg or two and some toast. While sipping and munching, they gazed down over the balcony rail at the latest fashion in bonnets and bald heads, all bowed in preliminary prayer. When it came time for the first hymn, they set down the coffee cups and melted the congregation to tears by the clear perfection of their tones, and the devotional quality of their interpretation.

CHAPTER II

The Home in Old Weehawken

I

FATHER took his family to New Jersey because he had decided, in 1883, to move his expanding business there. Having started to build his new factory, he planned a new home, close by.

The factory was in Union Hill, on Kossuth Street, near Pleasant Avenue. Union Hill, now Union City, adjoins Weehawken, the township which stretches along the Palisades from Hoboken to Fort Lee.

Pleasant Avenue is a short street running down a hill into the Boulevard, the main artery of traffic from Union City through Hoboken to New York. Father built our new home at the point where Pleasant Avenue meets the Boulevard. The factory was finished before the house, and to be near his work Father rented a house in Hoboken, and there we waited for the Weehawken masons and carpenters to get out and let us in.

My memories of Hoboken during that temporary residence are dim and few, but they are of experiences I lived and felt for myself, my earliest conscious sampling of the world at first hand. Even in 1885, Hoboken was important for its railroads and its shipping, but it still had certain romantic village qualities, now almost or quite obliterated. I was not conscious of the transatlantic German liners which docked on our shore, nor of the excellent hotels, some like Meyer's still in use, where travelers came from New York and spent the night, to enjoy excellent food and drink, and yet be on hand for an early sailing. Where or how the Delaware, Lackawanna, or the Erie, or any other road got its patrons to the ferries, and so to New York—these and other such matters were hidden from me. But I remember peaceful broad streets, lined with shade trees, and spacious substantial brick houses, very attractive to those New Yorkers who had begun to weary of brownstone fronts. From the river would come the sound of a boat whistle, from the sidewalks the brush of a footstep or the tap of a cane, from the cobblestones, at long intervals, the rattle of a delivery wagon or a private carriage.

Along the river there were parks, with restaurants or pavilions, where on Saturday afternoons and Sundays excellent music was dispensed, and probably more excellent beer. The largest of these playgrounds was called the Elysian Fields. I appproved of it. Whenever Mother or Nanna, or both, took us to walk there, I pestered them until they let me take off shoes and stockings, and wade among the low slippery rocks along the shore. Helen looked on from her baby carriage, or slept in it; Sister, always my devoted guardian, hovered about with cautions and advice. I fear I have repaid a lifetime of affectionate warnings chiefly by heeding them as little as possible. One day the counsel to avoid all slippery rocks was reinforced by Mother's plain order to have nothing to do with one rock in particular, a green slime-covered boulder. I had not noticed it before, but from what Mother said I judged it might be interesting. When the family eyes were turned elsewhere, I stepped boldly up, and without loss of time bumped down again, and disappeared into the water. Nanna fished me out, and Mother went home for dry clothes. I can still feel the ignominy of being stripped naked and dried off in public by my resolute aunt, who would restore circulation and save me from pneumonia, even though she rubbed off my hide. Where she found the towel, I cannot say, but she polished me in full view of passing grownups, whose superior smiles made me wish I had drowned.

My memories of the home in Bloomfield Street are connected with the living room, behind the parlor. We must have been on the west side of the street, since the living-room windows looked out, across a garden, on sunsets. I have no image of the parlor, and none of the dining room, but against the northern wall of the living room was Mother's square piano, and along the southern wall were bookcases and a sofa. It must have been the family habit to gather here on Sunday afternoons and holidays; I remember it always by daylight, and always full of people.

In this room I made my first contact with the problem of spelling. I can see myself near a window, studying a page of large black letters, the charm of which had nothing to do with words, nor with the meaning of words; those letters were worth while, just for themselves. By this time

I must have seen many pages of music, yet I have no such memory of notes as I have of letters. I suppose I was busy taking music in through the ear, with special attention to Father's voice as it came upstairs to me in my bed, the nights when an accompanist played for him. If I can truthfully say I could read music before I could read letters, I must add that I was an atrocious speller.

Hoboken had two Episcopal churches, Trinity and St. Paul's. My parents first attended Trinity, for the reason that they had known the rector, the Reverend George C. Houghton, in New York. When Dr. Houghton returned to Manhattan to be Rector of the Little Church Around the Corner, we transferred our patronage to St. Paul's, over which the Reverend William R. Jenvey presided. I rather liked being taken to church. I liked the music. Perhaps I liked the prayers and the sermons too, or absorbed profit from them unconsciously. But on everything except the music, memory is a blank. That is, with two exceptions. In the congregation at St. Paul's there was a tall boy, who seemed to me a grown man, and Father said he played tennis well. I did not then know what tennis was, but later I found out, and when Richard Stevens became a figure in tournaments, a specialist in long drives from the base line, I thought of him as he was in boyhood, at St. Paul's. And an older person caught my attention in the same parish, a tall serious young man who rarely if ever smiled, and Father said he spent long hours in a room he had constructed in his cellar, for the strange purpose of splitting stones and studying them under a microscope. Father said it was important work, and I might as well remember the young man's name, because he would be highly thought of. So I learned the name by heart, for future reference—George F. Kuntz. Years later I met him often again in New York, when his preëminence as expert in precious stones was established. But he had not learned to smile, not easily. Perhaps a knowledge of diamonds does not necessarily produce an inner sparkle.

Father's best Hoboken friend was Dr. Romeo Chabert, a French surgeon, noted in his day, the leader of his profession throughout Hudson County. He served us devotedly as family physician while we lived in New Jersey. In appearance he resembled the elderly Frenchmen in Daumier's drawings. He was stocky in build, his chin and his upper lip were shaved clean, and he wore side whiskers, well combed out and flowing. His grandfather had been a surgeon in Napoleon's armies, and Dr. Chabert, like Balzac, was proud of the historical distinction. This, of course, I learned much later.

He was a remarkable linguist. In addition to his beautiful French, he commanded fastidiously correct English, and his Spanish, Italian and Portuguese were certainly fluent, and no doubt otherwise admirable. His library contained works in all the languages he spoke. On my own shelves today are some of these books, the gift of his family in remembrance of him. I value particularly a Pickering edition of *The Decameron,* in three volumes, 1825, and a large French-Italian and Italian-French dictionary, in two volumes, which for forty-five years I have consulted constantly, improving myself, I hope, in two languages at once.

Dr. Chabert was the first gourmet I knew, and of a type no longer extant. His exquisite consideration of the palate was carried to lengths. Not only must his food be carefully selected and properly cooked, but he insisted that it be served at the right temperature, and kept there. I discovered this philosophy of his early, soon after I observed his whiskers. Invited, with other children, to his lunch table, I beheld food served to all guests, whether young or grown, on hollow plates filled with hot water.

2

We moved up to the new home in the autumn, though it was not yet completed, and the grounds continued rather messy until the following summer.

The house, though large and comfortable, was architecturally atrocious. Whoever persuaded Father to put up such a mistake must have been a doubtful character. But the location was superb. Some fifty or seventy-five feet above the Point, it provided a long view up the Boulevard, and a still longer one down the ravine through which the Boulevard sank toward Hoboken. In the distance beyond the Hoboken shore we could see the river to lower New York. At the Boulevard end of our property stood a large oak tree, under which we spent many hours in warm weather. Here on a sleepy Sunday afternoon Father would organize his telescope and set his watch. In his factory there were chronometers of extreme accuracy, but it amused him to take his time from the face of the City Hall clock.

Since Pleasant Avenue, in front of our door, was the dividing line between the two townships, our home was in Weehawken, and the factory, which we could see from our windows, was in Union Hill. We children realized before long that we were living on the edge of a strong contrast. Across the street was a thriving settlement, promising some day to be an industrial city, but on our side along the Palisades stretched a row of large estates, the residences of old families who had roots in the history of the Hudson River Valley, or of New York, or of Staten Island. Union Hill, we felt, had a vigorous future, and meanwhile its crudities might be overlooked. Weehawken, on the other hand, had a ripe, aristocratic past. Perhaps we believed, I am sure I did, that Union Hill as it grew in age, would mellow and change its nature and become stately and patriarchal, like old Weehawken.

Of course Union Hill was aristocratic in its own way. The inhabitants, were almost all German, and their chief local industry, until the coming of several silk mills, was the manufacture and consumption of beer. The William Peters brewery, a large structure, could be seen, and in a favorable wind smelled, from our house. Mr. Peters himself was a familiar and honored neighbor. Indeed, the old-fashioned Germans connected with the brewing business made an impression on me so fine and so lasting that I have never felt at ease among prohibitionists or teetotalers. I saw among the Union Hill families great loyalty and affection, warm comradeship, fondness for music, especially in choral groups, and lovely traditions, especially at Christmas time.

Father's silk weavers were German and Swiss, with a few French, all of them artisans of great skill, since he specialized in fancy ribbons and sashes, which had to be made on complicated Jacquard looms. The weavers and the machinists got on well with the beermakers. The community maintained a Schützen Park, a mile or so south of the factory, and on Saturdays, Sundays or holidays the male citizens would march off in a body for a little target practice. They usually paraded past our house, in the middle of the dusty street, their wives trudging along the sidewalk, admiring Papa, dragging the children after them, and carrying heavy lunch baskets. The men always marched in companies. For uniform they wore Prince Albert coats and derby hats, and a broad sash across the bosom and over the shoulder, tied in a bow at the left side, where a sword would have hung if they had worn swords. Since most of them were rather stout, they seemed like cartoon figures out of *Fliegende Blaetter*.

I was too young to be invited to any of these *Fests,* though Father's weavers treated me as if I belonged to them, and would gladly have taken me along. I cannot say how good their marksmanship was, nor how keen was their interest in it. I think they enjoyed picnicking with their families, and talking among themselves. I wish I had been old enough to know what they talked about. No doubt it was politics, but I wonder if it was American politics, or European.

Of the estates which gave Weehawken its character, Mr. Gracie King owned the one furthest south, Highview, overlooking Hoboken, with a distant but clear view of the Stevens estate, on Castle Point. North of the King acres came the Duer estate, and north of that a succession of large places, stone houses suggesting English manors, and parklike grounds. Hawkshurst, the home of Mr. Edward Duer, was nearest, in a grove of stately trees, directly across the Boulevard from our modest home. Father and Mr. Duer were associated in neighborhood philanthropies, and isolated though all families were along the Weehawken Palisades, the Duer children were to some extent our playmates and companions. Sunday mornings we went to church and came back together, filling a good part of the car which plied between Weehawken and Hoboken. Once, when Helen was old enough to come with us, Mother placed her on the car seat between Sarah Duer and me, Sarah being of my advanced age. Helen wanted to stand on the seat, for a better view out the window, and I told her to sit down. I probably wanted to impress Sarah with my sense of decorum. But my small sister, having a mind of her own, continued as she was, and Sarah gave me a sympathetic smile, as much as to say that children will be children.

Mr. Duer was tall and held himself very erect. My sisters and I noted his resemblance to the Earl in *Little Lord Fauntleroy*. His family had been leaders in New York State since before the Revolution. William Alexander Duer was President of Columbia College from 1828 to 1842, and a daughter of his became Mrs. Gracie King. Weehawken reeked with ancestry and genealogy. Mrs. Edward Duer, a granddaughter of Martin Van Buren, was a gracious and sweet lady, who managed to seem delightfully cordial even while holding herself aloof from the world, especially from her own children, to whom she referred as "those Duers." On the churchgoing trips to Hoboken, she always sat in the opposite end of the car from them.

On Pleasant Avenue, two or three blocks from us, on the Weehawken side, another series of spacious homes began, but they lined a private avenue or lane, which was entered through a gate, and they stood fairly close together. I remember little about this secluded neighborhood, except that a Mr. Stagg lived in one of the houses. He stays in my mind because he rode a fine horse, and always waved to me as he pranced past.

And with my own eyes I once saw what these sequestered mansions were like inside. The Episcopalians of Weehawken and Union Hill, having traveled enough on the Hoboken car, were raising money for a church of their own. There was a welter of fairs and bazaars, and I wanted to do my share of ticket peddling from door to door. At five-thirty or six on an autumn day I rang the bell at a house in Mr. Stagg's lane. When I told my errand, the maid said that Mrs. So-and-So might not be at home, but she would speak to Miss So-and-So. The names have gone from me, forever. While she was reporting me and what I came for, I had a good look at an immense entrance hall. The floor was laid in squares of black and white marble. There was a heavy walnut staircase. Against the wall were tables or chests with mirrors above them, flanked by tall candles. I noticed the candles because our house was lighted by gas. Probably this house was too, but at the moment candles burned. Then down the stairs came a beautiful lady of mature years, perhaps twenty-two or twenty-three. She transported me to bliss by buying four tickets, the price being a quarter, but she saddened me by conveying by subtle hint the possibility that though she had invested so much in the entertainment, she might not attend. So far as I know, I never saw her again.

Perhaps the influence of all the Weehawken memories kept me for years from observing real life, from seeing the America of the moment, which foretold the future. When Father built his home between Pleasant Avenue and the Boulevard, he believed, as I often heard him say, that a district so lovely, with vistas of the great city, its rivers and its bay, would always contain the homes of those who like quiet and solitude. He guessed wrong. The houses in Stagg's Lane have long since been torn down. The people who lived in them have no place in history. They were well-to-do and cultured, but they were trying to live in an age which was already passing. I remember them as charming ghosts.

The larger estates along the Palisades have also disappeared. The Duer home, the noble house and the deer park behind it, have been wiped out by the spread of population and business. Over the very spot where our house stood, runs the northern Jersey approach to the Lincoln Tunnel. As I write, however, the factory building on Kossuth Street still stands, now occupied by candy-makers. In the brick wall of Father's old office the scars still show where once the brass plate was fastened, with the name, John Erskine and Company.

3

No sooner were we moved into the Weehawken house than our parents started Sister and me on our education. Let me record in gratitude that they understood education in a large and broad sense. To educate me they provided several governesses, an intelligent horse, and a goat.

Since there were no schools in the neighborhood, the governesses were imported daily from Hoboken. They were rather remarkable women, all of them, and I owe to them a good beginning in languages, history and literature, subjects to which I was naturally disposed. The first teacher was Miss Etta Burhorn, a native of Switzerland, if I remember correctly. She wrestled with my primal ignorance, and gave me, Heaven knows how, a taste for European culture. She also subjected me to my first consecutive music lessons. Our second teacher was Miss Antoinette Chipchase, as lovable and affectionate a person as I have met, who continued her interest in her pupils through long and happy years, until her death, August 20, 1943. She was a thorough teacher, with a gift for persuading at least one indolent child that he ought to work. Her argument was based on the practical consideration that no subject is hard if you master all the steps, but whatever you skimp or skip will prove later the one thing you need.

Our next and final governess was Miss Mary Steele Harvey, who lived with her widowed mother and her brother Carroll. Mrs. Harvey taught the Duer children, and Miss Harvey taught us until my sisters and I went to school in New York. She then entered upon an interesting career in social work, at the end of her life holding an important post with the police department of Baltimore. She said it was contact with me that turned her thoughts to the wayward.

In 1886 Father bought us a horse. In the stable at the factory there were horses for the business wagon and the family carriages, but he wished us to have a small and gentle animal of our own, at whose expense we could learn to ride and drive. He found for us Bessie, a paragon. She played a notable part in our upbringing, and until her early thirties she was a member of the family. She would have been a valuable mare, had she not been a little short in front; her legs from the knee down were badly proportioned to the upper structure, and her step, consequently, was slightly staccato. Father gladly overlooked the defect because of her unusual intelligence. When she came to us, in her extreme youth, she already had enough tricks for a circus career. She could drink beer out of a glass, and was glad to do so. She was schooled in gaits, and if you said good morning to her, she would hold up her right forehoof to shake hands, and if you then said you would rather shake the other leg, she obliged at once with the left.

Father did not encourage her beer drinking, but we taught her all we could, and she taught us much more. She always knew who was driving her, and who was in the carriage. If Sister or I had the reins, with Nanna along as protecting passenger, Bessie did what she thought good for us, choosing her own speed, and at each stop pulling as close to the curb as she wished, but no closer. But if Father was with us, her behavior took on style and precision, and she obeyed the gentlest hint. We were taught to harness or saddle her, and if we wished to take her out, we were supposed to go to the stable and do this work for ourselves. If one of the stablemen wished to put the bit in her mouth, she would raise her stubborn head and resist, but when we children went into the stall with the bridle, she held her head down and let us slide the bit in. She had what in a human being would be called grandeur of character.

One dark rainy night I was sitting beside Father, as he drove the buggy rapidly. Streets were not lighted then, and at a place where the darkness was thick, Bessie put down all four feet and slid till she came to a stop, pitching us forward. Father got out to see what had happened. In front of Bessie a small boy was picking himself out of the mud. While running across the street, he had stumbled without our seeing him, but Bessie had turned herself into a sort of cow-catcher, and rolled him over and over.

She was with us, as I said, for many years, but the stay of the goat was fortunately brief. He was enormous, husky enough to pull an undersized but fairly heavy cart, and it was Father's kind idea that every morning our gardener-coachman should harness the beast, bring him over to our place, and hitch him to something until I should be free and disposed to play with him. I remember that goat with vividness and horror. His smell was terrible, and his manners were shocking. When I got into the cart and pulled a rein to guide him, he simply turned his head until his neck was folded back parallel to his spine, and in that posture he defied me to pull his head off. If I tried to start him, he declined to budge, but when I had given up in despair, more likely than not he would bolt off in a direction not of my choice, and nothing could stop him. One day, seeing another goat in the distance, he spilled me out of the cart, went through the fence and disappeared across Pleasant Avenue, taking a few pickets with him. Quite illogically, the prospect of losing him plunged me into tears, but the gardener caught him and brought him back.

Father, made thoughtful by the hole in our front fence, suggested that the goat might enjoy the run of the factory yard for a few days, until he became used to us and settled down. But there was an addition to the factory in process of building just then, and the contractor carelessly spread the plans on a table in the open air. The goat ate them all. From that moment Father's attitude was even less sympathetic than mine. I saw the goat no more. What disposition was made of him, Father never told me. I never asked.

CHAPTER III

The Home in Eightieth Street

I

BETWEEN 1886 and 1890 I discovered some remarkable facts about my parents. They had once been children more or less like me, and they too had had parents, who previously had had parents, and so on backward into a remote past, with which I, neither through merit nor through choice, was somehow bound up.

All this was revealed to me on visits to my grandmother's house in New York, at 128 East Eightieth Street—and on visits to Lansingburg, on the Hudson River above Troy, where once had lived another grandmother, whom I was not to see. In the Eightieth Street house my father had spend his youth. In Lansingburg my mother had spent her girlhood.

The house in Eightieth Street was for my childhood indescribably alluring. Though full of long-accumulated memories, it was free from any museum or mortuary atmosphere. On one side of the living room or back parlor was a two-manual organ, which at an early age I used to pump up and run over the pedals, hoping in vain to touch them all before someone stopped me. In a corner of the bookcase was Uncle Arthur's flute, carefully laid away, just as it was when he last played it. My grandmother liked to recall days when her large and still unbroken family had made music together, one child at the piano, one at the organ, my grandfather with his violin, Uncle Arthur with his flute, Uncle Will with his 'cello. There were one or two left over who played no instrument, but they all would sing.

My grandmother was six feet tall, and straight as an Indian. I recall in

affectionate detail the length of her black skirts, the snug-fitting black bod-
ice, the white ruching at neck and wrists, the white cap which always covered her white hair. She was everything a fabulous grandmother should be,
inventor of delicious surprises, storehouse of family legend and anecdote,
incomparable playmate. On our visits to her, on her visits to Weehawken, my sisters and I tried to conceal our confidence that she had
presents for us. Our manners may have been transparent. She wore an
underskirt as long as her gown, with a deep pocket on each side. After
the first greetings were over she would sit straight in her chair and talk
with Mother, about anything at all, as it seemed to her grandchildren,
and being a grand tease, she talked at length. Then, as though absent-
minded, she would reach down, grope among her voluminous garments,
and discover to her own surprise a toy for each of us, and a box of candy.
That accounted for one pocket! An hour later she would think of the
other, and behold, it would produce better results than the first!

She was born in Lanark, Canada, the fifth of thirteen children, all of
whom, after her mother's early death, she cared for, cooking for them,
making their clothes, cobbling their shoes. Her grandparents in Govern,
Scotland, had been persons of local consequence, but during her childhood
and youth she knew nothing but hardship and poverty. There was one
brightening moment when her father brought his large brood to New
Hartford, New York, but the moving accomplished, he immediately died,
and she was left to look after her brothers and sisters as usual, incidentally
working in a mill for a small wage, and getting herself, on the side, some
sort of education. She wrote well, but I doubt if she had much acquaintance with books. She had been rather busy. But she had wisdom of
another kind. When I was graduated from kilts into short trousers, she
gave me my first grown-up outfit. Mother and she took me to Brokaw's,
then on Astor Place. The trousers and the jacket fascinated me chiefly
from the social and esthetic points of view, but Grandma fingered the
goods as though there were nothing to a suit but wearing qualities. For
the moment, I feared she lacked imagination.

The first night I ever spent away from home, I spent with her. There
must have been debate as to my ability to prove a contented guest without
Sister or Mother or Father, but Grandma wanted me, and the experiment
was made. Mother brought me in from Hoboken, and with heartless
contentment I saw her start back again alone. Had I thought of it, I
might have contrived a tear or two, or at least a troubled glance, but I

really was enjoying myself immensely. As night came on I talked rather more than was necessary, less to entertain Grandma and my aunts than to demonstrate that I was fit for the great world, and could stay awake after eight o'clock. But the demonstration bogged down, and I accepted an invitation to retire, asleep before my head touched the pillow. Grandma had me sleep in her bed for safety.

After the edge of drowsiness had been taken off, I heard the roar of the elevated train over on Third Avenue. The cars were then drawn by real locomotives, which burned coal and made a startling racket. The city uptown was almost as quiet as Hoboken, and during the night it was rare that a footstep disturbed the street. Out of this stillness the elevated train approached with a far and faint rumble, gradually grew louder, passed with a roar, and then, by a well-managed decrescendo, disappeared into silence again. The effect was marvellous. I can see the room even now, the massive bed, my tall grandmother asleep beside me, the moonlight striking through the window and sending to the ceiling a reflection from the mirror on the dresser. By watching this reflection I kept awake till another train rose out of the night, and sank back again. I intended to listen for a third, but it was too long in coming.

Aunt Lizzie, Aunt 'Cilla, and Uncle Charlie, lived with Grandma. Uncle Will, like Father, had married and gone from the old house. Uncle Charlie, most attractive of bachelors, had a room and study on the top floor, and near the study window was an old-fashioned desk chair, a large comfortable seat with a swinging arm which you could draw in front of you to form a desk. I suppose Uncle Charlie used that desk in his student days, but I never saw him in it. I was in it myself whenever I could get to his room. Study or literary work was far from my thoughts, but the desk arm, when pulled around in front, offered a sunken inkwell, a choice of pens, and several well-sharpened pencils. Mechanical sharpeners were then unknown, and a point was whittled with a penknife. Uncle Charlie, like Father and Uncle Will, kept his knife in razor condition, and could sharpen a pencil with six strokes, equally spaced and ending miraculously in a point.

From our earliest years we were devoted to Uncle Charlie, and I connect him in memory with Weehawken, where he visited us frequently, always leaving behind him a new sense of his courtliness, his good humor, his love of a bright story. It seemed fitting to us children that when he married it should be to a woman as kindhearted as he, and strikingly handsome—Josephine Lucy Gillespie, our Aunt Josie.

Though Uncle Will was already married, he continues in my memories as a member of Grandma's household, perhaps because she loved to tell of his boyhood pranks. He was a very funny man, funny rather than humorous, and funny people, like funny books, are extremely rare. He resembled Father and Uncle Charlie in being courtly and genial, a person of essential dignity, but his instinctive solutions of problems and his comments on life provoked laughter. I believe his funmaking was automatic and unconscious. He had talent for machinery and for mechanical techniques, but he was not otherwise intellectual, any more than Grandma was.

Once when he was small he wanted to go out and join a game of marbles, but Grandma, who had shopping to do, told him to stay home and rock the baby's cradle, the baby being Uncle Charles. He obeyed with such eagerness, with so slight an air of grievance, that she lost confidence in him, and hurried back. Coming down the street she saw the game of marbles going strong in front of her house, Uncle Will quite plainly the liveliest player. But after each turn at the marbles he would pick up a piece of string and give it a pull. The cradle was on the third floor. He had threaded a ball of twine through a series of pulleys, down halls and up staircases, until he could rock the baby without missing the game.

When he was seventeen or eighteen, he went out one afternoon with a boy of his own age, and did not come home until dinner time, or later.

"Where in the world have you been, William?"

"I attended a funeral, Mother."

"Whose funeral?"

"A man's or a woman's, Mother. It seemed best not to ask which."

"Mercy me! What have you done?"

He and his friend, on an aimless stroll, had stopped respectfully as a casket was carried out of a house, and the funeral party got into the carriages. Uncle Will could look serious when he tried, and naturally he was mistaken for one of the mourners. There was one carriage left over, and the undertaker appealed solicitously to the bystanders on the sidewalk.

"Anyone else?"

"Come on, Ed," said Uncle Will, and they accepted the kind offer. At the cemetery they joined the group by the open grave, lifting their hats slightly, and once Uncle Will applied his handkerchief to the corner of his eye. He thought the bereaved family were diverted from their grief, trying to recall which distant relative he was. At the conclusion of the ceremonies he shook hands with those who wore the deepest mourning, taking care that his emotions made speech impossible. They in turn respected his sorrow and asked no questions. The ride back was delightful, and the carriage set him and his friend down at their separate homes.

In Father's family there was a clear-cut division of temperaments, which as I grew up I began to notice. In childhood I assumed uniformity among my relatives, since their affection for each other was obvious. But as I began to acquire intellectual interests, I saw that Father and Mother followed my doings with sympathy, and that Aunt Lizzie was ready to meet me on whatever ground I wished to explore, but instinctively I intruded neither my ambitions nor my new ideas upon Uncle Charlie, or Uncle Will, or Aunt 'Cilla. When I spoke of it to Father, he remarked that human beings usually differ, and he added the illuminating suggestion that perhaps Uncle Will had noted with regret my indifference to machines and the manual arts. His estimate of relatives Father always kept in the key of general principles.

Mother, however, never let charity spoil her aim when there was a nail to be hit on the head. She told me that after my grandfather's death and Uncle Arthur's, Father had been somewhat lonely among his people. He and Arthur, and to a less extent Aunt Lizzie, had inherited from Grandfather eager minds and scholarly tastes. Lovable though Grandma was, she and the children who took after her were perhaps unaware of my father's deepest interests. He had, I think, a genius for education, both the insatiable urge to acquire knowledge and the equal need and the ability to impart it. He was ready for college so early that my grandfather thought a year in business would mature him, and make later study more profitable. But Father found such pleasure in working with Grandfather, and he promptly made for himself so large a place in the business, that he could not leave it. With time he realized his loss, and he envied Uncle Charlie his course in the College of the City of New York, in the same class with Walter Damrosch and Vernon M. Davis— both good friends of mine years later.

Though Father came to regret his lack of thorough training in scholarly methods, he was not at first unhappy in business. On the contrary. The creative aspects of his ribbon making delighted the artist in him. He personally designed every piece of goods he made, and in this highly technical work his fellow manufacturers recognized him, I believe, as a master. But the day came when he saw the fashion move away from elaborate patterns and pure silk, to a plain synthetic product which could be turned out cheap on speed looms. He could make ribbons that way too, if nothing finer was wanted, but it broke his heart. I doubt if his brothers knew why he cared. They were fine sensible men, but they were not artists.

When I decided to give my life to books and teaching, Father encouraged me, though he might have been glad to see the business carried on by the son who was named after the founder. Once when I asked him what sort of person my grandfather was, he said quietly, "You have his tastes." When I reported this remark to Mother, she looked up with her usual protective alertness whenever one of her children received a possible head-turning compliment. "Your father flatters you! Your grandfather was an excellent man to have for an ancestor."

2

A crayon portrait of my grandfather hung on the living room wall in the Eightieth Street house. It hangs in my home now. It shows a large broad-shouldered man, with high forehead, prominent nose, large ears, mouth large and firm, dark brown hair sprinkled with gray, thick beard, the upper lip shaved clean. All the Erskines had that brown hair, with a slight tendency to curl, all except Uncle Will, whose hair was red. In sharp contrast, Mother's people were all black haired, slightly swarthy, with high cheekbones, as though they had somewhere met a Spaniard, long ago.

Grandma was vague about the early history of the Erskines, perhaps because for her the important member of the clan was the one she married. But Uncle Charlie liked to know what he came from, and in my childhood and at intervals thereafter he passed on his information.

I had a great-great-great-grandfather, Archibald, who sided with the exiled Stuarts in one of their attempts at a comeback, and after the customary defeat and collapse he took refuge, of all places, in Tyrone Country, Ireland. This legend may be founded on fact, but to me it makes little sense. Later Erskines were Presbyterians most of the time. At least that was the church they stayed away from. What Archibald was doing in the Stuart camp, I cannot imagine. And if he needed refuge, why did he seek it among the Protestants of Tyrone? And why did the family stay out of Scotland so long beyond the time necessary to cancel a political error?

Archibald had a son John, my great-great grandfather, born in Tyrone about 1755. His son, another John, my great-grandfather, was born in the same place in 1788. This John, at the age of twenty-six, married a girl named Elizabeth Clark, and for some twenty years he and she, with their offspring, shuttled back and forth from Tyrone to Glasgow, from Glasgow to Belfast, from Belfast to Glasgow again. I suppose he was following opportunities in his craft, which was linen weaving, in days when weavers were not factory hands but moved in society freely, individuals like other artists, setting up their looms in their own houses, and marketing their goods as they thought best. In 1836 this great-grandfather of mine, still bent on improving himself, left Greenock, suburb of Glasgow, for New York, on the sailing vessel *Glasgow*, Captain Griffith commanding. The crossing took seven weeks and two days. He made his first New York home in Perry Street, where there was a Scottish colony.

He must have been well supplied with energy, but the strong character in his household was his son John, my grandfather, born in Glasgow, May 4, 1815. It was he who at the age of twenty-one persuaded his elders to migrate. He wanted a more complete life than the old country could promise him. In particular he wanted music and books. On the sailing ship he brought along his violin, an undersized instrument of considerable age and good tone. Grandma told me that when they were first married he would practice in the kitchen, at the end of the day. He liked to smoke his pipe as he played, and in the kitchen he could send the smoke up the chimney. He was always, she said, a considerate man. I have his violin. His books were divided among his children, and I recall one of them on our Weehawken shelves, with marginal annotations in a firm hand.

He bequeathed to us his love of Scotland and Ireland and his respect for the English, with certain reservations. Music influenced his attitude. Brought up a Calvinist, he rebelled against that theology, still more against dreary psalm singing. In Glasgow there was an Anglican church, where he used to slip into the rear pew to enjoy the cheerful music. But he was a weaver, not one of the gentry, and perhaps his dress showed that he worked for his living. One Sunday some ass of a sexton got over to him the idea that all the pews, including the rear one, belonged to his betters, and perhaps he would be welcome in the Methodist chapel down the street. He became a Methodist. Never again did he set foot in an Anglican church, and only once in an Episcopal one, when years later in New York City my parents were married. I have from him a dislike of privileged or ruling classes and of snobs. Even now, when England talks to the United States about our common interest in democracy, the remembrance of my grandfather blunts for me, somewhat, the edge of the fine idea.

He prospered in business, weaving laces and silks instead of linen, and by the time he was twenty-six, five years after his arrival in New York, he owned his own factory, on Gansevoort Street. In 1856 he sold this factory to Fisher, the piano maker, and built another at 316-320 West Thirty-fourth Street. Here during the Civil War he made hoop skirts and bonnet wire. Nine years later he sold this second factory to the Steck Piano Company, and built a third on West Forty-fifth Street, from that time making only ribbons and sashes.

On July 3, 1843, he married Orcilla Graham. Their first home was on Twenty-eighth Street, but in 1856 he built at Riverdale the house now occupied by the headmaster of the Riverdale Country School. This location, however, proved too remote, and at the beginning of the Civil War he moved his family back to the city, to the house in East Eightieth Street.

CHAPTER IV

Lansingburg

I

IF THERE was a division of temperament in my father's family, there was a wide gulf in my mother's. I began to understand it only when Sister and I were taken on visits to Lansingburg. A hundred years ago, before the railroad out-distanced the canal, this quiet village seemed destined to thrive and grow. It attracted settlers from Great Britain, it boasted a few modest industries, such as book publishing, and some larger ones, chiefly brush- and varnish-making. When I first visited the place I noticed the ivy-covered churches, of a style I had seen in pictures of England. Most of the homes, I also noticed, were spacious and comfortable, but to what extent they showed English influence, I cannot say.

When we visited Lansingburg, we went up on the Albany boat, taking with us Bessie and the surrey. From Albany we drove the rest of the way, to the home of James McQuide, a distant relative and close friend of Mother's. The McQuide house was large, remarkable in my eyes for its outdoor summer kitchen. At the end of the garden was the McQuide brush factory, where I learned that paint brushes are themselves painted, and varnished besides. The information did me little good, since brushes are now made somewhat differently. But Mr. McQuide's son James had a tall velocipede, which he put at my disposal in the most comradely spirit, and I neglected the study of brushes in order to ride the machine up and down Lansingburg's brick sidewalks, under thick shade trees. On Sundays I was taken to church, and several times on weekdays to the churchyard, where Mother's mother lay buried, and Mother's brother

Robert, who died in the Civil War. I knew, before I was plainly told, that Lansingburg had once been Mother's home, and overhearing fragments of her conversations with Mrs. McQuide I gathered the gist of what had happened to Mother's mother, and I might have grasped more if my thoughts had not been on Jimmie McQuide's velocipede.

Mother was born, not in Lansingburg, but in Castle Wellan, Ireland. Castle Wellan is on the East coast, above Dublin. It pleased me to think that Mother was Irish, and consequently I was disappointed to learn that her folks came from Yorkshire, and that she was descended from Sir Charles Scarborough, Court physician of Charles II. Gradually acquiring information about the Merry Monarch, I was perplexed that a relative of Mother's had ever got into such bad company. My grandmother in the Lansingburg churchyard was Anne Scarborough. Her father, John Scarborough, was a British revenue officer stationed at Castle Wellan. His duties must have made him unpopular with the Irish.

On my first Lansingburg visit I was stunned, as you might say, to learn that after Anne Scarborough died her husband married again, and was still living. To think that I had an extra grandfather, perhaps just around the corner, whose acquaintance I had not made! I never saw him. Memmen and he exchanged letters, I believe, but Mother and Nanna had a grand feud with him, and kept it up till the day of his death. He was a varnish manufacturer, and in his later years an explosion in his factory rendered him stone deaf. Otherwise he might be living still, for he was essentially an indestructible person. But when well past eighty, crossing a railroad track one day, he inadvertently collided with a fast-approaching train.

Did I say Mother had a feud with him? More precisely she hated him, to the same degree that she worshipped and perhaps idealized the memory of Anne Scarborough.

Unless she exaggerated, this grandmother of mine was beautiful, with the bluest or grayest of eyes, the whitest of skins, the blackest of hair. I think this description indicates Mother's love for her parent, since neither side of my family has excelled in good looks, but I dare say my grandmother was fascinating, since all Scarboroughs are that. At Castle Wellan, Anne Scarborough fascinated a young curate. Also, she lost her heart to him. They both were, it might now seem, exasperatingly correct young things, according to the best Victorian or pre-Victorian models. They carried decorum, delicacy and sensitiveness to tragic exaggeration. Though they understood each other, the curate postponed any outright declaration until a hoped-for advancement in his profession might make his offer more attractive.

At Castle Wellan lived a gifted but erratic young English-Irishman named William Hollingsworth, a small man with an amazing mind and still more amazing audacity. He too loved Anne Scarborough, and whether or not he had more money than the curate he lost no time in proposing to her, and she lost none in rejecting him. But he was the last person in the world to be discouraged. He knew, of course, who his rival was, and he took pains to cultivate the curate's acquaintance, until he thought the poor fellow was ripe for plucking. Meeting him one day, apparently by chance, he took advantage of a casual reference, made by himself, to poison the curate's romance once for all. He did it by saying approximately this, that Anne Scarborough was a fine creature except for a weakness which often occurs in young and good-looking girls—she was a heartless flirt. When the curate protested, Hollingsworth smiled.

"Has she not permitted you to believe you have some claim on her hand?"

When the curate admitted that he hoped to marry her, his diabolical adversary kept after him.

"Did she ever tell you she is engaged to me?"

Thereupon the curate, being a sensitive and gullible soul, without giving Anne Scarborough a chance to defend herself, packed up and disappeared from Castle Wellan to parts unknown. My grandmother, in the dark as to what had happened, grieved for years, until convinced he had left for good. Meanwhile William Hollingsworth persisted in his courtship, and at last, following a dubious pattern to be found in old novels, she said there was perhaps no reason why at least one of them should not be happy.

So William Hollingsworth had his opportunity to be my maternal grandfather. Why he brought his bride to Lansingburg, I do not know. Perhaps he feared the curate might come again to Castle Wellan. But the curate, to bury his weak self and his unnecessary sorrow, came to America, and one Sunday, after Anne Scarborough had had her elder children and had made some progress toward resignation, he preached in the Lansingburg church, and found her in the congregation. They met for a few minutes alone, and she learned what William Hollingsworth had done.

Mother was Anne Scarborough's youngest child. William Hollingsworth took his wife back to Castle Wellan on a visit in order that this child might be born there. When she was a few weeks old they returned to Lansingburg, where the other children had been left. Why was this difficult trip undertaken, with its two ocean crossings? Did my grandmother crave one more sight of the place where she had dreamed of happiness? Was my grandfather at all eager to grant her wish? The story fades out at this point. Anne Scarborough died when Mother was about twelve. What became of the curate I do not know, but I am glad not to have him for an ancestor. I must be grateful to William Hollingsworth, however questionable were some facets of his character. Much of him, good and bad, reappeared in Uncle Wee-wee his son, and perhaps still shows up in later generations. With all his strength of will and sharpness of mind, he was not a happy man, and neither was Uncle Wee-wee. They caused unhappiness to others, and perhaps they could not explain to themselves why they did.

When my grandfather remarried, Nanna, who had plenty of his talent for making a bold decision, immediately brought his other children, Uncle Wee-wee, Memmem, and Mother, to New York. I doubt if they had much money, but Nanna found jobs for herself and Memmem in a department store, and started Uncle Wee-wee in his brush business, while Mother did the housekeeping in their small rented flat. They prospered, and they made many friends. Before Mother was twenty, she met Father.

She was not proud of her Hollingsworth blood. Loving her mother as she did, she leaned rather exclusively on the fact that she came from the Scarboroughs, of Yorkshire. Out of compliment to my father she always spoke highly of Scots in general. She would go so far as to suggest that in remote times more than one Scarborough may have chosen his bride from across the Border. Mother could express an opinion, even about the past, in such terms that you felt sorry for history, if it did not bear her out.

2

What the temperament of my grandmother and my mother might have been like, if William Hollingsworth had not shadowed their lives, I think I can imagine. The Scarborough character in its unspoiled condition was exhibited by my grandmother's younger brother John, who followed her to this country, and became Bishop of the Episcopal diocese of Southern New Jersey. I think he was the man Mother admired next to Father. She always referred to him as "Uncle John," in an indescribable tone of loving respect for his intrinsic worth far more than for his many honors. He was a wholesome character, very much a Yorkshireman, with the qualities that have made England great. Morally and physically he was sturdy, clear sighted and sensible, full of inner peace and cheerfulness, being in harmony with himself. As a young man he was embarked on a successful ministry as rector of a rich church in Pittsburgh, but the New Jersey diocese called him, and he felt it his duty to accept, though he knew he was choosing a hard and comparatively obscure life. His parishes were scattered along the seaboard, and their congregations were small, except when summer vacationists filled them out. In winter he was always visiting his churches because it was their bad season, and in summer because it was their good one. All that I ever heard of him illustrated for me the work of apostles and bishops in early Christianity, who were personal pastors of their flock, knowing and caring for every individual.

His home was in Trenton, within a few steps of the railroad station. His diocese maintained a beautiful old house in Burlington as a bishop's residence, but Uncle John knew his parishes would need him, and he insisted on living near the train. He had the temperament of an empire builder. Our family used to tell characteristic stories about his Pittsburgh days. One had to do with the beginning of his friendship with Andrew Carnegie. Needing a new parish house, or something of the kind, Uncle John went down the street, laying the project before various steel magnates. Mr. Carnegie resisted the appeal. "I'll be frank with you, Dr. Scarborough," he said, "I am not a church member, perhaps not in your sense a believer." "And I will be frank with you, Mr. Carnegie," said Uncle John, "it's not your soul I'm after this morning, but your pocketbook."

The sexton of the Pittsburgh church at one time was a likable fellow who unfortunately could not leave the bottle alone. After a number of incidents Uncle John served an ultimatum. "The next time you enter any part of the church building in that condition, I will lift you out with my own hands and drop you in the street." A few Sundays later, as the eleven o'clock service was about to begin, the sexton, completely befuddled, reeled up the center aisle toward the chancel. Uncle John took off his surplice and strode out to where the wretch was making himself dizzy, walking round and round the litany desk. At sight of the rector he started a maudlin argument, but Uncle John gave him a push, tripped him up, lifted him by collar and trouser-belt, carried him down the aisle and dropped him on the sidewalk, to the astonishment of late arrivals.

My last memory of Uncle John is of his later years, when he was visiting my parents in New York. It was midwinter, and late one afternoon he started out for some public reception or other ceremonial gathering. He had gotten himself up in his dress clothes and his silk hat, which he always handled so carelessly that it never was shiny, and though there was snow on the ground, he was stepping out in well-polished shoes. When Father, concerned for his health, suggested rubbers, Uncle John spoke up like a naughty boy. "I wore the things till I was seventy, but now that I'm on velvet, I'll enjoy myself!" Which he did for another ten years.

He had five daughters, remarkable women all of them: Helen, Kate, Anne, Bess and Margaret. Anne, Bess and Margaret I have known best, but they were all held up to me as models of what people should be, and in spite of that fact I loved them. Helen married Charles Hewitt; Kate married the Reverend Edward Knight, who became Bishop of Colorado; Anne married Charles Gummere, and let me play the organ at her wedding; Margaret married Charles Roberts.

3

The political opinions held by my parents were colored by their experience of the Civil War, which was a fairly recent occurrence when I was born. Robert Scarborough Hollingsworth, Mother's favorite brother, died in that conflict, and among Father's relatives there had been a fierce loyalty to Abraham Lincoln, for whose sake, it seems, as much as for the country's, several of them enlisted. Father was a child in the Eightieth Street house when Lincoln was shot; he told me how his brother John, one terrible morning, brought in the paper, saying, "The President is dead!" My parents would be sadly disappointed with me, after the upbringing I had, if they knew I once stepped outside of the Republican Party, which they continued to think of as Lincoln's. I was first aware that I might disagree with them, when I heard a humorless visitor remark one afternoon, on our summer porch, that beyond question the Democratic Party was the invention of the Devil. Child though I was, I expected someone to laugh, but nobody did.

Ten or more years later Mother amazed me with an opinion which showed that either the political climate was changing or I had missed the sweep and independence of her mind. She said she never could see why the Southern States had to be kept in the Union by force. "They were insane to secede," she said, "and if they had had their will, they would have been ruined, but they were ruined in any case, and why should they not ruin themselves in their own way, if their hearts were set on it?"

CHAPTER V

Six Children

I

ON MAY 11, 1886, my sister Lois was born. There was a great stir in the house and I made myself a nuisance, hanging around the door of Mother's room, until Dr. Chabert said, as he came out, "John, there's a fine sister for you in there!" I received the news as favorable on the whole, but I noted that the house was filling up with girls.

Helen was now three; we called her Das, short for Daisy. I was six; Das and Sister called me Brue, short for Brother. Sister was almost eight. Three fine girls, with—or against—one boy, who began to have serious matters to think about. I could no longer ignore differences in character between their sex and mine, I being by assumption a typical example of masculinity. Sister was conscientious, unselfish, always keeping an eye on Das and me with a natural mothering instinct. I thought her admirably grown-up but inclined to be overstudious, yet when in difficulty with any of my lessons, I went to her shamelessly for help. Das was fun loving and funmaking, precociously witty, always exercising her brain on what was close at hand. From the moment she was able to talk, Father was sure she would be a satirical novelist. Toward me she had the younger sister complex; she respected me more than I deserved, because I was older, and defied and challenged me, for the same reason. Lois too had a happy disposition, but there was in her appearance, as in her speech and her manners, an elfin, otherworldly quality which set her apart. She was healthy, full of animal spirits, decidedly a romp, and at the end of the day she would fall into deep slumber, but in the middle of the night she would appear anywhere in the house, a white noiseless ghost. She was an incurable sleepwalker. Once when Father was alone downstairs, absorbed in some ribbon designs, he was startled by a light hand on his arm, and there was Lois, staring appealingly at him, open eyed but fast asleep. He picked her up without waking her, carried her to her bed, laid her on the pillow and watched her relax, as though glad to be home again. Next morning, as always, she was cheerful, ready for the day, with no recollection of her wanderings.

On September 11, 1889, my brother Robert Scarborough Erskine was born. He was named after that soldier-brother of Mother's, and Uncle John came to Weehawken to baptize him. I was old enough to be impressed by the ceremony. Lois was then three, Das six, I ten, Sister twelve. Bob became at once a masculine ally, very different from me in temperament, rather silent and self-contained, but liking many things that I did, always in his òwn way. We both loved music and books, but not the same music, nor the same books. In early boyhood he was much as he now is, a mature man. I have known no other person who changed so little during a lifetime, or had so little need to change. He had and has an extraordinary talent for loyalty.

On May 23, 1893, my sister Rhoda was born, the youngest and most gifted of the family. She had a subtle and keen mind, and skill in several arts and handicrafts, but her health was never robust. Like Lois she impressed us as somewhat elfin and otherworldly, though she was not a sleepwalker. She had another peculiarity; from time to time, usually at an interval of years, she would fall into a deep faint, from which she would not wake for perhaps an hour. No doctor told us the cause, and we grew almost accustomed to this terrifying habit, since it seemed not to worry her. She was peculiarly dear to us, since she had many of Mother's traits, with her own special qualities of courage and faith, her substitutes for health, which made possible the achievements of her short life.

She and Lois had much in common, but they never met. Lois died just before Rhoda was born. The new sister seemed a heaven-sent consolation for the child who had been taken away, but perhaps Rhoda suffered from coming into the world just then, when Mother was crushed with grief.

Our large family were so united and had so much happiness together, that my memory of childhood takes little account of differences in age, or of small variations in our daily routine. After the morning recitations there remained some study for the afternoon, but this we were free to do when and as we chose, and we had the same freedom to dispose of the rest of our time. I think of those years as the only period when I could do exclusively as I liked. Yet I know now that Mother and Father guided us with strong hands, surely also with rare wisdom. Instead of commanding us to do what they wished, they planted the idea so skillfully that we imagined we had thought of it ourselves.

Wishing us to know good books, they turned us all into insatiable readers. They began by seeing that each had his or her small bookcase, a few shelves, and a strictly private set of books, enlarged by gifts on birthdays and at Christmas. They knew that a child will read a book it owns more readily than a book which is common property. Later on, a large general library will have its appeal, but even then, a book reader who has been started right will remain a book collector.

In our house the architect had not handled well the landing of the front stairs on the second floor. There was plenty of space, but it was so shapeless as to be almost unusable. The best of it was over the front door and the vestibule, where the welcome spread of floor was further increased by a bay window, vine-covered. Here was our family library, book cases, shelves, comfortable deep chairs, and a smallish round table holding a lamp and magazines. At dusk that lamp was always lighted. Day or night, until bedtime, we children might curl up on the red-upholstered chairs, and read whatever tempted us.

My earliest literary adventures were in my own diminutive collection, composed chiefly of English books for the young. I sampled *Tom Brown's School Days* and *Tom Brown at Oxford,* enjoying but not understanding those genuine masterpieces. Then I went through most of Charlotte M. Yonge's books, and for the moment liked them, terrible though they are; also, I read the works of Mrs. Ewing, distinguished above other amiable ladies who have hoped to uplift the world, by the extent to which she reeks sentiment and false pathos. All her stories would now be called tear-jerkers. I have thought of reading one or two of them again, just to see whether a memory so unfavorable can possibly be just. The one I might try, were there not so much other reading to be done, is *The Story of a Short Life.* Whether or not the story would still stand up, at least I learned from it the Latin motto, *Laetus sorte mea,* happy in my lot, which impressed me then as a noble philosophy. Now I think the best thing to do with one's lot is to improve it.

When I was ripe for the grown-up books in the family library, real books, I began on each shelf at the left and read straight across, mowing down whatever came in my way—Scott, Dickens, Thackeray, Macaulay, Shakspere, Fenimore Cooper, Hawthorne—every volume in every set. The less accessible shelves at the top were inevitably the more alluring. Macaulay's essays were bound in red, and alongside, perhaps because it was of the same color, stood what threatened to be a collection of sermons. It was called *Advice to a Wife and a Mother*. Baffled but intrigued, I petrified the family at dinner by saying the book had no plot. Later in the evening I returned to it hopefully, but it was gone, and I never saw it again. My parents did not believe in censorship, and this is the only blot on their record.

I read much poetry—Burns and Byron, Tennyson, Tom Moore, and oddly enough, Owen Meredith. Tennyson's chief work I knew almost by heart before he published his final volumes. Though I read and liked Longfellow and Poe, I remained ignorant of Emerson and Whitman. I reflect now, with the sense of having missed an opportunity, that while I was reading comfortably on a red chair in the bay window, I might have seen Walt face to face, at the cost of only a short trip to Camden.

2

Mother and Father had firm opinions about the educative value of the dinner table. My sisters, my brother and I were expected to dress for the evening meal, not simply to wash up, but to get into different clothes from the ones we had played in through the day. Here the girls had certain advantages. For reasons which puzzled me then and still do, girls can keep cleaner and wash up more quickly than boys, even when engaged in the same dusty occupations. At Weehawken, in summer particularly, I became humble every afternoon between five and six, when my sisters came downstairs and walked on the lawn in fresh laundered dresses, with perfectly tied sashes, and a ribbon in their well-brushed hair. Mother would appear just before dinner, in flawless white. I remember the contrast with her black hair, then beginning to show streaks of gray.

She and Father believed that to be dressed for dinner put us in the mood to behave better at table. They were right—and the principle holds for older folk as well. We had frequent dinner and luncheon guests. Father would bring home business friends when they came to the factory.

The first telephone I ever saw, a line from the wall beside his office desk to the first landing on our back stairs, was used chiefly to warn Mother how many extra plates would be needed. Hoboken acquaintances might drop in at any time, unannounced. If there was room, and if they were interesting people, we were allowed to sit with the grown folks. But if the table was too crowded, or if, as on a few occasions, Mother thought it appropriate to keep us out of sight, we ate in the sitting room, next to the dining room, with the door open between, so that we could hear the conversation.

Our parents treated us, so far as they could, not as infants but as their contemporaries; they understood and encouraged the natural ambition of children to grow up quickly and take their place in the world. When guests arrived for lunch or dinner, or on any errand not strictly private, we were expected to present ourselves in the parlor, not to be shown off as the family prize packages, but to do our part in the hospitality of the house. And when there were no guests, Father would talk with Mother in our presence about business problems, or political events, or something that caught his particular attention in the morning paper, and it was not out of order for us to comment or ask a question, provided we waited for our turn and otherwise tried to be adult in our manners.

3

I remember 1892 as the critical year of my youth. All that had gone before was easy and full of sunshine; what followed, was difficult and increasingly shadowed. I knew that some of my ancestors had not been happy, but it did not occur to me that my parents could have deep trouble; at no time did trouble ever seem further away than at the beginning of that year. We were all in health; Father had success and wealth, so far as I knew, and in his talk we caught glimpses of hopeful plans.

On April 15, Grandma ended her long and useful life. As she lay in her coffin her majestic height was impressive. She was the first dead person I had looked at. Uncle Will came and stood with me beside her coffin, and startled me by revealing the depth of his affectionate heart. "This is not my mother!" he exclaimed in a passion of grief. "She is gone. This is only a cadaver!"

Father went to Europe that summer on a business trip. The night before he sailed some friends came in for a farewell dinner party, at the end of which Lois stole shyly up to him with a box containing a handsome watch, a gift from Mother. My son Graham wears that watch today. Mother had another gift to welcome Father on his return; her old square piano was moved into the sitting room, and a Steinway baby grand stood in its place. At that prosperous moment Tiffany watches and Steinway pianos came as easily as happy thoughts. And of course Father had purchased in Europe handsome gifts for us all. To me he brought a fine bow for my grandfather's violin, which I was beginning to play.

A few weeks later, on September 3, my sister Lois died. On the morning before, she had felt strangely tired, and Mother sent for Dr. Chabert, who advised that she stay in bed. She had grown fast and was now tall for her age. She needed a good deal of rest, the Doctor said; she must not overtax her heart. Next morning she felt even more tired, and Mother called the Doctor again, this time with alarm. By noon Lois had faded away painlessly, and was gone.

4

I said that we children followed closely the grown-up interests which occupied our parents. Somewhere in my eighth or ninth year we heard much talk about a new mill Father was building in central New York, at Norwich, Chenango County, between Binghamton and Utica. As soon as the mill was completed, we were taken up to see it, and in time Father rented a house, which became our summer home.

Norwich was and still is a lovely town in a picturesque valley. Father chose it as the site for his second factory, partly because of the clear water he could find there for his dye shop, and partly because of other advantages, which I have forgotten. Being near New York City was not one of them. This Norwich mill was perhaps Father's great mistake. The factory at Union Hill had earned wealth for him, but he branched out at a bad moment and in, for him, an unfortunate direction. Goods of rare design and quality can hardly be produced in quantity, and in a remote district like Chenango County it was unreasonable to look for the kind of weavers his kind of ribbons needed.

Perhaps he was attracted to the country by a dream he had of a new type of factory, such as could not be developed in or near a large city. His own father had begun life as a hand weaver; Father hoped some day to provide his men with homes on the village street, in groups of two houses, each two houses having a large garden in common, and behind the garden a weave-shed, with looms run by electricity. There would be a central distributing and collecting station; a wagon would take the silk to each weave-shed and bring back the product; and the weavers, paid by the piece, could work as much and at whatever hours they wished. Dear individualist that he was, he believed that workers would always like to be independent masters of their time and their condition, eager to escape the factory lock-step, and get ahead at a speed set by their own skill and their own industry.

Even if this dream of his had been practical, the ribbon business in 1892 was in a bad way. Ribbons were disappearing from women's hats, as sashes were from their dresses. Tailor-made suits, as they were called, were the new vogue. Quite stubbornly Father persuaded himself, against sound advice and overwhelming evidence, that tailored suits were a transient fad, and that the demand for ribbons and sashes would return. Women, he said, would never deny themselves true beauty of costume—true beauty being found only in a ribbon-trimmed dress. From 1892 until my graduation from college in 1900, he was pouring every cent he had into the business, to keep it afloat on the wrong basis. When it was all over and he had nothing left, not even the Weehawken home, he told me that if he had set fire to both factories in 1892, had burned them to the ground with all their contents, and had collected no insurance, he still could have retired with a competence. But by 1900 I doubt if his capital amounted to more than a few thousand dollars.

From the beginning of our financial shrinkage he and Mother discussed the situation frankly with us children. I have always been grateful to them for their confidence. Though our prosperity continued outwardly for several years, Sister, Das and I knew our reserves were dwindling, and that Father put his hope in a turn of fortune that Mother had the good sense to know would never come. She was wiser than he in practical affairs, and she did not approve of the course he was taking. It was the artist in him who had succeeded, and when art was no longer desired in his business, he was through.

But the most precious part of their children's education may have been the privilege of watching the continuing love and trust between these parents, although on matters of such consequence they did not agree.

CHAPTER VI

Grace Church, Union Hill

I

A S I said before, the Episcopalians of Weehawken and Union Hill,
weary of traveling to Hoboken for Sunday services, at last organized a parish of their own and built Grace Church, in Union Hill, at the
corner of the Boulevard and Gardner Street. Among the leaders in this
work, perhaps the chief inspirers and maintainers of it were Father, Mr.
Duer, and Robert Dixon, the best architect in Union Hill.

Grace Church enriched the lives of us children in many ways. Just
because it was a small parish, surviving only by the loyalty of all its members, it provided for us a closer acquaintance with our neighbors, and
perhaps our first insight into the collision of temperaments inevitable in
all society. There was difference of opinion about the architectural style
of the building, about the size of the chancel, about the shape of the pews.
The resulting dramas were more human than religious, and best of all
were the diplomatic efforts of Mother and Father and the other sensible
folk to nip these arguments quickly and bind up whatever wounds befell
from lively words.

There were minor excitements, which to our childhood seemed heaven-
sent. One excellent member of the congregation, who never missed a
Sunday morning, held that "paper money," though legal tender, was
unsanitary. She would have made her offering in gold or silver, if those
metals could have been carried conveniently, in the right denominations,
but the world being as it was, she always put a dollar bill on the plate,
and every bill in her possession was soaked in carbolic acid before it went

49

into her pocketbook. When Father and Mr. Duer took up the offering, the odor of carbolic acid told the worshippers that the good lady had brought to the altar a perfectly safe dollar. Afterward the dollars and the carbolic smell came home with us, since Father was the parish treasurer, and kept the money in his strongbox until the bank opened on Monday.

Then there was always the excitement provided by Mr. Duer, teaching his children to behave. His large family filled a pew, and those furthest away from him thought themselves safe, especially during a prayer, when Mr. Duer got down on his knees with considerable effort, because of rheumatism or arthritis or some other aristocratic infirmity. But he was not a man to accept defiance. He always carried a cane, which, once he was seated, he laid away on the floor, under the pew in front of him. As soon as any of his children started trouble, the stiff but angry gentleman got up his stick, which at the end of his long arm could control the entire pew. From there on, my sisters and I watched with unneighborly zest, to see which of our dear friends would be tapped or poked.

2

For some time after it was started Grace Church had no permanent rector, and Father and Mr. Duer, chiefly Father, were busy finding temporary supplies. We were in the diocese of Newark, and the Bishop of Newark was the Right Reverend Thomas A. Starkey, a stately old gentleman with a beautiful voice, highly anglicized, who is spite of much charm did not direct his diocese with Uncle John's vigor. I marvel now at a situation where a few laymen and a few devoted ladies were left to organize and run a parish with so little oversight or guidance. We might have been stranded mariners, trying to continue the ways of civilization on a desert island. But the fact that Father secured most of the visiting preachers was a pleasant thing for Father's children, if a little hard on Mother and our cook, for naturally Father asked the ministers to dine with us, and many of them were men of talent, some of them widely known in their day. Listening to their conversation, I learned much that is of value to me today. A number of them were professors at the General Theological Seminary, presumably scholars, and not a few quite eloquent. One in particular was unforgettable, Dr. Walpole, an Englishman, of a noble appearance. I was always delighted when he came to our house. Once or twice he brought with him a son, a small boy slightly younger than I, whose name was Hugh. In time Dr. Walpole returned to England, to a succession of important posts, until in 1910 he became Bishop of Edinburgh. His small son grew up to be Hugh Walpole, the novelist.

I have taken pains, for two reasons, to indicate the religious atmosphere in which my boyhood was spent. In the first place, my family traditions were British, the first books I read were British, and I went to school and college with a body of ideas which would probably have been mine had I been brought up in England or Scotland. For that reason, when I decided to teach literature, it was English literature that I taught, not realizing until much later that the literatures with which my sympathy is strongest are the Greek and the French. In the second place, it is somewhat the fashion for American writers to describe their early contacts with religion as intellectually stultifying and spiritually depressing. I risk the contempt of these colleagues by telling the truth, that whatever may have happened to them, my experiences in the field of religion were stimulating and happy, a large and profitable part of my education. I thank my parents that they presented to me the spiritual ideals of the Old and the New Testaments, so that I could appreciate not only their beauty but their mastering importance in the progress of the human race. Though I was brought up a Protestant, I have my parents again to thank that the history of Christianity was neither withheld from me, nor warped to favor any sectarian view. I was encouraged to read freely in the accounts of the Early Church and of the Middle Ages; I knew that the beautiful cathedrals of England had been built by Catholics, in a Catholic civilization; that the English liturgy and the English Prayer Book were adaptations or translations from the Catholic manuals, and that the English Church owed its separate existence altogether too much to that buccaneering and murderous old goat, Henry the Eighth. Neither of my parents thought well of Henry.

To be sure, I discovered for myself that many ministers and preachers are dull men, but in time I discovered also that many scholars and professors are likewise soporific. I even made the acquaintance of some iconoclastic unbelievers, and some of them too turned out to be thick-skulled and crude. Evidently it was possible to find intelligence and humility or stupidity and arrogance among the supporters of either side in almost any argument. My respect began to lean always to those who had a reasoned point of view, a method of thinking, a philosophy.

Here at last, as in some other matters, my love of music led me fruitfully. In the little church at Union Hill I became interested in ecclesiastical music, at first in the works of inferior composers, at last in the motets and masses of Palestrina. From very modest beginnings I progressed inevitably to a study of the liturgy which his music served. Encountering in my reading occasional references to the *Summa,* I had the curiosity to investigate, of course in the most superficial way, the profound pages of St. Thomas Aquinas. I began this reading at the end of my college course, and I have continued it ever since. Now in my later years I am glad to watch the widening appeal that the great Scholastic makes to laymen—curiously, if I am not mistaken, more often just now to Protestant than to Catholic laymen. No other study has been for me more worth while. I am no doctor in the stupendous philosophy, but it has revealed to me some of the potential reaches of the heart and the mind.

3

The music at Grace Church was provided by a volunteer choir of men and women. Father organized it, as I need hardly say; his love of choral singing would not miss this opportunity. Some of the voices were very good, his own and Robert Dixon's, for example, both tenors. There was a fair balance in the other parts, though diplomacy was called for, as always in volunteer choirs in small churches, to deflect the energies of willing friends who thought they could sing but could not.

The organist and choirmaster was Frank Fruttchey, a young man of talent, who had begun his musical career as a choirboy in Old Trinity, New York City. Father discovered Mr. Fruttchey in Union Hill before the church was established, and engaged him as his accompanist, and also as my piano teacher. Then he engaged him to play for the choir and train it. So long as we lived in Weehawken, Father met the whole cost of the music at Grace Church. When Mr. Fruttchey, in 1892, was called to a New York parish, I pleaded for permission to replace him. Though Mother objected that I was too young, Father sided with me and I had my wish, helped out by the fact that there was no other organist in the neighborhood. I was simultaneously saving money for Father, and pleasing myself!

For four years Father drilled the choir, to my accompaniment. I began at once to persuade him that we should get rid of the women singers. In a year or two I was allowed to introduce a few boys, whom I trained, to save Father's time. By the time I was sixteen the choir was entirely male, and I drilled it. We had one rehearsal on Friday nights at the church, and on Tuesday evenings the thirty men and boys would squeeze into our sitting room, where Mother's square piano now stood. After the Tuesday rehearsal there were always refreshments—ice cream and cake, coffee or soft drinks. Then the boys would go home, and the men would stay for talk with Father, or perhaps for a little more singing. In summer Father provided the boys with equipment for a baseball team, and arranged games for them. In spring and autumn, on Sunday afternoons, he frequently took them all to New York, to hear some noted choir sing a service, perhaps at Old Trinity, or Trinity Chapel, or St. Agnes'. Whatever advantage this was to the boys, I know what I learned—as perhaps Father hoped I would—from great organists and choirmasters like Arthur Messiter, Walter B. Gilbert, George Edward Stubbs.

The organ at Grace Church was a three-manual pedal instrument, excellent for a budding organist to practice on, but sadly deficient in tone, since it had no pipes. It was a reed organ, of a kind I should like to think no longer exists, but I fear examples may still be found. It could be played very soft or quite loud, but neither way was the tone improved. I feel ungrateful to the old box, telling the truth about it now.

4

Attendance at Grace Church made me aware of friends whom I had merely taken for granted, as children will. Now I really noticed and greatly liked the Duer girls, Elizabeth, Sarah and Angelica, and their brother John, of my own age. From time to time some attractive cousins of theirs came to visit them—Alice (famous later as Alice Duer Miller) and Caroline (a gifted writer too much overshadowed by her sister). But in 1892 my favorite was Sarah, a splendid character even in childhood, who influenced me more than she was likely to know. Unusually thoughtful, she had feminine charm in abundance. We used to go for long drives together, I being then twelve, she a year older. I would walk over to the Duer house to ask if she were free. She usually was. I would then go to the factory stable, harness Bessie to the buggy, drive back to the

Duer house, and start off proudly with Sarah. We usually drove toward Fort Lee, or through the woods on the Duer estate. It was not locomotion I wanted, but talk. What Sarah did for my groping mind, I cannot adequately measure. I wish I could think I did anything for her, but even by childhood standards I must have been, outside of music and books, amazingly green, and she was impressively grown up.

On one of our buggy rides I proposed marriage to her. It must have been at a moment of extreme elation, the cause of which I have forgotten. Perhaps she agreed with me in an argument, thus indicating that we were destined soul mates. I believe I told her something of the kind; I had not been reading romantic novels for nothing. I am quite sure I said I could never love another, and would be extremely obliged if she would let me know how she felt. She turned on me her brown eyes, and asked why, oh why, I had spoiled a beautiful friendship. Fondness for argument prompted me to inquire what had been spoiled, and how, but Sarah shook her head, saying that nothing would ever be quite the same between us. Moved against my will to sudden penitence, I apologized for having spoken out of turn, and promised never to do it again.

5

Among the ministers who came from the Seminary to help out for a service or two at Grace Church, was the Reverend Horatio W. P. Hodson. He was about forty, Father's age. He had begun to practice law and was on the straight road to success, apparently, when some deep experience persuaded him to abandon these prospects and spend the rest of his days in hard work in small parishes. He made an impression at once upon Father and Mr. Duer and the other men of Grace Church, and when they asked him to be their rector he accepted.

In the lives of all my family he counted for much, so long as we remained in Weehawken. He was a powerful character, of a type not often met outside of fiction. On the slightest acquaintance even a casual observer could see that his was a vigorous and highly trained mind. He was an experienced organizer and executive, and he could handle men. But those who knew him better found him surprisingly emotional, swayed always by feelings or outright passions, not easy to foresee or explain. Perhaps his emotional tempests were related to that personal experience, whatever it was, that made him change his life. Though he was a warmhearted friend, he remained mysterious and stormy, subject to moods of almost terrifying melancholy.

I enjoyed his society, since he held vigorous and exciting views on everything I was interested in, and he was a grand talker. He was well read in general literature. He liked music too, but there his taste was abominable, and to listen to his opinions was a discipline in diplomacy. He tried to persuade me that my duty and my opportunity in life was to enter the ministry, hinting at the rewarding satisfactions he had found in it. Whatever those satisfactions were, peace of mind was not among them. He gradually became difficult, especially in his dealings with the ladies of the parish, who pronounced him, perhaps with justice, a woman-hater, and one of them told him to his face that he should have been a monk, not a parish priest.

Though he caused me to think seriously of entering the ministry, his own experiences warned me to stay out. Or he may not have influenced me. Perhaps my decision against the priesthood was inevitable. I have no talent for celibacy, nor for the cloister, nor for sweetening up the women's auxiliary or the sewing circle.

CHAPTER VII

Music Teachers

I

FATHER himself gave me my first piano lessons while I was still very much a child, starting me off on scales and simple exercises. Miss Burhorn got me a little further, but I made no progress till Frank Fruttchey, father's accompanist and the Grace Church organist, took me in hand. He was tall and rather good looking, with a kind manner, helped out for me by the glamour of his considerable talent. He had no difficulty in kindling my love of music until it was the dominant interest in my life. He had some ideas of teaching which were far ahead of his time, or perhaps they were so ancient that they had become neglected. He wished me to learn music, not simple piano playing. Along with my pieces he taught me harmony and counterpoint. Out of each lesson he saved at least ten minutes for what we should now call oral harmony. With my back to the piano as he modulated, I was expected to call out each successive chord, naming the notes in their position. Thanks to him, music became for me a clear language, easy to follow intelligently.

But though he excited me about music, he did not teach me to play well. As performer and as teacher of technique he was erratic. He could play anything himself, and he did, without discrimination. I heard him, in our parlor, play one of the later Beethoven sonatas, and also something of Chaminade. He played everything brilliantly, with feeling and sparkle, and somehow he made all pieces sound alike, as though he had composed them. He liked best, I think, to improvise, which he could do well. He let me play what I chose. He would not insist on Bach if I preferred

Schumann and Chopin and Liszt, which I did. From him I acquired neither a love of practice nor an understanding of how it should be done. I simply played by the hour. I had a natural facility in memorizing, and no kind of performance is uncongenial to me, but I spent my time trying to compose, an activity which he applauded on principle, no matter what the result. It was years before I learned that a composition may be correct in harmony and counterpoint, and yet be worthless.

Later, after I had passed my twelfth birthday, my approach to music became suddenly more serious and more intelligent. I was conscious of the change. I spent every minute I could at the piano acquiring a repertory, or studying the great oratorios of Handel and the symphonies of Beethoven. Father saw that I needed better teaching than I had had, and since Mr. Fruttchey was now busy with his New York choir, it was arranged that I should study with Carl Walter, the old friend from St. Bartholomew days. I began going to Mr. Walter's house at 795 Lexington Avenue for a weekly lesson.

2

Carl Walter was a remarkable musician, once widely known in New York, but now forgotten except by my friend Dr. Walter Timme and a few others who join me in honoring his memory. He was as attractive and whimsical in his character as in his appearance. He was not good looking, like Mr. Fruttchey, but far more arresting. He was short, with a remarkable squarish head, and he wore his hair in a bang, a style which I envied, since there was no need to comb or brush or part. When Carl was reading a book, or was otherwise thoughtful, he had a habit of stroking down the top of his head, from crown to forehead, and at the end of a few quiet minutes his hair lay smooth. Like Uncle Wee-wee and Father he was an enthusiastic swimmer, and I have seen the square head bobbing around in the water, the bang clearly defined, since the hair was wet.

His father had come from Germany to conduct an orchestra in Cincinnati, and Carl had grown up in that city. In youth he moved to New York, prepared for a concert career, but the United States then had small welcome for even fine musical talent unless it came directly from Europe with the established reputation of a Rubinstein. After a brief experiment Carl Walter saw that his future lay in teaching, not in virtuoso touring. He made a characteristic decision at once, to teach and to enjoy teaching

—also to play more than ever, but not in public. He was lionized by wealthy New Yorkers of his day, and wherever he knew that his host and hostess were sincere music lovers, he was glad to play for them. He said it was pleasanter to play for nothing in the house of friends than to rent a hall in order to play for strangers. These spontaneous recitals of his were celebrated. He had a rich repertory and he practiced constantly, not to prepare for any particular performance, but because his piano was his life.

I never came away from my weekly lesson without some quaint advice, not necessarily about piano technique in any limited sense. "When you are asked to play in a home," he once said, "play anything you wish, if you have never played there before. But if it is the second time, recall what you played the first time, and play it again. They will not quite remember it, but it will sound familiar, and good music, when it is familiar, gives pleasure."

His own playing was remarkable for the beauty of tone more often cultivated by Russian than by German pianists. I used to think he was fortunate in being left handed. His runs, octaves and trills were extraordinary, and apparently it made no difference to him which hand executed them. Many a time during a lesson he would lean over the piano and show me with his left hand how he thought a right-hand passage should be played. He had strong opinions about what the great composers intended, and it was disconcerting to observe that, when judged by those opinions of his, practically all editions were wrong. He would amend them boldly. He always had a pen and an eraser within reach, and as you played for him, he was busy rewriting the text of your music. If you were reading a piece for the first time, he worked over your shoulders, eraser in the left hand, pen in the right, or the other way around. I doubt if he had special knowledge of the original editions; he simply trusted his intuitions. I still possess copies of Beethoven sonatas and Chopin ballades and polonaises rewritten or improved in his hand. The procedure sounds outrageous, but the result was always, to say the least, thought-provoking, and in a large number of cases self-justifying. He thought it was an error not to print music as pianists were sure to play it, especially in the assignment of notes to the different hands. After he had made what he considered the intelligent redistribution, there was sure to be as much work for the left hand as for the right.

Though his technical equipment was extraordinary, his attention was always on the interpretation, on the musical meaning, on the mood and the style. It could not be said of him, as of Frank Fruttchey, that he made all composers sound alike. He worked hard to make me understand— better, to make me feel—the great difference between Schumann, Chopin, and Brahms. While studying with him I continued to compose, and he was always ready to look over my work, but he never flattered me about it. He did think I might be a player, if I worked hard enough and followed the right models, by which he understood the right interpretations. One day he told me I must hear a concert announced for the following week. The pianist was a long-haired Pole named Paderewski. "He plays Bach correctly, romantically." Here I must say Carl Walter spoke prophetically; Paderewski became the most poetical piano player—at times —that I ever heard, but the concert to which my teacher sent me was full of heroic pounding.

Perhaps as a logical consequence of his sensitiveness to musical style and his insistence upon correct interpretation, Carl Walter believed that a talented German should study music in Italy, and a talented Italian should study in Germany. He prophesied lean days for opera, because cosmopolitan versatility among singers was going out of fashion. This pronouncement was made before Wagner occupied his present large place in the repertoire; few singers then expected or wanted a career in nothing but Wagnerian rôles. Carl Walter, though a German, had no enthusiasm for Wagner, who he told me was a master of orchestration, rather than a great musician. "Most of the time he sounds as if he had more to say than he has." Carl's idol in opera was Mozart, and he ranked Bizet very high indeed, not only for *Carmen,* but for his songs.

His most intimate friend among the musicians in New York was Emilio Agramonte, composer and singing teacher. Carl and Agramonte belonged to a group who composed, and gave periodical recitals of their works, which they rarely published. Carl's piano pieces were strongly influenced by Gottschalk, for whose work he had considerable respect. In general he liked the music which appealed to Spain and to South America. Let me say frankly that I now think his taste is likely to seem better with passing time; his originality and his independence gave him immunity to the heavy-footed domination of German music which in England and the United States followed and exploited the deserved triumphs of Mendelssohn's authentic genius.

After I had studied with him a few years, Carl Walter startled me one day by saying, at the close of the lesson, that I must come to him no more. As he spoke he closed down the piano lid, in an impulsive and sentimental gesture, and I saw that his eyes were moist. For a moment I was baffled. But he said that if I wished to be more than an amateur, my father should send me to Europe without delay, where I could study at a great conservatory, among many students of my own age, from whose playing and practicing I might learn almost as much as from my teachers. "Music," he said, "is learned best in the world of music. No private teacher is a world!"

When he said this to me, I realized that I was already so deeply interested in books that I must hesitate to abandon my plans for college study. Later I told him I was committed to literature. "You are wise," said he. "You could not compete with the Poles. In Poland, when there is no revolution, they practice piano or violin. It is remarkable how much time there is, even in Poland, between revolutions."

I owe to him far more than music. He was thoughtful, his observations of life were keen, and he expressed them with dramatic force. Once he asked how much I was practicing daily.

"Three or four hours."

"In long stretches, or a little at a time?"

"An hour at a time, or half an hour."

"You make a mistake," he exclaimed. "When you grow up, there will be no long stretches. Practice in minutes, whenever you can find them—five or ten before school, after lunch, between engagements. If you spread the practice through the day, piano-playing will become a habit, part of your life."

When I became a college professor I wanted to write, but recitations, theme-reading and committee meetings filled my days and evenings, and for several years I got nothing down on paper. My excuse to myself was that I had no time. Then I recalled what Carl Walter had said.

During the next week, whenever I had five minutes, I went to my desk and wrote as much as I could. At the end of the week, to my astonishment, I had a sizable manuscript for revision. Why not, after all? Most of us take no more than fifteen minutes to write a note to a friend, and the note may have three hundred words in it. Three hundred words would fill a page, as prewar books were printed. Fifteen minutes a day would yield in a year a volume of three hundred and fifty pages.

When I began to write novels, it was by this piecemeal method.

Though my teaching schedule had become heavier than ever, there were minutes which could be salvaged. At last I took up piano playing again, finding that the intervals of the day provided time enough for both writing and practice.

But there is an important trick in this time-using formula; you must get to work quickly. If there are only five minutes, you cannot afford to waste four of them chewing your pencil. You must make your mental preparations beforehand, and concentrate on the task almost instantly when the opportunities come. Fortunately, rapid concentration is easier than most of us realize. I confess I have never learned to let go easily or happily at the end of five or ten minutes, but life can be counted on to supply interruptions.

3

The men who taught me music in my early years—Frank Fruttchey, Carl Walter, Edward MacDowell—all died young, in every case the victim of a nervous collapse which affected the brain. Here was more than a coincidence. My boyhood occurred in what seemed to me a fortunate period, but another verdict might have been pronounced by older people, by musicians in particular. In the America of the 1890's many a true artist, though financially successful, had cause for dissatisfaction with his life. Now, after many years, I think I can discern a tragedy in Carl Walter's advice to go abroad and study with someone else. I have wondered why he did not organize his serious pupils into a class, so that they might enjoy among themselves that interchange of encouragement and inspiration which he knew could be found at European conservatories. But others in America had tried that experiment, with little success. Perhaps he feared he would fail, for the same reason. How many serious students had he? I may have been the only one, and I gave up a musical career. Yet I was not a typical American. The rewards of business and industry did not tempt me; I gave up the doubtful fortunes of a pianist for the assured indigence of a college professor.

CHAPTER VIII

Columbia Grammar School

I

IN 1893 Father decided that it was time for his three eldest children to go to school in New York. Mother agreed with this decision, but I believe Father made it. He had been worrying about me. I heard him say that unless I soon got from under the soft discipline of governesses and learned to make a place for myself among boys, I might have a hard time when I went to college. If I were to leave our domestic schoolroom on the top floor of the house, Sister and Das might as well leave it too. So they were entered in the Comstock School for Girls at 32 West Fortieth Street, and one morning in the late summer Father took me to the Columbia Grammar School, 34-36 East Fifty-first Street. After a brief interview, the two principals, Mr. Benjamin Campbell and Dr. Richard S. Bacon, accepted me as one of their flock.

Mr. Campbell was a short man with graying sideboards, rather handsome, very alert, a vigorous teacher. I believe he had been something of a boxer while in college, perhaps the lightweight champion. At that first meeting I was aware of his challenging, all but pugnacious, manner. Later I had reason in plenty to appreciate his strong character and his kind heart. It was not by accident that the Grammar School was located only a block away from Columbia College. It had been established in the eighteenth century, only ten years later than the original King's College, to serve as its preparatory department, and that had been its chief function ever since. When the College went to Morningside, the Grammar School felt the difference, and Mr. Campbell moved it to the West Side, but he could not then find a location near enough the University to continue the old relation. I entered just in time.

Dr. Bacon was a large heavily bearded gentleman of terrific solemnity. Since his nose was more than a little red, it was inevitable that his pupils should malign him by inventing a marvelously detailed myth about a certain closet in the school office. The door, as I remember, was in the left-hand corner, as you entered. Here undoubtedly were kept the books containing all our marks. Both Mr. Campbell and Dr. Bacon were seen at various times entering the closet to consult the records. Since Mr. Campbell had been an athlete and still kept in training, he escaped our puerile scandal-making, but Dr. Bacon's nose dedicated itself to be our target. In certain moods we were convinced, and said so, that when he stepped reverently into the closet to verify our academic standing, he verified something else.

The victim of our malice had indeed one defect; he was entirely without humor. Such pomposity and gravity I have seen in no one else. But he was a great teacher of Greek, so overwhelmingly superb that before we left school most of us held him in deep respect, tinged with puzzled awe. To him I owe something more than acquaintance with a language; he planted in me an enduring love of Greek civilization and culture. Though Father had not gone to college, he was so much in the British tradition that he thought it absurd to come up for a university degree without Greek as well as Latin. Our modern degrees, bestowed for no classics at all, he considered an imposition on youth. He wanted me to be drilled in Latin and Greek, and he expected me to perfect myself in French. There would be other languages, when I had time for them.

But among all the language teachers I had, then or later, Dr. Bacon was in a class by himself. He never mentioned to us the direct method, and perhaps the term had not yet been coined, but at the end of each recitation he had us stand with our hands behind our back, and answer in Greek the very simple questions he asked in that tongue, taking the words and constructions from the page on which we had just recited. I know that classical Greek is not modern Greek, and that Dr. Bacon almost certainly pronounced classical Greek in a way that Homer would not have understood. We did not learn to speak Greek. But words which are familiar to lips and ear, become easy for the eye, and I entered college with such a reading command of Greek that I elected the subject through the four years as a snap course. I never had a comparable facility in Latin.

2

The distance of the school from our Weehawken home was formidable. To get to my first class in the morning, I had to take the car down the Boulevard to the Fourteenth Street-Hoboken ferry, a trip which consumed at least half an hour. To cross the river, with the usual wait at the ferry dock, took twenty minutes. On the New York side the Fourteenth Street horsecar got me gradually to Fourth Avenue, where I changed to another horsecar, which carried me up through the tunnel and past the old Grand Central Station to Fifty-first Street. I missed few days even in bad weather, but under the best conditions I had to leave home shortly after six-thirty in order to reach school a safe number of minutes before nine. The trip both ways took more than three hours a day, and for most of the school year, having left home in a dim light if not in darkness, I got home only at dusk. I was growing fast, and after half a year of this schedule began to look like a wind-worn scarecrow. My parents were worried, and Mr. Clarence H. Cook, one of the upper-form masters, stopped me in the hall one day and asked what was the matter. I resented the question, but he cross-examined me until he learned how far away I lived. A few days later Father had a letter from Mr. Campbell suggesting that I reach school at ten instead of nine. From that time my Columbia Grammar experience was altogether happy. Just how the lost hour was made up I cannot now recall.

Mr. Campbell had on his staff a group of teachers who were, as much later I realized, answers to a headmaster's prayer. They were all strong and attractive personalities, they were all first rate in their subjects, they all knew how to teach, and as the incident with Mr. Cook shows, they all watched us closely and with a kind interest, out of class as well as in. Those who worked most over me were Mr. Campbell, in mathematics and Latin; Dr. Bacon in Greek; Dr. Charles Moore in mathematics and English; Dr. Odell in English and Latin; and Mr. Cook in Latin and mathematics. Mr. Cook had us also for a few minutes after lunch on Fridays, in public speaking. It must have been a wretched end to the kind gentleman's week. Our oratorical talents were pathetic, and our choice of pieces to recite was too grotesque for any teacher to endure with equanimity. On Fridays, immediately after lunch, Mr. Cook always lost his temper. His habit was to record marks with a soft pencil, and he pressed the pencil heavily, to make the marks decisive. Marking us for public speaking he sometimes drove the pencil through the paper, and once when I tried on him Longfellow's *The Children's Hour,* he exclaimed, quite loud, "My God!"

While Father and I were talking with the principals, on my first visit to the school, a tall young man of striking appearance came into the office. He had a noble face, a magnificent head, deep-set eyes, and a fine voice. He was still in his twenties, but his hair was prematurely white. Father said to me, as we left the building half an hour later, that he was still thinking of that young man's face, one of the most remarkable he had ever seen. I gave my opinion that he looked like an actor. I was not so far wrong, at it turned out. The handsome young teacher, my deeply prized friend ever since, was George C. D. Odell, Professor of English at Columbia University, and successor to Brander Matthews there as Professor of Dramatic Literature. He taught me a year in the Grammar School before he joined the faculty of Columbia College. He was my teacher again in my undergraduate years, and when I myself became at last a teacher at Columbia he was one of the colleagues with whom I was most closely associated. I have memories of him, therefore, at all periods of my life, but naturally I attach special importance to a chance incident in his classroom at the Grammar School which started me off as a writer. Perhaps I should have tried to write sooner or later, even if I had never met Dr. Odell, but he applied the match which ignited me.

He was explaining to us the English sonnet, the kind that Shakspere wrote, and also the more complicated Italian sonnet which Milton practiced. Superficially the difference is in the rhyme scheme, and as Dr. Odell spoke I was wondering whether the well-planned Italian pattern, just because it was more artificial, might not be easier to write. I offered the idea for the consideration of my teacher and my classmates. The classmates showed no interest. Dr. Odell disposed of me by saying that the Italian sonnet form was extremely difficult. I should have stopped there, if silence had ever been easy for me. I said firmly that I could write an Italian sonnet myself, if I tried. Dr. Odell retorted that he would like to see my attempt. My classmates laughed at me. I brought him the sonnet next morning. He conceded that the rhymes were properly arranged. It was probably the worst poem ever concocted by a fourteen-year-old boy, but my schoolmates were impressed, and my reputation as a literary fellow spread from classroom to classroom. Consequently I was chosen—I can't recall by whom—as editor of the school magazine. I have been writing ever since. At the end of my second year a prize was offered for English composition. I entered the competition and won it, surprising myself and my teachers. They told me so. At the end of my third and last school year another composition prize was offered, and again I came out ahead. After that I was incurable.

In the class ahead of me at Columbia Grammar was William Aspenwall Bradley, my predecessor as editor of the school paper, and already a competent writer. In his too short life he went far. He was of a serious temperament; he had some humor, but how much, I was never sure. His ideals, in life as in literature, were very fine, he was a tremendous worker, and in several fields a precocious scholar. Even in school he was making himself an expert in book designing, by mastering the history of printing types and the relation of the style of type to the size and the shape of the page. Perhaps he had already begun, what he continued in college, the study of French engravers and etchers.

In my own class I met three boys of unusual character and mind, all of whom entered Columbia Grammar when I did, went through college with me, and ever since have been my friends—Melville H. Cane, Alfred E. Cohn, and Harry Hull St. Clair. In time St. Clair married my cousin Ethel Erskine, Uncle Will's daughter. In school he overawed us by his fondness for efficient, up-to-date methods. He learned shorthand, in order to take better notes. He solved sciences and languages as another would now solve a crossword puzzle. He had boundless curiosity, the exploring temperament.

Alfred Cohn was also an explorer, but of a different kind. He knew from the beginning what he wished to make of his life, and though he was fond of the arts, had some training in music, knew several modern languages and was well acquainted with history and general literature, we took it for granted that he would be a specialist in some branch of medical science, preferably in research. Melville Cane at school was altogether a poet, and at heart he has remained so. His early poems were very serious, and his best work still is, but he has written clever light verse, and I think I can name the occasion when he discovered by accident his resources of wit and satire. It was during the second meeting of our freshman class at Columbia College. At the first meeting, a few days earlier, Melville had risen to address himself with considerable gravity to some issue important to the extremely young. That day he was wearing a new derby hat, which, when he stood up, he placed carefully on the chair he had just vacated. At the end of his speech, diverted by his own eloquence, he sat down on the hat. When he rose again at our next meeting he was greeted with applause and with emphatic advice as to where to put his hat. Immediately he stole the thunder of the teasing classmates by saying funnier things about his mishap than they could think of. After that, wit was expected of him, and he always obliged.

I describe these school friends, not only to indulge an impulse of old affection, but to indicate my double good fortune in having extraordinary classmates as well as rare teachers. What a child gains from school depends to a large degree on the other children there. A wise parent considers that fact in choosing a school, but not even a wise parent can foresee the quality of the children who will arrive later. When Father entered me in the Grammar School, he did not know, nor did I, that Melville, Alfred, and Harry St. Clair would also enter that autumn. Mother used to say I was born with a silver spoon in my mouth. Fate has been generous to me.

3

Columbia Grammar was an old-fashioned preparatory school. Dr. Campbell and his staff may have been preparing us for life, but they never said so, if my memory is correct. They hoped to prepare us for college, nothing more and nothing less. In those days each college held its entrance examinations late in the spring. In two successive Junes my Columbia Grammar classmates and I appeared at the College, a block away, first for our preliminary, then for our final examinations. After the daily ordeal we went back to Fifty-first Street and showed our teachers what questions had been asked, and what we had answered. They were not worried, nor, to tell the truth, were we. The school had prepared us well, and we could go home with easy minds.

On the first day of our preliminary examinations, the first time I sat in the halls of my future Alma Mater, the subject was Latin. I came in from Weehawken as usual, took the Fourteenth Street car over to Fourth Avenue, then changed northward. Those horsecars were small, and the passengers noticed each other. Opposite me, seated next to the front door, was an elderly gentleman of whom good manners might be expected. As we turned into Forty-second Street an excited person, evidently fresh from

a train, rushed out of the old Grand Central, jumped on our front platform, and tried to open the car door, which happened to be latched on
the inside. The frantic arrival pounded for admittance. He wore a tan
box coat and a brown derby, too small for his moon-shaped face, which
was embellished by ridiculous side whiskers and mustache. He wore a
flower in his label, his eyes protruded, the lenses of his glasses were very
thick, he carried a brief case and a sporty cane, with which he did his
pounding on the car door. He seemed bound for the race track, or for
an appearance in a minstrel show. The old gentleman at the end of the
car looked at this apparition, then turned to the rest of us and winked.
The door latch then gave way, and the freak came in unhelped.

Half an hour later I sat in the examination room with my sharpened
pencils ready, and my pink examination book open before me, waiting
for the question paper to be distributed. Junior instructors patrolled the
room. Suddenly an incarnate magnificence entered, in cap and gown and
a hood reminiscent of Joseph's coat. I recognized the moon face, the
mutton-chop whiskers, the protruding eyes, the general thyroid effect.
The student sitting next to me whispered reverently that the gentleman
was the head of the Latin department, Dr. Harry Thurston Peck.

This strange man, fantastically gifted and fantastically ill-starred, was
then at the height of his career as scholar, teacher, historian, orator, editor
of a well-known classical dictionary, editor of *The Bookman,* a literary
review notably well informed and entertaining, an occasional essayist on
such subjects as the psychology of perfume. He was endowed with everything but discretion, judgment and taste. From my contacts with him at
Columbia I learned to appreciate his general human kindness, and I
know how highly he was esteemed by men who worked with him, like
Arthur Bartlett Maurice, assistant editor of *The Bookman.* But when I
saw him on the car platform that morning, and in the examination room,
prinked out in his millinery, I caught no suggestion of intellectual power,
and certainly no hint of that fatal charm which tangled him with too
many ladies, and at last, almost twenty years later, made a self-inflicted
death seem to him the only way out.

This was my grotesque introduction to the academic world. For a
while it put me rather on my guard against much that I wanted to believe in.

My last memory of Harry Thurston Peck is like that early glimpse in
the streetcar, slightly bizarre, and in view of his end, slightly tragic. Dur-

ing my final year at the University, I was president of the Graduate English Club. We wanted Professor Peck to address our spring meeting. He consented cheerfully, but when the date approached, Professor Price, the head of our department, was very ill, in fact dying, and I called at Professor Peck's office to say the meeting had been called off. To my knock on the door he responded with a cheerful "come in!" In I went, and got a shock. On a couch at one side of the room, he was seated next a rather handsome young woman, going over a Latin text with her. The book lay across his knees, spread open. She leaned down also somewhat across his knees, for a view of the text; and he, nearsighted man, necessarily had to lean down for a good view. With one hand he held the book steady, his other arm was around her waist. Whether he was translating to her, or she to him, I cannot say. As I came in, both straightened up, but without apparent embarrassment. He did not withdraw the encircling arm. I admired him for that. The lady too seemed pleased.

I told my errand. He expressed regret and sympathy for Professor Price. I walked out. They resumed their grappling with a difficult text.

CHAPTER IX

The College on Forty-ninth Street

I

IN THE late summer of 1896 I received a notice to appear at the
College within certain dates, and register for the freshman class.
Father decided he would come along and see how registering is done,
so Bessie was harnessed to the buggy, and crossing by the Forty-second
Street ferry, we drove to Forty-ninth Street. Since no other vehicle was
in sight that afternoon, we hitched Bessie to a lamppost and entered the
campus. The Registrar presided over a small room where those who
wished to purchase education could step up to a window or grill and pay
in advance. Anticipating a rush of business, he had caused a rail or fence,
at least three feet long, to be built in front of his window bars. I found
a place inside the rail without difficulty, no other candidate for registration being present. I signed my name, the Registrar accepted Father's
money, we untied Bessie from the lamppost, and thoughtfully drove
home.

Shortly after the term opened I made the acquaintance of the Dean,
John Howard Van Amringe, a figure in Columbia history. Van Am was
a gentleman of fine presence, who looked taller than he was. His white
beard, parted at the chin, lengthened him out. The beard had once been
red. He took almost military care to walk erect, and on occasion he literally leaned backward. He had a high voice, which in spite of huskiness
and a natural squeak, was penetrating. When dealing with a mere student who was not an athlete, he assumed a fierce manner, straightened
up, and glared down through his glasses, which because of the heavy

chain or cord attached to them, always slanted across his nose. Theoretically he held that teacher and student are and should be natural enemies. As I have implied, he favored athletes. It would be misleading to say that he wasted no attention on the studious, but he certainly had something like scorn for a grind. He was credited with saving the college from coeducation. His argument was simple. "You can't teach a boy mathematics if there's a girl in the room, or if you can, he isn't worth teaching." To conscience-stricken youths who wished a private word with him, he snapped, "Put it in writing!" It was remarkable how many of our petitions, when spread on paper, evaporated. He seemed a master hand at disposing of bluffs, but in fact he was oversoft. For those who cared to study his moods and wait for the right one, it was ridiculously easy to pull his leg.

He had an office boy, named, as I recall, Willie. Whether Willie had been trained by Van Am or whether he was the spontaneous product of nature, is not for me to say. If you knocked at the Dean's door, Willie opened it an inch or so and told you to put it in writing. According to widely circulating rumor he was not above suggesting that a package of cigarettes would help your case. He favored Sweet Caporals.

Van Am was perhaps a histrionic character, as many a man is without knowing it. His great popularity among the students may be explained by the fact that he gave an admirable performance of the part which undergraduates in those days thought a dean should play. Students like myself, ambitious to write or practice any of the fine arts, were a new type just beginning to appear in numbers on the American campus, and Van Am, who cared little for innovations, endured this one philosophically. Whatever the limitations of his interests, for me and hundreds of other boys he was a human and reassuring institution. Some of his casual remarks, thrown off with blustering emphasis, stuck in our memory like bits of folklore. "Don't eat crow unless you have to; but if you have to, say you like it!"

2

The President of Columbia when I entered was Seth Low. It was not till my senior year that my acquaintance with him went further than a passing salute, yet I remember him more easily at Forty-ninth Street than in the neighborhood of the Library building which he erected at One Hundred Sixteenth Street in memory of his father. He represented the old Columbia rather than the new, he was cautious in an expansive period, and though he took many wise steps toward the future, he did not always go through to the end. The development of the University was brought about gradually by younger and bolder pioneers. But he was a very courteous gentleman of a vanishing day, high minded and devoted to his ideals. If he had been less stiff in manner, and if he had had a stronger sense of humor, Columbia men might remember him more nearly as he deserves.

During freshman year I saw him once or twice in morning chapel. Attendance was not compulsory, and a few experiences of the curiously unwarming service were enough for even the resolutely pious, but it was characteristic of Mr. Low that he attended regularly. It was also characteristic, unfortunately, that he neither reformed the ceremony nor abolished it.

The chapel was a longish barren room in one of the inner buildings. Up this bowling alley there was a single aisle, with pews on each side for students, if any should come, and a seat at the end for the President. In front of the President's seat was a lectern, from which the Chaplain read the Scriptures. The Chaplain was the Reverend George R. Van de Water. Against the wall near the lectern was an extremely small organ. Beside the organ was an upright piano. The organist, Dr. George William Warren, played the organ until it was time for a hymn, then switched around to the piano, on which he could make more noise. The service consisted of Scripture reading, prayers and hymns, in no discernible order. After ten minutes of this miscellany, Dr. Warren deserted the piano for the organ, and began a soft postlude; Dr. Van de Water vanished into the closet where he took off his vestments; the students stood facing toward the aisle; and Mr. Low marched out. As he passed each pew we bent ourselves in an academic salaam.

3

Edward Alexander MacDowell became Professor of Music at Columbia the autumn I entered as a freshman, and his classroom was the first experience which justified my dreams of what a college or university should be. After I had registered for the prescribed courses, I found a copy of the thin folder which announced the new offerings in music, and immediately waited on Dean Van Amringe for permission to study advanced harmony and orchestration. Having got past Willie, the office boy, I found myself in an atmosphere which was intended to be, and was, heart-chilling. The idea had not yet penetrated the academic skull that music is a house-broken subject, deserving polite toleration if not hospitality. For most of the cultural high priests, music was still something you "took up" on the side, a mental discipline less rigorous and possibly less rewarding than poker.

Van Am glared at me. "You have plenty of real work, you know." I admitted the weight of my schedule.

"Well, won't that keep you busy? Why do you want to study music? Why must you study it now? Why not wait till you have more time?"

I explained, as youth can, that the essentials should never be postponed.

"It's against my judgment," said he. "You're here to get an education!"

I suggested that if MacDowell's instruction were not good for me, the Trustees had erred in providing it. That argument finished him. He was not convinced, he merely gave me up, with a shove toward the perdition my heart was set on.

"It's at your own risk."

I remember the words, the only benediction my Alma Mater pronounced on my zeal for the fine arts. This was nearly fifty years ago. I recite the episode as throwing light on MacDowell's misadventure in the academic world. It was one of the best of my many good fortunes that he began teaching at Columbia just as I began my studies there, and I admire the University authorities for the fleeting illumination they had when they called him. But they must have wanted him, not music. They belonged to their time. In my three years at Columbia Grammar School not a note of music had disturbed our tradition-keeping halls, not a word about music was uttered by either principal or by any teacher, and no one but Melville and Alfred knew my interest in music. I whispered to them that I played the piano; they whispered back that so did they.

Not only my early months at Columbia College, but all my years, were colored by knowing MacDowell. Had I begun to study English literature in the usual approach, I should have tried to admire, simply because my teachers and even more famous critics told me to do so, a number of authors who were not really first rate. But after a few hours in MacDowell's classroom I saw that literature is an art, like music, and every art should be studied in its masterpieces, from the standpoint of an apprentice who hopes some day to practice what he has learned, not simply to collect opinions about it.

Carl Walter was an artist, but MacDowell was the first top-flight genius I knew. He taught composition as he taught piano playing, with the assumption that his pupils had professional standards and wished not primarily to make money but to live out a philosophy. He made me realize that music or any other cultural activity is mean indeed if it is not a sincere way of life. The authentic spirits practice their art because they neither could nor would do anything else. The point came home; I studied music because it was a function of me to study music. What difference did it make, that the University as yet gave no credit for music study?

With Van Am's reluctant but written permission, I called on Mac-Dowell during his office hour in Carnegie Hall, in the rooms of Sargent's Dramatic School, where for the first year his classes met. The distance from Forty-ninth Street implied no precautionary isolation or quarantine, but Columbia had outgrown its buildings, and not even a grace note could be squeezed into the old Hamilton Hall, to say nothing of a piano. The Carnegie Hall suite was rather attractive, full of sunlight, smart and neat. The building then was new.

MacDowell sat at his desk, kind but keen, slightly quizzical. His questions probed deeper than Van Am's, but they had points of resemblance.

"Why do you wish to take these courses?"

"I want to study music."

"All of it?"

That threw me off a bit, but I said I did not expect to exhaust the subject, even though I studied as long as I lived.

His eyes twinkled. "Why go into your latter end? Why not tell me of your studies at this end? Have you begun? Do you know anything yet about music? You didn't say you wished to study further."

Unbalanced by the teasing, I began an idiotic outpouring of my accomplishments, my studies in harmony and counterpoint, my work at the piano, my organ playing and choir drilling in a small church, my—

He interrupted. "Then you know the different keys?"

I thought I did.

"What's the key of two flats and a sharp?"

For the life of me I couldn't answer, never having seen a mixture of sharps and flats in one signature.

"But don't you use the F sharp when you play the G minor scale? It's there, isn't it, whether or not the signature says so?"

At that point of complete deflation my examination stopped. The result seemed not unsatisfactory to him.

"Come along—we'll see what happens."

It is an argument against university posts for great musicians that in a large institution the chance is strong that some of the professors may know how to lecture. This puts the musician, by comparison, at a disadvantage. Lecturing is a branch of literature, not of music; it is a vestige of minstrelsy with the harp-playing left out. Musicians lecture well only if they possess an extra talent, not necessarily related to their art. For prolonged discourse their special medium is not words, and when they use words for musical interpretation their comments, even when helpful, are likely to be disjointed, a series of lightning flashes, bound together by the structure of the music they illuminate.

MacDowell was stimulating, as only genius can be, but his teaching was most effective with students who were already well grounded. I had the impression that his point of departure each day was not the precise frontier of our knowledge or ignorance, but some musical problem which at the moment engaged his attention. He would begin the hour standing up, often leaning comfortably against the piano, but in a moment, finding words inadequate, he would sit down and play. Then, apparently because our inactivity troubled him, he would ask one of us to write a theme on the blackboard and do something or other with it, but he often forgot to say what the theme and its development were to illustrate, and if we asked for information, our questions were likely to start new directions of thought, which however brilliant left us breathless.

If at times he puzzled us, we must have puzzled him still more. In the classes which I attended there was a fantastic range of preparedness and sheer ignorance. William Henry Humiston stood out in professional capacity and experience; he was already a fine pianist and organist, shortly he was to be the program annotator for the New York Philharmonic, and a few years later the assistant conductor of that orchestra. After him, at a distance, came a group of serious and fairly competent youngsters, among whom, of course, I range myself. Somewhat uncertainly I recall from those days Lewis M. Isaacs, who may have joined the group one year later, but he was an ambitious young composer, and though the responsibilities of his law practice diverted his energies, he remained a

MacDowell disciple, and for years was secretary of the MacDowell Association. In the harmony-counterpoint class were Angela Diller, composer and teacher, and her cousin George Matthew, a fine singer, one year ahead of me in college. Here again, perhaps, my memory slips; these two may have joined MacDowell's classes in the autumn of 1897, but whenever they came, they lifted our musical level. There were also, I must add, a number of MacDowell admirers, diffuse esthetic enthusiasts, eager to give the fine arts the benefit of their approval. They should have been spending their time elsewhere. One lady, in some respects mature, combined the Wednesday afternoon class with social engagements afterward. When she came to class dressed for a tea, in black satin and white gloves, MacDowell's teasing instinct invariably responded. We learned to watch for the moment when he would imperil the costume by sending her to the blackboard, himself in a gesture of chivalry handing her the chalk and the powder-scattering eraser.

From these exciting hours I cherish a miscellany of recollections, each of them full of his personality. One of us, for example, made a slighting remark about Liszt, and was promptly rebuked. MacDowell's estimate of the permanent contribution Liszt had made in the cause of music, and his discriminating admiration for Liszt's compositions, would now be considered orthodox, but fifty years ago they seemed overgenerous. And I am still amazed at his reply when I asked him which composer he would name to illustrate modern tendencies. I knew that Debussy and he had been fellow students, and when I asked the question Debussy was just coming into fame, but MacDowell made no reference to contemporaries. "For harmony," he said, "the kind that all periods must reckon with, study Palestrina. For modern music, study Bach. After that, use your own judgment." I found it difficult then, and still do, to relate this advice to his own compositions, much as I admire them.

In the classroom, as I have intimated, he was at the piano constantly, working out whatever was under discussion, and though the playing was of necessity intermittent and casual, I still think of it as prodigious. More than in his recitals the extempore performances of the classroom transformed the piano, made us forget the instrument and hear the music.

In the composition class one day he spoke his mind about the material we used. Our work, when of good enough quality, he said might pass for that of Europeans. Neither our themes nor our rhythms suggested that we lived in New York. He hastened to add that he set no value on conscious or deliberate nationalism, but an artist must accept himself for better or for worse. What we whistled, sang or played in moments of relaxation, more often than not was ragtime. Well, if syncopated rhythms were natural to us, why not try to make of them something important? "I would do it myself," he went on, "if I had not lived so long in Europe. Ragtime is not instinctive with me as it is with you—though I did make an attempt at it in the scherzo of my *Second Concerto.*"

That was the first good word for jazz I ever heard, and I remember it in connection with a remark of Charles Martin Loeffler, just before his death, that if he had his work to do over again, he would explore the rich possibilities of the jazz orchestra, as Ferd Grofe used it.

When Columbia moved to Morningside, MacDowell was installed in West Hall, a building now destroyed, a vestige of the old Bloomingdale Asylum, running north and south on part of the ground now occupied by Earl Hall. On the lowest floor were a bookstore and a lunchroom, on the second floor the Music department, above that the offices of the modern language professors, and on the top floor the undergraduate magazines and a large room for the use of the Glee Club.

Much of my time was spent at the Glee Club piano, and one afternoon a tenor was exercising himself to my accompaniments from memory. He spoke of MacDowell's song, *Thy Beaming Eyes,* regretting that it was in F, much too low for him. I transposed it to A flat and we started off, but before we had gone far MacDowell came up the stairs two steps at a time.

"Erskine, you know better than that! It's in F! If I had painted a landscape in one tone of gray, would you come along with a can of paint and make it lighter or darker?"

After he disappeared, I reflected that he permitted his publishers to bring out his songs in several keys, a procedure which blunted his point. Yet I felt then, and still believe, that he was essentially right.

A few days afterward I met him on the campus. His eyes had recovered their friendly twinkle.

"You're one of the stars of the Glee Club, aren't you?"

I explained that in that firmament I was only a shooting star.

"Well, shooting or fixed, will you do me a favor? Persuade those gentlemen to keep their piano tuned! If necessary, say I implore them, for the love of God!"

His appearance on that day was as I like to remember him. He seemed an out-of-door man, full of energy and health. When he strode across the campus in his tweed suit, with his cane hooked over his arm, even the least musical passer-by looked at him twice. Yet in spite of this wholesome impression, the deep-seated nervous trouble which eventually destroyed him, already began to show itself, on occasions. Some of his friends not at Columbia have suggested that the University overworked him, but I believe that is not so. I would not say that the average professor is overworked, and MacDowell taught fewer hours than the average. His schedule was light, and he had as assistants Leonard Beecher McWhood, to look after the elementary classes, and Gustav Hinrichs, admirable and experienced musician, to train and lead the College orchestra, conduct the music at academic ceremonies, and organize a chorus at Barnard. In the middle of each winter MacDowell had leave of absence for concert tours. He also conducted the Mendelssohn Glee Club, which had nothing to do with the University, and during his six Columbia years he did much composing, some of his best. If he was extremely busy, it was the urge to create which drove him, perhaps also an inner awareness that his great powers were soon to fail him.

But for the moment he radiated cheerfulness and inspired youth to stronger faith in its ideals. Like all poets he unconsciously communicated a philosophy. He made us feel that if music is a way of life, the musician, like other men, must assume the obligations of common sense and morality. He told me one day that he was glad I was going in for music, and overstimulated by the apparent compliment, I asked if he thought I had any special talent. "No," he said, "nothing special, but enough to make a good craftsman if you work hard. Would a law student ask his teacher the chances of his becoming a member of the Supreme Court? An honest, hard-working lawyer has a creditable place in society, and without many such men in the profession, perhaps there could be no great judges. Until we have thousands of well-trained musicians, there will be no adequate foundation for genius to build on when it arrives."

I recognized the truth, but I interpreted it my own way. He spoke of foundations, but perhaps he meant paving stones. I had said goodbye to music, in more ways than I realized, when I decided not to take Carl Walter's advice and go to Europe. Then, and when MacDowell spoke to me, perhaps it was easier to be modest about my musical talent precisely because confidence was growing that I might do something in literature.

After my sophomore year, though I took no more courses with Mac-Dowell, I saw him constantly and continued to learn from him. As long as I was in college I attended faithfully the recitals of original work by his composition class. One evening, in the small Barnard theatre, I heard three lovely songs by Angela Diller, beautifully sung by a young lyric tenor who had come from the South to study with MacDowell. His name was Hugh Martin. After years of vocal study abroad the lyric voice became heroic, and Hugh, returning to this country, joined the Metropolitan Opera Company as Ricardo Martin.

We have had in the United States, I think, two great composers, Stephen Foster and Edward MacDowell. Widely though they differ, they both had the authentic inspiration and the authentic dedication. When I try to name the quality which the great in art always illustrate, dedication is the word which comes to mind. Intellectually and spiritually Mac-Dowell was dedicated. In his Columbia classroom we were aware of something which cannot be analyzed in program notes.

4

Though MacDowell provided the great experience of my freshman year, two or three others helped to make it memorable. With Dr. Odell, my teacher in Columbia Grammar, friendship continued and grew. His associate in the teaching of English to freshmen was William Tenney Brewster, very tall, whimsically self-controlled and self-possessed, who fascinated us by his preference for Boston over New York. This judgment was always indicated involuntarily, since he was of an impeccable courtesy, yet the suggestion did come through that the ways of thought and feeling which were acceptable to Boston and Cambridge would naturally commend themselves to persons of the best taste. He was our first Harvard man, as splendid a citizen and as true a gentleman as can reasonably be expected in the rough world, where he has long played a distinguished part with stoical fortitude, understanding and humor. He, Dr. Odell and Edward MacDowell contributed to our education by treating us always with such courtesy that we had to improve our manners in order to respond in kind. Because of them, I have never had patience with those guides of youth who conceive of themselves as animal trainers.

In the first term of freshman year we read Horace's *Odes,* and our Latin instructor, Henry Jagoe Burchell, startled us by interpreting Horace, that ancient worldling, as a modern and human character. Mr. Burchell was very young, not much older than some of those he taught, but perhaps for that reason he understood us, and we felt he knew life. Of some other teachers we were less sure, but Mr. Burchell, we were convinced, was the real thing. In senior year some of us had another course with him, this time reading Catullus, and we were convinced again. A short time later he withdrew from teaching. He had all the desirable qualities which Harry Thurston Peck lacked. Perhaps that is why the Latin department did not make a stronger effort to keep him.

Since much of my study and writing has been concerned with the classics, I might as well say here what I think in general of the teaching of Latin and Greek in Columbia College while I was a student there. During the First World War, I heard James Hazen Hyde say he owed his love of the French to the nurse he had in childhood; she was a German. I can say that perhaps I owe my lifelong interest in the content and the spirit of classical literature to the preoccupation of my teachers with other matters. They conveyed to me their conviction that Latin and Greek should be studied as a moral obligation, in order to keep a tradition alive and hand on something precious, but only Dr. Bacon in school and Mr. Burchell in the College had the ability to indicate just what should be kept alive, and why it was precious. Mr. Burchell revealed to us so much contemporary vitality in Horace, that the question of keeping him alive did not occur; all he needed, all that any poet needs, is not to be killed off by unimaginative teaching, masquerading under the honored name of scholarship. Latin and Greek are not dead languages unless we assassinate them. But many professors of the classics are conservatives of the worst kind; they conserve the wrong thing. Aware that they have a precious thing in their keeping, they hate to admit that the precious thing is merely life. Life is so easy, so unscholarly! Mr. Burchell made Horace a contemporary, as Gilbert Murray a decade later made Euripides, and a popular contemporary at that. But some professors of Greek took pains to suggest that Gilbert Murray's scholarship left much to be desired—in other words, that his gorgeous translations were not the kind of translation they would have written, had they written any. And though Mr. Burchell left Columbia, other teachers remained to carry on a strictly scholarly tradition, by exhibiting Herodotus and Sophocles, Vergil and

Lucretius, as though each were that triumph of the conserving art, a mummy.

5

Among my freshman classmates I made a number of new acquaintances, and some lifelong friends. Joe Fackenthal, a whimsical keen-minded Pennysylvanian, sat next to me by alphabetical destination in every classroom. Henry Sydnor Harrison, kindly humorist, later the author of *Queed,* sat a few chairs away, and further off John Muirhead and Charles J. Ogden. Muirhead came from South Amboy, where his father was Mayor, and where he organized unforgettable house parties during Christmas holidays. Always whimsical, too modest or too indolent to set down on paper the subtle appraisals of people and experience which make his conversation remarkable, he has spent contented years teaching English, and other matters, to the students of Hobart College. Charley Ogden came from Wilton, Connecticut. After graduation he took a degree in Greek, taught that subject for a while, gave himself to the study of Persian with Professor A. V. Williams Jackson, and became secretary of the Oriental Society. These friends were in our not too large group of real scholars, along with Simeon Strunsky, and of course Alfred Cohn and Harry St. Clair, from Columbia Grammar. The determined writers of the class included Harold Kellock, quiet and thoughtful, and the strangely gifted Henry G. Alsberg, poet and 'cello player.

But the friend to whom I was closest during college days, was George Malin Davis Kelly, tall and commanding in appearance, blessed with many talents and abundance of personality. We had tastes in common, both loving music and books, but in background and temperament we were a contrast. He was the only son of Dr. Stephen Kelly, then president of the Fifth National Bank. His mother, dead in his childhood, had been a Mississippi Davis. From her he inherited an estate and a famous house in Natchez, to which even in his youth he was drawn by ancestral loyalties. He was a Southerner at heart, at home in the landscape, the climate, the sociable and not too strenuous life. He might have been a great singer. His voice was a baritone of range and power and magnificent tone, and like myself he studied music with some thought of making it his profession. After we met he did some further piano work with Carl Walter. He might have gone far in opera, since his precocious voice continued to develop even beyond its promise, but he was held back by his love of Natchez, which, whatever else it can offer, furnishes no career for opera singers. After a while he married and settled there permanently, to enjoy life with his family and manage his estates. He died suddenly, in April, 1946.

CHAPTER X

The University at Morningside

I

DURING the summer of 1897, Columbia moved up to the new buildings on Morningside Heights, and in the complicated migrations a few odds and ends were mislaid or lost—among them a course in chemistry which Harry St. Clair and I had elected. It dropped out of the curriculum, and we spent hours looking for it. Charles Frederick Chandler was to have been the instructor, and his name had attracted us rather more than the subject. We took our problem to Van Am. Chandler's course had lapsed, he admitted, but fortunately there was a substitute, Professor Charles Pellew's lectures for medical students. Pellew was Chandler's son-in-law, and since we were not to have Chandler, it was something to study with so close a relative.

Pellew gave his lectures at the end of the afternoon, from five to six, so that the boys from the College of Physicians and Surgeons could get uptown. The installation of the new halls was incomplete, especially as concerned electric wiring and bulbs. Pellew's large amphitheatre, after five, faded rapidly from dimness to blind dark. Chandler's son-in-law must have been a chemist or Chandler would not have had him around, but as a lecturer he was nothing at all. Only at intervals could he be heard, and then a certain affectation of speech and manner prevented him from being understood. Some years later, in 1923, he inherited an English title, went back to claim it, became Viscount Exmouth, took his seat in the House of Lords, or wherever viscounts are employed, and no doubt was in his proper place at last. He died in 1945. But meanwhile in 1897, his five o'clock medical students, in grief at his inaudibility, threw spit-balls and howled catcalls until six, when they raced for seats in the crowded horsecars southward bound.

Early in November I sought Van Am's permission to desert this kind of chemistry for Professor Ogden N. Rood's physics course, even though it was almost the middle of the term.

"If you change now," said the Dean, "you will flunk."

"I'll flunk if I stay!"

"If it will make you happier," said Van Am, "to do your flunking in Physics, speak to Professor Rood about it."

Rood was a great scientist, and I learned much simply by watching his methods. Research was his passion, but he could teach, as far as was necessary. The physics class came on Mondays, Wednesdays and Fridays, and between sessions the Professor resumed his interrupted experiments. In his laboratory, which was next door to his classroom, he had a couch, where he slept when his experimenting held him too late to go home. On Mondays he came to us fresh and tidy. By Wednesday he looked wilted, by Friday dilapidated. Then he would go home for the week end, and on Monday he would begin the cycle again, refreshed and tidied.

2

The undergraduates at Columbia had a newspaper, *Spectator,* and a magazine, the *Literary Monthly*. When the college moved uptown a third publication was added, *Morningside*. To this last I began to contribute, Melville Cane aimed at *Monthly,* and Sydnor Harrison joined the staff of *Spectator*. By the time we reached senior year each of us was editing his favorite publication, and we all were writing for the two strictly literary magazines. *Monthly,* a conspicuously serious review which permitted itself no more humor than a British quarterly, contained essays, poems (romantically lyrical, tragic, or epic), stories and criticism. *Morningside,* a handsomely printed brochure appearing every three weeks, accepted neither essays nor literary criticism, but showed the broadest kind of hospitality to fiction or verse of any style, provided it had quality. George Hellman edited *Monthly,* in succession to Joseph Proskauer, and Bill Bradley, from Columbia Grammar School, edited *Morningside,* which owed its attractive format to his knowledge of types and page-designing. Though he and Hellman were my academic elders by a year,

I learned rather easily to accommodate myself to their exercise of the authority which derives from long-accumulated wisdom.

Of course I am prejudiced, but I think the contributors to *Morningside* were a superior group, some of them to be numbered surely among the great of their time: Hans Zinsser, class of 1899, bacteriologist; Fred Keppel, class of 1898, successor to Van Am as Dean of the College, then Assistant Secretary of War under Newton Baker, then President of the Carnegie Corporation; Joel Elias Spingarn, poet and critic, one of the great authorities on the Renaissance, Assistant Professor of Comparative Literature at Columbia. Every number of *Morningside* had a fresh cover, drawn in black and white by some obliging artist who happened to be studying architecture, almost always by Huger Elliott, long a staff-member at the Metropolitan Museum of Art. Without Huger, *Morningside* would have missed some of its habitual excellence. He had talent, and he had the wholehearted joy in our enterprise which marks the true and lovable bohemian, predestined citizen of the Left Bank.

3

Halfway through my sophomore year *Morningside* published some verses of mine, fanciful and light, of no importance except for the impression they made on one man. A few days after the issue came out I found in my mail a flattering note, in a neat but miniature hand, suggesting that I call on the writer in room 509 Fayerweather Hall. That was the building in which I was studying physics with Professor Rood, but the English department occupied an upper floor. I was not sure of the signature, but it seemed to be Thomas R. Price. With an undergraduate's haziness about his elders, I had no idea who Thomas R. Price was, but since he evidently appreciated my peculiar talents, I was glad to encourage him by the sight of me. In this inadequate mood I climbed the stairs and met one of the noblest gentlemen and one of the best friends who ever inspired a sophomore to make the most he could of his life.

I can still see Professor Price, as he opened the door of his office. His manner had a courtliness from another time and place. He was of medium height, rather bald and slightly stooping, with a thick mustache and remarkable black eyes. His sight was not good, but his eyes seemed keen. He received me with expressions of pleasure, and wished me to a seat with something like deference, which overwhelmed me then, and seemed even more incongruous as I learned, through months and years, how great a man he was. But he had a fantastic respect for anyone who could write, especially for anyone who could put verses together.

He was one of the two or three most profound scholars then teaching the English language and literature in America. He had begun as a precocious student at the University of Virginia, with a particularly high record in mathematics. At the age of thirteen he had mastered all of that subject then taught at West Point. After taking his M.A. at the age of nineteen, he went to Germany to study Greek and Oriental languages at Berlin and Kiel, but upon the outbreak of the Civil War he ran the blockade, and received a commission on the staff of his cousin, General J. E. B. Stuart. Immediately after the war he married, and spent his honeymoon in General Lee's house; because of Lee's example, he went into education, to help in the restoration of the South. He taught English and modern languages at Randolph-Macon College, then succeeded Basil Gildersleeve as professor of Greek at the University of Virginia, when Gildersleeve went to Johns Hopkins. At Virginia, Professor Price also taught Hebrew. He had a reading knowledge of some twenty languages, half a dozen of which he could speak fluently.

From my little poem he got the impression that I was destined to be a writer, and he never wavered in that amiable opinion, which no one else then held. He was not himself a writer of the kind he thought I might be; I was later to profit by the instruction of a remarkable poet, and never cease to remember the inspiration with thankfulness. But only Professor Price, before I had accomplished a thing, believed in me, and taught me to believe in myself.

A few weeks after this very first meeting with Professor Price I received from Mrs. Price an invitation to tea. I went, and found myself in a choice representation of the Southern colony of New York City. Professor Price's loyalty to Virginia was extreme. He was never reconciled to the outcome of the Civil War. He and Mrs. Price led their social life either in the University circle or among Virginians who like themselves had come North. I remember the impression made on me that afternoon at tea by the large number of good-looking girls and handsome ladies, and by the prominence of the Southern accent. Mrs. Price was a gracious hostess, and her daughter Elizabeth—Mrs. Frederick Houston—then a young girl, flitted around the room with two or three others of her age. I had not then acquired a gallant philosophy, and to tell the truth, I went to the tea in the hope of seeing the Professor who appreciated my writing. I found him in a corner of the drawing room completely surrounded by the most beautiful girls at the party. As I came up, I saw he was balancing a glass of punch in his fingers without drinking it; he was too busy talking. Obviously his talk was witty, for he had his audience in laughter. When I drew near enough to hear his words, I discovered he was discussing the oddities of Danish grammar. I learned at once two of his main characteristics. He was a born courtier, and preferred not to waste a moment on a man if he could be talking to a woman. And he could turn the driest academic subject into bright material for social purposes.

Whether he was a typical Southerner of the old régime, surviving from pre-Civil War days, I cannot say. I met no one else, whether Northerner or Southerner, quite like him. It was easy to see that he had traveled abroad; he was more likely to speak of Europe than of our own country. If he could, he would avoid all references to American politics. Within the walls of his own home, if he spoke of the President, you knew he was referring to Jefferson Davis. Otherwise he would say with great respect, Mr. McKinley, or Mr. Cleveland.

We had no teacher who was more courteous, but almost my last memory of him illustrates his loyalty to a prejudice. Half a dozen of us in one of his seminars were writing an examination paper. He thought it ignoble to proctor students who were undergoing a test, but the walls of his classroom were lined with cases of books from his overflowing library, and while we were writing he came in to consult a volume. As he turned the pages the janitor came up the stairs with a gentleman who wished to call on Professor Price. The Professor offered the gentleman a chair on the spot, and for a moment they conferred in low tones, the caller explaining his errand, the Professor listening without enthusiasm. All at once something went wrong. The caller arose and backed apologetically toward the door. Professor Price followed him out and across the hall to the staircase. At the top stair the gentleman took a hasty farewell and hurried down, but Professor Price stood there talking after him vigorously, raising his voice to catch up with the fast-disappearing visitor. We in the classroom heard something like this: "No sir! If at any time you ask a favor for yourself in your private capacity, I shall be delighted to oblige you if I can! But as to the present matter—it would be impossible for me to think of anything to say at the funeral of your dead friend which his relatives would care to hear!"

4

With Professor Price, admirer of writers, were associated Professor Brander Matthews and Professor George Edward Woodberry, two younger colleagues whose reputation was well established. They differed sharply in background and temperament, and both differed from Professor Price. Woodberry was the product, somewhat narrowly, of Boston, of Cambridge, of Harvard. Brander was just as narrowly the product of old New York, of that merchandising society—respectability founded on exports and imports—which Henry James and Edith Wharton described. Woodberry, born at Beverly, Massachusetts, from five generations of sea captains, had been brought up in a atmosphere of high thinking but of decidedly plain living. Brander Matthews, heir to a sizable fortune, had been conditioned by social contacts and by wide travel for the life of a cosmopolitan, the kind of world citizen who would feel at home anywhere in the best clubs, the best restaurants, the best theatres. Through my college days Woodberry took his vacations at Beverly, on the ancestral North Shore, or in Italy, which was his spiritual home. Brander liked to rest up in his London clubs or in the Paris theatres.

Brander was a skilled and graceful man of letters. He regarded writing as a craft, an honest way of earning a living. I doubt if his soul ever yearned for self-expression in a more profound sense. His novels were not important, and his plays did not hold the stage, but he was a warm-hearted friend, his acquaintance among celebrated people here and abroad was wide, and he was an excellent raconteur. Also, and perhaps this was his greatest charm, he was of a loyal temperament, and in all his loyalties he remained to the end of his days rather sophomoric. His affection for Columbia, his Alma Mater, expressed itself in typical undergraduate gibes at rival institutions and in exaggerated rooting for the home campus. In this respect, as well as in his love of the theatre, he had points of resemblance with Professor William Lyon Phelps, of Yale. The best portrait of Brander which I have seen is in Lloyd Morris' autobiography, *A Threshold in the Sun*.

Woodberry was a thoughtful scholar, a philosopher, or as Brander would say, an idealistic dreamer—and Brander could say nothing more severe of any man. Woodberry's office in Fayerweather was next door to Price's; Brander's was at the opposite end of the corridor. The two men found each other uncongenial, and the department was threatened with a serious division. Professor Price grieved that his colleagues could not get on together. He was devoted to Woodberry, who admired him greatly. Though he always spoke of Brander with punctilious courtesy, I doubt if he cared much for the New Yorker's self-confident exuberance. Brander was not above telling jokes at the expense of the old and defeated South.

5

In the second semester of sophomore year Will Bradley told me I had been elected to the editorial staff of *Morningside*. From then on I began to learn the routine of getting out a small tri-weekly, and at the board meetings I had good hours with Bradley himself, with Henry Alsberg, my classmate, with Hans Zinsser and Huger Elliott and the Barnard representative, Virginia Gildersleeve, talented and well poised, who contributed fiction to our pages and good sense to our discussions.

One incident made on me a lasting impress. We are often told that the training of character is as important as the training of the mind, but less frequently do we hear just how character can be trained. I had one teacher who knew how to do it. His ostensible but less important job was to acquaint me with the events of American history. He was Harry Alonzo Cushing, afterward Dean of our Law School. A hard worker himself, he apparently hoped to make slaves of us; the amount of reading he assigned weekly was formidable, and we were to make notes on every page we read and bring our notebooks to class with us, so that Mr. Cushing could examine them immediately if our recitation was unsatisfactory. Unless the volume of our notes convinced him of our industry, we were in trouble. In case a poor recitation was contradicted by a good notebook, I suppose Mr. Cushing attributed to us some defect either of mind or morals. For this disciplinary system of his I had no liking at the time, and I have no respect now. It was based on a number of false premises. The ability to take notes as you read is of no more value than the ability to keep a diary in the midst of exciting experiences. Copious notes, like any other form of long-windedness, can hardly be interpreted as indicative of intelligence or scholarship. In childhood I learned to read with concentration, and the reading which Mr. Cushing assigned was not always uninteresting. When I became interested I forgot to take notes.

But Mr. Cushing did give me, as I said, a lesson in character, in moral responsibility. Columbia in those days had two literary societies, which frequently met in public debate, and for lack of more experienced debaters my society put me on its team. I found the preparation of my speech more alluring than the lengthy report Mr. Cushing had called for, to be handed in on the very day of the debate. I unfolded my problem as he was writing on the blackboard just before class. He was busy, he had his back to me, he showed no eagerness to turn around.

"Mr. Cushing," I called, "may I hand in my report a week late?"

He glanced, without pleasure, over his shoulder. "Why not hand it in on time?"

I explained why not.

He resumed his blackboard writing. Then with cold deliberation, his back still turned: "You have already decided to debate. If you can also find time for your classwork, do so! If you can't, don't bother me!"

I took my part in the debate, and I handed in the report promptly, and I thank Mr. Cushing for teaching me not to shift, or try to shift, moral responsibility.

6

I heard from Melville Cane and other classmates many respectful or even excited references to Professor Woodberry, whose course in Elizabethan literature they were attending. I would have elected that course myself, if my attention had not been centered on MacDowell and Professor Price. I resolved to study with Woodberry for the rest of my college years, and to visit his classroom at once, for a taste of his quality. When I went to his office to ask permission, I found myself talking to a quiet person of less than average height, who wore thick glasses but whose glance concentrated on me. He enunciated with leisurely precision, not so much because he wished to be understood as because he loved words for their own sake. He showed no interest in the prospect of an auditor, he may even have been a little on guard, as though I were an intruder, but at last he said I might sit in the back of the room.

There was no need to specify the location of my seat. While he spoke, the good places were already taken. Though the lecture period would not begin for another five minutes, eighty or ninety boys were already assembled. The wiser ones, knowing that Woodberry's voice did not carry well, liked to keep free the hour before his lecture, so that they could arrive early and seize a chair well forward.

I waited patiently with the others until Woodberry came in, about ten minutes past the hour, and the room quickened with a thrill of expectation. At Columbia a teacher who arrived late usually found no class; the students could leave without penalty after five minutes. But for Woodberry they always waited. They knew that when he began at last they would hear at once some quiet-seeming remark which would open their eyes and start them thinking. It was so that morning, as Woodberry lectured on Shakspere's *Sonnets;* it was so the following year, when I elected his course in nineteenth century literature; it was so in graduate years, when he lectured on epic poetry.

Others have described the method and the effect of his teaching, and though their accounts seem to me less than adequate, my own attempt may fall just as far short. The truth is that his fantastic success in the classroom was not to be expected and it remains difficult to account for. Of any pedagogical science you might say he was wilfully innocent. His voice was so low that it hardly reached to the last row of seats. He might have spoken louder, but he preferred not to make the effort. He was so nearsighted that he could not see what was going on in the classroom, but he probably did not care, so long as a decent silence prevailed. In later years deafness overtook him, but at Columbia his hearing was acute.

He was a fascinating and noble teacher only because what he said to us was fascinating and noble. He always lectured on a high plane, with the obvious assumption that for others as for himself the masterpieces of poetry and the deep things of life would be of consuming interest. His students responded to the generous compliment.

To many scholars imaginative literature is merely one of the graces of life, and the study of books merely a professional occupation, to be pursued during working hours and at other times laid aside. For Woodberry literature was life itself. It could be created by those who were steeped in life, and by no one else; on the other hand, he was concerned with life chiefly under those eternal aspects which are the star dust of poetry. He who would do laudable things in poetry, Milton said, must himself be a true poem; Woodberry believed the doctrine, and his work and his life were of a piece.

We were aware of this unity when he entered his lecture room. Other men, more obviously brilliant, could illuminate literature from the outside, but he made us feel that he was availing himself of an opportunity to speak to his fellow man about what was uppermost in his thought and nearest his heart. His teaching was the overflow of a lifelong preoccupation.

Such subject matter, presented by a teacher so unemphatic, might well have been an excuse for inattention, or even the occasion for classroom disorder. There was indeed a legend at Columbia that Woodberry's first classes, in the early nineties, found something ridiculous in this dreamy, soft-spoken man who conferred with them on equal terms about the spirit of Shelley, or the imagination of Milton, or the moral grandeur of Sophocles, or the divine myths of Plato. Those first students of his, we heard, started a riot, just to see what he would do. In surprise and sorrow he gathered his books and his notes, and retired to his study. He told me of the incident years later. President Low sent for him, and said he understood there had been trouble in the class.

"Indeed there has been!"

"What do you intend to do about it, Mr. Woodberry?"

"Nothing, Mr. President."

Mr. Low was astonished at this detachment.

"No," continued Woodberry, "you invited me to lecture at Columbia on literature, to persons, presumably, who wished to hear. Of course I can lecture to no one against his will."

That held Mr. Low for a moment.

"Perhaps," suggested Mr. Woodberry, "a little discipline might render the students more attentive."

"And who," asked the President, "is to introduce discipline into your classroom?"

"You," said Mr. Woodberry. "I am a teacher. The disciplinary function resides in the college executive."

"Let me ask one more question," said Mr. Low. "When you speak of discipline, what have you in mind?"

"The guillotine."

I asked Mr. Woodberry what happened next, but he had forgotten, or perhaps he never knew. He continued to lecture as before, and his students became aware of what they were listening to. For the word-music of poetry, the phrasing, the verse form, he had extraordinary sensitiveness. Yet the content of the poem was always more to him than the technique, and the spirit more than the content. He had a unique gift for making even an unread youth appreciate, at least to a degree, how in some passage of Shakspere or Keats a very human experience produced in the poet a poetic emotion, and how that emotion dictated the form of the poem. Many of us learned in his classroom, what mature artists sometimes need to re-learn, that technique cannot be acquired or applied from the outside, but must grow out of the experience which the artist hopes to express.

We did not always understand the subtleties of his interpretations, but he imparted the faith that they were not beyond our reach, if we tried. When his students describe him as stimulating, they mean that he sent us away after each class still thinking of the poem or poems he had discussed, and still pondering his criticisms. Though the bell had rung, we could not put his lecture out of mind.

We felt then, what we have thought of more precisely since, his unusual gift for speaking of a poet in the very mood of the poet's own work. This skill of his resembled the art of a musician who can interpret various composers each in his distinctive style. When Woodberry spoke of Shelley, the atmosphere he created was in sympathy with Shelley's genius. When he spoke of Milton, or of Walter Scott, he put us in the mood of those very different writers. Interpretation of this subtle kind is easy to feel, but hard to describe.

No memory of him in his Columbia days would be complete if it did not include his friendship with A. V. Williams Jackson, Professor of Indo-Iranian languages, who collaborated with him in the course on Elizabethan literature. In personality and temperament the two friends supplemented each other. Jackson had a social gift as marked as Woodberry's reticence, and a lightness of touch which offset Woodberry's seriousness. The relation of these two unusual men seemed to us an illustration of those chivalrous loyalties which we had learned to admire in Sidney and Greville, and the other great companions of poetry.

Woodberry was far from being what is called a practical man. His contacts with politics or business or ordinary housekeeping were slim. He was temperamentally destined to the cloister or the study. But it was only in later years that we realized this, and none of us thought the discovery important. We had had teachers in plenty who knew more of the practical world than he, but they taught us far less. He was preoccupied with poetry, in the era of Mark Hanna, but from his lectures on poetry we derived a conception of life in the highest sense realistic. He was the first teacher from whom I got the notion that the public life of the citizen is important as an expression, even as a test, of his private aspirations, and that the business enterprises of a country cannot in the long run be separated from its essential religious or spiritual faith. Having learned from him that poetry is the flower of life but still an integral part of it, we went on to learn that all human activities are related, and—unless one is stupid or a hypocrite—must be harmonious. Perhaps the humanity of this point of view is too magnificent for the jaded or the overcautious or the world-weary, but for boyhood it was a thrilling vision, and in its power many who sat in Woodberry's classes have tried to live.

It was a rare experience to be studying literature with a man who was producing it. In 1899, my junior year, the campus was stirred by *Heart of Man,* and a year later we were quoting to each other lines from *Wild Eden.* I see no reason to change my opinion that *Heart of Man* is one of the great books of our literature. Indeed, it seems more timely now than when it first startled us, more than forty-five years ago. Our country then was dangerously prosperous and self-satisfied; the silly little war with Spain had been won, we were inflated with commercial interpretations of our Manifest Destiny, we were about to shed almost as much blood to subdue the Philippines as more recently to liberate them, and our people were stirred by few moral questions more significant than whether Admiral Dewey should have given to his wife the house which his fellow citizens had presented to him. It was a bleak moment for poets or for youth, but just then, when the need was greatest, Woodberry reminded us that men cannot be, as we have learned to say, isolated; he showed us that poetry, religion, and politics in any noble sense are all rooted—not in the genius of any one race or country—but in the general heart of man. Long before the war agony from which we now emerge, he taught us, and no one has presented the truth with warmer eloquence, that democracy can be limited by no border, no frontier, since all mankind are born into a single world, and in some degree must share a single fate. As though he were speaking to his boys, he reminded his readers that how to live is the main matter, whatever else we may study; our highest intelligence would be to understand our human nature and the ways of our heart; our best fortune would be to share the common lot. And by common lot he made us understand not the constrained inheritance of mediocrity, nor the limited vision of merely local issues, but the whole drama of human experience.

It seemed to many of us a tragedy, the burden of which fell more on us than on him, that when the revival of poetry took place around 1910 the new poets did not value Woodberry's work, and some of them were studiously hostile to it. He had prophesied the revival and had done much to bring it on, but more than one of the younger group took pains to suggest that he was out of date. The verdict described truly enough the external aspects of his art. He spoke with the accent of the older Boston culture, and he had a feeling for the English rather than for the American language. It is true also than he was in the best sense a singer; poetry for him was not conversation but music. But he remained consistently generous toward writers of a different tradition than his, and toward the future in which he might have no part. In one of our last talks, after he had withdrawn from teaching, he asked me what sort of literary background the modern college boy has. I told him my Columbia students came to college with a good fund of reading, but not the reading in which I had been brought up, with slim knowledge, for example, of English literature, or of Greek, or of the Bible. But some of them were widely read in Russian literature, of which I was practically ignorant, and most of them kept up with modern books from all quarters of the globe. Woodberry smiled. "It's not important," he said, "that they should have the same background as you and I. They will belong to another age. Their turn will come to grow old. There will be many other ages."

I must set down here one more memory of the first lecture I heard him give. As he talked he held in his hand a folded sheet of letter paper on which was an outline of what he wished to say, with page references and other reminders. As he came to the end he folded and refolded these notes, and then, as if unconsciously, tore them to fragments and tossed the scraps toward the wastebasket. All his lectures ended with this tearing up of the notes, and I wondered at the destruction of material which a lecturer, I imagined, would be glad to keep. When years later I asked him about it, he said that if he had kept his notes, he certainly would have used them again another year, but his point of view might change. By tearing up his notes, he made sure of having something fresh to say.

7

In my junior year Woodberry's students organized, I believe at his suggestion, a literary circle which we called the King's Crown, after the symbol of royalty on Columbia's eighteenth century seal. There was also a crown of iron on the old King's College flagpole. King's Crown met twice a month, and he showed further his understanding of his boys in the choice of a meeting place and in the arrangement of programs. Once a month we met in one of the larger classrooms to hear an address by a distinguished writer, a friend of Woodberry's, whom he had persuaded to come. After the talk we adjourned to the College Tavern, for beer and pretzels and an opportunity to exchange ideas with the visitor, if we could think of anything to say. Evenings with William Dean Howells, Edmund Clarence Stedman, Weir Mitchell, John LaFarge, Thomas Wentworth Higginson were a privilege we did not undervalue, nor soon forget.

But I learned even more from the alternate meetings, which were entirely informal, with no guest speaker and no program, but entertainment of quality was sure to offer itself spontaneously. Professor Jackson was always there, and Woodberry himself, and a keg of beer in the middle of the room on the second floor of the Tavern. How much of my education I owe to the Tavern! I grieved when it was torn down to make way for the Union Theological Seminary. Woodberry and Jackson kept the talk on worth-while topics, and drew us into it. We learned then, if we had not known before, how to be both cultured and comfortable. It would be hard to exaggerate the value of an undergraduate "bull session," where boys speak their minds and unconsciously help each other in their gropings. The talks at the King's Crown were, if you please, "bull sessions," with this distinction, that two wise teachers and true gentlemen were present, to set an example of honest thinking, of good taste in thought and speech, of courtesy in discussion.

If any student was called on for a special contribution, the result was memorable. Woodberry was alert to the work of us all, and he usually knew if a boy had something up his sleeve. On one memorable evening Henry (Hank) Alsberg read us a story which, as I happened to know, he had thought of during one of Woodberry's lectures. My seat was next to Hank's, and when Woodberry read a passage from Tennyson's

"Lucretius" I heard a muffled exclamation, "God, what a story!" These were the lines:

> Then, then, from utter gloom stood out the breasts,
> The breasts of Helen, and hoveringly a sword
> Now over and now under, now direct,
> Pointed itself to pierce, but sank down shamed
> At all that beauty.

Hank's story was about a beautiful but wicked queen who plotted to kill her husband and give the kingdom to her lover. The loyal prime minister discovered her plan and drew his dagger, but could not strike anyone so beautiful. She remembered the dagger, and as soon as her villainous lover had seized the realm, she put out the minister's eyes and turned him adrift, to beg for a living. Years later, as he crouched in his hovel, he heard a woman's voice praying for shelter. Unable ever to forget that voice, he told her to come in. The country had revolted, her lover was dead, vengeance hunted her. The blind man felt his way along the wall. She did not recognize him till his fingers were at her throat. It was useless for her to scream and struggle; by destroying his sight she had robbed herself of her only defense.

Hank always read his stories bashfully, but this one was superbly written, and its effect was powerful. Woodberry gave it his accolade. "I wonder how you sleep of nights, Mr. Alsberg!"

8

Among the good things of junior year, on another plane, was Professor George Rice Carpenter's course in daily themes. The idea of daily themes was thought up by Harvard teachers, and their pupils went out from Cambridge in all directions, for several decades, preaching the advantages to be derived from writing one page every twenty-four hours. The daily-theme course was not equally successful everywhere, but as Carpenter gave it, at Columbia, it was a remarkable experience.

For the first half-year we handed in a theme every day, each theme being a page in length. The second half-year was devoted, all of it, to writing one essay, of at least five thousand words. The writing of short pieces constantly either left you with not another idea in your head, or it taught you how much there is to say if you keep your eyes open and think about what you see. No doubt the daily themes were good for me, but I learned still more from the long essay in the second half-year. Professor Carpenter asked us to choose a subject, and he gave us a week to think it over. Then he discussed the subjects in public, before the whole class, and in private consultation. He asked us whether our subject was of such significance to us, that we needed five thousand words to do it justice. Then he asked what interest it would have for readers at large. From these preliminaries I learned once for all that nothing worth while can be written on less than a large idea, a great crisis, a genuine problem.

From the subject we passed at once to the treatment—that is to say, to the form. He asked us to bring in a skeleton of the essay, paragraph by paragraph, each paragraph being represented by a single sentence. By the time we had shaped this outline to his satisfaction and our own, nothing remained but to fill out the paragraphs and smooth away the angularities of the frame.

To this day I use no other method in preparing any piece of writing, whether short or long. After training so sound, I do not care to begin a novel or an article before I have worked it out completely in outline. It is easy to write the first sentence when you know what the last sentence will be. I cannot estimate the amount of time I should have wasted, had I not taken that course with George Rice Carpenter.

He taught me other things. He was a gentle soul, with humor and common sense, and he was content to give his life to the teaching of composition because he conceived of the writing process as an exercise in sincere thinking and sincere feeling. Many of my classmates, like me devoted to Woodberry, avoided the daily-theme course because they thought it inculcated a mechanical approach to an art which they conceived of as pure inspiration. I believed they were wrong then, and now I am sure they were, for the simple reason that without the mechanics of writing, which they declined to learn, it is hard to do any writing at all. Many of them have much to say and occasionally squeeze some of it out, but their intervals of silence are too long. A writer is one who writes, as a singer is one who sings—and in either case habitual performance is understood.

Carpenter was no Woodberry, but he loved poetry, and his favorite poet was Dante. He was a good Italian scholar, and he knew the Florentine's compact verses by heart. At the time I wondered at his taste, he coming from New England with much American realism in his blood, but in my graduate years he made one remark which explained himself and opened up to me the essential quality of Dante. I happened to say something about Shakspere, something full of admiration youthful and undiscriminating, something probably trite and banal, since Shakspere had been thoroughly admired before I got at him. "Oh yes," said Carpenter. "Very interesting, that Elizabethan poet! He did much for the theatre. But I'm not an antiquarian. I can understand a modern poet like Dante."

9

That fine story of Alsberg's was published in the *Morningside*. The little magazine was at its peak in these years, while the writing fever was running its course in Columbia College, and with almost the same intensity in Barnard. Grace Goodale joined Virginia Gildersleeve to represent Barnard on the editorial board, and they in turn were succeeded by Jeannette Bliss Gillespy, one of the ablest writers in either college, born in Lansingburg, Mother's early home. Miss Gillespy's verse was of a poignant quality much admired and envied by the rest of us. She had a boldness of thought which we could not imitate, and we attributed it to some deep experience withheld from normal mortals. Board meetings of *Morningside* were exciting when she was present; she would say wise things about the manuscripts we considered, she was full of high spirits, when occasion demanded she had a mordant wit, and she might even stoop to a pun. Campus legend declared she had raised the question in a literature class whether "Sphere-born harmonious sisters, Voice and Verse," was not an allusion to the precarious New York pronunciation.

But she was a true poet, and the world lost something when she, mysterious as ever, abandoned the cultivation of her talent, and hid herself in silence.

This miniature foretaste of the writing world suddenly became of secondary interest. At Columbia the seniors each year composed and presented a musical show of variable quality, but always with whatever entertainment value results from seeing female rôles played by boys. In the years preceding our graduation the Varsity Shows had been excellent, and several teams of composers and librettists were grooming for the 1900 production. When the call was sent out for scores and manuscripts, Melville Cane suggested that I write the music to a book by him. Within half an hour Syd Harrison proposed that he write a book to music by me.

In another half-hour we had consolidated forces, and in twenty-four hours—I am sure not later—we were hard at work on *The Governor's Vrouw,* a musical comedy which we said would be in the Gilbert and Sullivan tradition. Syd and Melville were to do the book, Melville the lyrics, I the music. Since the accompaniment would be played by the University orchestra, I had at least one opportunity in a lifetime to score my music and hear what it sounded like.

The book had a good idea, lifted from Washington Irving's *Knicker-bocker History.* William Kieft, the Governor who preceded Stuyvesant, was a small man with a quick temper, who had a large wife with a violent tongue, and both of them jointly had a beautiful daughter named Katrinka. My friend George Matthew, from MacDowell's classes, sang Katrinka. He was a gymnast, a specialist on the flying rings, and his biceps were so developed that when he dressed up as a Dutch girl we cautioned him to relax, so his arms would look merely fat. I gave him a tender lullaby, which made quite a hit, especially when he was singing high notes pianissimo. Stage nervousness might at any moment cause him to clench his fists bravely until the astounding biceps ballooned out.

According to Syd and Melville, Governor Kieft won the enmity of the Indians by forbidding the sale or use of tobacco on Manhattan. Mrs. Kieft didn't like the smell. To pacify the Indians, the Governor made wampum legal tender, whereupon the Connecticut Yankees manufactured wampum by the cartload out of discarded oyster shells, and in no time sound money was displaced by bad. The Connecticut Yankees had Amsterdam's gold, the Amsterdam treasury had oyster shells—and Kieft, alas, still had his wife!

The Governor then agreed with the Indians to lift the ban on smoking if they would oblige by abducting Mrs. Kieft. They took her one evening when she stepped abroad for a moment to look at the moon. The Governor called out the trained band, first making sure that they were short of ammunition. To put a proper face on his villainy, he promised to give his beautiful daughter, Katrinka, to any brave gentleman who would rescue her mother. That was the end of Act I.

The handsomest of the Yankees took up the Governor's offer, gathered a few friends, and started out. Before they had gone far they met the Indian band bringing back the unendurable Mrs. Kieft. The young Yankee made a deal with them; they promised to swear he had rescued the lady only after heroic effort. He then took her home, they perjured themselves for the sake of the tobacco trade, the Governor fainted, and the Yankee got Katrinka. Everybody, Indians and all, joined in a loud and amicable chorus, and the friendly audience insisted on many recalls.

The Governor's Vrouw was given for a week at Carnegie Lyceum, beginning Monday evening, February 19, 1900, and for one performance the following Monday in Brooklyn, at the Academy of Music.

My musical and theatre-minded friends were prominent in the cast. George Kelly played the Captain of the trained band, Rutger Planten was the amorous Yankee trader, and William de Mille was the Indian chief.

William C. de Mille had begun his studies in the School of Mines, but toward the end of his course he decided to be a dramatist instead of an engineer, and came over to the College. He was the only non-amateurish actor in the cast; perhaps for that reason he helped himself to the part of the abducting savage, a muscular and gymnastic rôle without dialogue, which as William expanded or inflated it, furnished the exciting moments of the play.

The Governor's Vrouw brought my undergraduate career to a close. At Commencement the award of the Proudfit Fellowship in Letters enabled me to go on to the Graduate School. There would be no break in my life at Columbia but merely, as I assumed, a progress in maturity. I was not likely to think seriously again of music as a profession; I would be a scholar, a teacher—and in time perhaps a writer.

CHAPTER XI

The Graduate School

I

IN THE autumn of 1900 I did indeed go on in my studies from where I had left off in the spring, but there was a sharp change in our home. Father sold his factory in Union Hill and the house in Weehawken. All that pleasant life, indoors and out, the friendships, the church work, the choir training and the organ playing, came to an end, not because we wished it so, but because New York was a different world from New Jersey, even though there was only the river between. We moved to an apartment at 340 West Eighty-fifth Street. For the next three years our summers were spent at Norwich.

The apartment in the city brought us close to three new friends, Miss Minnie Harris and her sisters, Ida and Stella, who lived in a brick house, an old-fashioned private residence, at 500 West End Avenue, just around the corner from us. Sister and I had met them on a summer trip to the Thousand Islands. They were English, children of a sea captain, who bequeathed to them an enormous zest for travel, and the means with which to satisfy the urge. They all sang well, Minnie superbly, and Father's voice was still in good condition; together we had evenings of music, with cosmopolitan talk about European and American art, or whatever else appealed to people who knew the concert stage, the theatre and books, in that far-off world, forty-five years ago.

Because the Harris sisters inspired Father, we had even more music at home than usual, and some of the time that had gone to choir training was now given to piano practice. I believe I played better during the three years of graduate work than ever in my school days. Also, for the first time I had at serious moments the authentic urge to write, the sense of something that had to be said, rather than the mere wish to see myself in print. *The Century Magazine,* then edited by Richard Watson Gilder, offered a prize for the best short story, for the best essay, and for the best poem written during the year after graduation from college. In the competition for graduates of 1900, I won the poetry prize with "Actaeon," which appeared in the *Century* for January, 1902, and later gave the title to my first book of verse. This success opened doors for me. Mr. Gilder and his associate editor, Robert Underwood Johnson, continued to publish my work, and Bliss Perry, then editing *The Atlantic Monthly,* took some of my poems. But I had set a mark in "Actaeon" which for a long time I could not equal. Though I still had faith in myself, I began to doubt my talent for verse; if I were to go far, it might be in fiction or drama. I tried my hand at a number of short stories, all disappointing. Just one of them got into a widely circulated magazine. After the publication of *The Private Life of Helen of Troy* this indiscretion of mine was discovered by the editor of a fiction anthology, who wanted to reprint it. I promised to sue him if he did.

In my Graduate School years our old writing crowd from *Monthly* and *Morningside* continued to meet in an informal club which called itself The Society of Bards and Prophets, or more formidably *Societas Bardorum Vatiumque Columbiae.* We gathered in rathskellers attached to breweries or other places favorable to letters and to good-fellowship. Fortified by a stein, a slice of rye bread with cheese on it and a dab of mustard, we listened to each other's compositions patiently, and read our own in retaliation. Melville Cane would be there, and George Wharton, melancholy humorist, one of the early contributors to *Morningside,* and Bradley and Hellman and Joel Spingarn, all constant attenders, with three or four variables.

Bradley and Hellman, having taken the Master's degree during my senior year, were now publishing and editing *East and West,* a magazine of their own invention. It came out once a month. In the first number its ideals were clearly stated. Since the trend of the modern magazine was toward articles of a reportorial nature, and since more and more of the page would be given to illustration and advertising, *East and West* hoped to be "entirely literary, containing well-written stories, good verse both serious and light, and essays of contemporaneous interest." Young writers would be welcome, but the elders would not be discouraged. Looking over the beautifully designed pages, which are a memorial to Bradley's youthful skill in such matters, I cannot now recall which were the young writers and which the veterans. But it was a good list—Gustav Kobbé, writing on art, Louise Betts Edwards, Arthur Ketchum, Richard Burton, George C. D. Odell, writing even then on the New York theatre, Percy Mackaye, Clinton Scollard, Curtis Hidden Page, Howard Chandler Robbins, Alice Duer Miller, Madison Cawein, Arthur Colton, Hans Zinsser, Meredith Nicholson, Christian Frederick Gauss, Frank Wadleigh Chandler, W. P. Trent, Edith M. Thomas, Gerald Stanley Lee. All these, and others in the book, I already knew or came in time to know. They didn't seem then so settled in tradition as they may seem now; Gerald Stanley Lee's brisk essay on "The Habit of Letting One's Self Go" was considered daring, almost too much so. The kindly philosopher, mind you, advised us all to let go. Knowing the threat of nervous tensions in modern times—and the second year of the century seemed modern times —he was advising us to relax before it should be too late.

East and West ran for a year with surprising success. Those of us who merely contributed, thought the editors should have continued indefinitely, in the interest of culture and for the wider distribution of our works. But the fact that the magazine had not lost money did not in itself promise the editors a future. They had the sense to stop in time. Bradley became book designer for McClure, Phillips and Company; Hellman went into the art business.

My earliest memory of George Hellman dates from autumn of sophomore year, when Columbia had just moved up to Morningside and the campus grounds were not yet in order. Stumbling along one of the temporary wooden walks near the present Engineering Building, I was startled to observe a solemn slender youth, wearing a red beard and with a conspicuous cane draped over his arm, standing under a wretched tree that had lost its leaves early in the summer, and gazing heavenward at one forlorn bird perched on one naked twig. I thought I was looking at a caricature of Alfred de Musset in process of getting himself an inspiration. But I learned that the bird-worshipper was Mr. George S. Hellman, of the junior class. We became friends forthwith, companions in worthy and exciting causes all our lives. He does trim his beard to look like Alfred de Musset, and he understands that no lonely bird on a bare twig should be left uncontemplated by a romantic poet. But he's a grand fellow, and I shall love and tease him, while breath is in me.

2

My graduate studies in English were under Professors Price, Woodberry, Brander Matthews and William Peterfield Trent, who joined the Columbia faculty in 1900, coming to us from the University of the South, at Sewanee. He was a tall Virginian, lank and bearded, full of courtesy and humor. He became at once a beloved figure on the campus, all the more attractive because of more than one resemblance to Don Quixote. In the first graduate year I took his course in seventeenth century literature, from which I recall chiefly his passion for Milton and the rotund fervor with which he read great passages out of *Paradise Lost* or *Samson Agonistes*. He was primarily a historian, and the values he found in Milton were not those which Woodberry had revealed to us. But I was glad to be initiated into the fruitful tradition of English political thought, and the beauties of Milton's combative prose. With Brander Matthews I had a course in Molière, profitable in itself, and memorable because William de Mille was in the class, and George Philip Krapp, of the English department, later my colleague at Columbia, and William Albert Nitze, lecturer in Romance languages, later my colleague at Amherst. Any class that Brander conducted would be scintillating, and in this course he was dealing with his favorite dramatist, and the presence of solid scholars like Krapp and Nitze insured discussion of high quality. With Professor Price I began a thorough exploration of Middle English, which continued through the two following years, until I had my Ph.D. The course with Woodberry was a series of extraordinary lectures on the epics, which later were the basis for his study of literary tradition in *The Torch*.

In addition to work in English, my major subject, I studied Italian, my minor, and during that first graduate year I applied myself rather desperately to German, a language which I never cared for, and had been allowed to neglect, but now I began to foresee trouble at my final examination. Candidates for the doctorate were required to demonstrate their ability to read German at sight, unless they had passed sophomore German with a high mark. Why sophomore German was equated with the ability to read that language at sight, I did not know and preferred not to ask; even at that late hour I would take German with the sophomores, unless some kill-joy of a disciplinarian stopped me. My usual good fortune held; the sophomores that season had their German from Professor William Addison Hervey, humane gentleman and first-rate teacher. By attending closely to the sounds the sophomores made, I was able in a few days to pronounce German as well as though I had taken a preliminary course, and I learned the grammar from Professor Hervey's patient and thorough correcting of my written exercises. He gave me an "A" at the end of the term.

In Italian too I took a short cut. During the summer after my graduation I studied Italian grammar by myself, and so armed I elected Professor Speranza's reading course in Dante. I do not apologize for my irreverent attitude toward language courses which are designed chiefly for the eye. Declension forms and conjugations are not hard to learn; the rest comes from hearing the language spoken and from speaking it yourself, whether or not you make mistakes. My three years of graduate study in Italian were happy and to this extent profitable, that I have read and spoken Italian since with satisfaction to myself and with no visible distress to others.

Carlo Leonardo Speranza, my teacher, was a rare person. His father's estate, in the north of Italy, had been appropriated by the Austrians, both the Speranzas, father and son, having thrown in their lot with Garibaldi. My future teacher joined the fighting as a boy, was promptly captured, and after a swift trial was locked up to await execution, but the struggle came to an end, and he and Italy found themselves free. I asked him how it felt to brace yourself for death and then be let off; he said he was disappointed. He had a fine speech carefully memorized, to impress the firing squad, and no one cared to hear it.

He was no longer youthful and not at all a martyr when he taught at Columbia. Never very tall, he had put on weight with years, and his early political enthusiasms had been tempered by much experience and the kind of humor Chaucer liked. He was not a trained scholar, nor— and this should be reckoned to his merit—a trained teacher. His knowledge of Italian literature was wide, precise and deep, and he loved it in the same way and in the same measure that he loved life. A strong social sense accompanied him into the classroom, and it seemed to him and to us logical that he should interrupt the recitation to comment on any significant experience suggested by the text.

We were reading the *Purgatory* one day, and had our heads crammed with ideas of divine justice, when Professor Speranza suddenly put down his book, took out his handkerchief, cleaned his spectacles, leaned back in his chair, and said he was reminded of a landlady in New Haven. On first coming to this country he had boarded at her excellent establishment and must have caused her to grieve, since he liked Chianti with his meals and had his bottle on the table, in the sight of the other boarders, some of whom lacked his courage. The landlady believed the millennium would be brought in by the local temperance society, over which she presided.

But the unfortunate woman had an attack of flu which left her in an anemic condition. "Madam," urged Speranza, "if you would drink at lunch and dinner one glass of this red wine, merely as a tonic, you would recover your vigor. In my country we take it as medicine."

She said no, but in the end she ventured a sip or two and found the wine satisfying as the Italians do, merely as medicine.

When Speranza left New Haven to teach at Columbia, he offered her a farewell gift, a case of Chianti to protect her against a return visit of the flu. She accepted on condition that the case be marked "Sarsaparilla." She feared some neighbor might misunderstand.

As it happened, her brother was a druggist, and the expressman, seeing the marking on the box, thought it must be for the store. All the clerks were present when the Chianti was revealed.

I can see the broad smile on Speranza's face as he restored his spectacles to his nose and picked up the *Purgatory* where we had left off. "The precaution, gentlemen, advertised the hypocrisy, did it not? What says the proverb? There is a God in heaven!"

On academic occasions Professor Speranza wore the usual black gown, but with bold stripes on the sleeves, and a hood which was a burst of color. I asked him what degree was represented, and from what university.

"I gave myself the degree," he said pleasantly, "and I designed the garment. The law school I attended was near Florence. The makers of gowns and hoods have not heard of it, but they prepared a costume from my description of what the graduates of the institution would wear if they were teaching at Columbia. The consequence is satisfying, do you not think?"

3

On the evening of December 14, 1900, Professor Woodberry's students, past and present, tendered him a dinner at Sherry's, which in those days was at Forty-fourth Street and Fifth Avenue. The occasion was the tenth anniversary of his coming to Columbia. Joseph Proskauer presided, and introduced President Low, Professor Price, and of course Woodberry himself. Mr. Low described the circumstances of Woodberry's first coming to Columbia, Professor Price paid a tribute to his younger colleague, and Woodberry spoke in his characteristic vein of idealism and friendship.

The attendance at the dinner was large, and we were all happy, but I doubt if any of us realized half the significance of the evening. No one thought of it as the close of an epoch; we assumed Woodberry would round out another ten years at Columbia in natural sequence, and that his influence would increase and spread. Though I had reason for gratitude to other teachers in the literary departments, and first of all to MacDowell in music, yet I felt with my classmates that Woodberry's contribution was unique. I assumed that his attitude to literature and education would be in the spirit of the future. Had I not thought so, my preparations for a teaching career would have been troubled, for my greatest wish was to hand on in my own way, as I could, something of what he had given to me. For the moment, the zest with which we celebrated his tenth year carried over into enthusiasm for the University, and the committee which had organized the dinner retained its formation long enough to found the Columbia University Club, which began its existence in August, 1901.

On April 19, 1902, Nicholas Murray Butler was inducted into the presidency of Columbia, Mr. Low having become Mayor of New York City. The ceremonies of the inauguration at the University and the alumni dinner for the new President that evening at Sherry's, constituted altogether the most exciting public exercises Columbia had ever held. Though Dr. Butler was then only thirty-nine, his achievements as organizer and administrator were already prodigious. The President of the United States, Theodore Roosevelt, attended the ceremonies, morning and evening, and the pageantry of his military escort and the presence of famous scholars and statesmen surrounding him at the dinner filled us, who were still young, with pleasant visions of what our University might become.

Of course we were all familiar with Mr. Low's benign but careful way of speaking, and we knew the clear-cut perfection of Dr. Butler's lectures on philosophy, but I was not the only one who remarked, as we talked over the brilliant ceremonies afterward, that the new President had made one of the coolest and most efficient speeches imaginable in one so young, faced with so large a responsibility. Since then I have heard Dr. Butler speak many times, and never in any other manner. His activities have taken him to most parts of the Western world, and he has exercised his extraordinary talents in many ways, in many communities on behalf of many causes, but it seems to me that except for the ripeness and the subtlety that come with years, he was at the beginning all that he is now.

Philosophy was his subject, but he was never content to be a mere historian of other men's wisdom. Action, not meditation, was his sphere. As quickly as possible he made himself what he was born to be, an empire builder. Convinced early in life that our country, like the rest of the world, needed education more than anything else, he conceived of education as a science which, to be applied, would need thorough organization. Theories of education were still too largely theories; there must be experimental schools to try them out. Teachers in all grades must be properly trained, standards of entrance to colleges and graduate schools must be overhauled and brought into line, methods of research must be perfected, opportunities for advanced study must be made available for women.

Columbia University today is the outgrowth of the small schools which clustered at Forty-ninth Street. The entire development is marked with Dr. Butler's foresight and practical power. He was the first head of Teachers College and of Barnard College. He organized and for a long time administered the system of standard entrance examinations known as the Middle States Board. He organized, and in its first years directed, the Columbia Summer Session. He founded and long edited the *Educational Review,* which spread his ideas through the country. Those ideas, of course, were not unanimously applauded. It would be surprising if he and his accomplishments had not received occasional criticism, especially from other university presidents. His success at last reached a point where his rivals were excused from admiring him, and were free to envy.

But at his inauguration dinner many of the young alumni were far from happy. They admired him personally, they had no other candidate for the presidency, the speeches had been interesting, and one of them, that by President Edward Anderson Alderman, then of Tulane University, had been notably wise and eloquent; but something was present in the atmosphere, or absent from it, which prompted an ungracious comparison with the Woodberry dinner. In place of warm humanity, there was noticeable a slightly blatant efficiency. The impression was perhaps created first of all by the presence of Squadron A on their horses, in the morning, escorting President Roosevelt to the Library steps. Perhaps it occurred to us that so Kaiser Wilhelm of Germany might visit his universities, rattling his saber. President Roosevelt and Dr. Butler, as we knew, thought rather well of Kaiser Wilhelm in those days. We had hoped that our tradition would continue the spiritual humanism which Woodberry had taught as the essence of whatever was civilized in the Western world. We had no knowledge then of the altercations and misunderstandings that were soon to separate both Woodberry and MacDowell from Columbia, but our intuition was correct that some fundamental antipathy must exist between those two men and others like them, and the spirit which somehow articulated itself in the inauguration of the new President.

Time proved us both right and wrong. It seems now that the loss of Woodberry and of MacDowell was inevitable for reasons chiefly in themselves. The humanistic spirit finds more than one avenue of expression, and in his own way Dr. Butler has always been a supreme humanist. He has made education serve, not simply the literary ideal, but also the political and the social, and more men would agree now than forty-three years ago that social and political questions are among the most vital and urgent. His work for international conciliation was motivated by no sentimental or theoretical pacifism, but by fairly precise knowledge of the danger into which the world was moving fast. Inside the university, as I know by experience, his justice and his loyalty to his colleagues commanded their respect and their loyalty in return, however widely they disagreed as to specific measures.

Yet the danger which we scented, the night of the inauguration, was really there. It lurked under the satisfaction of Trustees and older alumni in having at the feast the President of the United States, this particular President. Here in person was that so-called Manifest Destiny, physical, vigorous and forceful, which Woodberry implicitly opposed in the *Heart of Man,* and which Rodó attacked directly in *Ariel.* Our University would grow, its graduates would be legion, its endowment would become fabulous, its degrees would be well thought-of—but would it produce great personalities? Would there be a place on its staff for original minds? The question has been asked of all large institutions, highly organized. The great man, the genius, may be dismissed; more often he is promoted; in either case he may lose the career for which his talents fit him. On the other hand, is idealism really incompatible with practical sense? Why should not a poet like Woodberry be a man of action, competent in daily affairs? These questions, posed by swift changes at Columbia, filled my head almost as much as my studies.

4

At the beginning of the second graduate year I had to choose a subject for my doctoral thesis and get the approval of Professor Price and the other professors of English, since my fellowship was in their department. All the undergraduate courses I had taken with Woodberry had been in English literature, but by what seems a silly distinction he was Professor of Comparative Literature. His best students were already producing admirable theses on worth-while subjects—Spingarn with his *History of Literary Criticism in the Renaissance,* Frank Chandler with his *Romances of Roguery,* John Garrett Underhill with his *Spanish Literature in England Under the Tudors.* Later there would be John Smith Harrison's *Platonism in English Poetry of the Sixteenth and Seventeenth Centuries,* Horatio Sheafe Krans's *Irish Life in Irish Fiction,* Lewis Nathaniel Chase's *The English Heroic Play,* and Martha Pike Conant's *The Oriental Tale in England.* The English department had on its side of the line only one thesis, Ferris Greenslet's excellent study of *Joseph Glanvill,* and Greenslet and I were inspired by Woodberry and devoted to him. My youthful admiration for the man seems all the more justified now when I review the record and see that not only in undergraduate teaching but in the promotion of graduate studies, he had no rival in the English department.

My thesis, like Ferris Greenslet's, would for a technical academic reason be written under Professor Price, and since his health was beginning to fail, the English department promised me the help also of Professor Trent. I chose to write about the Elizabethan lyric. There was no comprehensive account of song writing in Shakspere's time, and since many

Elizabethan lyrics were written to be sung, and were set to fine music, I wished to explain why such a marriage of music and poetry always lasts for only a short time. This problem has recurred more than once in literary history—in Antiquity, in the Middle Ages, in the Renaissance; after a period when poetry and music are enjoyed together, poetry leaves music behind and is enjoyed for its own sake. No one knows why, and few besides myself have tried to find out.

The proposal of such a thesis subject staggered the English department, who not having much experience with thesis subjects of other than the strictly Germanic type, wanted to begin on something easy. I must admit that a question involving music would have staggered even Woodberry. There was no teacher of humane letters at Columbia just then who cared much for that art, or knew anything about it. Dear Professor Price once admitted that music was for him only the least disagreeable of noises, and in order to be undisturbed when at his work, he had trained himself not to hear it. He therefore advised me, to the relief of his colleagues, to make a purely literary and historical study of lyric poetry as published in the Elizabethan age, and to condense my notions about the music into a short introductory chapter or preface. There they sleep harmless, to this day.

The other graduate students were also, of course, wrestling with this problem of a thesis subject, and since most of us exchanged ideas freely, there was a wholesale revelation of human nature, and among my companions in the seminars were a number of unusual characters. Taking Professor Trent's course with me were William Ellery Leonard, poet and later professor of literature at Wisconsin University—and Ludwig Lewisohn—and Marion Tucker, later head of the English department at Brooklyn Polytechnic,—and Miss Barnette Miller, historian of the Near East, for many years on the faculty of Wellesley College—and Edward Graham, who later, as the youthful president of North Carolina University, reorganized and developed that institution until it became a model for other State universities in intellectual and social leadership. In the course which Woodberry gave on epic poetry, I met Graham and Lewisohn again; also Upton Sinclair.

Edward Graham was a man set apart by peculiar gifts for a large task. He had good looks and an excellent mind, courtesy, tact, humor, whatever are the ingredients of charm. Having taken the Master's degree, he called on Professor Price for guidance as to further study. Immediately after this interview, happening to meet him, I noticed the half-smile on his face.

"I've been talking with the Old Man," he explained. "He rather forced me to look at myself in the mirror. I wasn't sure I ought to stay on for the Ph.D., and he asked why not.

" 'Perhaps I'm too old, Professor.'

" 'What *is* your age, Mr. Graham?'

" 'Twenty-four, sir.'

"He put his black eyes on me. 'Mr. Graham, perhaps you are right! Young men today are slow in starting. At your years I had studied in Germany, I had fought through the war, I was married, I had a child, I already occupied my first teaching post.' "

For once I thought Professor Price was less than just, but Graham stood up for him. "I'm glad he spoke plainly. I'll think it over."

Shortly afterward he left the University, returned to the South, and began his remarkable work. He may have been a little old to waste time on a Ph.D., but he had finished his task and was at rest in his early grave before some of us had got started.

Leonard and Lewisohn were congenial spirits; I remember them always together. Leonard had just returned from study in Germany, and had brought back with him two accomplishments, the ability to improvise limericks in Latin, and a knack of insinuating, or shouting from the housetops, his contempt for his native land. I confess that he and Lewisohn bored me by their jibes at American ways and American people. But no one could fail to recognize in both men a remarkable capacity for scholarship, and in Leonard something approaching genius as a writer. We were well prepared for his accomplishment in poetry, and we were not surprised that his life was burdened by more than one man's share of trouble, or that some of the trouble may have been imaginary.

5

Professor Price's health continued to fail, and I turned to Professor Trent more and more for guidance in my work. Toward the end of my third graduate year it became evident that I should never show the completed thesis to the friend who had encouraged me at Columbia from the first. Professor Price recovered temporarily from a serious operation, but died on May 7, 1903, at the age of sixty-four.

At the Ph.D. examination I was saddened by his absence. Professor Speranza was there to ask me questions about Italian literature, Professor Trent examined me on my English studies, and the eight or ten present from various departments asked questions in any subject they chose. Halfway through the ordeal an unwise remark of mine started an acrid debate between Calvin Thomas, Professor of German, and Adolphe Cohn, Professor of French. Professor Thomas was apparently the only examiner who had read, or at least remembered, that introductory chapter of mine containing the ideas about music.

"Your theory, as I understand it, is that musical quality in words is obscured when the words are put to actual music."

That, I agreed, was my idea.

"And therefore, if the words have in themselves a high musical quality, the tendency is to drop the actual music, so that the musical quality of the words may be enjoyed."

That, I admitted again, was my argument.

"Well then," he concluded, "I should like to hear you illustrate your theory from German lyrical poetry. Will you be so kind as to give one example where the words are highly musical, and another where they are not?"

Intending neither disrespect nor facetiousness, but merely telling the truth, I said I did not know the German language well enough to be sure when it was musical and when it was otherwise.

Professor Cohn gave a mean laugh, and remarked that great men had lived before Agamemnon, but none had left the recipe for catching German in its musical moments. Then Professor Thomas retorted that there could be no such doubt about the French language, since thoughtful Frenchmen always served notice in advance that they would now be musical, or pathetic, or profound, or humorous, as the case might be. Then these two fine scholars consumed the rest of the hour insulting each other's subject. Their colleagues, listening in, were amused, and when everybody had enough of it, they gave me their solemn opinion that I deserved to be a doctor of philosophy.

Before Commencement Day arrived I had one invitation to teach at Amherst College, Massachusetts, and another to teach at Kansas University. Still later Miss Carey Thomas, knowing nothing about me but having heard somewhere of my thesis, asked if I cared to consider a position at Bryn Mawr. But I had already accepted the Amherst offer.

As I learned years afterward, it came to me in a queer way. At Amherst the Reverend Heman Humphrey Neill was retiring as professor of English Literature, and the Trustees were looking for a successor, preferably for one who already had, or who might eventually accumulate, some reputation as a writer. At the same time the Reverend John Franklin Genung, Professor of Rhetoric, having had enough of the freshman mind, was withdrawing from the correction of paragraphs, sentences and spelling, in order to lecture on biblical literature, and the President of the College, the Reverend Dr. George Harris, was looking for a young instructor who could and would teach freshmen, and do it cheap.

So he wrote to Professor Trent at Columbia about the instructor, whom he was willing to pay a thousand dollars, or in the case of quality, twelve hundred. Mr. George Plimpton, chairman of the Amherst Trustees, wrote to Mr. Woodberry for the name of some creative person eligible to be a professor of literature at a salary of three thousand dollars. Both Trent and Woodberry nominated me, neither knowing that the other had been approached. When the authorities of that Yankee college compared the two letters, I was promptly called—at the lower rate. Having found an unexpected bargain, they sought no further addition to their faculty—or their budget. I was to teach all the freshmen, impart classroom instruction, read themes, hold private consultations. There would be about one hundred and twenty boys in the class, it would probably be desirable to meet them in sections, there would be at least one theme a week. If after all this I should find that any strength or ambition remained to me, I might consider myself free to teach all the literature that ever had been written. President Harris outlined my opportunity not precisely in these terms, but approximately so, and I girded myself to take possession of as much of my destiny as I could.

This time I had indeed come to the end of my youth. From now on I must be a mature person. I had a row of diplomas which I could frame and hang up for students and other visitors to admire. On occasions of academic ceremony I was entitled to wrap myself in the gown and the hood of a Ph.D., and balance on my head a mortar board with a gold tassel. Beyond doubt I was a professor! The cap and gown and hood were graduation gifts from those dear friends, the Harris sisters—a parting gift in more than one sense, for the home at 500 West End Avenue was now breaking up. While I had been involved in my degree-getting, Minnie Harris had married the Reverend Pedro Mèsny, and from now on would live in Guernsey, Channel Islands. Stella was marrying Mr. William Hill, and would live in Cork, Ireland. My own home was changing. Aunt Nanna had suffered a paralytic stroke, and was crippled for the brief remainder of her days. The younger children were growing up fast. Robert and Rhoda were well along with their school work, and my sister Helen was almost at the end of her Barnard course.

But I am afraid I was occupied with little except my personal affairs when I took the train to Northampton and the trolley across the Connecticut Valley to the college town on its lovely hill. As the car came over a rise and I caught my first glimpse of the chapel clock tower, I said to myself that there, in all probability, my life would be spent. I liked the prospect.

PART II

1903—1909

CHAPTER XII

Amherst College

I

DURING my Amherst years I roomed in the house of Mrs. Baxter Marsh, on the south side of Main Street, just east of the Common. For the first two years I ate at the boardinghouse kept by Mrs. Aurelia B. Hinsdale Davis, at the corner of Pleasant Street and Northampton Road. In sharply different ways Mrs. Marsh and Mrs. Davis represented in essence the spirit of the town.

Mrs. Marsh rented rooms to bachelor instructors. Her clients therefore were young, but she was not. She was tall and thin, and she carried the scars of a lifetime of toil. Her husband, an invalid in his late seventies, wore an immense untrimmed beard which floated around his face like a gray mist. His voice was high and cracked, the ghost of a voice. Mrs. Marsh adored him. By years of dressmaking she had accumulated enough to build her house, with a home for them on the ground floor and apartments above for the teacher-tenants. I had a study with fireplace on the second floor, at the northwest corner, and a bedroom on the top floor.

The house was in fine condition always. Mrs. Marsh did her own work. Never could she have accomplished so much had she not known how to plan her day and save time. When she retired to her part of the house she always hung her false teeth over a nail just inside the door, to have them handy if anyone called. In response to a knock she would stick out her head, as it were unaccoutered, for a preliminary survey. If ceremony seemed appropriate she would duck back again and reappear smiling.

In the garden behind the house she raised chickens. The neighbors who bought eggs sometimes commented on her thrift. They said that she had been known to deliver eleven eggs instead of twelve, explaining that one egg had a double yolk. I do not believe this story, but there may have been significance in the fact that it was told.

At the beginning of my stay in the Marsh house my fellow residents were Ernest H. Wilkins, instructor in Romance languages and Latin, William J. Newlin, instructor in mathematics, and Curtis H. Walker, instructor in history. Wilkins, later President of Oberlin University, was the leader of our group. It was he who went downstairs and discussed with Mrs. Marsh the possibility of a little more coal in the furnace, whenever the mercury fell below zero, as in the Amherst winter it was likely to do. It was Wilkins also who let Mrs. Marsh know when a pie was needed. If one of us, perhaps toward the end of the evening, felt the pangs of hunger, and if the others felt the same, Ernest would go down stairs, seat himself on the lowest step in front of Mrs. Marsh's door, and begin to groan. The noise never surprised Mrs. Marsh. When she stuck her head out to Ernest and his groans, she always had her teeth in.

"Ernest Wilkins! Whatever is the matter with you?"

"Misery, Mrs. Marsh! Extreme misery!"

"Will you recover, or shall I notify your folks?"

"Don't worry them, Mrs. Marsh, unless you observe a change for the worse. There may be a remedy."

Here she would laugh and bring out a pie. "Ernest Wilkins, you must have smelled the baking this afternoon!"

Newlin, like other mathematicians, was drawn to philosophy, and still teaches that subject at Amherst. Walker is now Professor of History at Vanderbilt University.

Mrs. Marsh's house was so designed that after we four had rented the combinations of rooms which happened to appeal to us, what was left over could not easily be disposed of. There were extra bedrooms on the top floor but they did not connect and they had no fireplace. To this economic challenge Mrs. Marsh's mind responded promptly. She invited us, one by one, to give our approval. Two of the bedrooms, one of them next to mine, could be fitted up very comfortably for any occupant who probably would not spend all his time indoors. Two freshmen had applied. As a rule she did not take students, but these boys, she had been assured, were quiet, and if we were willing, she would admit them on condition that they disturbed nobody.

Of course we gave our consent, and the boys moved in. It was winter, Mrs. Marsh's top floor was cold, and we lived in peace, since for all except sleeping hours the freshmen were out of the house, somewhere, keeping warm. The boy whose bedroom was next to mine would have been a good neighbor even if the Marsh house had been more comfortable. He was studious and well bred, conscious of his responsibilities in the great world and resolved to bring on his family nothing but credit. The other freshman was all right too, but rather overendowed with energy, and I doubt if he shaped his conduct entirely for the benefit of any one's reputation, not even his own. He did not applaud the careful behavior of his friend, my neighbor; in fact, he called him "Mommer's Boy!"

In the course of time Mommer's Boy made a date with a girl at Smith College, and boasted of it to his comrade, whom we might as well call Imp of Satan. When Mommer's Boy was safely on the trolley for Hamp, Imp of Satan removed six hens from Mrs. Marsh's coop, brought them upstairs, tied strings to their legs and fastened the ends of the strings to the footboard of Mommer's Boy's bed. Simultaneously he also removed from the room all the electric bulbs.

At one o'clock Mrs. Marsh's house rocked and reeled as from an earthquake. Mrs. Marsh rose hastily without stopping for teeth, wig, slippers or shawl, and came directly from sleep to the center of the hurricane, wearing a nightgown which years and much laundering had made transparent. The poor woman was calling on God to save her home, and the rest of us sprang from our beds and joined her. From Mommer's Boy's room came the sound of falling objects and ferocious ejaculations or protests or oaths. Wilkins, our dependable leader, forced the door. Indeed, it was not locked. The room was pitch dark, but Mommer's Boy emerged into the hall light, his face scratched and bleeding. The birds would have followed him lightward, but they were detained.

"My hens!" screamed Mrs. Marsh. "What are you doing with them in your room?"

"Would it not be well," asked Wilkins, "to turn on the light?"

"*You* turn it on!" said Mommer's Boy, quite out of his manners.

At this point the Imp of Satan, roused from oblivion, came out rubbing his eyes, and when he saw that Mommer's Boy had been robbing the chicken house, he apologized so handsomely to Mrs. Marsh that she remembered in what company she was, and with such scanty covering.

Her husband, Baxter, who did not come upstairs, must have had an immediate report when she went down. I met him on the street the next day. He stopped, steadied himself on his cane, tilted up his beard and aimed his eye at me; "I hear"—the high wheezy voice had its own gusto —"I hear you had the privilege of beholding one of Mrs. Marsh's lunar appearances!"

2

Mrs. Davis was perhaps older than Mrs. Marsh. She was a dear little lady, with the whitest of hair and the kindest of dispositions. She had once been fairly tall, but now she was shrunken and bent. Her husband had been well-to-do but the provision he had made for her turned out to be almost nothing at all, and after his death she took students and faculty into her home as boarders. When I reached Amherst her table had been for twenty years the best in town, and also the most expensive. No one grudged the price, since the quality could not be matched elsewhere. She charged five dollars a week.

She had a quite remarkable cook and a capable waitress, two sisters, French Canadians, but her cuisine was strictly New England. It would not have occurred to her to serve dinner at any other hour than noon. There were afternoon classes, but we prepared for them by eating a heavy meal. At night there would be supper, in the strict Puritan tradition— creamed codfish or scrambled eggs, hot biscuits, stewed fruit, and strange to say, coffee. Strange to say, because the older Amherst did not approve of coffee after noon dinner, when we College folk needed it most. I bought myself a machine for making drip coffee, and set it up in my study, on a table near the fireplace. In time I had another table, to hold a tea set.

The students who boarded with Mrs. Davis ate at the long table in the dining room, some thirty of them, and she presided at the head, with a generous tureen of mashed potatoes in front of her. The meat was carved in the kitchen and served with the other vegetables, but the mashed potatoes, creamy and hot, with plenty of butter, were something special. The faculty boarders were segregated in a small room, off the parlor. We usually numbered six or seven. There were the quartet from the *Maison Marsh,* and Joseph O. Thompson, Professor of Physics, and perhaps a visitor, or a married colleague whose wife was in Springfield for the day. And at the head of this table, also with a tureen of potatoes, sat Miss Katharine Hinsdale, Mrs. Davis's niece.

Only an impish fate could have brought Professor Thompson and Miss Hinsdale into juxtaposition, or contrast, or, as you might say, conflict. They were both from New England, but the professor was proud of that fact, and Miss Hinsdale was not. Joseph Thompson—his students called him "Toggles," was a tall angular person of great force, moral as well as physical; his kindness and his sincerity had at times a terrible quality. He earned the reputation of a wit by telling the truth and nothing else, even about himself. He was integrity incarnate. He had studied in Germany and he revered the memory of some great scientists he had known, but in general he thought his own land was good enough for any reasonable person, and if there was a better spot than Amherst, it must be the township of Weymouth, Massachusetts, where he was born. He was incurably absent minded and consequently, beyond intention, entertaining. On a winter day he would come shivering to lunch, without hat, overcoat or galoshes, having left those articles in his locker at the physics laboratory, with the key to the locker in his overcoat pocket.

During one famous class hour he was tapping his watch against his teeth while a pupil recited. Sometimes he tapped his upper teeth, sometimes his lower, and there were moments when it seemed as though he were aiming at his tonsils. Then the cover of the watch flew open, caught against the back of the teeth, and the watch was in for good. They say Toggles was magnificent. He held on to the watch chain and for the benefit of the student drew a rapid diagram on the black board, with these directions: "Pull watch forward by chain until lower side of case rests on tongue at *A;* insert pencil over cover of watch at *B;* exert gentle pressure downward and forward until cover closes upon case at *C*."

The student followed instructions, the watch came out, and the recitation went on from where it had been interrupted.

Miss Hinsdale, like her aunt, had once been wealthy. She had traveled abroad, had gone to school in France, and there she would have spent her life, but hearing that Mrs. Davis had lost money she came to Amherst, perhaps merely to learn the sad facts, perhaps to help the old lady, of whom she was very fond. While on this Amherst visit she lost most of her own fortune, and she never could go back to France. Perhaps her income, however shrunk, still made it possible for Mrs. Davis to conduct her boardinghouse not as though she were feeding college boys but as though she were entertaining guests. Miss Hinsdale and she were perhaps partners in the enterprise. Certainly the niece had the best quarters in the house, an airy apartment on the ground floor stretching along Pleasant Avenue, where she installed her library of French and Italian books, where she made coffee for herself after lunch, excellent French coffee, and where she entertained her friends. Her bedroom was upstairs; her living room was her world, except when she took the head of the table, to serve mashed potatoes.

Her appearance was striking. She was large, very tall, of heroic build, and her deep-set eyes, ringed with shadows, suggested tragedy. Unhappy she certainly was. She belonged to that class of American who, in the final decades of the nineteenth century, thought that culture and social standing could be obtained only by marrying a European. This was not difficult for a rich American girl, since quite a number of Continental and English titles needed cash, but cash in quantity, and a woman like Miss Hinsdale, whose wealth was never excessive, could not buy her way in. She would remain on the fringes of European society, a cultural waif or exile, uprooted from her proper land and underestimating its virtues and its progress, yet savagely derisive of fellow Americans abroad, whose luck in husband-buying had been better than hers. All that Miss Hinsdale had got from her travel years were, so far as I could see, an excellent command of the French language, a genuine appreciation of French character, and a bitter undervaluing of Americans—in particular a sarcastic humor toward those who resided in Amherst, whether faculty or townsfolk.

With all this, Mrs. Davis's niece had considerable warmth of heart. I found her an exciting friend, rich in knowledge of things I cared about, and an inexhaustible source of Amherst gossip. The information she gave me had often a lemonish flavor, but usually it was accurate.

At our table I sat opposite Toggles, at the end nearest the window. Miss Hinsdale sat at the other end, with her back to the door. She preferred not to see who came into the dining room; she wished not to be noticed by the students, who for their part were a little in awe of her. Unless our conversation at the faculty table took a cosmopolitan turn, she withdrew into herself, but we usually made her come out again. Professor Thompson's method was extremely courteous; he would engage her in a discussion of some innocuous subject of interest to himself and therefore presumably to others. He wanted to know, one day, whether she enjoyed straw rides, and it did seem as though, if her reply were encouraging, he might organize that form of entertainment for her. He held the firm conviction that cold baths are injurious to health, and one noon, expounding that doctrine to us, he electrified the table by asking Miss Hinsdale, as a typical case, whether she bathed in cold water or hot.

3

The Amherst faculty at that time consisted of two sections, the survivors of the group who had made the College famous, and new accessions to replace them. The replacements, ranging in maturity from me to several men of forty, were beginning to outnumber the old fellows, but not, alas, to outshine them. Professors Emerson, Crowell, Tyler, Genung, Garman and Elijah Harris were giants, teachers of teachers. Their pupils held professorships in many universities, and they managed to pursue, in a small college, ideals of science and scholarship which usually are cherished only in larger institutions.

Some of the older teachers had begun life as ministers, but they had studied in Germany, and could match any German-trained scientist in thoroughness of method. Charles Garman made his course in philosophy the central influence of senior year; Benjamin K. Emerson, geologist, sharpened the wits of his colleagues by his vigorous thought and his trenchant speech; John Tyler, called "Tip," the biologist, and Anson D. Morse, historian, were not only great scholars but gentlemen of rounded culture, whom it was an education merely to know. George Olds, Professor of Mathematics, later President of the College, deserves a word in another place, and with him, since they were inseparable friends, I shall speak of William L. Cowles, Professor of Latin.

Of this older group I naturally saw most of Professor Genung, who was the head of the English department. A strong stocky figure, with a thick beard, a succulent deep bass voice, and a twinkling eye, he was one of Amherst's most picturesque characters. He used to tell of his boyhood, that he was brought up on a farm self-sufficient in economic and other ways; the household provided itself with food, with shoes, with clothing, with all its physical comforts and with almost all its spiritual satisfactions. This remembered way of life became with him, I think, an ideal. In whatever he did, he liked to begin as close as might be to the raw material, and he worked always on a generous scale, having in mind as it were the needs of the whole household. Few scholars in his generation had a finer training in the ancient literatures and languages, as well as in English, and few were more thorough, yet he had no mind for specialization; he went after the whole subject from the ground up. I heard him say how rich life was when the clothes on your back, the room that sheltered you, the chair you sat in, the candle that lighted you, the food on the table and the table itself, were all produced or fashioned by your own hands. He would have liked nothing better than to write, print and bind his books, with pen and paper, ink and press and thread, all of his own manufacture.

He wrote with a quill pen, and he illuminated his manuscripts like a medieval scribe. He was an accomplished musician, and played his beloved viola in the College orchestra and in many an impromptu trio or quartet. He gave me one day an illustration of his self-sufficiency and perhaps of his humor as well. He had been asked by a society of clergymen to give a talk on "The Best Hymns." "Of course," he said, raising his eyebrows, "it's of little use to discuss hymns without giving examples, so I've arranged to have four or five hymns sung. Do you know," he added, with his own chuckle, "I'm writing them myself, words and music."

Inclusive spirit that he was, he would thank me for remembering him completely. I must therefore say here that his hobby was not really music but architecture. He designed house after house, undiscouraged by the reluctance of his neighbors to build from his plans. There was a legend that only two structures of his ever went up. One was a backhouse for a farm. The other was an addition to a church.

His relations with his students, even with the worst of them, had always a merciful humor. In his study were two files with cryptic labels which signified two kinds of ass, one kind much worse than the other. The cards in these boxes bore the names of his laziest students. He would come back from a particularly provoking class, shift a few names from the file of the less to the file of the more execrable, light his pipe and survey the two groupings in sorrowful meditation, until his blood pressure went down and he could return to his writing with equanimity.

"This brings me up to the mark, I believe, Professor," said a hardened reprobate, as he handed in his written work about three-months overdue.

"To *your* mark," corrected Professor Genung, and the boy was safe, having been the occasion of wit in his softhearted and wit-loving teacher.

Among the younger men on the faculty my closest friends were Nitze, from Columbia, now head of the Romance department at Amherst, and of course my neighbors at Mrs. Marsh's, and Harry DeForest Smith, Professor of Greek, and William P. Bigelow, Professor of Music. Biggie and Genung were bosom companions, and as time went on I turned to Biggie for advice on all literary questions. He had extraordinary good sense, and his love of reading made him, for me, a choice companion. Arthur Baxter, an Englishman who taught Italian, helped Nungie and me to use up Biggie's spare time. I soon formed a habit which may have been hard on the music professor. Late in the evening I usually wrote a letter home to my people, dropped it in the post office just before midnight, and then went around to the Bigelow home to exchange ideas about literature and music and the fascinating question, How to educate the young, or that other question, Can they be educated?

He had been born in Amherst, the son of the leading physician. After graduation from the College he had taken his tenor voice to Germany to prepare for the operatic stage, but after a few years, realizing that his gift was for teaching, he had come home and begun again. He provided Amherst boys with such training in music as few undergraduates ever enjoy.

CHAPTER XIII

The Dickinson Feud

I

WHEN I went to Amherst I had read some of Emily Dickinson's poems, but I knew nothing of the important position the Dickinson family held in the history of the town and of the College, and I knew even less of the feud which had grown up over the editing of Emily's poems. But now I could remain ignorant no longer. On the northern side of Main Street, some two hundred yards east of the *Maison Marsh,* was the former home of the exclusive Emily, who in her poems was on easy terms with Nature and God, but in life held converse with her fellow man only if she couldn't help herself. There was the garden where once the poet's white-clad form was glimpsed without enthusiasm by the neighbors she ignored or scorned—by Mrs. Marsh, for example. I asked Mrs. Marsh for her opinion of Emily. It was not high. She said Emily never set foot outside her father's place, which was small. She understood Emily had written a good deal, but she had been too busy to read any of it. She doubted if Emily ever did anything useful. In every small place, she reminded me, there were likely to be a few queer people.

At Mrs. Davis's boarding establishment I gathered my first real information about Emily and the feud. Mrs. Davis had known Emily slightly, and Emily's sister Lavinia more intimately. She had also known the old Squire Dickinson, Emily's father, and Austin, Emily's brother; and even more intimately, Austin's widow Susan and his daughter Martha, who during my first Amherst year were traveling in Europe. Mrs. Davis disliked scandal, and I learned directly from her nothing about the incipient feud. I still have copies of Emily's poems and her letters in the first edition; I bought them at the sale of Mrs. Davis's library after her death. The little books had been presented to her, inscribed by Emily's sister Lavinia. Mrs. Davis told me that Lavinia was only less remarkable than Emily herself.

As I said, Mrs. Davis disliked gossip, but a number of people who came to her house did not. I soon learned the embroidery which the popular imagination was giving to a few simple and unquestioned facts. Emily Dickinson had died in 1886. Four years later Mabel Loomis Todd, assisted by Thomas Wentworth Higginson, made the first edition of Emily's poems. In 1891 the same editors brought out a second series of poems, and in 1896 Mabel Loomis Todd, unassisted, brought out a third series. Emily's letters, edited by Mabel, appeared in 1894 in two small volumes. These were the volumes which I acquired from the library of Mrs. Davis.

Mabel Loomis Todd was the wife of David Todd, who professed astronomy in Amherst College. According to local report, Emily Dickinson died without providing for her own literary debut, and though she knew the Todds, it was not she who asked Mabel to take charge of her immortality. Mrs. Todd's election to this honor was due, it was said, to her acquaintance with Emily's sister, Lavinia, or more probably, to her friendship with Austin Dickinson, Emily's brother.

Popular report went on to say that Austin had a brilliant wife, Susan, whose disposition was in every respect cordial until Austin contracted, or developed, the habit of spending his spare time in Mabel's company. He also evinced a strong inclination to bestow on Mabel, by gift or bequest, a modest piece of real estate, but before this transaction had been completed in orderly fashion, he died, in 1895. Gossip added two items, one more easy to believe than the other. The incredible one was to the general effect that after Austin's death, Mrs. Todd was involved in some kind of lawsuit over the land which Austin intended to give her but didn't. This rumor we now know was true. The other was that when Austin died his wife, Susan, was planning to sue him for divorce. I should hesitate to recall this gossip if it had not been stated in full in the account of the Dickinson feud given by Mrs. Todd's daughter, Millicent Todd Bingham, in *Ancestors' Brocades,* published in 1945.

When I first heard these legends, whether true or false, I had not yet laid eyes on a Dickinson. I had, of course, gazed with proper respect on the outside of the brick building where the immortal Emily had resided.

Across the lawn, to the west, stood Austin's house, which at the time of my arrival in Amherst was unoccupied except for a caretaker. It was a large building, and the grounds surrounding it seemed ample. Like Emily's home, it was protected from the dust of Main Street by a high hedge. David Todd I met at the first faculty meeting of the year, which occurred the day after I arrived in Amherst. He was a short man, genial and courteous, with a pointed beard which gave him a distinguished appearance. On Saturday morning of my first week, as I was walking to breakfast, I met him again, this time in front of the post office.

"By the way, Erskine," he asked, "you play the piano, don't you? Would you care to play some hymns tomorrow night at Mrs. So-and-So's?"

I hesitated, and he explained.

"She's a fine woman, elderly, an invalid. She likes nothing so much as hymns. I go around every Sunday night with four of the students to sing for her. One of the boys plays the piano, but the flu has got him down. Be a good fellow and help us out."

Weakly I said I'd be glad to, but I didn't think much of the invitation, and when I spoke of it at the breakfast table, there was a general laugh, especially from Professor Thompson and Miss Hinsdale. She made no comment, though she was one of the local authorities on all aspects of the feud, but Toggles said that David was up to his usual tricks. The invalid lady had wealth, he wanted a legacy for the astronomical department, and I had been invited to help pull her leg. By the time we had finished breakfast I was disgusted with myself for being an easy mark, and I wrote Professor Todd at once that though I had said I would gladly play, I wished now to withdraw. Later in the day when we met in the village, he crossed the street with a pleasant smile.

"Erskine, you have a remarkably interesting handwriting. Has no one ever called your attention to it? One of the most interesting handwritings I've seen!"

The subject did not come up again between us. The old lady died, there was no legacy, and so far as I know, Professor Todd sang no more hymns. But after this introduction to him I paid attention to the criticism his elder colleagues bestowed on him quite freely. Toggles had the gift of moral indignation, but some of the others merely laughed. They seemed to doubt David's ability as an astronomer. A wealthy alumnus would lend him an ocean-going yacht for eclipse expeditions to remote parts of the earth. The scientific value of such a trip I was not competent to estimate, but apparently there were a good many eclipses, all in pleasant seas. Professor Todd also took an interest in Mars, and from time to time newspapers ascribed to him a plan to go up in a balloon high enough to wave a flag or something at that planet on the chance that someone there would wave back at him. Mrs. Todd I met at faculty receptions and at other more or less public gatherings. She and her husband did not seem to mingle much with general Amherst society. I constantly heard of their daughter, Millicent, who at that time was away at school or college, and who, as I was repeatedly told, had a fine mind and an admirable character, and would some day be heard from. Because the Todds at that time were living a retired life, I have only a faint impression of Emily's editor, but Mrs. Todd seemed to me endowed with a good deal of that feminine charm which operates without words. She must have done her share of the talking, but I cannot remember a single remark of hers. I got the impression that her interest in books or in writing was not great, and I thought she avoided rather than cultivated the society of the students. This attitude was unusual in a small college, especially since she was attractive, and her husband in his own way was popular with the boys. They took him even less seriously than did his colleagues, but they were genuinely fond of him. During my Amherst stay they made up a song about him, a parody of "Everybody Works But Father," which they sang lustily whenever he appeared. Two local allusions in the text need annotation; the College Chaplain, Professor Preserved Smith, was known as Pickles; President Harris had recently got into the newspapers by telling the alumni he'd be glad if every student had a dinner coat. Now the classic will be clear.

> Everybody works but Davy,
> He sits 'round all day,
> Gazing at the stars,
> Now and then drawing his pay.
> Prexie works for dress-suits,
> Pickles works for God,
> Everybody works in Amherst
> But Davy Todd,
>   The —— old loafer.

Professor Todd's pleasure at being so immortalized seemed genuine.

If he came on a group of boys singing, in a fraternity house or out of doors, he frequently asked them to sing "his song."

From town report I learned that Austin Dickinson had been a remarkable man, in his time Amherst's leading citizen, as his father Edward had been before him. His widow Susan was well known in the household of Mrs. Davis—that is, to Mrs. Davis and Miss Hinsdale, and to some of the old graduates who visited Mrs. Davis whenever they returned to Amherst. I gathered that Susan Dickinson had a mind much above the ordinary; those who knew her agreed that in her prime she was a proper mate for Austin, his equal in culture and his superior in social grace. By all odds she was, they said, the most brilliant talker in that part of the state. From Miss Hinsdale, from Professor Bigelow, and from Dr. Frederick Jones Bliss, one of the old graduates, I gathered details about the daughter Martha, or Mattie. They all said she was tall, self-willed, perhaps erratic, with more than her mother's talent for extraordinary conversation. Miss Hinsdale and Biggie denied that she had any charm, but they persuaded me that she had a good deal, for Miss Hinsdale was jealous of her, and Biggie could not hide the fact that as a boy he had admired her, and perhaps she had not sufficiently admired him.

"Martha Dickinson?" he exclaimed when I asked about her. "Why, she and I played together when we were children! Many a time I've strapped the skates on that girl's ankles! She's a snob, that's all the matter with her."

Miss Hinsdale poked fun at Martha for going to Europe so often— accused her of hunting a husband there, and of having hunted a long time, in vain. In the winter of 1903-1904, Martha was thirty-eight. But I knew that Miss Hinsdale herself, for whatever purpose, would have been glad to see Europe again.

Dr. Fred Jones said frankly that during his College course he had been madly in love with Martha and was still proud of his good taste, but she was too much for him. He and she both, at the age of eighteen or nineteen, were ambitious to talk like the characters in George Meredith's novels. Martha believed it was an art and therefore could be learned, so she had him over, quite frequently, to sit on the Dickinson porch and practise Meredithian conversation. But one day, after a few minutes of it, she stood up and told him to go home. He gasped, but she meant it. "I told you to go home, Fred! You are not subtle today." Then he laughed at her, but it did him no good. "Fred, you weary me today—you are not subtle!" He took his hat and went, but as he slammed the gate, looking back angrily at the tall figure, he called, "I am too, subtle!"

If a personal tragedy had not befallen Martha, the Dickinson feud might have remained a fairly simple affair, involving only Emily's manuscripts and Austin's susceptibility, but I saw for myself the dramatic episode which caused a rift between Martha and the people of Amherst. Letters from Mrs. Dickinson to Mrs. Davis began to hint that the European wanderings were overclouded. The whisper spread that Martha had met a mysterious gentleman whom she was determined to marry, though her mother disapproved. In time a formal announcement dropped into all the prominent households, that Martha was the wife of a certain Captain Alexander Bianchi, a Russian of old family in spite of his name, and if you please an officer in the Czar's private guard. The Captain's military duties necessitated the spending of practically all his time on the Riviera.

Amherst was delighted. The general verdict was that a proud Dickinson had been taken in by a foreigner. The townsfolk wished Martha would hurry home so they could look him over and decide who had caught which. In the spring of the year Martha obliged. She brought him home, and at once invited a select group of residents to a reception in his honor. Everything went wrong from the start. The hand-picking of the guests was a triumph of public relations in reverse. It was reported that she wished her husband to see Amherst at its best, and was therefore introducing to him only those neighbors who were cultured and widely traveled. The Todds were not asked.

At the party the Captain courted disaster by wearing a super-gorgeous costume, which Martha said was the dress uniform of the Czar's favorite guard, but which local connoisseurs recognized as the best suit of the Springfield bandmaster. A new Steinway stood in the drawing room, the Captain's wedding gift to Martha, but once more Springfield provided corrective information. Those acquainted with piano dealers there were prepared within a week to venture the opinion, or something more than opinion, that the check which paid for the Steinway had been Martha's. The refreshments at the reception were generous, and in a gush of sentiment for her native New England Martha had rather played up cider and doughnuts, but the Captain declined, announcing in a French which Amherst could understand that he drank nothing but champagne.

In short, he gave an atrocious performance, and the anti-Bianchi faction would have been glad to engage him for a reappearance. Martha never forgave Amherst. From that day she had on her hands not only the major quarrel over Aunt Emily's manuscripts, but a private vendetta with those who had taken one look at her romance and laughed. The Captain did not last long. He disappeared, having made heavier inroads on the Dickinson patrimony than ever Emily's editor could have meditated. But perhaps Martha clung to her infatuation. Years later she went abroad for what she told her friends would be a short trip, but she stayed indefinitely, in the Alps. When asked why she did not come home, she answered that a distant relative was dying of tuberculosis, and since she had no other obligation in the world, her mother being then dead, she would stay where she was needed. If this distant relative was the Captain, the kindness was entirely like her, but it was also like her to insist on being addressed as Madame Bianchi, to the perplexity of etiquette experts in Amherst and elsewhere.

2

At the beginning of my second Amherst autumn, she and her mother were back in their house, living quietly, as though the Captain had never upset them. I was surprised one day to get a note which, as I learned later, was from Martha. No Dickinson ever wrote so that more than two words out of three could be deciphered, but I solved the puzzle; I had been invited to lunch with Mrs. Austin Dickinson and her daughter. I went, of course, and for the rest of my years at Amherst I prized the Dickinson hospitality with a correct premonition that I should meet nothing quite like it again.

It was as much as anything a hospitality to ideas. Martha and her mother could be found any evening in the library reading before the open fire, ready for visitors who brought something for the mind. The long library table was covered with current magazines of the most formidable kind, journals of philosophy and history, quarterly reviews. The library was a small room on the right as you entered the large hall. It was crowded with books, and so was every other room on the ground floor —the large parlor on the left, the various offices which disclosed themselves as you penetrated deeper into the house. Austin Dickinson's home was altogether a library. There were many paintings, but the books impressed you most. And they were a true library, for use rather than show. Martha could be described adequately by calling her a reader; Mrs. Dickinson was a scholar. I once expressed my amazement at the difficult reading I found on her library table. "It's a conviction of mine," she said, "that two women who live alone, with no man in the house, should keep near them something tough, to get their teeth into."

Martha had less than her mother's social charm, being in that respect all Dickinson. She had also in full measure the Dickinson strength of will and eccentricity. But in conversation she had her mother's genius. Emily could write, but she was not much of a talker. On occasion, it is said, she made profound remarks, but what the occasions were, and what the remarks, and who heard them, is imperfectly recorded. I doubt if any other person so inarticulate ever achieved so much fame as a poet. Her niece Martha, on the other hand, though she wished to write, had no gift for it, but she was one of the most stimulating talkers I ever met. She was curiously observant, and her reflections on what she observed were unconventional and unforgettable.

Both these women were dear friends of mine, and I honor their memory. As the Dickinson feud grew and gathered venom, the admirers of Mrs. Todd have dealt unjustly with Mrs. Dickinson, "Susan," and they can hardly be excused by the fact that few of them had the privilege of knowing her. She was cultured, intelligent, and kind. In gifts of mind, and rather obviously in gifts of heart, she was superior to her detractors. Their envy and jealousy can be understood. In the scramble to exploit the dead Emily, Susan had the misfortune to be in the way. To get at Emily's poems Mabel vamped Austin, leaving to posterity in excuse some poisonous hints that his wife didn't deserve him.

After Susan's death in 1912, Martha began getting out new volumes of Emily's poems, at first singlehanded, later with the collaboration of her friend, Alfred Leete Hampson. Admirers of Mrs. Todd thought that these instalments of Emily were less well edited than those which Mabel Loomis Todd and Thomas Wentworth Higginson had presided over, but we now know from *Ancestors' Brocades* that the liberties taken with Emily's text by her first editors might be thought excessive, and Martha Bianchi, at her death, willed away the manuscripts in her possession, so that it is impossible at present for scholars to form an opinion as to the accuracy of any edition. In the years through which I followed the course of the feud, while at Amherst and afterward, the motives on both sides seemed natural and rather pathetic. From all that has been disclosed about Mrs. Todd in *Ancestors' Brocades,* it is evident that the defeat in the lawsuit over the Dickinson property hurt her deeply. The rumor in Amherst, recorded by her daughter, that Austin Dickinson cared more for her than for his wife, was not unflattering and could not have been entirely displeasing, but it called for some sort of comment, and the attacks on Susan's character began, which are little short of a disgrace to American biography. Unpleasant things were said about the social status and private character of her parents and remoter ancestors; her lack of wealth in her youth was stressed, and Mrs. Todd's personal testimony was quoted to prove that Austin spent evenings in her home because he couldn't endure the society of his wife.

Martha Bianchi was loyal to her mother and would have moved heaven and earth to defend her and to get even with her detractors. Both she and Mrs. Todd were fighters, the difference being in what they fought for, but Martha, unfortunately, had that score to settle with Amherst for the derisive guffaws at her matrimonial experiment. It embittered her life in the place where three generations of her people had been honored. The town wanted Austin Dickinson's house as a library or museum, or something of the kind, but Martha directed in her will that it should go to her collaborator, Mr. Hampson, and when he wanted it no longer, it should be torn down. The attitude of most people in Amherst and near by, remained derisive toward her rather than hostile. In 1931 Amherst College gave her the honorary degree of Doctor of Letters. On the Committee to make the award was Calvin Coolidge for the Trustees, and Professor Bigelow, among others, for the faculty. Biggie told me how Coolidge exercised his humor at Martha's expense. He asked first of all what she had done to deserve a degree. He was reminded of her volumes of verse, of her four or five novels, and of her editions of Emily Dickinson. The ex-President, having spent his life in the neighborhood, probably knew as much as anyone about the history of the Dickinsons and about Emily's poems, and the feud over the editing. He probably knew the famous lawsuit by heart, but he pretended ignorance, asked who Emily Dickinson was, said he had not read any of Martha's original books, and asked whether they were popular. Committee members, to bolster Martha's case, reminded Mr. Coolidge of the great services rendered to the College by her family. Her brother Edward had served in the Library, her father was Trustee and Treasurer, her grandfather was Treasurer and one of the founders of the institution.

"Well," said Calvin, "if her grandfather was Treasurer, and her father was Treasurer, I think the College has done enough for that family."

Martha got her degree, but Coolidge's joke circulated with it.

Martha died in New York, after a brief illness, in December, 1943. I was present at the funeral service, which took the form—amazing in her case—of a requiem mass at the Church of St. Mary the Virgin. She was always allergic to dogma and ritual, and how she got into St. Mary's, I cannot imagine. As the incense enveloped her and the priest sprinkled holy water, I watched the casket somewhat nervously, half expecting a tall figure to push the cover away and sit up and make a few Dickinsonian remarks.

She is buried in the modern cemetery at Amherst, with Austin and Susan, her parents, and quite near Mrs. Todd.

If you are hasty you might think the feud at an end—both feuds, the one between Martha and the Todds, the other between Martha and the village. But the editing feud is not yet completely out of everybody's system; and when Martha's will was read, the town knew she had got even, in a regrettably savage way. To recapitulate: she gave Mr. Hampson her father's famous house and everything in it—all of Emily's manuscripts in her possession, with full power to dispose of them—Emily's piano, and everything else connected with her. Two of the executors named in the will declined to serve, and even the least malicious of Martha's critics asked why she would destroy, by scattering the manuscripts, her last chance to prove that her editing had always been competent and in good faith.

Now, since Mrs. Bingham published *Ancestors' Brocades* and its companion volume, *Bolts of Melody, New Poems by Emily Dickinson,* we know that Mrs. Bingham had in her possession all along, and still has, manuscripts of Emily's poems, the existence of which was concealed from Martha, who had good reason to think she inherited all the manuscripts at her Aunt Lavinia's death. Amherst residents, those who look hopefully for another spicy chapter in the feud, wonder what rights in the Bingham manuscripts Mr. Hampson has, and whether he will care to claim them. At the present writing, so far as it is known, he has made no disposition of the property. One Amherst opinion is that the Austin Dickinson house should become a museum or shrine, and that all of Emily's papers, those that Mrs. Todd and those that Martha had, should rest in safe peace in one place.

The feud could have a happy, even a noble ending if Mrs. Bingham and Mr. Hampson now turned over the manuscripts in their possession to some permanent institution. The Austin Dickinson house is not fire-proof. I wish the papers might all rest in the Library of Amherst College, which Emily's father and her brother Austin helped to found and main-tain, and which is already the custodian of library treasures.

Emily is the one who counts. Her genius has won its place in spite of her editors. She ought to be secure in that austere and lofty seclusion which during her lifetime was hers by choice. But the mean little feud about which she never knew a thing, still feeds indirectly on her great name to keep itself going. Not long ago a group of Martha Bianchi's partisans met at her grave for a commemorative tribute. One of them said a few words of affection and admiration, bringing in the name of Aunt Emily to put the ceremony on a high level. Almost immediately one of the Toddites, a relentless professor, exposed in the local paper his grounds for believing Martha Bianchi was not an admirable editor, and that her mother, Susan, was not an admirable woman.

CHAPTER XIV

My First Students

I

FOR the first three years at Amherst my teaching schedule was heavy, because of my wish to give courses in literature. These years were also rather stormy, because of inexperience in handling boys. I dare say I impressed the freshmen as a queer addition to what they had understood to be a restful, tradition-loving community. I have a photograph taken the week I met them, and looking at it now I can understand their point of view. I was tall and slender; to be precise, I measured six feet one and a half inches, and my weight was a hundred and forty pounds. Several in my earliest classes were as old as I, or nearly so, and I looked younger than I was. For these handicaps I had to compensate by a venturesome disposition and a strong will, and here I was fairly well equipped. My hair was black, my nose large, my face long and my cheekbones high; I was becoming accustomed to hear the guess that Spain had something to do with my ancestry.

President Harris, when he engaged me, said the Amherst freshmen for twenty years had done little work in their English course, and perhaps that condition ought to be changed. I concluded, perhaps too hastily, that the reform was my task. I speak of the matter with so much doubt because when I made the boys work and they rebelled, President Harris did not support me.

At the end of my first week, no one had written a page for me, though I had announced that there would be weekly themes, and had set the date when they should be handed in. No change in the situation at the end of the second week. I made the class a very serious speech. Either they would give me a theme a week, or they would fail the course. Since accident or illness might befall the best of us, I would allow this leeway, that for cause they might miss two weeks in the year, but three misses would be fatal. Practically to a man the class loafed for two weeks more. I devoted the time in the classroom to a discussion of the art of writing in general. When they wrote at last, after the fortnight of grace, I marked their papers savagely, suggesting that the faults probably came from lack of practice. Then one of them, having no more leeway, brought in his essay a week later, and I refused to accept it. At the end of the semester he had a deficiency in English. He already had a failure in mathematics, which he considered a normal misfortune, but why should anyone fail in English? Besides, he was captain of the track team, and two failures would disqualify him for the spring meet with other New England colleges, and without him the team would lose. I heard this argument from him, from prominent alumni, and from President Harris, who had requests from the alumni that I be dismissed. At last I was asked by the President to appear before the executive committee of the faculty and explain what I was doing to the College. I explained. When I had no more to say, President Harris spoke very gently. "John, I suppose I am in a way your chief, as the head of the faculty." I agreed. "Then I suppose I could order you to give this boy an examination or do something else which would enable him to pass." I answered that doubtless he could give such an order, but I hoped he would not, since I should have to resign. "In that case," said he, "the order will not be given." So the captain of the track team was unable to compete, and without him the team lost, and for a while I was thoroughly disliked by most of the boys. But those who studied with me did their work, and in time we were all friends.

I know now that there are other methods of securing discipline besides threats and ultimatums. My later classes gave me no trouble, not necessarily because they were superior in brains or more docile, but because I learned how to get what I desired even from stubborn and skittish youth. And I must not leave the impression that all my students made trouble for me; in each year there were a number of grand workers, some of whom have gone far. Among them were Bruce Barton and Joseph Bartlett Eastman, transportation expert; Walter Walker Palmer and William Sargent Ladd, physicians; William Ives Washburn, David Franklin Goodnow, and Richmond Mayo-Smith, publishers; Horatio Elwin Smith, William Haller, George Frisbie Whicher, Christian Alban Ruckmich, and Talbot Hamlin, college professors; Claude Fuess, headmaster of Phillips-Andover; Eustace Seligman and Mason Huntington Bigelow, lawyers. I name only a few, but many faces rise before me as I write— Adolphus Merigold Milloy, Louis Joseph Nicolaus, Marston Hamlin, James Shelley Hamilton, composer of *Lord Geoffrey Amherst,* and Roscoe William Brink, determined individualist. George Plough and Burt King Taggart died long ago. Chilton L. Powell, sound scholar and fine teacher, certain of a useful career, died suddenly after the First World War. They were all boys of promise, and some of them were permitted by fate to use their gifts.

Amherst, during the presidency of George Harris, had something of the family atmosphere more often found in country boarding schools than in colleges and universities. The citizens of the town, when the institution was opened in 1821 with forty-seven students, made the boys as comfortable as possible, turned their homes into eating places, and mothered those youngsters who seemed to need extra care. As late as 1904 the townspeople still took a personal interest in the boys, and the boarding-houses were all known by the names of the ladies who maintained them. There was no other place to eat except the hotel, which was in a condition of polite decay.

Over an institution so intimate, all but domestic, it was fitting that a man like Dr. Harris should preside. He was paternal, a true pastor, the incarnation of kindness. He had many other attractive qualities, but perhaps he was not intended to be a college president. The unpleasant duties of such a post, he neglected or ignored. Toward disciplinary problems, he had one consistent attitude; he postponed solving them. Yet in his own gentle, procrastinating way he did much for Amherst College, and I remember with gratitude his friendship, the gracious humor with which he dispensed the hospitality of his home, and the whimsical detachment with which he watched, as it were from the sidelines, the attempts of his faculty to make the College a center of light and learning. Loving music, he gave Professor Bigelow magnificent encouragement in the development of a College orchestra and chorus. He was at his best, perhaps, when he received on the campus distinguished men of arts and sciences; he had read much and traveled widely, and he was far more scholarly than he cared to admit. He was not really opposed to work, but I never heard him say much in favor of it, and he had the saving wit of the indolent. One autumn he rose in chapel to address the students at the first assembly of the year, but after a sentence or two he got tired and broke into a happy smile—"I intended to give you some advice, but now I remember how much is left over from last year unused." With that he took his hat and walked out.

2

At Amherst in my time the alumni were only a little less influential than the faculty or the President. On the whole they did not exercise this influence to encourage the intellectual life. They usually concentrated on athletics. This type of alumnus was in those days a blight on all the small colleges. But another type, less noisy and less conspicuous, enjoyed the advantages of intelligence. At Amherst I met both types. Toward the end of that troubled first spring, when I had weathered the storm but at the price of being regarded by many alumni and students as a menace and a nuisance, I was starting to cross the Common one morning in front of the post office when I was stopped by a slender, courteous gentleman with a kind voice and still kinder eyes. He shook my hand as though we were old friends.

"My name is Babbott. I am one of the very ancient alumni." He laughed at his own joke, and I recall the youthfulness of his appearance at the moment. "I have heard the boys talking about the new English teacher. Do you like your work?

"I happen to know," he went on, "that the Library allowance for the English department is not large. I suppose you need some books which you have no money for?"

I had already discovered this condition, common to all colleges.

"Well," he said, "I want you to have a fair chance here. I'll send you a check for books for your department, and when you need more, let me know."

The next day his check came, a very generous check indeed, and each year after that, while I was at Amherst, I would report to him how the money was spent, and he would renew the gift for the coming season. Frank Lusk Babbott was one of Amherst's great men. He was a leading citizen of Brooklyn, New York. I might as well say he was one of the strong influences for everything fine, not only in New York City, but in the State and the nation. Few rich men have used their wealth so wisely. His generous gifts always followed careful study of particular needs, and there was hardly a field of human interest in which he hadn't deep and well-trained sympathies. All social causes appealed to him; so did all forms of noble art. His private collection was notable. He was a devoted and scholarly reader, and a lover and patron of music; and he gave his time and strength to the cause of education, not only in his own college but in Brooklyn and Manhattan and many other places. His notice of me at the end of my first Amherst year put me far along my way. He was a faithful friend until his death in 1933.

He told me once that Americans underrate the possibilities of the retired life. The man in the background, he thought, has the advantage of a detached viewpoint, and avoids the disadvantages of official responsibility. He said that many a man can do more good out of office than in. He was thinking of himself, and the remark explains him. I admired him for it, since I knew how sincere he was. But I knew also that his philosophy could not be mine. I was beginning to see how much of life is a warfare, and how embarrassing it is for a soldier to have a retiring disposition.

Some fortitude was called for in putting Mr. Babbott's gift to use. The English department needed more money for books, but Professor Genung, the head or at least the senior member of the department, might well have expected Mr. Babbott, a former student of his, to give the money to him. There was a third teacher in the department, older than I but younger than Professor Genung—George Bosworth Churchill, a forceful character with an excellent mind, but not particularly a literary person. Anything that Churchill undertook he would accomplish efficiently, but his inclination was toward law and politics. He rather neglected his opportunities as teacher and scholar, but he served with distinction for many years as moderator at the annual Town Meeting. From 1917 to 1919 he was a member of the Massachusetts Senate, and a few years later he was elected to Congress. He supported me while I was the target of student wrath after the track-team episode, yet he was somewhat startled and not a little hurt when Mr. Babbott entrusted to me his departmental gift. The fact was that Mr. Babbott wanted the teaching of literature at Amherst to be much more vital than it was, and since Genung and Churchill had been there for some time, he preferred to make his experiment with the new instructor.

I tried to ease the situation by handing the fund over to the College Treasury, and by assuring Genung and Churchill that it was for us all to use as a department. I doubt if Nungie remembered the incident more than a few hours, but it troubled Churchill. I suppose there was more to say for his point of view than at the time I realized. Amherst was his Alma Mater, he was an ambitious man and had worked hard, and if his efforts now failed to make the impression he wished, he would be the last person likely to understand the reason.

He had many interests outside his College work, and at the moment I had none. In addition to his other distractions he began to build a new house, and he liked to be on hand every minute to see that the masons and carpenters committed no error. He found it difficult to fit this exhaustive backseat-driving into his teaching schedule, and except for his classroom performances, the campus for a while saw little of him. We had in the English department a literary club which held fortnightly meetings, where papers were read by students or faculty, and addresses were sometimes made by distinguished visitors. Churchill, Genung and I had agreed to be responsible for the programs in rotation, but the housebuilding threw Churchill a bit out of step.

It was his turn to arrange for a meeting, and when nothing happened I offered to arrange it for him. He accepted, slightly embarrassed, saying he would be ready next time, but next time he was busier than ever. I walked down to the new house and found him on a ladder, inspecting the laying of beams on the second floor. I offered again to take charge of the club program. I did not mean to plague him, but my offer had that effect. With a touch of heat he asked why the matter was so pressing, and I told him it would be a pleasure in any circumstances to help keep the club alive, and to that end it was essential that meetings should occur on the dates we had previously announced to the students.

Churchill had by nature a good deal of senatorial dignity, and from his ladder he admonished me not to be impertinent, not to inflict my advice where it was not wanted, not to imagine and certainly not to imply that he was neglecting his duties, and above all not to entertain the idea that I was the head of the department. I then withdrew, and he resumed his house inspection, but in a day or two, since nothing happened, I arranged for the club meeting, and after that, whenever the department interests were neglected, I stepped in. The President seemed to approve, and Professor Genung did not care so long as he was undisturbed in his own studies, but between Churchill and me no love was lost. When my own University, at the end of six years, called me back, I went around to his house, no longer new, and told him of the invitation. Never have I seen a man try so hard not to look happy.

3

One of the most stimulating speakers we had at our literary club was Herbert Vaughan Abbott, son of Lyman Abbott, and husband of Zenda Berenson, who was the sister of Bernard Berenson, the famous art critic. I name Herbert Abbott's relatives for a special reason; having always lived in the society of notable people, he had gradually acquired a marvellously flattering manner which intimated that, since you and he had met at all, it must be because you too were notable. He was a courtly gentleman but short of stature and slight of build, and while he talked he curled up in his chair in a shrinking posture and carefully massaged one of his ankles. He fascinated me. He always came conscientiously prepared, though for the early part of his talk he seemed casual and unorganized. That may have been because he brought his notes on a pack of small cards which he held in his left hand, and as he finished a topic he lifted a card from the top of the pack and slipped it in at the bottom. But his remarks were thoughtful and searching, and so well planned that, as the minutes went by, an almost architectural structure unexpectedly took form.

Gerald Stanley Lee did not, like Herbert Abbott, teach in Smith College, but he lived in Northampton, and so did George W. Cable, whose acquaintance I made through Professor Joseph Thompson, who took me to call on him. Since his health was not robust, Mr. Cable had ceased to give lectures, and we could not have him for our literary club, though he was easily the most important writer in our neighborhood. But Gerald Stanley Lee gave us a remarkable talk. Just what the title was I do not recall, but Mr. Lee spoke always on the same subject. He believed that few of us realize our powers, that we fetter ourselves with chains which would drop off if we relaxed or, in his pet formula, let ourselves go. He carried on a tireless crusade against so-called inhibitions, against the false modesty which is really cowardice, and against the kind of self-restraint which is indolence.

Two important lecturers came to Amherst during my first winter there and addressed not the literary club but a large general audience from the whole College and the town. These two were William Butler Yeats and Frederick J. E. Woodbridge. Yeats was then making what I believe was his first tour of the United States, and one of our alumni, an Irishman, provided the college with the opportunity to hear him. On November 19, 1903, the poet dined at Professor Churchill's, I being the other guest, and from there we went to the lecture in College Hall, and afterward to a supper party at the President's house. Yeats was in good form all through the evening. He stood then at the threshold of his fame. Our ears still found the music of his verses full of a novel magic, which with time to some extent wore off. Yet he still seems altogether the greatest poet writing in English during my life, and in his fresh youth he was overwhelming. His conversation at that time was spontaneous and inevitable; in later years it became somewhat studied.

At Professor Churchill's table he poured a stream of mischievous comment on men prominent in the literary world of the day. Of one writer he said that the fellow had a talent for uttering platitudes, and since that was what he was born to do, he did it complacently, even with pride.

He said there are two wonderful things in the universe, the vanity of popular novelists and the sensitiveness of unrecognized poets.

He defined a popular novelist as a man who has a little genius and an infinite amount of vulgarity. In everything but his gift of expression he is identical with the multitudes who read him.

He told us that when George Moore saw Beerbohm Tree in *Hamlet* he said, "Remarkably poor play! So out of date, you know." But when he saw Forbes Robertson in it, he exclaimed, "Amazing play! So well constructed! Holds your attention first and last!"

He said the laureateship was offered to William Morris, who declined it. William Watson should have had it, since he was the only living Englishman who invariably rose above himself when he wrote on patriotic subjects. But Watson happened to be out of his mind at the moment, and of course the English are conservative; they like to know in advance what their laureate will say. Yeats thought nothing better could happen to them than to have a mad laureate.

As for Alfred Austin, he said the first thing Austin did after being appointed laureate, was to write to Salisbury, the Prime Minister, saying he would be delighted to spend a few days with his Lordship whenever that plan fell in with his Lordship's convenience.

In short, Yeats was all Irishman that evening, with an Irishman's ability to tell the unpleasant truth, even at the expense of his friends, and with a dogged persistence in tracking down all the opportunities, even the unpromising ones, to disparage England. Since he expressed the wish to visit an American fraternity house, some of the Alpha Delta Phi boys called for him at the close of the President's supper party, Churchill and I coming along. For an hour and a half he talked with the boys, and asked to hear their college songs, which they gladly sang for him. When we left the house and were crossing the Common, they sent a cheer after him, and sang a parting song. He stood in the moonlight listening, then moved on with a remark which neither Churchill nor I expected: "How natural and how beautiful! What a contrast to the vulgarity of Oxford!"

The other important lecturer, Frederick Woodbridge, was an Amherst graduate who had been Professor of Philosophy at the University of Minnesota, and now was Dr. Butler's successor in the same chair at Columbia. Charles Garman, the great teacher of philosophy at Amherst, Woodbridge's own teacher, was absent on a sabbatical vacation, and his ablest pupil had been called back to give in his absence a series of public lectures on the major thinkers from Plato and Aristotle to Spinoza. It was my first sight of Sheddy Woodbridge, as Amherst named him, and I saw him on an occasion which brought out the finest of his gifts. He had lost his heart in youth to his College as a home of ideals, and even as a boy his character had so impressed the community that now on his return he was greeted with something like veneration.

CHAPTER XV

Woodberry at Amherst

I

MEANWHILE my old world in New York was changing fast. During my first winter in Amherst, Nanna died of another paralytic stroke, and at the University the resignation of Professor Woodberry was announced early in 1904, and immediately the resignation of Professor MacDowell. I doubt if Columbia ever recovered from the mistake of letting these men go. No university can afford the reputation of being inhospitable to genius.

George Arthur Plimpton, the Amherst Trustee who had been Woodberry's schoolmate at Phillips-Exeter, immediately arranged for him to lecture at Amherst during the academic year 1904-1905. Mr. Plimpton wanted him for the whole year and hoped the appointment might be permanent, but Woodberry was much depressed by the close of his Columbia chapter, and did not care to commit himself again to a long stretch of teaching. He would give one course at Amherst during the spring term of 1905. The departmental announcement, issued in June, 1904, said the course would deal with modern literature, would meet three times a week, and would be open to juniors and seniors.

The spring of 1904 was the first I had spent in New England and I thought other springs would be like it, which none of them were. Through the winter of 1903-1904 we had heavy snows and more than ninety days below freezing. Some weather expert, looking up the record, may prove me wrong, yet I remember the severe and protracted cold, and certain pleasant advantages of it. Those of us whose studies were on the second floor looked out on deep covers of snow upon the porch roof, and into these drifts we stuck a few dozen bottles of beer, secure against observation from the street, and confident that our refrigerator would not vanish in a sudden thaw. That spring the snow on the sidewalks, instead of melting, simply wore off in the dry cold, and when the sun at last was high we could put away our overshoes. I wrote Woodberry descriptions of the fine weather, and prepared him for a climate that knew neither mud nor slush. But the next winter was warm and rainy. Every time he tugged at his galoshes he gave me a reproachful look.

He planned to stay at the Amherst Hotel, at the northwestern corner of the Common, where Main Street crosses Pleasant and becomes Amity. I engaged a room and made what preparations I could for his comfort. The car from Northampton stopped in front of the hotel, and I waited for him there on the evening of February 9. It was raining and his train had reached Springfield late. At seven o'clock the trolley brought him in, wearing a heavy coat with a cape, carrying a large bag, and looking as though he had been exiled to the Arctic. He was as fond of warmth as a cat.

The hotel managed to assemble a fairly good dinner, after which Woodberry took a brighter view of the universe, lighted a cigar, and found a comfortable chair in the small parlor one flight up—Amherst hadn't yet learned to call it the "Mezzanine." After a while President Harris came in, with Nungie and Churchill, and all four smoked and talked till ten-thirty.

Next morning I showed him around the village before his lecture, which came at a quarter to twelve. Then we had midday dinner at our faculty table at Mrs. Davis's, with coffee in my room afterward. One night of the hotel had been enough. He wanted to eat at Mrs. Davis's and if possible live in the same house; since Mrs. Davis had no room, he found comfortable quarters that afternoon at Mrs. Lindsey's home, on Northampton Road, only a few yards away. For the rest of the term he came to my study daily after the heavy midday dinner, and we had coffee and a good talk over his cigar. My pleasure would be hard to describe—so many hours, on terms so intimate, with a teacher for whom I had a regard so profound!

The lectures were given in the large room at the east end of Walker Hall, on the second floor. About eighty students registered for the class, and ten or twelve of the faculty were present daily as auditors. The

College was soon talking about the Woodberry point of view and the Woodberry style of lecturing, the faculty as well as the students recognizing at once his unusual quality. The old magic was working again.

After the lecture on the second day, James Walter Crook, Professor of Political Economy, called at my study early in the afternoon to talk about the revelation which the course had already been to him. Woodberry was lecturing on English literature in the nineteenth century, and he used the first hours to discuss poetry, and what he conceived its function in life to be. Professor Crook, somewhat more than middle aged, considered himself a scientist. I doubt if he had ever heard a strong argument for the part played by imagination and emotion and ideals, not only in our personal lives but in the broad evolution of society. That afternoon he was a man who had just been struck by an idea, and he was almost unnerved by the blow. He asked me what Woodberry himself had written, and I handed him a copy of "Agathon," a long poem which shows how much Woodberry owed in his youth to Milton and to Plato. Few readers know it today, few knew it in 1905. Professor Crook began to read it aloud. The music of the lines gripped him, and he read on and on. At the end, to his astonishment as well as mine, he broke into tears. Great poetry reveals us to ourselves. Crook told me that as he read he had discovered a number of things.

He was an interesting man, a Canadian of rather heroic character, who had grown up as a boy in a logging camp, and after his youth was gone, he got himself an education, and at last, having studied with leading economists here, made his way to Europe to learn from economists there. But nowhere in his long and difficult climb had he encountered poetry or any esthetic experience. For the rest of that semester he remained one of Woodberry's most diligent students.

2

The reason or reasons why Woodberry left Columbia have never been made clear, and perhaps they are not ascertainable now. He and Brander Matthews were out of sympathy, and he had the impression that Professor Price was the only colleague who played fair with him. More than once he said that Professor Price had not been appreciated at Columbia, a statement with which I did not agree. But most often in our talks over the coffee urn in my study his regrets about Columbia were impersonal, merged in a general sense of defeat. He was living, he felt, in an age hostile to the finer things. Of President Butler and the Trustees he spoke always with respect, but with the implication that they shared the spirit of their time, and must therefore slight that side of man's nature which goes into the arts. It is no use trying to combat so strong a trend, he would say; life is a dirty game. This formula he repeated so often that at first I was concerned for him, but gradually, as the bad weather of that year set in, Amherst mud contributed humor to his pessimism. "Life is a dirty game," he would groan, leaning against the wall to pull on his galoshes.

At Columbia he had served for a while as faculty member of the Athletic Committee. One day we talked of college sports; I dare say I was telling him my adventure with the alumni when the captain of the track team failed in English. Woodberry said, almost with violence, that it was useless and perhaps harmful to make boys live a—for them—unnaturally ethical life which later they would be compelled to give up as soon as they got into that other life, which, as he insisted, is a dirty game. When I told him I had no sympathy with such ideas, he laughed. The momentary excess of pessimism was caused, I found out, by lack of sleep. The radiator in his room had been noisy.

As the days went by and the success of his course became too obvious for him to be overmodest about it, I hoped he would be more cheerful, and at some moments he was, yet he continued to have dark moods. He had no plans for his future. He probably would not teach again except for brief engagements; he distrusted all institutions; the administrators of universities, he said, were no different from business executives. If they were not expected to earn dividends for investors, at least they must produce winning football teams and enunciate only those economic or social principles which the alumni would enjoy hearing. I reminded him of his obligation to write what at that moment he was telling me; could he remain silent about his sincere convictions? He invariably replied that to oppose the spirit of the age is vain. Provoked by this determined defeatism, I told him one day that he was putting up a strong argument for suicide; if life was such a dirty game as all that, why should I endure it? Or why should he? He said it was a good question. He himself had no impulse to live longer. Suicide was usually an awkward performance; if you used a pistol you messed up the room, and if you jumped into the river, someone would be greatly inconvenienced fishing around for the body. But death, if it came of itself, could not come too soon. Just at that moment my coffee machine blew up. The death-loving poet, in three lightning strides, got from his chair next the coffee table to the door. And there he stood laughing.

During one of the last snowstorms of the winter the Connecticut Valley enjoyed a visit from Henry James, who had come back from England to tour America with his lecture on Balzac, and was to tell the girls at Smith all about Balzac on the next Friday evening. The Amherst authorities did not engage him to enlighten the boys, perhaps because most of the boys would be at Hamp anyway on a Friday night, but we had a gratifying link with Henry James even though we didn't hear him; he and Professor Emerson, our geologist, were cousins. Newlin and I, never having laid eyes on Henry, thought we might as well brave the snowdrifts. Woodberry admitted that he too had never seen the man, but writers, he argued, should be read rather than looked at, especially in bad weather. For two days we argued the point until he gave in and said he would come with us, but late Friday afternoon more snow began to fall, and when he arrived for supper he was triumphant.

"I knew it would not be necessary!" he exclaimed. "I have already seen him! I am satisfied."

We asked where the meeting had occurred.

"A little way down the Northampton Road, near Orchard Street. He was looking for the home of Professor Emerson. I directed him."

We were excited. "Did he know who you were?"

"Why should he? I told you we have never met."

"Then how did you recognize him?"

"By his words! 'Can you tell me where is Orchard Street—if, perchance, there be an Orchard Street?'"

So Newlin and I went over to Smith alone. President Seeley, who also was related to Henry James, introduced him. The novelist sat well down in his chair gazing at the ceiling, with one leg crossed over the other, the broad sole of the elevated shoe sticking out well forward and obscuring the rest of him. The introduction over, he rose quickly, spread out his manuscript and began, turning each page firmly down on the speaker's desk as he finished with it. The lecture was afterward published, but I have not read it, nor, I am sure, has Newlin. Perhaps it would be easier to read than it was to take in through the ear, but one sentence remains. I repeated it to Woodberry the next morning, and Newlin agreed that those were the precise words. An ordinary mortal might say that Balzac must be judged by no one of his novels, but by all of them taken together. Henry James put it this way: "It was not given to him to flower, for our convenience, into a single supreme felicity."

3

It was somewhat a surprise to me, who had known Woodberry only in the Columbia academic circle, to see how he blossomed out among New Englanders, his own people. Churchill and he got on famously, and the new house was put to its happiest use, or so it seemed to me, when Churchill gave one of his large "Woodberry parties." I remember a particularly genial and expansive evening, when all the literature and language teachers—Greek, Latin, Italian, Spanish, French and German—gathered at Churchill's in Woodberry's honor. Nitze and Biggie and deForest Smith, an Athenian spirit born in Maine, matched my old teacher in wonderful talk. That night I was proud of the Amherst faculty.

One week end we assembled a large party for dinner at Rose Warren's, in South Deerfield. Many a Saturday evening do I remember with Nungie and Biggie, with Churchill, deForest Smith and the others, at that attractive hostelry as it was forty years ago. But this time, because Woodberry was coming, we were joined by Preserved Smith, Amherst's scholarly Chaplain, by Professor Olds and Professor Cowles and others of the elder group for whom Rose Warren's steaks and onions would not have been, in themselves, a compelling attraction.

Rose Warren's was a small hotel, more precisely a roadhouse, owned by a man named Warren and managed by his middle-aged and highly executive daughter Rose. Tom the bartender excelled in his speciality, and could be counted on for efficient bouncing whenever a gentleman dropped in after visiting too many bars further up the road. In the course of nature, Mr. Warren died, leaving the property to his child. However mature and matronly her appearance, yet she was a New Englander, with sensitive regard for appearances. Could she, a spinster, administer a roadhouse in solitary association with Tom, a bachelor? She invited him to choose between matrimony and search for another job. He married her, and business went on as usual.

It was a question whether Tom ever made a decision, or whether Rose made it for him. When we dined at her place, she would come to the table and recite briskly the options for the evening—steak, chops, chicken, roast lamb, trout—whatever the season provided. We should have been glad to think it over, but Rose never allowed more than thirty seconds, and when the time was up she would announce the selection we had not yet made. "Professor Churchill will have steak and onions, Professor Genung, roast lamb; steak and onions for Professor Nitze—now if Professor Genung will make it unanimous, steak and onions for everybody." She convinced us that we got what we wanted. On the occasion of our big dinner she organized our choices as usual, and when Woodberry heard what he had asked for, he was slightly bewildered, but on reflection he perceived that Rose had read his mind correctly.

At all our Amherst parties and especially at the Rose Warren dinner he showed a love of fun and a gift for good fellowship which some of his New York friends did not think he had. Perhaps he never found at Columbia the hearty sort of comradeship to bring out this side of him. Even when he unbent, he remained the highminded gentleman we had met in the classroom, but he could be warmly human, and he loved as much as anyone a walk into the country, a meal well cooked and served at the New England roadside tavern, and the brisk walk under moon and stars to the midnight car which Biggie always engaged to wait for us across the river, at the other end of the bridge.

4

During Woodberry's stay at Amherst he gave lectures at Mt. Holyoke College and at Smith College, and a series of lectures at Johns Hopkins. My diary for that period reminds me how active he was, but if I trusted only my memory I should say he did little of importance in addition to drinking coffee with me in my study at noon. Because his lecture came at the end of the morning, I saw to it that the bulk of my work was scheduled early, leaving the afternoons fairly free. On our way from lunch to coffee we stopped at the post office for his mail, and while the coffee was making he would read his letters and talk about whatever interested him. One day it was the news that the Oxford Press had asked Spingarn to edit a collection of seventeenth century critical essays. Another time there was a letter from his friend Professor S. H. Butcher, of the University of Edinburgh, who the year before had delivered at Harvard his lectures on Greek subjects. But if there happened to be no letter to set him talking, he would draw on Columbia memories, Columbia being at the moment constantly and sadly in his thoughts. He spoke at length one day of J. Russell Taylor, the poet, then in the English department of Ohio State University, and of Herbert F. Small, of the class of 1901, who showed promise as a writer, and who also—though this meant nothing to Woodberry—was an excellent violinist, and a member of the University orchestra which played for the performance of *The Governor's Vrouw.*

The entries in my diary do not explain by what transition Woodberry passed from these names to the problem of class discipline, but it was then that he told me of his early difficulties at Columbia and of the talk with Mr. Low in which he named the guillotine as the ideal monitor. Still less can I now recall by what shift he began to speak of the futility, perhaps the wickedness, of trying to impose our own sense of duty on other people; "compelling them to come in may be at first a hospitable impulse, but in the end it may also be some form of inquisition. Rules may be useful in general, but the individual boy ought to have many chances." He illustrated by an incident at Columbia in his first days there. One of the students had made himself a public nuisance, and though frequently warned by the Dean, developed a remarkable facility in going from bad to worse. As often happens in such cases, the young rascal was extremely likable, and Woodberry shared the hope of his colleagues that here the guillotine might not have to fall. But the young man seemed bent on perdition, and the faculty met to pass sentence. The list of offenses was read out, astounding both for number and for variety. Woodberry said it rather made him gasp, but the Professor of Germanic Languages, Hjalmar Hjorth Boyesen, the Norwegian writer, rose in his place and told the Dean there was something wrong with this indictment.

"Please explain yourself," said the Dean, a bit put out.

"How old is this hardened sinner?"

"He is sixteen."

"Well, Mr. Dean, I am only a novelist, not like you a criminologist, but since I write for grown men and women who know life, I would not put into a story of mine a character so young and of such complicated depravity acquired during one year of attendance at Columbia College."

Woodberry told the story with zest, but I asked him how his guillotine would ever have a chance if all professors were as shrewd as Boyesen. He laughed, then spoke of his own education. He had come early, he said, and so had escaped being overtaught. Never was any theme of his corrected by anyone, and never had he taken any course in literature. He thought he had learned to spell after he took to writing as a profession; proofreaders taught him by pointing out his mistakes. "Even now," he added, my grammar is frequently assailed, but"—here he seemed conscious of merit—"I always change it when they call my attention to it." From boyhood he had read books, for love of them. Most of his Harvard study was in philosophy; in that subject he took his degree. Once he visited the classroom of Francis James Child, the great Harvard Professor of English, famous for research in several fields; and once he had listened to Agassiz, in order to see a first-rate scientific mind at work. But next to philosophy the subject which had meant most to him was history. He counted it his golden fortune to have been a student at Harvard while Henry Adams was making his researches and giving his extraordinary course in medieval life and law. Woodberry thought it the finest course he took at Harvard; he said there could not be a better course.

When he said this, few Americans knew anything about *Mont-Saint-Michel and Chartres,* privately printed only in 1904, and we had to wait for *The Education of Henry Adams,* even in its private printing, until 1907. Talking with Woodberry then, I could not realize how profoundly Henry Adams influenced him for good—and perhaps for not so good. Adams, he said, had taught him scholarly methods. The course in the Middle Ages was conducted not by a series of lectures, but by reports from the students on assigned topics, with incisive comments from the reserved professor. Woodberry said that when his topic was assigned, he did not know what it meant. Adams told him to look it up in the encyclopedia, and go on from there. By hunting down the sources listed and pursuing all the bibliographies, he came at last to the ultimate manuscripts or inscriptions. It was a terrific way of mastering a subject, but it is the scholarly way, and Woodberry learned it well. The evil which I believe he derived from Henry Adams was the unreasonable disposition to find fault with the times in which he was fated to live. Henry Adams enjoyed every kind of good fortune, but he was discontented by nature, and he made himself more discontented by study and practice, until his vast culture rendered him chiefly this service, that it enabled him to find fault always on a high plane, so escaping the reputation of an ordinary whiner or grouch.

There were sad moments in Woodberry's life, but not more than in most other lives, and since he was gifted and fortunate, he ought to have been happy. At Amherst I saw him, as I have tried to indicate, in one of his happiest phases, surrounded by good will and esteem. But when the College asked him to return in the autumn and become a permanent member of the staff, he refused. I forget now what reason he gave; I doubt if he had any. Perhaps he thought it was the thing to do. Henry Adams had hesitated to teach for fear he might not teach well; then having proved himself a great teacher, he gave up teaching once for all.

Woodberry, on the day he spoke of Adams, had something to say of Emerson. He thought Emerson's poetry had the quality of permanence; you could live with it. He saw Emerson once, that is heard him, the last lecture he ever gave. Emerson's daughter sat by and handed him the pages to read. Emerson constantly forgot what he was saying. Why should a man wish to live beyond his brain? At this point Woodberry laughed, perhaps remembering his inconsistencies on the subject of suicide. In younger days he had asked himself, he said, why a man should live beyond his eyesight, and since his own eyes very early threatened serious trouble, he made up his mind that when they gave out at last, he would kill himself. But each time he needed stronger glasses, by some coincidence it always happened that he had found a new interest in life.

5

For some reason which I cannot now recall, Woodberry went home a few days before the end of the term, leaving an examination paper for me to give his class. At the day and hour scheduled by the Registrar I wrote the questions on the blackboard and sent the examination books on to Beverly for him to read. Here are the questions—the last paper he set for any class, typical of all his examinations, which never inquired specifically into the reading done, but gave the student an opportunity to show his powers.

1. The traits of Scott, as a man and as a writer.
2. What is your own impression of Shelley's 1) life 2) teachings 3) poetic charm?
3. Describe some poem by Keats and exemplify his literary qualities by it.
4. Distinguish the personal and social elements in the genius of some author dealt with in the course, and illustrate by the discussion the difference

between psychological and sociological criticism as a means of interpreting and understanding a literary work.

5. Explain and comment on the doctrine—"not the fruit of experience but experience is the end."
6. What, judging by the things said in these lectures, makes a great book? How does its greatness pass into your own life and become a part of your own vitality?

When we said goodbye I thought he was off as quickly as possible for another one of his European journeys, and hardly expected to see him again for a year or so. But the day before Commencement, at the end of June, President Harris sent for me, and when I arrived at his house, Mrs. Harris asked me to dine with them that evening and take charge of Mr. Woodberry afterward; he was coming up for his honorary degree, Doctor of Letters. This was happy news. Mrs. Harris seemed particularly pleased about it, reflecting, I suppose, the President's mood. She said Mr. Woodberry had written "such beautiful letters about his honor."

At seven I went to dinner, and when the President and his wife left to make the round of the Class Day receptions, Woodberry and I talked for a while in the library. Then he put on evening clothes, and we began with the Delta Upsilon reception. Though he was there but a short time, an incident occurred which pleased and moved him. One of the guests, a girl, came up and introduced herself; she was the niece of Clarence Leighton Dennett, the friend to whom *The North Shore Watch* was a tribute. Whether he had met her before, I do not know, but they talked for a while, she evidently impressed by the meeting, and he stirred by memories. Then we went to the Theta Delta Chi reception, where some of the boys, particularly Clarence A. Stone and Winfield A. Townsend, students in his course, made much of him. After visits to the other fraternity houses, we walked back to the President's, and Dr. Harris gave me the diagram of seats for the Commencement platform, telling me I was to be the faculty marshal.

Next morning the honorary guests assembled at the President's house about ten o'clock. After what seemed to be very serious talk with his old schoolmate, Mr. Plimpton told me that Woodberry would leave his name on our faculty list, promising, or at least encouraging us to believe, that in the autumn of 1906 he would be with us again. Of course this plan came to nothing, but for the moment it gave us pleasure.

The faculty marched into College Hall with more formality than Amherst usually indulged in. When each guest received his degree, the seniors and other students applauded, but for Woodberry they gave a cheer, a tremendous one.

At the alumni luncheon he sat at the head table with the other guests of honor, and afterward he suggested a call on Mrs. Davis, to say goodbye. He had a new straw hat, very white and stiff, and I remember him sitting in Mrs. Davis's parlor nursing the hat on his knees and gazing up at the old lady in friendly understanding. Miss Hinsdale sat by, approving. His presence in Amherst that half-year and the daily meetings with him at the table had probably consoled her somewhat in what she considered her exile. Then as we left Mrs. Davis's, he suggested one more talk in my study, where I made coffee for the last time, and he smoked a cigar.

In the evening at the President's reception he was surrounded by faculty and students, but I had a characterirstic word from him; he told me not to expect him to write. "Letters bother me."

CHAPTER XVI

Expanding World

I

WHEN I went to Amherst the number of students was about four hundred. We liked to think a superior kind of growth was in process, an intellectual quickening, which of course might be expected first in the faculty and afterward, through well-organized irrigation or through seepage, in the students. There were new faces in the faculty room, in Walker Hall, and new ideas in the faculty debates. After the third year, Will Nitze left us for the University of California, and to replace him we had Carrington Lancaster, now Professor of Romance Languages at Johns Hopkins. Carrington took the room across the hall from mine at Mrs. Marsh's house. To the German department came Clarence Willis Eastman and Otto Manthey-Zorn, and to the Latin department, Harold Loomis Cleasby, and afterward Lewis Parke Chamberlayne. Charles W. Cobb came to teach mathematics, Robert Palfrey Utter to teach English, and Frederick Lincoln Thompson to teach history.

In the autumn of 1906 I returned to the campus as Associate Professor, with a new instructor to share the composition work with me. Through Professor William Allan Neilson of Harvard we found Bob Utter, a Harvard graduate who had gone into newspaper work, and from there to an editorial position in a publishing house, and at last had returned to teaching, his first love. In his youth he had seen much of the Far West. In a splendid sense he was a scholar and a gentleman, and the Amherst faculty knew his quality at sight. After the armistice of the First World War he taught with me at the Army University at Beaune, where his

colleagues elected him chairman of the English department. On returning to this country he became Professor of English at the University of
California. His French-American wife, Madeleine Bocher, brightened
Amherst by her wit and her sturdy character, as Bob gave it flavor by
his acquaintance with the world in more than academic activities.

Carrington Lancaster and Lewis Chamberlayne, our two Southerners,
were picturesque comrades, Carrington very tall, Lewis rather short, Carrington deliberate of speech, Lewis earnest, intense, at times fiery. In a
few years Lewis went to teach Latin at the University of South Carolina.
He belonged to the South, which he loved with many kinds of pious
affection, but in Amherst he was remembered and missed.

Charles Cobb, mathematician of great originality, poetry-lover, musician, tireless student of rhythms, soon became an intimate friend and dear
companion. Our collaboration in music I shall have occasion to describe
when I speak of the Amherst choir.

Among all these newcomers Fritz Thompson may not have been the
outstanding scholar or the best teacher, but he was certainly the strongest
influence in the College life. Like Bob Utter he owed some of his power
in the community to his wise wife. Marietta Thompson had known
Fritz from childhood, and in many tactful ways had influenced and
directed his career. Fritz was an Amherst graduate, as his elder brother
Dan had been, but Dan was tall and good looking, an excellent student
and an experienced educator, first as head of the English department at
Lawrenceville School, then as headmaster of the Roxbury Latin School,
whereas Fritz was short and fat, always a bit overawed by elder brother
Dan, until Marietta brought him out. Dan is now remembered as the
father of Randall Thompson, the composer. Fritz, left to himself, would
have spent his life too modestly teaching history to schoolboys, had not
Marietta lured or pushed him into serious graduate study at home and
abroad, and into travel all over the globe which without her he never
would have undertaken. When they came to Amherst they took the old
brick house which the Nitzes had just vacated, just south of the President's home, and there in the comfortable study during the winter and on
the side porch in warm weather an extraordinary amount of College business was informally but efficiently disposed of.

I owe much to both these friends. Marietta had to a remarkable degree
the teaching ability as it can be applied to husbands and other grown-up
men. Having developed Fritz's talents and enlarged his career, she could

meet no young man without looking him over with all her kind intelligence to see what could be made out of him. Though I learned this only years afterward, she decided that I might be developed into a public speaker or lecturer. During her first winter in Amherst she told me one day in her husband's study that the Women's Club of the town had commissioned her to ask a favor of me—they wanted some lecturers on nineteenth century English literature, to be given in one of the College's larger classrooms, one afternoon lecture a week for ten successive weeks.

I may have hesitated, but not long. When I said I would ask the department of Buildings and Grounds for permission to use the room, Marietta laughed; she had attended to that already. So I gave the lectures, and to my surprise and pleasure found before me an audience of size, with President Harris and many of the faculty, and with visitors from the neighboring faculties at Mount Holyoke and Smith. I worked hard on the talks, and enjoyed giving them. They must have been overpacked and stiff, but they were an education for me at the moment, and they led immediately to the public lecturing which has occupied much of my life. At the conclusion of the Amherst course, Miss Bertha Young, Professor of English at Mount Holyoke, invited me to give a series of lectures there the following season.

It had not occurred to me that the talks to the Amherst Women's Club were what is sometimes described as a professional engagement, and when Marietta, again in Fritz's library when the course was over, handed me a tidy little bag of gold from the ladies, I was embarrassed, but I got over it. The money was spent in books, and my library took an immense leap.

If news of this public lecturing reached my old teachers at Columbia, it may have suggested to them that I had some surplus energy which might be put to use. Professor Carpenter sent me an invitation to give two courses in the Summer Session of 1906. The fee for the six weeks was four hundred dollars. My Amherst salary as an associate professor was now sixteen hundred dollars, and it seemed handsome of Columbia to offer, for so little work, one quarter of what I earned in the whole winter. I mention finances merely to recall the low cost of living in a small New England college town forty years ago. The senior professors in Amherst lived comfortably on the top salary, three thousand dollars, owning their houses, bringing up their children well, entertaining their friends simply, but with charm and grace, and laying aside a little for books and travel. One or two citizens lived in something like affluence, at the rate perhaps of five thousand dollars a year, and Churchill and Nitze, our two well-endowed colleagues—perhaps I should add Fritz Thompson, may have had even more, but their way of life was thoughtful and in good taste, and they never let their wealth separate or isolate them.

Though the cost of living rose, even in those days, I was aware of no economic problem. Mrs. Davis's table was now only a memory; I could no longer get board for five dollars a week. At the Amherst Hotel, where I shared a table with Toby Baxter, the weekly rate was one dollar a day, and the special table for faculty bachelors which Professor Crook's wife was planning in the house next to Mrs. Marsh's, might be still more expensive. But I should still pay for board and lodging in Amherst, from the end of September till the end of June, no more than four hundred dollars. The addition to my salary took care of this amount, so that the summer could be faced with twelve hundred dollars in my pocket—and the summer could be paid for, if I chose, by teaching at Columbia. Whatever a man earned in that far-off millennium, was clear gain unless he owned real estate, and since I owned none, my only direct tax was two dollars to the township of Amherst, for the privilege of voting.

I earned money now by my pen—not a large amount, but I gathered it in with a sense that the world was growing kinder and more discriminating. Mr. Gilder, at *The Century Magazine*, and Bliss Perry at *The Atlantic Monthly*, were accepting my verse at the gratifying rate of twenty-five dollars a poem. Furthermore, Professor Carpenter, general editor of "Longman's English Classics" for school use, invited me to edit some selections from the *Faërie Queene*. Since I have always loved Spenser's beautiful but difficult poem, the preparation of this text brought me lively pleasure—and a fee of one hundred dollars. My self-confidence began to show resemblances to conceit.

2

Of my two classes at the Columbia Summer Session, one was a writing course, parallel to the sophomore work in the winter, and one was a course in Elizabethan literature. The fact that the students were adult, some of them experienced schoolteachers, was a challenge and in many ways an inspiration. My students could hardly have learned more than I in those six weeks; when I returned to Amherst it was with new ideas for the conduct of literature classes. I had always believed that the art of writing is learned by writing, by the solution of problems as they arise in practice rather than by memorizing in advance rhetorical doctrine or sets of rules. After the Columbia Summer Session I was convinced that the teaching of literature should also be based on writing. At one moment in a course the student's interest in the subject reaches a peak; and that moment occurs immediately after the student has taken his final examination. Preparing for the ordeal, he puts his mind on the reading, he has ideas about it, and he will stop you in the hall to compare your opinion with his, and to start an argument. I resolved to get my pupils into this frame of mind before the course was over. If the examination woke them up, then the course must be converted into one prolonged examination. That autumn my students in literature gave me an essay on each successive author before I lectured on him. I read their opinions before I gave mine, and in the classroom we argued with self-respect on both sides, since we had all read the material we argued about. In a sense the students gave the course; I criticized their presentation.

Perhaps none of us can name the moment when he realized what his personal philosophy must be, or the direction in which his temperament would drive him; no doubt I was already committed to the active life rather than the contemplative, so far as there is a mutually exclusive opposition between them. But the autumn of 1906 was the season in which I determined that for me literary scholarship must be creative, that I must practice the subject I taught, and my students must practice it too. From then on I have been increasingly distrustful of colleagues who lecture on poems or novels or plays and put the authors in this or that pigeonhole, but cannot themselves write a page that anyone would print or that anyone would read. I grant that even those incapable of writing may be able to drill dates and titles into youthful heads; for that reason our school and college courses in literature are useful to this extent, that they tell who wrote what, and when. But the convenience of printing has long ago been invented, and it is a saving of time and money to acquire elementary facts from books, rather than from teachers who recite from books. And after you have drained the book of every fact in it, you don't have to give it a pension.

I will not labor the point here, but having perceived that my students should acquire their own original ideas about the books we studied, I went on to the insight that I, their teacher, had the right to come before them only if I brought original ideas of my own.

I saw also that I must bring the writing courses into closer relation to the art as professional authors practice it. The students who took their literary urge seriously were content to fill the *College Monthly* with critical essays, praising or reproving current books and plays for satisfying or for not satisfying the undergraduate taste. These judgments were firm, unqualified and final, as though the Recording Angel were handing out marks. I recall one terrific lambasting of Edith Wharton's *House of Mirth,* by a boy who knew nothing of the world Edith Wharton wrote about, but he was sure Edith Wharton did wrong in portraying people who were less than admirable; such attention might encourage them. I would not imply that my best students in their daily life were pharisaical, but in their literary criticism they were. Not once did they concede that the author was trying to work out a problem, never did they give evidence that they knew what the problem was, and having made their point that the book was not well written, they rarely ventured any other suggestion for improvement except that it should not have been written at all.

Now I began to discourage critical writing and to advocate creative work of any kind within the student's capacity. The supply of poets just then was meagre, as it has always been in Amherst, strange to say. That beautiful landscape provokes poetic moods which might be expected to articulate themselves. But Amherst has generated or attracted to itself no school of poets, and no school of painters. Frank Babbott used to say that the distances across the valley are too vast and too magnificent. In essence the effect is Alpine—dramatic. My students, once they ceased to promulgate their severe opinions of other men's work and to do some work themselves, turned to short stories and one-act plays.

But until a play is produced, neither the dramatist nor anyone else can tell whether it is good or bad, and we had no theatre in which to try out our experiments. We surmounted this difficulty by deliberately writing the little plays for a given setting—one end of the Student Lounge. There was a fireplace, with a door at each side; all our dramas occurred in front of a hearth, sometimes cold, sometimes aflame. All our exits and entrances had to be on one side or the other of this family altar. Or the hearth might not be a shrine; by moving the table and the chairs this way and that, we could set the scene for a business office, a police court, or a clergyman's study. We gave the plays before the Literary Club, and the dramatists and their friends were the actors. Bert Taggart,

I recall, was one of the best, particularly in female parts. Costumes, of course, were not always in period. The matter of make-up should have bothered us, but it didn't; William Ely Hill, the cartoonist, already practicing his talent in satiric sketches of campus life, prepared each cast by painting their faces with water colors. The Student Lounge was cold in winter unless a good fire burned on the hearth. Toward the end of each piece the make-up, set afloat by perspiration, became perpendicular stripes.

Though the boys were ingenious in devising plots for the stationary and permanent setting, they showed no other tendency to gather their material from the life around them. The Amherst environment set them dreaming, but they did not dream of life in Amherst. Why that was so, I cannot explain. In my teaching I had two ambitions, to make scholars of my students, and to make writers of them. These purposes were not mutually exclusive, and to the best of my knowledge I tried as hard in one direction as in the other. But on the whole my best Amherst students became teachers, and my best Columbia students became writers. Perhaps the city, which can seem hostile to art, is really favorable to it, or to the active life, of which art is one form.

3

With Wilkins, Toggles, Cleasby and a few other intimates, I had been singing in Professor Bigelow's chorus. The Music department gave annually a number of really splendid concerts, some by virtuoso artists engaged for solo performances, others by the College chorus and orchestra. Monday night of each week was reserved for rehearsals, and since Biggie always put on a work of major importance and major difficulty, he wisely had his orchestra rehearse every Monday with the chorus. Sometimes I left the bass section to perform on a two-manual melodion which could substitute approximately for clarinet and oboe when those instruments were absent. Biggie copied the parts from the score, and I played one part on each manual, using stops which at least suggested the color of the instrument.

To complete the chorus Biggie brought in young women from the Amherst High School, from the village choirs, from the whole landscape. Altogether he assembled a chorus of three or four hundred, a well-balanced group, strongest naturally in the basses. When we came to the final performance of each work, there would be professional vocal soloists from Boston or New York, and our College and village orchestra would be supplemented or salvaged by the first desks of the Boston Symphony. Biggie was a Napoleon of educational strategy. He knew what it would mean to our local clarinetist or flutist to play side by side with an experienced artist. The anticipation of this privilege at the final performance guaranteed faithful attendance at rehearsals. The quality of the singing and playing was surprisingly good, and the works performed were all masterpieces, some of them too rarely heard. In my years the *Messiah* was given, of course, and *Elijah;* also the *Creation* and *St. Paul,* and *Hymn of Praise,* and Mozart's *Requiem.* There were several more, Haydn's *Seasons,* Handel's *Acis and Galatea*—but I remember most clearly and with most gratitude the Mozart *Requiem,* which we all loved, and our enthusiasm for the amazing music enabled us to surpass ourselves.

In the series of visiting artists I heard for the first time Josef Hofmann and Olga Samaroff, and others with whom I have been associated through later years in common musical interests and in friendship. The Hofmann concert was extraordinary, remarkable for the program as well as for the matchless playing. Josef Hofmann was then in his early prime, with a large and well-practiced repertoire. His manager submitted four or five programs to choose from, and Biggie asked me which program I'd rather hear. Each was built around one large piece. The minor things that filled in were of course important in their way, but the big piece dwarfed them. There was, for example, the *Appassionata,* and all the Chopin *Préludes* played as a suite, and the Schumann *Fantasie.* I suggested that we ask for a performance of the big pieces alone, a composite program, and though we hardly expected Hofmann to agree, he did and most cheerfully, and he played a concert that set the audience cheering, ordinary handclaps being inadequate for undergraduate enthusiasm. After the performance Biggie and I walked with him to the President's house, where there was a supper. On the way Hofmann asked a question which he said had tantalized and perplexed him.

"What kind of people live in this town, who want a program like that? Nothing but curiosity made me play it!"

4

My interest in music began to involve me, in the spring of 1907, with choir work in the Episcopal church of the village—Grace Church, named like the little parish at Union Hill. Bishop Frederic Huntingdon, of the diocese of Central New York, a graduate from Amherst in 1839, had wished his decidedly Congregational College town to have a church of the communion to which he belonged. Some friend or friends of his gave the money for a replica of an English parish church. The ivy-covered stone building is handsome inside and out. To reach it I had only to walk a few yards from Mrs. Marsh's, around the Town Hall to Spring Street. It had seats for four hundred or more, but in my time all the Episcopalians in Amherst could be counted on two hands. The fortunes of the parish were then rather low, and there were hardly enough men in it to form a vestry. For that reason I was soon elected to that body, and came to know well the few but strong and devoted, who kept the parish afloat until it moved into smoother days. I remember especially Dwight Billings, a leader in the town, manager of the hat factory; and Professor George F. Mills, head of the English department in the State Agricultural College, at the northern end of Amherst; and Dr. Frederick Tuckerman, retired physician, of an old Massachusetts family. His father was that F. G. Tuckerman mentioned in the *Memoir of Alfred Tennyson* by his son. Dr. Fred Tuckerman kept in his box at the Amherst bank a manuscript copy of "Locksley Hall" in the poet's hand; he got it out to show me one day. In his study he had on display a souvenir which he prized more highly than I did, one of the church-wardens which Tennyson liked to smoke. The elder Tuckerman had carried it off at the end of a Farringford evening, after watching the Laureate puff the bowl black and tint the stem.

The choir at Grace Church consisted of a few young men and women, more women than men, all with fair voices but quite untrained. There was a small two-manual organ, an excellent instrument, for unexplained reason in good condition. The organist was a girl who slaved on the choir according to her lights for one hundred fifty dollars a year. Early in 1907 she married and moved away, and her young brother, who pumped the organ, moved away too. There was no other available organist in town, and for a moment it looked as though Grace Church must approach God only in prayer, postponing praise until better times. But Mr.

Billings, Dr. Tuckerman and Professor Mills showed me my duty to take the choir in hand and make something of it, and for inducement Mr. Billings offered to install an apparatus for pumping the organ by water. Since the choir had no music library, I made a counterproposal to drill the choir through the College year for nothing, provided that 1) Mr. Billings provided the pump, and 2) I might draw on the Treasurer for the annual purchase of music to the amount of one hundred fifty dollars. On this basis I was organist and choirmaster for the rest of my time in Amherst. We soon had a fine choir, rather large for the building. Two afternoons a week the sopranos and contraltos came to the choir room for some voice training. One afternoon, late, the basses and tenors came, and Friday evenings we had a full rehearsal. Remembering the schedule now, I marvel at the leisure of that simple Amherst life. Since the choir work was interesting, it didn't seem then that I gave too much time to it. Perhaps it was all the more engrossing because I had not thought to do much in music again.

At first my ambitions for the choir were very modest. In size it outran what I hoped for; attracted by the training, however elementary, high school girls joined, some of them from Biggie's chorus, and I persuaded Amherst College tenors and basses to help me out. But for a while I was satisfied if they sang on pitch, with good tone and good rhythm, and with the words correctly and uniformly pronounced. But at the end of the year Charles Cobb raised my standards for me. He had been a choir singer at the Church of All Angels, New York, under the direction of Clement R. Gale, and after he had heard my choir one Sunday afternoon he preserved a stony silence, he having that kind of uncomfortable integrity. I knew he would have admired if he could. When I pressed for an opinion he gave it firmly; the tone and the rhythm were all right but there was no interpretation, no expression, the music said nothing.

I was irritated, but Cobb had given me an idea. The choir room was in the basement of the church, and it contained an antique square about which little could be said except that I kept it in tune. It was pleasanter to rehearse upstairs in the choir stalls with the organ, but after Cobb made his criticism we rehearsed in the basement, unaccompanied. After I had played a piece through, the choir reading and humming the parts, I would leave the piano untouched, except for the passages assigned to the organ alone, which had to be memorized like the *tutti* of a concerto. Standing away from the piano to conduct, I worked on effects which until then I had thought beyond the capacity of my amateur outfit. Progress in this *a capella* singing was at first slow, afterward quite rapid, and having demonstrated my will to be in a musical way of grace, I asked Charles to help us with his bass voice, and he couldn't well decline. His experience and taste inspired us, and the choir attracted a larger congregation, particularly of students. What this meant in terms of pure religion, I did not pause to ask; the music was becoming fine indeed, and I was glad to have a hand in producing it.

CHAPTER XVII

British Isles

I

IN THE summer of 1907, with my sisters Anna and Helen I made a little tour through England, Scotland and Ireland. Much as I loved the history and the arts of France and wished to visit that country, I gladly devoted my first journey abroad to the land from which my people had come, and the literature of which I studied and taught. The decision was fortunate. Had I seen France before I saw England, small wish to spend precious time anywhere else would have been left in me. I felt in my bones as I started out that something in me belonged to France and would some day insist on going home. If Stella Harris had not married Will Hill and gone to live in Cork, I doubt if my sisters and I would have visited Ireland, and certainly we had no reason for including Guernsey in our plans, except that Minnie Harris had married the Reverend Pedro S. Mèsny, Rector of Castel, one of the quaint parishes on the island. We seized the chance to see again these friends of 500 West End Avenue.

We crossed on the *St. Paul,* of the Red Star Line. In those days schoolmasters and college teachers went abroad, if they could, for their summer vacation, and so did their pupils. Our boat was full of them. The schoolmasters were easily recognizable as such by the way they took their constitutional around the deck. They had so long been setting an example to small boys that they had to walk with head up, chin in, shoulders back, and spine of a ramrod stiffness. The college professors relaxed and slouched as much as they wished.

Our attitude toward Europe in those pre-First War days begins now to fade altogether from memory. Europe was then supposed to possess a culture and a civilization which we, if we tried hard enough, might acquire through imitation. The German Empire did not seriously rival the British, but the preëminence of German science, German scholarship, German education and German music was conceded—except by a minority, among whom I wished to be counted, who suspected that the Latin genius still had something which the German spirit had failed to acquire, and for which it was no substitute. But the difference, we hoped, could be bridged over; we tried to admire both Germany and France, each for its peculiar merits, and we persuaded ourselves that wise Germans and Frenchmen, in spite of irritations persisting from 1870, would teach their countries to live side by side in amity. England was still mistress of the seas, and what was more important, she controlled the world's finances. She was the great creditor nation and we were in her debt, to remain so until the First World War. Her true laureate was Rudyard Kipling, singer of the British troopship as symbol of a genius for getting around wherever desirable property needed appropriating or protecting.

> "What he thought 'e might require,
> 'E went and took."

Though North Americans were bumptious enough after the Spanish War, confident of a gigantic future, it was an article of our educational and cultural creed that until we caught up with our destiny we should visit Europe and take lessons. History made it natural that England and France should be our tutors—in spite of our strong sympathy for Ireland and our delight in the Celtic Revival, known to us through the work of Yeats, Lady Gregory, Douglas Hyde, and Synge. For Italy we had a friendly esteem, an admiration at low temperature. What we chiefly liked about her was a great past. Rightly or wrongly we failed to reckon her among the makers of a modern world.

We knew little of Russia except that the Czar was always fighting off revolution and the Russian intellectuals were always fomenting it. The Russian writers best known to us were those who had left their country to live in Paris. We had heard little Russian music, though Russian singers and pianists toured America. A few Americans, like my friends the Harris sisters, had indeed traveled in Russia, but they must have missed its great qualities, for they brought stories chiefly of the espionage and general tyranny which, under the Czar, Russians as well as foreigners had to endure.

We may say, then, that the American seeking to improve himself took a trip to Great Britain as an elementary course, a trip to France as a course somewhat more difficult, since a language was prerequisite, a trip to Italy as a special course in history, and a trip to Germany as a finishing course. Those who went to Russia were insatiables, looking for graduate work.

2

At Southampton my sisters and I had to wait for the Guernsey boat, and to fill in the time we crossed to the Isle of Wight and took the miniature train to Farringford to the home of Alfred Tennyson at the end of the island. The monument to the poet rises above the cliffs from the downs where he took his walks, wrapped in his long cloak, but the house in which he lived could not be visited, and indeed could hardly be seen through the thick foliage and the fine trees of the little park. We had been warned that Farringford offered nothing for tourists, but we walked the length of the road or lane which encircles house and lawn, and one or two glimpses we did catch of the sprawling, comfortable home, and of the doorway through which had passed many of the wisest and most celebrated, coming to pay homage to the author of *Maud,* and *In Memoriam,* and the *Idylls.* Then we walked to the village church, to see the Tennyson memorials there. I came away wondering why the entrance to the church was almost blocked by the buildings which have grown up in front of it. The reason, whatever it is, doubtless springs from some ancient custom or privilege, but I could not learn what.

We reached Guernsey by an overnight voyage in a crowded boat not much larger than a tug. There were two sleeping cabins, one for men, the other for women. Never before or since have I heard so many seasick men in one spot, but the trip was short, and when we climbed up to the deck in the morning the weather was gorgeous, the colorful harbor of St. Peter's Port, more French than British in atmosphere, made us forget the night, and Pedro and Minnie were there on the dock to welcome us. Though I had met Mr. Mèsny in New York, I understood him only when I saw him in his home. He was altogether an Old World product, a native of the Channel Islands, and an incarnation of the twofold culture, French mingled with English, which gives the Islands their character. Guernsey and Jersey in those days were far more reluctant than Canada or Australia to accept the fact that they were part of the Empire. Guernsey insisted that it gave its allegiance to the reigning monarch, not as King of England but as the descendent or successor of William the Conqueror and other Dukes of Normandy. It had its own parliament and in many matters was entirely self-governing. For one thing, it coined its own money, a circumstance which would impress an American, since the denial of that privilege was one of the irritations which drove the American colonists to revolt. With the perversity of ultra-independent people, the Guernsey folk stuck to pounds, shillings and pence, but took care that the Guernsey shilling was not equivalent in value to the English. If you had English shillings in your pocket, any small purchase in a Guernsey shop would give you a mathematical headache. To establish its independence further, Guernsey had its weekly half-holiday on Wednesday instead of Saturday, arguing that since Sundays are full rests, there is an advantage in spacing the half-rests between them.

Mr. Mèsny's congregation at Castel, like all Guernsey folk, spoke among themselves a Norman patois, but they knew English well, and on occasion they showed a surprisingly critical appreciation of pure French. Though the parish belonged to the Anglican Church, English was the language only for the morning service; in the afternoon and evening a French translation of the English Book of Common Prayer was used, and the sermon was in French. Mr. Mèsny told me his congregation worshiped God in the morning; at the later services their attention was on the rector, to catch him if his French had an English idiom in it.

Mr. Mèsny knew what things we'd like to see, and thanks to him we gained a concentrated impression of Old World characters and customs. We visited, as all tourists do, Hauteville House, where Victor Hugo lived in exile; we attended a charity bazaar and a church fair, we had tea one afternoon with the owner of a very old house, we attended tennis parties, and we played croquet. It was interesting to see Victor Hugo's house just after our bird's eye view of Farringford, the homes of the two chief figures in English and French poetry in their time. Farringford expresses a reticent temperament, Hauteville does not. Hugo wrote *Toilers of the Sea* and other masterpieces in the room on the roof of the house, enclosed in glass. He also took his baths there. He liked to work and even to sleep within sight of the French coast. Of course he came

downstairs occasionally, perhaps several times a day, certainly whenever
he walked up the steep and narrow street to another house a few yards
away, where Juliette Drouet shared his exile with him. I confess that
I had no great admiration for Hugo after this Guernsey visit; his house
as he had kept it, one crowded illustration of bad taste, and the legends
of his love for Juliette, a queer jumble of Byronic romance and Mrs.
Grundy domesticity, roused in me a prejudice from which I did not
recover until the First World War, when I learned from soldiers in the
French Army how prophetically he had been the voice of his people's
suffering, their anger, their courage, and their hope.

I had heard of the English fondness for music-making in the home.
I began to think they would rather make it themselves than have a musician make it for them. The heartiness of the singing was extraordinary.
The women stood very straight or leaned back slightly. They held their
music away from them, at arm's length, and glared at it as though their
feelings had been hurt. Almost everyone sang from music, though they
repeated their songs so often that they must have known them by heart.
But I wouldn't give the impression that these Guernsey amateurs always
escaped criticism; they made it impossible. There were three sisters,
worthy and spinsterish, who always operated as a team, one singing, one
playing the violin, and one the piano. They were referred to, behind their
backs, as Battle, Murder, and Sudden Death.

We saw the Parliament of Guernsey in action. An usher in sombre
uniform led us to a seat in the gallery, from which we looked down on
a moderate-sized chamber, not unlike a police court. At the end were
seats in a semicircle for the presiding officer and the dozen or so members. When we entered a bill was under discussion; apparently certain
improvements were needed in the coast defenses of Guernsey. Here was
something important! I thought the debate concerned shore-batteries,
patrol boats or even light cruisers. But suddenly the gentleman who
had the floor stated the total cost—something under fifty pounds. He
talked on, and we learned that his bill provided for some repairs in a
few feet of sea wall.

From Guernsey we went to Winchester and from there to Salisbury.
Winchester rather overwhelmed me with its cathedral, the first I had
seen. The gaudy Round Table in the old Hall offended me, as being
an obvious imposture, which straight-dealing Englishmen should not encourage; surely there were enough relics in England, without synthetic

additions. Salisbury Cathedral from the outside, in the midst of the famous landscape, seemed beautiful indeed, but inside not at all so. Then we spent a couple of days at Cambridge, a disgracefully short time for so many memories and treasures.

I did wish to look at the Tennyson manuscripts displayed in the Library of Trinity College. Since the guidebook said the Library was open from two o'clock on a certain day, Tuesday perhaps, during the summer, I was at hand at two. The Library was indeed opened at that hour by a custodian or superior janitor, who admitted two scrubwomen with their mops and pails, and began to shut the door in my face. Through the diminishing crack I protested that the Library was advertised as open at that hour; imperturbably he admitted the fact, but this was the one day when the room was to be cleaned. I told him I had never been in Cambridge before and could not soon be again; I asked him to give me ten minutes at the case which contained the manuscripts; surely the women could begin on some other part of the floor. But he said again that the room would now be cleaned, and having established this truth to his own satisfaction, he finished locking me out. If the old boy stands in my memory for dumb-headed inflexibility and bad manners, I must add that he stands also for some practical good sense. It's all very well to preserve Tennyson's poems in a glass case, especially in the Library of his college, but one need not look at such things. Who ever was the happier or wiser for reading a great man's poetry before the typesetter and the proofreader had remedied the minor errors? What had I learned from Dr. Tuckerman's manuscript copy of *Locksley Hall* except that Tennyson always wrote the possessive of "it" with an apostrophe, as though it were the contraction of "it is"?

From Cambridge we went directly to Cork, where Will Hill met us with his car—a very early car, a Renault. A short drive down the harbor brought us to his summer place at Currabinny. The house was large and comfortable, on an elevation overlooking the water. There was a garden and a lawn, and a tennis court on which Will exercised me daily. He practiced the double profession of architect and engineer, as was then the custom in Ireland and doubtless still is. One of his duties was to look after construction for the railway between Cork and Dublin, and in addition to designing houses and office buildings, he had on his hands when we visited him some important work for the British Government. The Land Act was going into force just then, making possible the purchase of small plots on a long-time installment plan. But the opportunity for disputes and quarrels, even feuds, was large; at the end of twenty years or so, neighbors who had lived in peace for generations might be at each other's throats over a boundary. Surveyors' maps would mean nothing to them; they would rely on their memories, and their memories would not agree. To avoid such tangles, if possible, engineers were sent into the different counties to pace the boundaries with the prospective land-buyers, wife and children tagging along, so that the whole family, please God! and the neighbor's family as well, might understand, at least in the beginning, who precisely owned what.

Will was assigned to this work in Kerry County, and he and Stella took us on a three days' jaunt in their car, stopping every now and then to do some boundary-pacing. A more intimate way to see Ireland could not be contrived, and we came back with vivid memories of huts with peat fires, of poor people with princely manners, and of children who had never been off the bog, yet whose voices, because or in spite of that, were pure music. Will saved time out for a visit to Killarney, which remains one of my most convincing memories. The lake and the castle and strange light on that landscape are all that the poets have said, and it's rare indeed that nature justifies the praise bestowed upon it. Ireland is evidently an unhappy place to live in, for the old legends are full of grief, long before the English were heard of in the land. To be sad is an Irish gift. But the same men who find life too hard in the south of Ireland can go to New York or Chicago or Boston, or to any country in South America, and take charge of the place like the born administrators they are—outside of Ireland. The Irish export well.

From Cork we went to Dublin, where the memory of Swift led us to his cathedral, during an afternoon service. The choir-boys wore soiled collars and dirty cottas and sang off-key, and from the wall the stone effigy of savage wrath glared down on us. Trinity College ought to have been interesting, but was not. On the whole, the charm of Dublin seemed to lie exclusively in memories of the eighteenth century, and in the beautiful English for which the city is famed, even among non-Irish. I have never heard such perfect speech elsewhere.

From Dublin we crossed to England, and took the train to the foot of the Lake Country, traveling then by coach to Grasmere. For me this was a high point in the trip; I wanted to see Dove Cottage, where Wordsworth lived some of his great years with his sister Dorothy. The effect of this little shrine is uncanny, as many a visitor has testified, but I cannot explain the mystic influence. For whatever reason, here is one spot on earth where the former dwellers are still the soul of their house. In the small rooms with ceilings so low that I couldn't stand up straight, the kettle seemed left on the hearth by William and Dorothy only a few minutes before, and if the door had opened I should have turned to face them.

In the Lake District showers alternate constantly with sunshine, and the mountains change shape as the clouds and mist move about their shoulders. Nature here is alive and breathing, a personality and a presence. It was a revelation, and something of a shock, to realize that though Wordsworth's nature poems are true of this landscape, they could not be equally true elsewhere—in Arizona, for example. But Wordsworth is not primarily a nature poet, anyway, though he may have thought he was. His insights turned inward; he was a psychologist.

In Edinburgh I noticed at once that the Scots, like the Irish, count it a merit to be anything an Englishman isn't, but I thought they had the advantage of the Irish in squeezing more fun out of their prejudices. When I was walking on Calton Hill, one long twilight, a tall white-haired man came toward me, brandishing his cane and calling "Hi!" I thought he was warning me off the grass, but he explained that he walked abroad on favorable evenings, and when he saw a palpable stranger he joined himself to him as guide, and the stranger he hoped was none the worse, and he might be slightly the better. Understanding each other, we started out. He would point to a monument or building and say, "That belongs to the reign of George II of Scotland," or "George III" or "William IV." He kept this up till I asked the right question: "Are these the same as George II, or George III, or William IV of England?"

"Aye, of England too, on account of the Union!"

We visited Hawthornden near by, the home of William Drummond, poetry-loving Scot in the days of Elizabeth and James, who wrote sonnets himself and pined because he was so far from the Mermaid Tavern when the giants met there. In 1619 Ben Jonson walked from London to Scotland for his health, and stopping with Drummond at Hawthornden for a few days, ate and drank enough nightly to take on again the weight he had walked off. That is of no importance now, but this is: after dinner he poured into Drummond's hungry ears priceless gossip, both scandalous and glorious, about the great Queen and about Shakspere and the other immortals with whom Ben, according to himself, had rubbed elbows, and about whom he, in most cases he alone, could report matters of astounding intimacy. Each morning, as we believe, while Jonson was sleeping off the night before, Drummond set down the golden talk while it was fresh in his mind. It was by way of thanks for that priceless note-taking that I made my pilgrimage to his house.

But for a Scot, there is only one first-class shrine in that part of the world. We spent a wonderful day at Abbotsford, with a side visit to Melrose. Sir Walter's home must have been enthralling when the novels were casting their spell over Europe, and the magician was writing his stint, thousands of words, every day before breakfast—then riding over newly acquired acres, to survey the progress of his tree planting. But surely, Abbotsford means more to the human race now. Though the noble home has declined into a not-too-extraordinary museum, yet the ghost of Sir Walter, the Sir Walter of the last heroic years, presides over the place and makes it both proud and sad. The large library is now a treasure cave for scholars to hunt in, but the small study opening out from it touches the heart. There is the table at which Sir Walter wrote, and on it the box containing his pen, paper and ink. On the shelves would be the volumes from the main library which he needed for each romance, and there is the little staircase, easy to reach, which led up directly to his bedroom. In the night, sleepless because of the appalling debt he had pledged his brain to pay, he would come down that stair with a shawl over his shoulders, seat himself at that desk, seize his pen, and fill page after page with humanity and swift action and courage.

From Edinburgh we came down to York. Since my mother's ancestors, the ones she liked best, came from Scarborough, many of those to whom I owe parts of my character must have walked in that minster, where I now walked, and doubtless worshiped there. I wondered what they prayed for. I attended the morning service and prayed with them. Seldom have I felt myself so strongly gripped by tradition.

While in London, we saw the Tower and the other show places, we went out for a day to Stratford, and for a three-day visit to Oxford. Perhaps because we had seen too much on our rapid tour, all impressions now were beginning to jumble. London, being a world in itself, should be visited frequently, for a year at a time. The recollections of my first hasty contact are fragmentary. The Abbey roused a miscellany of sentiments, pious and otherwise. I thrilled at sight of the places where

Wellington and Nelson rest; I did not thrill over the monument to Major John André. The British Museum had from me a passing gesture of homage, not the concentrated and prolonged inspection I really wished to give it. But the two things in London which demanded, and received, my wholehearted admiration, was the National Gallery and the choir singing at St. Paul's.

At a morning service at St. Paul's I heard for the first time what the eighteenth century used to call pulpit wit. The preacher was a short, not too impressive person, but no doubt he was well known to the other members of the congregation. He deserved fame. He read his sermon from manuscript, but every now and then he would look up quickly like a nervous bird, and emphasize a line to which he wished to attach importance. One sentence so underlined I have not forgotten. "Too many of us, my dear brethren, hope to come in for the widow's blessing by imitating the widow's mites."

I have loved fine churches all my life, and nothing in Stratford was so rewarding as the unusually large parish church there. Guidebooks and Shakspere biographies make too little of it. Of course they say the poet is buried in the chancel, and they usually repeat the famous inscription about the bones, but they should remind us of what a boy of Shakspere's time would see and hear in that church—the fine rituals, the ceremonial pageantry, the splendor of the vestments, the nobility of the language, the religious mood of the chanting. Shakspere was familiar early with the atmosphere of worship and awe.

Stratford otherwise was so plastered over with blatant advertisements that it seemed a kind of literary Coney Island. After so many years I may do the place an injustice, but what I think of now is "Shakspere Ale," "Falstaff Beer," "The Hamlet Lunch," and "The Ophelia Tearoom."

The days at Oxford were gorgeous. We had at least a glimpse of the famous colleges, and of the Bodleian, and we felt, without being overwhelmed, the weight of history upon them all. For whatever it is that gives Oxford its unique quality, it cannot be mere duration. There are older edifices in the Nile Valley. What we admire in Oxford is timeless. It may be, as Matthew Arnold said, that Oxford is the home of lost causes and forsaken beliefs, and unpopular names, and impossible loyalties; but it is also true that Oxford whispers from her towers the last enchantments of the Middle Ages; and truer still and far more important, that she "keeps forever calling us nearer to the true goal of all of us, to the ideal, to perfection—to beauty, in a word, which is only truth seen from another side—nearer, perhaps, than all the science of Tübingen."

In September we returned to America but of the voyage homeward I remember nothing at all. I had too many impressions already, and I was too busy thinking them over, to take on any more.

I took abroad with me and I brought back, deep respect for the British people. I had expected to like the Irish, and I did like them, but a close view of their unpredictable temperament and their eccentric sense of values, stirred in me some sympathy with the English. I was prepared to admire all Scots, and my only criticism was that there aren't enough of them. If there were enough Scots to go around, they could run the Empire, to the great advantage of England and the rest of us. It's an aging Scottish joke, tolerated in *Punch,* that in London you find a Scot at the head of all departments, but it can't be true. The policy of the British Empire is still English. The impression I had of the English from this first breathless trip still seems to me essentially just. Whatever advantages can be derived from doing the same things over and over again, always in the same way—those advantages the English have. So long as they can stay in their groove, they are incomparable. But to pick their way through a disreputable world which has new ideas in it, and therefore new problems, is not what the English like to do. They do it like men when they have to, but they consider the necessity a bit of bad luck, and they get out from it as soon as possible.

I was thinking of all this on my voyage home because my life work was, and I thought it always would be, the interpretation of England and English literature to American students. Perhaps what I had taught until then might need revision.

One thing I do remember about the voyage home. My tall father was waiting in the crowd on the dock, and it was easy to pick him out as he waved his straw hat to welcome us.

CHAPTER XVIII

Amherst Graduation

I

IN A few days I was back in my study at Mrs. Marsh's, ready for any number of happy years at Amherst. I now was established as a teacher, my colleagues showed their friendship and confidence, I knew the townspeople, and they accepted me as one of them. Though the College was small, yet it could have whatever prestige the quality of its teaching deserved, and my opportunity, I believed, was to help make it, not a large school but a great one. My work in the classroom must be better; I must do more outside of class.

This year, 1907-1908, I began seriously to groom myself as a writer. I would always be at heart a teacher, but if a teacher is inspiring for four hundred students, he can be inspiring for four thousand, since students have a way of passing along the light they receive. At Amherst, Professor Garman taught philosophy to upperclassmen, but the freshmen and sophomores learned his point of view by contagion from their elders, long before they reached his course. In a small, closely knit college of four hundred boys a great teacher can influence every one of them, even though he meets only a hundred face to face. But if he hopes to reach more than the total four hundred, he must write. I had written poems for the pleasure of self-expression; I now began to write as a means of reaching the largest possible audience—or if you prefer, as a way of bringing the public into my classroom. I dare say I never wrote again for any other purpose.

To do much writing on a full teaching schedule is not easy, but I remembered Carl Walter's advice about using the moments instead of waiting for the hours. I began to cultivate the habit of taking up my pen as soon as I entered my study, and carrying on for a sentence if not a paragraph before I went out again. This was all very well, but Mrs. Baxter Marsh thought my desk should be dusted daily, and a writer can't readily pick up where he left off if he wastes five or ten minutes looking for his manuscript. Mrs. Marsh and I solved the difficulty by a compromise. I promised to write on a table if she would furnish the table; the desk would then be hers to dust, and I would leave on it no manuscripts, only bills and letters and whatever else might be tidied up and removed from view.

That year I produced as usual a number of short poems, but I also wrote at length about methods of teaching literature—of making boys love literature, as Woodberry had trained us to love it. One essay, on "The Teaching of Literature in College," I sent to *The Nation,* then edited by Hammond Lamont, with Paul Elmer More as his assistant. At that time I had met neither of them, but later I knew them well, and for half my lifetime I have enjoyed the friendship of Hammond's brother, Thomas W. Lamont. But while I was young and obscure *The Nation* set me forward handsomely by accepting my essay, and publishing it on September 3, 1908.

The avalanche of letters which descended on me from teachers, critics, publishers and novelists, made me realize the implications of what I had written. I had thought my point a simple one—in fact, I had feared it was too simple to interest a serious journal. The teacher of literature, according to me, should say as little as possible about the background of a poem or about the biography of the poet, these matters belonging rather to history than to literature; he should rather point out the admirable things in the poems, and should remind the student of the ideas and emotions which, in his own experience, parallel and illustrate the poet's message. There was nothing very new in the suggestion, but I probably overemphasized my dislike of the historical or biographical approach to literature, and since that approach was favored in practically all universities, I made myself a target. Of the avalanche of letters, a few hailed me as a champion of something-or-other, but quite a number recognized in me an idiot on the way to be a nuisance.

2

I continued to train the Grace Church choir, which improved rapidly, until its quality was high indeed. I spent unforgettable hours with my friends on the faculty, with Biggie and Fritz Thompson, with deForest Smith, Charles Cobb and Tom Esty, another mathematician as remarkable as Charles though of a different temperament. Tom's father, William Cole Esty, whom I had the good luck to know during my first days at Amherst, was in his time an active and important mathematician and a strong force in the College life. Tom inherited his father's gift of courtesy with a few extra attractions of his own. He and his brothers during their student days had a fine scholastic record, but were known even more for their astounding abilities as mimics and ventriloquists. Tom could—and did—address you in the voice of the President, or of any other person in the community. If your back happened to be turned, you could believe the impersonated had just entered the room. Amherst legend said that once at morning chapel Tom and two mischievous brothers, observing that three of the elder professors were absent, made a hasty agreement just before the recitation of the morning psalm, each brother making himself responsible for the voice of one professor. When the reading began, the congregation was electrified to hear the voices of the absent, unusually clear and strong.

Fritz Thompson's study became more than ever a meeting place for the younger faculty and the middle-aged. Morse Stephens, of the University of California, came on twice to give a series of lectures. He stayed at the Thompson home, and since he was one of the most copious talkers who ever breathed, Fritz used to ask us in relays to help him stand up against the volubility. On one occasion a plot was laid to get Morse Stephens on a subject where he would not be omniscient. One Amherst citizen had made, as he claimed, a special study of Freemasonry; Fritz invited him to join us, and at the proper moment to introduce the theme. Morse Stephens pricked up his ears, fixed an eye on him, and actually listened, but after a moment exclaimed, "If I am not mistaken, you have been reading the article on Freemasonry in Such-and-Such Encyclopedia!" Our expert admitted that he had given attention to that particular article, which he found thorough and intelligent. "Your opinion gratifies me," said Morse. "I wrote it."

During these years I had a number of visits from members of my family and from old New York friends. Father made me happy by dropping in at least once a semester on his trips to his Norwich factory. Instead of traveling directly on the Delaware, Lackawanna and Western, or on the West Shore Railroad, he would make a circuit to Amherst, and from there to Albany and Utica, and from Utica down the Chenango Valley. During these visits I watched his delight in the society of scholars and teachers, and realized again his natural bent for subjects far removed from his ribbon making. I believe it was at this time that I first saw the relation of my life to his and to my grandfather's. Books and music, books and music, for three generations we had craved a career in literature and scholarship, with some degree of expression in music, and thanks to better men before me, I had the chance.

Mother came and spent a week with me, an extraordinary tribute of affection since she disliked travel. Mrs. Marsh had a vacant bedroom for her, and during the day she spent hours in my study before the open fire, receiving friends who came in to call on her, or exchanging ideas with Mrs. Marsh about possible improvements in the room.

For most of her stay the weather was stormy, and since her health was beginning to be frail, I tried to keep her comfortably warm, well protected against drafts and dampness. But it wasn't in her nature to miss anything, and every day of bad weather she would mention some spot in the town or the landscape which I had mentioned in my letters, and in the end I always bundled her up and drove her around in the livery stable's best combination of horse and buggy. On the last night of her stay there was a full moon. We had been out driving that afternoon, and now we had come from dinner at the hotel, to rest before the study fire. I happened to say that on moonlit nights the view over the valley from the lawn behind the old College church was remarkable, and what a pity the ground wasn't dry enough for us to walk there. Mother agreed it was a pity, and we talked on, till she asked me in her dear determined way to bring her coat and her hat and her rubbers. "It will do me no harm at all to take a look at that valley in moonlight." So we saw the magnificent view, and she enjoyed it all the more because the path was sloppy and slippery, and it was a bit of an adventure getting up the hill on my arm. Any sane friend of hers, lacking her have-at-you temper, would have advised staying home and playing safe.

My sisters visited me, and Bob came up once after a heavy snow, and Professor Joseph Thompson, "Toggles," taught us to use snowshoes, an accomplishment which proved of small value. But he also lent us his bobsled, which was an immediate success. Between classes we coasted down South Pleasant Street, from the President's house to the Boston and Maine Station. It was a slide of some length, but a heavy sled on an icy surface could finish it in a few seconds. Most of our coasting time was spent climbing back to the top of the hill. My brother was a thoughtful guest, but I caught a note of regretful astonishment that I did not cut out the classes altogether, and give the day to the sled.

I prized visits from two classmates. Melville Cane gave a talk to the literary club, on vers de société. His readings from Calverley, Praed, and Locker-Lampson entertained us greatly, and set many of the boys reading light verse and trying their hand at it, so that Melville left quite a trail or wake in our poetic climate. I recall no discussion of Emily Dickinson on that visit, but Melville is now one of Emily's most versatile champions, lyrically serious when he pays homage, and humorously satiric when he polishes off her editors and detractors.

In the spring William de Mille came up and astonished my colleagues by his skillful tennis playing. Also he read to us, one night in my study, a just completed one-act play. Later the piece was produced, and he was immediately sued for plagiarism by a fancy-ridden gentleman who claimed he had written a play before William wrote his. There was no resemblance between the plots, and the plaintiff admitted that his work had not been produced, nor had the script been where William could have seen it, but since it was written first, William by some psychic process must have drawn upon it. Why the case got even a hearing before a referee, was hard to understand, but since the plaintiff set the date of his own composition some time after we had heard William read his play at Amherst, Carrington Lancaster, Fritz Thompson and I testified. I began to see that a successful playwright needs strong nerves.

I had visits too from my best friend in Norwich, John Prindle Scott, a graduate of Oberlin University, where he had specialized in music, and where he began the composing to which later he gave all his time. For several summers he and I gave a joint recital in Norwich, and in my two closing years at Amherst he came from New York to sing for the boys of the Delta Upsilon house at their annual Faculty Party. He had a voice of remarkable flexibility, and though he was a vigorous baritone he could sing with a delicacy usually reserved for sopranos and contraltos.

3

Professor Bertha Young, of Mount Holyoke College, who had heard my lectures to the Amherst ladies the year before, now invited me to give a series of four talks to her students. I took the invitation with extreme seriousness. I was to discuss Tennyson, Browning, Swinburne, and Rossetti. Because Woodberry always wrote out his public lectures and read them, I now did the same, and because I was to speak in the large hall, I thought I must wear my frock coat—just why, I can't recall. I'm afraid I also supplied the Mary Lyons campus something to comment on by appearing in a top hat.

In the autumn of 1908 the high school teachers of English invited me to give them a course in literature on Saturday afternoons throughout the year. By arrangement with the State authorities the course was to count for credit toward something or other. About the details I am now vague, but there were, I believe, twenty-five or thirty in the class, the books studied were those they had to teach, and I required papers at frequent intervals, and criticized their writing. It was heavy work and took time, but it forced me to re-study and revise my methods for students even more experienced and more ambitious than those I had met in the Columbia Summer School.

These teaching engagements at Mount Holyoke and Springfield brought invitations to give single lectures here and there in the neighborhood, and before I realized the change, my interests and activities spread beyond Amherst. My life still centered in the College and the town, my class hours were many and the students came so frequently to my study in Mrs. Marsh's house, that to protect myself I told them the shades would be drawn until half-past ten, but I would raise them at that hour, and a raised shade would mean that visitors were welcome. But in addition to this full and happy life I began to have a place in the larger world of education; at Yale I knew Charles Baldwin, Chauncey Tinker and Henry Canby, and Professor W. L. Cross and Professor Albert S. Cook. Committee meetings of New England English departments, and the annual gatherings of the Modern Language Association, brought me the acquaintance or the friendship of Professor Winchester of Wesleyan, Professor Gummere of Haverford, Professor Bright of Johns Hopkins, Professor Schelling of Pennsylvania, Professor Van Dyke of Princeton, Professor Kittredge, Professor Neilson and Professor Baker of Harvard.

President Harris seemed to regard me as a suitable person to represent the College on public occasions, and thanks to his good will I enjoyed even more travel than my lecturing would have occasioned. When the College of the City of New York dedicated its new buildings on May 14, 1908, Dr. Harris appointed me the Amherst delegate to the ceremony, perhaps with the thought that I would enjoy an extra visit to my people. John H. Finley, then President of the City College, had gathered a group of speakers of the quality he loved—Governor Charles E. Hughes, Oscar S. Strauss, Secretary of Commerce and Labor, James Bryce, British Ambassador, President Charles W. Eliot of Harvard, Joseph H. Choate, former Ambassador to Great Britain, and Mark Twain. I had never seen Mark Twain before, nor heard him. He was wearing his Oxford hood, recently acquired, and Mr. Choate or Mr. Bryce made a reference to him as "Oxford's youngest product." Mark said he preferred not to think of himself as the flower and fruit of Oxford's seven hundred years; let the noble university go on to still greater triumphs!

On January 19, 1909, Columbia celebrated the centenary of the birth of Edgar Allan Poe, and President Butler invited me to read a poem. Every commemorative conclave in those days had its official laureate, and the poems were pretty terrible, mine being no better, and I hope no worse, than the average. The other speakers who with me were to do Poe justice, were Brander Matthews and Thomas Nelson Page. My brother, then in his junior year, was managing editor of *Spectator,* and at dinner he greeted the family with the hope we'd get out of the meeting before breakfast; he had seen Mr. Page's typed script, and it was two hundred and fifty sheets. We thought Bob was joking, but he wasn't. Mr. Page brought on the platform the final draft of a book about Poe. His intention was to read no more than a reasonable quotation, but his work appealed to him so much that he kept on for an hour and three quarters. Mr. J. P. Morgan, conspicuous on the platform, frankly took a nap, and other Trustees made indirect comment by looking at their watches. I sincerely admired Mr. Page and his writings, but I never again heard him make a speech.

Four days later Richard Watson Gilder gave Amherst College a fine address on Abraham Lincoln. Learning that he planned a visit to Mount Holyoke, I persuaded him to spend a short time with us and speak to my boys, but the demand to hear him was so great that in the end he had the town for audience as well as the College. As editor of *The Century*

Magazine he had brought out "Actaeon," he was a close friend of Woodberry's, and like him had watched over my writing and advised me. When he returned to New York after his visit to us, he wrote a letter which I valued at the time and still read over when I need a little flattery to cheer me up; he told me for what qualities he liked my writing, or the promise of it, and he congratulated me on being where a poet could surely find happiness—in a beautiful landscape, occupied in work which gave opportunity for study, far from the distractions of life! Evidently he thought I was a fixture at Amherst. I was happy to think so myself. But on April 9, my old friend and teacher, George Rice Carpenter, died suddenly, and in the reorganization of the English department, Columbia called me home as Associate Professor.

4

The invitation came in a letter from Professor Trent, and I went at once to President Harris, who disposed of the matter in a way creditable to his kind and honest nature, but not, I hope, serving the best interests of his college. When I told him my news, his expression became for a moment even more paternal than usual.

"John, would you like to go back?"

I could hardly say no, and his question as he put it left me small room to say what I did want, which was to hear from him a strong wish for me to stay. So I told him the call from my Alma Mater was naturally attractive.

"Then you must accept it," said he. "I always knew you'd leave us sooner or later, but I hoped you would stay here through my time. However, if this is your destiny, take it at once."

I wrote Professor Trent my acceptance, and promptly had an amusing letter back, filled with his characteristic sense of fair play. Before he sent the invitation he told Mr. Plimpton of his purpose, and Mr. Plimpton made a wager that he could outbid Columbia and keep me at Amherst. When President Harris let me go, without making a counteroffer or reporting the matter to his trustees, Plimpton accused Trent of having played a trick and snatched me away. So Trent in this second letter handed me back my acceptance, and said we would now start over again. He renewed the call, adding the information that Plimpton was on his way to Amherst, to offer me a full professorship. If, having weighed both offers, I decided to stay where I was, my Columbia friends would still be my friends.

Half an hour after I read his message I put in the mail my final acceptance, sure that the situation would otherwise degenerate into inglorious dickering. When Mr. Plimpton arrived, the incident was already closed.

I know now that it was right for me to leave Amherst, or rather, it would have been wrong for me to stay. There are too few resignations in the world; we often fail to recognize the end of the chapter when we reach it. I had been fortunate enough to accomplish what Amherst wanted of me; I might have done nothing more than repeat myself. Providence, and President Harris, saved me from settling into a final pattern in my twenty-ninth year.

It was hard to say goodbye to the College, to the town, to Grace Church and my choir, to the marvelous landscape, which had taken possession of me once for all, as it does of most men who live in it for even a brief time. But I came away laden with gifts and memories of friendship. Town and College gave me a round of parties. At my last vesper service the choir sang their best—Stainer's *Magnificat* and *Nunc dimittis* in B flat, and Martin's two superb anthems, "Holiest, Breathe an Evening Blessing," and "Hail, Gladdening Light!" And Charles Cobb, true and unselfish, helped me pack my books. Two weeks before the date I had fixed for leaving, he implored me to make at least a start, by collecting enough boxes to hold my library. I did not realize how it had grown. With his aid I packed books till arms and neck and shoulders ached. Even so, I left town two days late.

PART III

1909—1917

CHAPTER XIX

The New Columbia

I

ON MY return in 1909 I found my Alma Mater very different from the University I had left in 1903. Outwardly and inwardly it was a new place. President Butler was then at the top of his powers, and though he was already involved in his work for international understanding, Columbia was still his chief interest. On South Field the first dormitories had risen, and the College classes, instead of being sifted over the campus, were housed in the new Hamilton Hall. Dean Van Amringe, picturesque and popular as ever, was approaching the retiring age, and in 1910 he was succeeded by Fred Keppel, who for ten years had served as assistant secretary and secretary of the University.

Undergraduate and graduate work were now clearly defined. The College English courses were given in Hamilton Hall, the graduate lectures and seminars in Fayerweather, later in Philosophy Hall. Ashley H. Thorndike was secretary of the department, in place of George Rice Carpenter, and comparative literature was now taught by Jefferson B. Fletcher and Joel E. Spingarn. Woodbridge, with his colleagues Wendell T. Bush and John Dewey, were stirring the philosophy department in many vital directions. Cassius J. Keyser, mathematician and philosopher, charmingly persuasive orator and writer, had caught the imagination of our whole academic community. James Harvey Robinson, formerly a specialist in the Renaissance, was making an entirely fresh reputation as a brilliant and caustic wit, with his attention shifted to the problems of the modern world. Closely associated with him, though differing from him and each other in temperament, were James T. Shotwell and Charles A. Beard. In economic history Vladimir Simkhovitch was pushing his own original studies, and furnishing his colleagues with entertainment and inspiration by his merry and unpredictable talk. With these I remember Michael I. Pupin, the inventor.

All these men taught me so much, through daily contacts here and there in the University, that I think of them as among the leaders of their time. If others do not rank them so high it must be for lack of my opportunity to know them well. At the Faculty Club they usually lunched together, and I found myself a place in the group or on the fringe of it. Such exchange of ideas I shall never hear again. It seemed then that the world was in a moment of great hope; each one of us personally was conscious of a large opportunity, our University was entering a brilliant epoch, our country had a future, at home and abroad the intellectual horizon was bright, the international mind had almost been awakened. Now, I wonder whether symptoms of approaching disaster were not already obvious, and whether the optimism on both sides of the ocean may not have been an effort of the will, an intensified appreciation of blessings which we half-knew would soon be taken from us.

Perhaps the students as well as their elders felt this premonition of the First World War. At Amherst the boys had been gifted in many ways, but not one of them was feverishly occupied with world ideas, nor was I, until I returned to Columbia. In the new Hamilton Hall I was reëducated by those I taught. Perhaps the nearness of publishers and editors in the large city stimulated the boys to get at their writing quickly, if they had an instinct for it; certainly they drew from the cosmopolitan atmosphere an extraordinary supply of current information. Randolph Bourne outshone all others by his articulateness and by his hunger for new ideas. He became at once the leader of a kind of youth movement, yet to call him young would be misleading. He was more mature than most of us who taught him, much shrewder in his appraisal of the prewar restlessness, much more keenly aware of revolutionary tendencies abroad in the world. His death at the age of thirty-two prevented a career about the ultimate quality of which we can only speculate.

In a partial sense he was, and would always have been a liberal, but never a young-spirited or happy liberal. He was born world-weary, and even in his first papers, published in *The Atlantic Monthly* while he was an undergraduate, he directed his lucid and provocative criticism against the elder generation without revealing precise hope or aspiration for his own contemporaries. Essentially he was a lover of tradition, an admirer of old cultures, and a critic of them only in so far as they had fallen short of what he liked to think they could have been.

Early in our acquaintance I disappointed him because I had not read Masefield's "Everlasting Mercy" as soon as he had. I remember the day he showed me a copy of the English magazine in which the poem appeared. He criticized the way English was taught at Columbia, and in particular the way I taught it, and since his points were all valid, I reformed myself as much as I could. Yet I confess to this degree of weakness, that I wondered why he felt called upon to be an indefatigable checker-up of other men's short-comings. It was Professor Woodbridge who sent one of his essays to the *Atlantic,* and so launched him as a writer. After graduation he went abroad on a traveling fellowship, to study the political conditions and the systems of government in England, France, and Germany. His report to the University on his return remains a shrewd and illuminating document.

Dixon Ryan Fox, pretending to no such genius as Bourne, was remarkable for wealth of ideas and for the ability to put them into practical form. Remembering what King's Crown had meant to me, I organized a literary club, to meet once a fortnight. From the beginning Dixon Fox supplied this group with a torrent of ideas and energy. Perhaps because he was engaged at the time in staging Elizabethan revivals for the Philolexian Society, he christened our literary circle The Boar's Head, after the tavern which Falstaff and his companions frequented.

Boar's Head soon developed resemblances to my Amherst group rather than to Woodberry's old club; we rarely if ever had an outside speaker, preferring to entertain ourselves. The discussion always began with books and writing, but before long we would be arguing about life, about current social and economic questions. Bourne and Fox ensured a good debate, since they were predestined to take opposite sides. Carl Zigrosser, even then far advanced in the study of art, would listen with a thoughful smile until he could keep out of it no longer. When he came in at last it was always to support the radicals. Bourne was more at home in modern music than in modern painting, but he valued Zigrosser as a strong ally.

Alfred Knopf belonged to the group but kept himself on the edge of it, being a liberal of such precocity that already he had become skeptical of mere talk. When I made his acquaintance Alfred was trying out his far from negligible powers as a writer, but with modesty which almost amounted to lack of self-confidence. Perhaps he suspected then what his true vocation would be. He found it a short time later when Professor Spingarn offered the undergraduates a prize for the best essay on modern literature. One of the suggested topics was the "Novels of John Galsworthy," and Alfred with characteristic liking for direct action, addressed a letter to Galsworthy asking for personal and specific information about his art. A lively correspondence followed, in which Galsworthy expressed the hope that Alfred would look him up, on some future visit to England. Who won the essay prize I do not remember, but Alfred went to England the next summer, and on his return he told me he'd like to be a publisher on the great eighteenth century model, the kind of publisher who reads his books and has a personal acquaintance with the authors.

As alert to the contemporary world as Bourne, but with a different emphasis, was Lloyd Morris, sensitive and enthusiastic. He must have been born with writing skill; I doubt if he needed teaching in the mechanics of composition, even in childhood. He was a liberal, a radical if you choose, yet I recall no opinion of his about the state of human society. He was on fire about new movements in art, in all the arts. He came to his freshman year fully aware of what was going on in the theatre, the dance, painting, sculpture, music. Imagine the excitement of having in your class a boy who knew Mary Garden and Isadora Duncan, who had the music of Debussy by heart, and Stravinsky and Satie, and wanted to talk about Brancusi and Toulouse-Lautrec. Lloyd called my attention to "291," the wonderful little gallery and exhibition room which Alfred Stieglitz maintained on Fifth Avenue, without charge, for the benefit of the public. Until the War, I saw every exhibition in "291," an incredible series which introduced to us, one week the drawings of Rodin, next week the water colors of a young man named John Marin.

Lloyd Morris remains today the same extraordinary character, and though his writing has shown steady growth through thirty and more years, I believe his best work is still to come. While an undergraduate he wrote a book on the Irish Renaissance which would have done credit to a much older man. Having read all the available material about Lady Gregory, Yeats, Synge, Douglas Hyde, and the others, he went to Ireland, became personally acquainted with them, saw the Abbey Theatre in action, came home and revised his book, which was then published by Macmillan under the title, *The Celtic Dawn.* His progress since that beginning is indicated by his recent book, *Threshold in the Sun,* a subtle and stimulating autobiography, notable for its portrait of the older New York in which he grew up.

When I first knew Lloyd, his father had recently died, and I think of him always as the comrade of his mother, a woman of beautiful tastes, who for many years wrestled heroically with a disease which she knew was mortal. Whatever the condition of her health, she shared and encouraged all her son's literary and artistic ambitions, made their home a brilliant salon for his friends—I first met Rebecca West there—and accompanied him on summer trips abroad which she knew would broaden his outlook and increase his acquaintance among writers and artists everywhere. When illness at last prevented travel and bound her to fixed and increasing agony, Lloyd paid back her love by his own devotion, complete and faithful. I have witnessed no human conduct more magnificent. In those days I saw much of him and knew the changes in his mother's state. She and my sister Rhoda were drawn to each other by the same fondness for the arts, and perhaps by the fact, vaguely guessed at, that they both were to die of the same disease.

2

I have known three great college deans—Van Am in my undergraduate days, Doctor Hitchcock at Amherst, and Fred Keppel after my return to Columbia. Van Am was, I suppose, the product of New York in the ninteenth century while the city still had some qualities of the small town, and a personality by sheer picturesqueness could make itself known and loved. Dr. Hitchcock, the "Old Doc" of affectionate remembrance, was a product of the Massachusetts landscape, by profession a physician, by heredity an educator—his father had been President of the College. He exercised over Amherst students throughout his long career an influence even stronger than Van Am's over us. His technique was different. His tall, long-bearded figure conveyed the thought of austerity, yet he had the warmest of hearts and his attitude toward all boys was pastoral and paternal. He never tried to awe them, he put up no barrier to protect himself from any appeal of theirs at any hour of day or night. As a doctor he was trained to answer all calls. Long before physical training, as distinguished from athletics, was understood or valued in most schools, Old Doc managed to get the modest Barrett gymnasium for Amherst, and in my time he had his office in a larger and more modern gymnasium, where he could keep his eye on the boys, believing wisely that the moral and intellectual care of them can often, if not always, begin most effectively with care of their health. In a college numbering little more than four hundred students, he could know them all personally, as in some cases he had known their fathers, or even their grandfathers.

One snowy December night when I was working at my desk in Mrs. Marsh's house, there was a knock on the door, and Old Doc came in. Already well past seventy, he was still a magnificent human being, tall and straight, with vibrant voice and a powerful New England accent. That night he wore rubber boots, the collar of his ulster was turned up, his broad hat and his long white beard were covered with snow. He explained that one of the freshmen was on his mind, so he stepped around to ask how the boy was doing in English. I looked up the record and was glad to give a good report—so good that I asked why Old Doc worried about him. "No worry! After supper tonight, resting for a moment, I thought of his grandfather. He and I were boys together—used to wrestle together. Thought I'd ask how the family stock is holding out."

On one occasion Old Doc watched over me with this same thoughtfulness. In my first Amherst year the freshman class outdid all human records in bad spelling, until I told them we'd meet for an extra period each week to concentrate on the rules of orthography as set forth by Noah Webster. The class grumbled, and with some justice, since I had no right to increase their attendance schedule, but they came, and at the first session, to my surprise, Old Doc came too. He sympathized with me in my attempts to get some work out of that class, and hearing the grumbling about the spelling session, he brought me his moral support. As he strode into the room he put everyone in good humor by exclaiming, "It's years since I attended a spelling bee! I used to be good at it. When I heard you were reviving the sport, I thought I'd come and check up on myself." From that moment spelling went up in undergraduate esteem, if not in practice.

Fred Keppel, though like Van Am a city product, had something of Old Doc's attitude to boys, together with some modern ideas about the management of his office. Van Am kept his door closed and could be seen only by appointment. Old Doc was very accessible, but in most cases the student took the initiative. Fred Keppel didn't wait to be looked up. In his room on the ground floor of Hamilton Hall, his desk faced the door, and the door was always open on the corridor, so that he could see every student and teacher who entered or left the building. If someone with whom he needed a word happened to pass, he would rush out and seize him. His spontaneous manners and methods distinguished him from Van Am; he resembled Old Doc in his direct acquaintance with all the students, with this distinction, that he cared more about their future than about their present condition. He liked those who did well in their work, but I think he liked especially the rare ones who knew what they wanted to do in life and were going straight for their goal. More than once I found a boy in one part of the country or another who could make good use of the college course, but who lacked funds or perhaps was incompletely prepared for the entrance examination. Once convinced that the boy had real stuff in him, Fred wangled the money for tuition, or disregarded the entrance requirements. I doubt if he was disappointed in more than one or two of those he took a chance on.

He knew the teachers as intimately as the students, and we often saw him on the fifth floor of Hamilton Hall, where undergraduate English courses were given and where we had our offices. He would appear as it were from nowhere, stick his head in the door and ask a question, and vanish again. The question was always about a student, but at the moment he may have had the instructor on his mind.

Dr. Odell and I conducted this undergraduate English work with four or five younger colleagues. Harrison Ross Steeves, like myself a Columbia graduate, was our mainstay in the administrative work connected with freshman and sophomore courses. Steeves was a meticulous scholar, a good teacher, an example to all of us in his reverence for decorum. I have rarely known a man so human at heart who went in for the proprieties on such a big scale.

Bayard Boyesen, another Columbia graduate, the son of the Norwegian novelist, supplied a stimulating contrast. He could match Steeves in fine manners, but he had no manner in particular; he was spontaneous, emotional, and imaginative; alive to fine things, within and outside academic territory. I was amused and delighted to hear him tell his section of freshmen that if they couldn't visit the Latin Quarter of Paris, they might find a mild substitute in the Café Lafayette at Ninth Street; he advised a dinner there once a week. Greenwich Village was earning its first reputation as the haunt of radicals, artists, and curious lookers-on, and Boyesen made it clear to all and sundry that he liked Greenwich Village, as indeed I did, but I didn't know it so well. He was a civilizing influence in the department, constantly reminding us that the work in the classroom is at best only a means to an end, a warming up canter for the real race, which will always involve a clash of ideals and personalities.

Knowing Hjalmar Boyesen, my classmate, I found it easy to understand Bayard, and temperamentally I agreed with him. He and Steeves co-existed in a polite state of armed neutrality. If Boyesen believed the classroom should never lose sight of the world outside, Steeves liked the classroom as such, and never concealed the importance he attached to purely academic experience. At times I wondered if permanent peace could or should be preserved between the Viking and the don.

Two others joined us shortly, Frank Humphrey Ristine and Carl Van Doren. Ristine was a sound scholar and a reliable teacher, somewhat on the Steeves pattern. In a few years he went from Columbia to a professorship in Hamilton College. Carl Van Doren was a remarkable colleague, energetic, ambitious, full of ideas, a prodigious worker. His special interest in American biography and American folkways distinguished him even then. Coming to Columbia from the University of Illinois, he brought to us the influence of Stuart P. Sherman, whose writings had already gained the admiration or the envy of most English professors. Stuart, Carl and I were later associated with Professor Trent in editing the *Cambridge History of American Literature,* but it was Carl's affectionate and frequent remarks about his teacher that first taught me to appreciate both Stuart's quality and his own.

More than anyone else in the department at that time Carl foresaw the coming vogue of American literature in academic circles, as a subject for graduate study, and the part that contemporary books by American writers would soon play in the national life. If I understood him correctly it was as a novelist that he first intended to take his place in this development, and one powerful story which I heard him read aloud is still a vivid memory. His splendid biography of Franklin and his editing of Revolutionary documents place him high among scholars and critics, but he has something to say for himself which has not yet been said, and his old students and associates, remembering him as he came fresh from the West, wait for him to say it at last.

3

When I returned to Columbia my parents, my sisters and my brother were living at 606 West One Hundred Thirteenth Street, and for that winter I stayed with them. Memmem remained in Norwich, to keep house for Father, on his visits to the factory. My brother Bob was a senior in College, preparing for the Law School. My sister Helen was a graduate of Barnard in 1904, and Rhoda was now in St. Agatha School, preparing to enter Barnard with the class of 1915.

My people, since the time they left Weehawken, had joined the congregation of St. Agnes' Chapel, Trinity Parish in West Ninety-second Street. Their religious interests, their old-fashioned disposition to be active in parish work, had not diminished when they came to New York City, and on rejoining the household now I found Father superintending the Sunday school at St. Agnes' Chapel with the same enthusiasm with which he had directed the much smaller school at Grace Church in Union Hill.

As I have said before, he had a natural delight in all forms of serious education, and one motive in his preoccupation with Sunday school was a conviction, which I shared, that such organizations are too often fairly close to pious frauds, since the teaching is usually done by those, however well-meaning, who have neither the temperament nor the preparation to teach, and the pupils therefore learn little besides restlessness and in-attention. Father would not have spent so much time in this work if the clergy at St. Agnes' Chapel had not welcomed and encouraged his ambition to create a real school. The teachers, of course, were as else-where volunteers, and a large number of them were amateurs, pedagogi-cally speaking, but a valued few were teachers by profession, and at least the curriculum was well planned and thorough. Because I sympathized with what Father was trying to do, and because during the Amherst years I had missed his companionship, I attended the Sunday school ses-sion with him, played the organ for the short service with which it began, and watched the working out of his educational ideas.

But though I didn't tell Father so, I could see no future for Sunday schools. Parents don't take them seriously. Their reason for sending the children is often no more than the hope to get them out of the way for a few moments on Sunday. After all, that is too often the parental rea-son for sending the children to school on weekdays. Parents are too likely to dread holidays, when the children have to be home. My own childhood had been exceptional in this respect, as in some others. My parents believed in education with a passionate sincerity, and they thought of church attendance as partly a form of education. Now we were in another day. The realization of this fact stirred for a good many years nostalgic memories of the life at Weehawken. I thought of those days more often than of the recent Amherst episode. But even so, I did not yet realize the influence that Weehawken memories would have on me always.

CHAPTER XX

Marriage

I

IN THE Christmas season of 1901, while a graduate student at Columbia, I went around to the St. Agnes Parish House one afternoon to help trim a large Christmas tree. The other volunteers were teachers in the Sunday school. I was assigned the task of draping ornaments around the top. Balanced on a high ladder, I distributed tinsel and colored globes where I thought they would do the most good. While the box of ornaments was still fairly full and heavy, I dropped it on the head of a tall girl, one of the teachers, who was working—as she thought safely—around the lower branches. She didn't seem to mind having her hat knocked off.

She was Pauline Ives, daughter of Theodore Milton Ives, then living in West Sixty-ninth Street. Several years later the family moved to lower Fifth Avenue, and on June 9, 1910, Pauline and I were married, in St. Luke's Chapel, Trinity Parish, on Hudson Street. Dr. William T. Manning, Rector of Trinity, performed the ceremony.

Pauline came of a New England family. Her maternal grandfather had been president, and I believe the founder, of one of New Hartford's insurance companies. To take an unnecessary risk was not in her character, and she hesitated long before she married me. We were not suited to each other, she said, without going into details. I see now that I did not attach sufficient importance to certain convictions of hers to which she clung as other folk cherish their prejudices. She thought that the life of a professor was precarious, and she suspected an element of instability, not to say a lack of moral fibre, in writers, musicians and other artists. She was a thorough and conscientious housekeeper, devoted to her children; she deserved and should have had a husband of her own conservative pattern, a fixture in the landscape and a member of the Republican Party. Because of a pious interest in the past, such as any scholar has, I sincerely believed myself conservative, not foreseeing at that time on how many questions, as I grew older, I should have to take the liberal or radical side. I married Pauline, therefore, with hopes of a lifelong happiness for us both. She was a strong personality, and she had unusual talent in the decorative arts; indeed she might have been herself an artist, if she had cared for such a career. Her skill in bookbinding, for example, is considerable, and she was at her best out of doors and close to nature. She is an expert gardener, whether with vegetables or with flowers, she loves horses and she rides well. And—what was most attractive to me—she has a beautiful speaking voice, and a natural sense for words. I did her an injustice by trying to impose on her my ideal of her, which was of course a synthesis of the ideals toward which I myself was groping.

Our first home was at 415 West One Hundred Fifteenth Street. There, on March 5, 1911, our son Graham was born, and my life passed into an entirely new phase. I had always been fond of children, within reason, and in theory at least I was prepared to feel a special interest in my own offspring, but when I heard Graham's first cry and held him in my arms, I was beyond expectation a changed man. Perhaps no one foresees what the parental relation will do to him; few try to describe the experience. I began to live chiefly in the future, planning for the boy as I had never planned for myself. The center of my attention was pushed forward.

Fortunately for Graham, not all my immediate plans for him worked out; he would have been overwhelmed. He hadn't been a completely separate individual thirty minutes before I was investigating his aptitude for music and taking the first steps to cultivate it. His bassinet had been carried into the living room for momentary relief of the strain on our small apartment, and after watching him as he squirmed and wriggled in his wrappings and coverings, a package of amazing energy, I played the piano softly. At once he stopped wriggling. He was sensitive to music! Or he may have been stunned. I tried a few chords to see which register appealed to him. He was most quiet—or stunned—when I played in the octave below middle C.

Though it was only March I began to think where to take him the following summer. This question became more acute each year until I bought a country place on my return from the war. Graham's first summer was spent at Redding, Connecticut, his second, at least a small part of it, at Sparta, New Jersey, his third in Ridgefield, Connecticut, his fourth at New Canaan, his fifth at Mannesquan, New Jersey, and the following summers, including the year 1919, at New Canaan. We liked that little town and thought of settling there. In 1917 I leased a house for three years, having discovered that it would cost me less to take it for a long period and furnish it myself than to rent it furnished for three months. When at last I went to France with the Army, my little family gave up the New York apartment they had at the time and stayed in New Canaan.

I give these statistics here, though the chronology of my story is interrupted. The point is that with the responsibility of making my own home, I fell at once into the way of life that makes Americans different from most other people; I was setting up a hearth and supplying my child with a miscellany of early memories in different places. During the winter too we were more or less nomadic. After a year at 415 West One Hundred Fifteenth Street, we spent a few months in One Hundred Thirteenth Street, and then found an apartment at 609 West One Hundred Fifteenth Street, where my parents by this time were living. Our apartment was on the same floor as Father's, and Graham ran in and out of both homes, to the delight of his grandparents, his aunts, and his uncle, who all spoiled him.

At 609 my daughter Anna was born on January 29, 1916. In the autumn of 1919, after the war, we returned from the rented home in New Canaan to 39 Claremont Avenue, where we remained for eight years, until we left New York for a new home at Wilton, Connecticut, the only spot of earth and the only roof which I ever owned. I expected to leave Nod Way Farm on the Wilton hilltop only when I should be carried to my grave, and I believed the houses I there built or enlarged were for my children and my children's children.

The years at 39 Claremont Avenue were singularly happy. I was as near to my Columbia office and classrooms as I had been to my duties in Amherst. Large though the University was, our community was compact. The other tenants at 39 were faculty friends, Graham attended Horace Mann a few blocks away, and all could walk to our daily appointments. My library was growing fast and I had shelves for many books at home, but for still more in my Hamilton Hall study, and if the book I needed any evening was there rather than at home, I took a short walk and got it.

At 39 Claremont Avenue, Dr. William Henry McCastline, the University medical officer, had the apartment next us, and Harold Jacoby, Professor of Astronomy, the apartment across the hall. Walter Henry Hall, choirmaster and organist at the University Chapel, lived on the floor below, and Professor Woodbridge two or three floors above. These friends and their families were the kindest of neighbors, never too busy for a word with Anna and Graham, who would have given them a high mark as intelligent grownups.

Professor Herbert Gardner Lord, of the Philosophy department, belongs in memory with this close circle, though his residence was several blocks away. Like Woodbridge he was an Amherst graduate and loved to talk about that place, and since his office in Hamilton Hall was next door to mine, I saw him from hour to hour, and we had much in common. He and Mrs. Lord more than most human beings had the zest of life in them; wherever they came they radiated happiness. Many an otherwise dull faculty meeting was saved at least in part by Professor Jacoby's trenchant common sense and Professor Lord's more subtle wit. Both men were endowed with intellectual honesty as well as the moral kind, and neither shut his eyes to the characteristic foibles of professors. I enjoyed their teasing even when I got in the line of their fire. I knew the deflation of my own professorial ego was wholesome, though incomplete.

2

In the prewar years, while I was still at 609 West One Hundred Fifteenth, we all became aware of increasing tension in the world and responded to it with a general speeding up of our serious activities. We hatched so many schemes for improving education and saving mankind that we bewildered ourselves. Perhaps because President Butler became active in the work of the Carnegie Endowment for International Peace, we were busy conditioning ourselves and our children to absorb pacifist ideals, soon to be kicked out of us again when the war broke and the

Government inaugurated the draft. But for a while we were full of good works and good thoughts. It was an exciting moment, an apparently fortunate one. The premonition of evil was not strong enough to be unpleasant.

Perhaps it was natural just then that there should be an almost frantic stressing of international cultural relations. Professors in quantity were exchanged between Europe and the United States, the ways and means being provided either by private philanthropy or through special lectureships in university budgets. The visiting professor became essential to the self-respect of any campus. His lectures, whether or not the students attended them, were reassuring. Like chapel services, they indicated that the academic heart was in the right place.

Two of our visiting professors taught me much, in different ways. Professor Gilbert Murray in April, 1912, came from Oxford to deliver the noble series of lectures which were published the following autumn under the title, *Four Stages of Greek Religion*. I never heard true scholarship articulate itself with more charm, and the incomparable presentation quite as much as the stimulating ideas captured me completely. I saw the Greek world in a new light, and found a new philosophy with which to face the contemporary dilemma. No doubt Professor Murray, as he composed these lectures, was better informed than most of us about the threat to European peace, and the austere loyalty to spiritual ideals, even to lost ideals, which he attributed to ancient Greece may have been a self-portrait. In their published form these lectures continue to persuade and inspire, and since the condition of the world is no better now than when they were first delivered, the need of them is as great as ever.

A few months after we had been listening to Gilbert Murray, Joseph Schick came from Munich, as Kaiser Wilhelm Professor to lecture on English language and literature. The contrast between the two visitors was ominous. Joseph Schick may have had a fairly clear notion of what was threatening the world, but he hadn't an ounce of philosophy in him, and if he had been a Prussian officer he couldn't have believed more firmly that Germany was on top and would remain there. His manners were military rather than cultured, but under all the saluting and heel-clicking the little man had a friendly disposition, and I enjoyed the frequent talks I had with him.

Gilbert Murray represented British scholarship at its best and I'm afraid Schick represented German literary scholarship at its best. His erudition was frightening, his capacity for work was incredible, but he didn't know where he was going, and he was entirely at ease with this central ignorance. He respected facts but he declined to ask what they meant. When he arrived in New York he had just published the first volume of what was to be an encyclopedic study of Hamlet in legend, in poetry, in art, and in music. I have the title page before me now: *Corpus Hamleticum. Hamlet in Sage und Dictum, Kunst und Musik. I Band. Das Glückskind mit dem Todesbrief. Orientalische Fassungen.* The story of the fortunate prince and the death warrant occurs universally in folklore, and in this volume Schick assembled the oriental versions of it, in the original languages, with translations. The excuse for this enormous and costly labor was the fact that, in *Hamlet,* the wicked King, his uncle, sends two courtiers to England with the Prince; they carry a letter to the English King, asking as a special favor to cut Hamlet's head off at sight. Hamlet finds the letter, erases his name and substitutes that of the courtiers, and the King of England executes them, out of good will to a fellow monarch.

Imagine a thick volume of over four hundred pages containing nothing but this episode in the ancient languages of India and China, in Turkish and Kurdish, in the Ethiopian dialects, the Egyptian and the Abyssinian, and in many another speech which few Western scholars could recognize either by eye or ear. It had taken Schick half a lifetime to learn all these alphabets and tongues sufficiently to study the versions, and he had traveled over much of the globe to find the type with which to print the texts. I asked what would come in *Band* II and *Band* III. More versions of the Prince and the Warrant, this time probably from Finland, Iceland, and Russia.

"Professor Schick," said I, "what is the significance of this very slight incident, that it must be tracked down so relentlessly?"

"It is a question," said Schick, "which I shall consider in my final volume, after I have collected every version in the world."

"But, my dear Professor Schick, I may die of old age before you finish the job. Will you not confide in me now the meaning of your work? I promise not to tell anybody."

He was shocked. "The meaning of my work? As a scholar I cannot now pretend to know what it is! Scientists can interpret a phenomenon only when they have all the facts which pertain to it."

The war put an end to Schick's uninterpreted labors. His English wife went back to England, he shouldered a rifle and went into the trenches, and the *Corpus Hamleticum, I Band, Orientalische Fassungen,* waits to this day for those other *Band*s to overtake it, especially the final *Band,* which was to contain the meaning of them all. *Band* I has by itself the significance of a work of art. It is printed in the blackest and costliest of inks, on the thickest and whitest of paper. The flyleaf of my copy contains half a dozen words in Schick's copperplate hand: "To Professor Erskine in friendly remembrance. J. Schick."

3

When Graham was four I entered him in the primary grade at the Riverdale Country School. Later he went to Horace Mann, but I wanted him to begin in the school which occupied the property once owned by my grandfather, where my father had lived in childhood. The school bus took Graham up in the morning and brought him back in the afternoon, but the first day I took him up myself, more moved perhaps than he by the occasion. I was meditating profound fatherly advice.

As we entered the school grounds a boy, twice the size of Graham, ran toward us to see what Riverdale had got now. Graham, to show his manners in the great world, took off his cap and held out his hand. The larger boy, overwhelmed, turned and fled. To distract Graham from his confusion, I plunged into my speech, approximately as follows:

"Son, now that you're going to school, you must get used to teachers. I hope you won't be afraid of them. Don't be afraid of anything on earth. Don't be afraid of me. I've known boys to cheat in their recitations or copy an answer in an examination, only because they were afraid of the teacher, or of their parents. Nothing is worth so much to you as self-respect and peace of mind, and a cheat has neither. I'll never criticize you harshly for a low mark. I believe you have a good brain, but I shan't remind you where you got the sort of brain you have. But if ever you do something wrong and get into a jam, come straight to me and tell the whole story, and I'll help you out and see you through. That's my bargain with you for life."

I don't think I've ever failed him, and I know he has never failed me.

In kindergarten he showed at once aptitudes and tastes which foretold his choice of a profession. When he and his classmates were to make miniature puppet theatres and write plays for them, he rather fell down on the play but constructed his theatre out of a wooden packing-box with the ingenuity of a born architectural engineer. And if he was less happy in his puppet drama, the reason may have been that he preferred man-size plays which he could act in.

For his own birthday party he composed an ambitious tragedy. The setting was one end of our living room; the audience, chiefly his school-mates, would occupy the other end. There were three characters, an extremely young Prince, played by himself, and his aged parents, played by Pauline and me. We learned our parts (they were extremely short), and rehearsed till even the much-demanding playwright was satisfied. I believe the performance impressed the audience, but at the conclusion Graham looked hot and puzzled, and by the time he was put to bed that night he was running a temperature. He had become an actor, a ham. The play was divided into five acts, each containing two speeches for the Prince and one apiece for the King and Queen. Graham's fever came from wrestling with the problem how to make his moment on the stage last longer. "I should have put more talk in it," he told us—"so the next act would not come so soon."

What wonderful years those were, with the excitement of watching him grow! In our New Canaan garden one year I set out some young tomato plants, and every morning Graham and I inspected them, until the day when they weren't there. Some creature had cropped them all off, close to the ground. "There must be a rabbit around," said I. "A little poison well sprinkled will take care of him!"

Graham said nothing, but his face took on an unhealthy flush, and by noon he had a high fever. At four o'clock I was sitting with him in the porch hammock, telling the stories which usually were his favorites. All at once he straightened up, with his large eyes. "Dad, the rabbit who spoiled the tomato plants—was me! I did some weeding, to help you, but I weeded too much."

I gave him a hug and said there were plenty more plants, and as soon as he felt like it he and I could walk up the street, get some, and set them out before night. In ten minutes his fever was gone.

His moral courage increased with the years until it became rather magnificent. After he had shifted over to Horace Mann, he went one afternoon to the office of the headmaster, Charles Tillinghast. "Well, Graham, what can I do for you?" "Mr. Tillinghast, I was awful in math today, and I'd rather hear now what you're going to do about it, than worry all night."

When he was almost five he decided that life would be fuller if he had a sister. His mother, listening to his evening prayers, heard the following addition to his reportory: "Please, God, send me a baby sister. Send her to 609 West One Hundred Fifteenth Street. Send clothes with her. And help me to be a good boy. Amen."

When the sister arrived in the course of time, Graham was repeatedly reminded by his aunts and his father that he was now a big boy, and must not depend on us longer for small services, like buttoning up his shirt front, which he was capable of doing for himself. Little Sister would share the attention which until now he had monopolized. The first time his mother was able to hear his evening prayers, they closed with an expression of gratitude: "Thank you, God, for that baby sister. She came. Amen."

"Graham, you didn't say, 'Help me to be a good boy.'"

"No, mother, I shan't ask that any more."

"Don't you wish to be a good boy?"

"Of course I do. But I find I begin to depend on God!"

Five years later, when he was ten, he and Anna were having a terrific quarrel at one end of the apartment while I was trying to write in the other end. I went to the door of the battlefield, and gazed at them reproachfully. Anna subsided, rebuked, but Graham sprang to his feet, looked me in the eye, one man to another, and shook his fist toward heaven. "Dad, to think I prayed for it!"

To a large extent I was his childhood companion. It took long for Anna to learn such easy terms with me, since I left for France soon after she was born, and when I came back at the end of the war, our acquaintance had to start all over again. But we made up for lost time. Today she knows me a little better than I know myself. But she has a broad mind and a sense of humor.

CHAPTER XXI

Experiments in Teaching

I

WHEN I came from Amherst to Columbia, Professor Odell had the oversight of the freshman English course. He generously offered to keep on and let me be responsible for the sophomores, but knowing that he was a little tired of elementary work, I took the first-year boys off his hands, and for a while at least he breathed freely. I taught one section of the class. Steeves, Ristine, Boyesen and Carl Van Doren taught the other sections.

There are two schools of thought among teachers of English composition. One hopes to correct bad habits in grammar, spelling, punctuation and the minor aspects of style, and refrains resolutely from any ambition to accomplish more; the other school aims at teaching the pupils to write. The difference goes far deeper than the innocent might suppose. Accuracy in spelling and good judgment in punctuation may be acquired and repeatedly demonstrated without having an idea, but it is impossible to be a writer or to learn the first principles of the art unless you have something to say. Great writers for centuries have remarked on the sadistic inclination of college instructors to put the composition courses in the early years, before the empty heads of the students have had a chance to fill up in history or philosophy classes. Milton in his letter to Samuel Hartlib on education in general, complains bitterly of this "preposterous exaction, forcing the empty wits of children to compose themes, verses and orations, which are the acts of ripest judgment and the final work of a head filled, by long reading and observing, with elegant maxims and copious invention. These are not matters to be wrung from poor striplings like blood out of the nose."

Milton refers to bad teaching in Latin and Greek, English composition in his day being learned not in school but from good example at home. But what he says of forcing empty wits to compose themes holds true whether the themes are in Latin or English. A theme is something that no sane person not under duress would ever compose. Those who have something to say write essays or articles or books, but not themes. In those colleges and schools where theme writing still persists the teacher is blood brother to the legendary music pedagogue who urged his pupil, "Play me something and give me plenty of mistakes to correct, so I can teach you to be an artist."

George Rice Carpenter had taught us in his daily theme course how to gather material, but he was exceptional. The Columbia freshman in 1909 or 1910 had been trained to manufacture themes of various kinds, narrative, descriptive, expository, but not how to draw ideas from daily experience; they seemed to think anything learned in their other studies would be unwelcome in their English compositions.

My associates and I plotted to make them think and excite them about the controversies then stirring in the world. With the advice of the university historians, philosophers and political scientists we collected a series of famous essays on ethical, social and political subjects, two essays on opposite sides of each question. The students read the essays and for a week discussed them in class. There was sure to be violent difference of opinion, to which we, the instructors, added fuel when we reasonably could, praising the argument when it had any degree of form or logic, and restraining it when it threatened to run wild.

At the end of the week each boy was yearning to express convictions for which the debate had provided not enough time; he went home and wrote his weekly essay—and in most cases, what an essay! The boys forgot to be literary, and learned to write as sincere human beings. So far as I could see, there was no falling off in spelling or punctuation. The teachers were as much interested as the students, since only live issues were argued, and the teachers of philosophy, logic, political science and economics smiled on us for bringing English instruction into some relation with life. But I have reason to remember that our elders in the English department presented us with no bouquets. Ashley Thorndike, our executive officer, began to have doubts of my eligibility for a place among serious scholars, and Dr. Odell, affectionate friend as he has always been, showed signs of distress or consternation whenever he felt it his duty to ask how the freshmen were coming on.

In 1913, Steeves and Ristine edited the dynamic material of the course, under the title *Representative Essays in Modern Thought*. By this time the results of freshman reading and debate began to show in the sophomore year, and Dr. Odell told me with disarming frankness that perhaps I should teach older students and he would take the freshmen again, since he believed he understood extreme youth better than I. So we changed, and I continued my effort to teach youth to think, merely starting a year later. How long the representative essays were still read and discussed in freshman year, I cannot now recall, but since they were all classics, masterpieces in their kind, perhaps Dr. Odell felt better about them when he could guide the debate or dilute it. I was not worried. A large group of boys had made the acquaintance of a few vigorous ideas, and an idea once let loose is hard to stop or recall.

2

The instruction which I gave in the College dealt with the Elizabethan age and the seventeenth century. In alternate years I was to lecture on nineteenth century authors, but I preferred the Elizabethan writers and after a while confined myself to them. I did not pause to ask why. I was extremely fond of Scott and Byron, of Dickens and Thackeray, of Blake, Keats and Shelley, of Tennyson and Browning. Ruskin had my warm admiration for his social vision, and my equally warm contempt for his art criticism. And Carlyle, in spite of his hysterical ranting, stirred me most of the time. But all these men, great though I knew they were, seemed not to belong to the England of their times. I found it hard to explain them as an expression of the country and the society into which they were born, but from which too many of them were soon exiled.

In the Elizabethan period, on the other hand, England was all of a piece. Elizabethan literature expresses Elizabethan England complete, without expurgation or apology—great poetry upwelling from the greatest moment, the most democratic moment of a great people. I continued to study Elizabethan literature and teach it because I was convinced it contains the genuinely modern ideals of those who speak our language, the most contemporary ideals, the most immediate. My feelings can be interpreted another way. I was interested in Frank Dobie's suggestion, in *A Texan in England,* that the spirit of the eighteenth century persists in the old country, and the Elizabethan in the new. That particular contrast I should not know how to sustain, but certainly the Elizabethans faced many problems which are ours in America today, and we should be glad to face them in the same way. Thirty years ago my Columbia students and I had the same feeling of kinship with the Elizabethans.

This literature class was quite large, some sixty or seventy. The boys elected the course in a hospitable optimism, giving me a hand on my return to Alma Mater, and our relations started off in a cordial atmosphere. I put into practice the new idea acquired just before leaving Amherst, that the students should criticize an author or a book before I spoke on the subject. At frequent intervals, therefore, there was a paper of some length, and at first I had nothing to complain of, but at last in one batch of essays I found two which had been cribbed.

Columbia had the usual punishment for such offenses, suspension or expulsion, which hurt the sinner without necessarily encouraging virtue in those who were innocent or not yet caught. After much thought and heart-searching I determined on a plan which if it worked might have a remarkable effect, but if it failed would leave me far out on a limb.

I went into class the next day, put my books and notes on the desk, took out my watch and laid it on top of the books, distributed the papers, handing back all of them, including the two which had been produced by dishonest work. I had given both the same mark, and I saw the guilty authors clutch them eagerly, glance inside for my comments, and look at each other with what I interpreted as a smile of relief. Then I walked back to my desk, made some suggestions about the essays as a whole, with a comment on their high quality in general.

"But in one respect," I added, "I didn't enjoy reading them. Two were cribbed."

The startled class looked up.

"Perhaps I should report this to the Dean, but I have no intention of doing so. I became a teacher because I love literature and like to exchange ideas with others who love it. I'm neither a detective of crime nor an executioner. Two of you fellows are not honest and not gentlemen, but you are safe from me. Unfortunately I am not safe from you. I don't enjoy the feeling that if I must go to my study for another book, I'd better pick up my watch and put it in my pocket. I'd be sorry to ask for your promise not to steal it. So it's no longer a pleasure to associate with you. I'm sorry not to meet this class again, but you understand why I say goodbye."

I took my watch and my books and walked out of the classroom. Ten minutes later, as I sat in my study wondering what would happen next, two penitent boys came in and apologized. If they hadn't, I wouldn't have met that class again. What the University would have done to me, I don't know. Of course I was neglecting to enforce an established rule. But at Amherst I had seen boys expelled for cheating, and once the cheating had been done in a class of mine, and there seemed to be no compensating benefit for a good deal of wretchedness.

At the next scheduled session the whole class were waiting outside the door to see if I would come. They took their places in silence, with obvious curiosity. I told them I had received two apologies, the incident was closed, and I was confident that nothing like it would recur. I had no more trouble.

For each of the advance reports on the reading, my habit was to suggest half a dozen topics, any one of which I hoped would be fruitful. To encourage independence of thought, I always added at the end of the list these words: "Or any topic of your own choice." I cannot now recall that any student ever availed himself of this large freedom. In order to propose a topic of his own, a boy would have to do some strenuous thinking, and his choice might not satisfy the teacher. It was better to accept one of Teacher's topics and play safe. But this criticism of my former students is not so severe as it may sound. I flatter myself that the topics I suggested were pretty good.

3

In the Graduate School I offered a course on the influence of American writers in Europe. Most of us know something of European influence on America, yet Fenimore Cooper, Edgar Allan Poe, Emerson, and Walt Whitman, affected Continental writing in many ways, and from this point of view they had not been studied adequately. My graduate students each investigated some aspect of the problem, and though most of them were handicapped by an inadequate command of languages, they turned up fascinating material, which together with the results of my own search made me decide to write a book on the subject. I ordered for the University all available translations, but knowing the quantity of material which could be got at only in the old country, I planned to spend a year abroad. Since my first sabbatical would come in 1916, I expected to go then. But when the time came, Europe was not to be visited for merely literary purposes, and after the war I was interested in other things. On my return from France I abandoned the course, and the book was never finished.

Yet while engaged in this study I came on many facts and insights for which I am grateful. The quite different, even conflicting, aspects of Emerson's genius appealed simultaneously to the mystics of Belgium and to the hard realists, even to the militarists, of Germany. Poe and Fenimore Cooper, who in the English original had no style to speak of, acquired in translation quite unexpected stylistic excellences. The fame of all Americans abroad depended upon the skill of their first translators. Poe owes his high place in European esteem to more than his own genius. His prose tales were translated by Charles Baudelaire, his poems by Stéphane Mallarmé, both of them writers of great distinction. Baudelaire, along with his other gifts, had the intellectual equipment to appreciate not only Poe's romantic mysticism but also the logic by which the enigmas in his mystery tales were solved. His translations improved Poe's style and at the same time did justice to his mind.

But in Germany the translators of Poe attended less to the ratiocination in his stories and more to their gothic qualities, the elements of ghostliness or horror. The German Poe is the writer not of philosophical fancies nor of detective stories but of weird thrillers or shockers. In order to make this limited appeal, the German translators in some cases omit entirely the passages of brilliant reasoning and stress rather the effect the problem makes on us so long as it is unsolved. In *The Gold Bug*, for example, the death's-head drawn on the pirate parchment, and the skull in the tree, become high points in the tale, but the working out of the cryptogram is slighted, as of little importance.

Most Spanish translations of Poe derive from France, and most Italian translations from Germany. Europe therefore is acquainted with two varieties of the American writer, both differing slightly from the original —a fact which deters few European critics from asserting, among their other eternal truths, that Poe is correctly understood in the old world but not in the new.

As my preoccupation with American authors became known, I was frequently asked to speak on commemorative occasions. On November

15 I made the address at the opening of the Edgar Allan Poe Cottage in the Bronx, and a few of my most devoted students, Lloyd Morris the leading spirit among them, came up and stood in a chill wind while I poured forth my eloquence to a handful of children and passers-by who paused to learn what the noise was about.

At the Metropolitan Museum of Art it was then the custom to hold a brief ceremony on January 19, Poe's birthday, in front of the bas-relief portrait by Richard Hamilton Park, and in January, 1914 I was one of the two speakers, the other being a representative of the French consulate. Fortunately, as it seemed to me, he came first, reading from a script that had been carefully prepared for him. He referred with pardonable pride to the share France had had in gaining for the American a recognition abroad which his own countrymen even now failed to accord him. It was the superb poet, Charles Baudelaire, faithful representative of the French respect for artistic genius, who taught the world, including the United States, to value at its true worth the subtle mind, the sensitive heart, the unfathomable soul, of Edgar Allan Poe.

I too had prepared a few remarks, but hearing this familiar half-truth, I plunged in and eased my mind impromptu. I agreed that the reputation of Poe owed much to Charles Baudelaire. I, a lover of France, would be one of the first to acknowledge the service Baudelaire rendered to American literature. Fortunately it would not be necessary to remind that audience of the circumstances in which Baudelaire had translated Poe, since poets in France received the recognition they deserved. But the gentleman from the consulate would perhaps permit me to say that a wise poet might prefer lukewarm attention to close and passionate study. Poe's countrymen neglected him, but they never tried, as Baudelaire's countrymen did, to put him in jail.

The gentleman from the consulate grinned, but as no one else knew what I was talking about, my sarcasms were wasted.

If I had not been engaged in a study of American literature as it fared in Europe I should not have known that everywhere throughout the old continent, even in civilized France, there are some good people who match or·outdo the New England Puritans in narrow-mindedness and in their readiness to persecute. Baudelaire is a poet too austere, too profound in thought and too exquisite in workmanship to be a threat against public morals, but he was arrested for publishing Fleurs du mal, and ordered to remove from the volume five or six poems which the magistrate could not approve, having read into them his own thoughts. The picture of the judge acquiring an acquaintance with poetry in order to find smut, would have been a subject for Daumier.

To the investigation of American literature abroad I owe other by-products, more worth while. From the lists of books annually published in Spain I learned the violent contrasts in Spanish tastes and loyalties. The most conservative books had a cordial reception, but so apparently had the most radical. The Spanish character has room in it for wide extremes. Had I been clever at reading the prophetic signs, I should have guessed before the war what would happen to Spain later on.

Two French poets, Charles Vildrac and Georges Duhamel, caught my attention not only by their verses but by their *Notes sur la technique poétique,* written together. Much of their work was in Walt Whitman's spirit, though their style was not his. Georges Duhamel became one of the most eloquent French voices during the war, in such books as *La vie des martyrs* and *Civilisation*. The Belgian, Emile Verhaeren, was producing his magnificent poetry in Whitman's manner and spirit, and Leon Bazalgette in France had already translated *Leaves of Grass* and written his biography of Walt.

Bazalgette was the only one of these writers whom I knew personally, at first through correspondence, after the war in a few meetings. He was the type of Frenchman who supplied backbone to the resistance movement in the second war. Continuous service in the first one undermined his constitution; when I met him in 1925, he seemed to me frail and already marked for death. But he was an intense spirit, passionately concerned about social justice and democracy. He could not, like Walt, loaf and invite his soul; he was a fiery crusader. Were he still alive, he would be found in the most advanced groups, a man of rare culture, spending himself to bring into existence a united and friendly world.

CHAPTER XXII

St. Agnes and St. Agatha

I

MY MEMORIES of St. Agnes' Chapel date from the autumn of 1900. Even during my six Amherst years my people kept me informed of the changes in this large parish, a chapel of Old Trinity, so that when I returned to Columbia in 1909 I had been continuously in touch with the congregation and the successive rectors for many years.

While we were still active in Grace Church, Union Hill, Father, as I have said, used to bring the choirboys to services at St. Agnes' to hear the singing, which like everything about the new chapel was of unusual distinction. The West Side promised in 1890 to rival New York's fashionable East Side, and there was a migration of wealth and social pretension to West Seventy-second Street, West End Avenue, and Riverside Drive. Knowing that Columbia College would soon expand into a university of unpredictable dimensions on near-by Morningside, the Vestry of Trinity Parish decided to build a chapel in Ninety-second Street, between Amsterdam and Columbus avenues. It was an elaborate and costly building, and its purpose was frankly to serve a congregation of the rich and the socially important. St. Agnes' was to be the West Side Grace Church.

This snobbish intention rested on the premise that those who could afford to do so would always live in the most desirable section of the town. The beauty of Riverside Drive, the gorgeous outlook on the river, the elevation above sea level, and the wholesomeness of the air, were appreciated. At least for a while. The West Side is still the best part of New York to live in, but fashion, prompted more or less by real estate operators, has swung now to the East River, where the apartment-dwellers have the vision not of sunsets but of sunrises, if they get up early enough.

St. Agnes' Chapel was dedicated in September, 1892. For fifty years, until it was closed and the building torn down in 1942, there was a gradual but steady deterioration of its fortunes. Members of the congregation had a tendency to move to the East Side or to the suburbs, and though they might retain their affiliation with the parish, they could not attend services in West Ninety-second Street. Those who moved into the West Side to replace them were in few instances Protestants or Episcopalians.

The first vicar in charge of the work was Dr. Edward Augustus Bradley. He came to Grace Church, Union Hill, several times to preach during Lent, and since he was a good musician and a kind gentleman, he always had something to say about our boy choir and about my organ playing. Of course I admired him.

His successor at St. Agnes' was Charles Tyler Olmsted, vicar from 1899 to 1902, when he was elected to the bishopric of Central New York. Dr. Olmsted was at the Chapel when my people first went there in the autumn of 1900, and I remember him as a man of wide learning, of unusual modesty, and of courtly but slightly austere manners. Even at that time, forty-five years ago, he seemed to survive from a remote era. Since it was under his administration that I first became familiar with the parochial work at St. Agnes', I think of him as presiding over the congregation when it was at its peak in numbers and in affluence. But perhaps it was during Dr. Bradley's administration that the Chapel had its golden years.

After Dr. Olmsted, Dr. William T. Manning was vicar from 1903 to 1908, when he became Rector of Trinity Parish. Under his vigorous leadership the work at St. Agnes' took on new life and showed again its early promise. Dr. Manning has distinguished himself in so many ways as bishop of New York that it may seem impertinent even to suggest my conviction that he is greatest as a parish priest, and that his revival of the work at St. Agnes', though temporary, was his most remarkable achievement. In his bishopric, as at St. Agnes', he has demonstrated his rare capacity for organization and administration, but he could hardly exhibit on the larger scene those qualities of heart which in the intimate work of St. Agnes' seemed to equal his grasp of affairs. Realizing fully that the West Side was changing, he accepted the change less as a problem than as an opportunity. If those who attended St. Agnes' were less wealthy than the earlier congregation, he saw the possibility of more immediate and more human service. Those were his lovable years, and I believe his happiest.

He was succeeded as vicar by Dr. W. W. Bellinger, who had been Rector of Grace Church, Utica. Dr. Olmsted also had come to St. Agnes' from the same Utica church, and perhaps Dr. Bellinger believed that he was following the same general pattern of usefulness and recognition and ultimate promotion. He certainly did not realize that the improvement which Dr. Manning had made in the condition of St. Agnes' could be only temporary. The changes in the neighborhood continued. The pleasant, private homes disappeared, to be replaced by cheap apartments not much better than tenements, and the former residents moved to the suburbs. Until his death in 1943 at an advanced age, Dr. Bellinger put up a gallant fight, but he could not make headway against the city's shift in population. He became saddened and somewhat embittered by the lack of support which he received from the mother parish of Old Trinity. Perhaps he expected that Dr. Manning, the new rector, knowing West Side conditions, would use the wealth of the Trinity Corporation to improve the residential properties around the chapel and modernize the parish house to cope adequately with new social problems within the neighborhood. But whatever Dr. Manning's own disposition may have been, the members of the Vestry which elected him rector hadn't a spark of missionary enterprise in them, and since they knew that the West Side was becoming what city planners call a blighted area, they made up their mind to invest no more in St. Agnes', but at the proper moment to close the work and tear down the building.

I speak of this with personal knowledge of the facts. On the death of Dean Van Amringe in 1916 I was elected to the Trinity Vestry, and because of affection for Dr. Manning, and knowing that my nomination had come from him, I accepted the honor. Since the beginning of Columbia University in the original King's College, some member of the faculty had always sat on the Trinity Vestry, and in a sense I was chosen to succeed Van Am, but I thought Dr. Manning wanted me because I knew St. Agnes' and its needs. I soon found out that the distinguished and estimable gentlemen then on the Vestry were practically with no exception living in an obsolete past. They cherished the memory of a time when all good Episcopalians in New York, like Philip Hone the diarist, were ornaments to Society with a capital "S," and possessed good bank accounts. They did not object to a sermon which reminded them that they, like other men, were miserable sinners, but they preferred not to hear too much about the poor, and they would have been quite content to let their beloved parish continue to derive some of its income from unsanitary tenements. They thought the building of a chapel on the West side had proved a business error. They wanted to take the loss and balance the books.

So far as the tenements were concerned, Dr. Manning was too strong for them. He engaged a competent social worker, one of the most severe critics of old Trinity tenements, to put all those buildings in proper condition. The cost of this operation was very great. Dr. Manning then persuaded the Vestry to sell all the tenements, pointing out that Trinity must choose between ministering to its people and deriving its income from them. Real estate holdings of Trinity have since then been largely office buildings and warehouses.

Whether this was the right way to solve the problem, I am not sure, but the Vestry did not make it for Dr. Manning an easy way, and I admire his courage for doing what he could. In the matter of St. Agnes' and other chapels the outcome was far less creditable. I belonged to a minority of the Vestry, who held that parishioners from the chapel congregations were as important as those who attended Old Trinity or St. Paul's, perhaps more important, since they could speak for new conditions and perhaps for new social ideals. My elder colleagues tolerated me with great courtesy, but I converted no one to the minority point of view, and gradually I perceived that it would be easier for Dr. Manning to proceed with the construction of the vast and costly Cathedral of St. John the Divine than to convert a chapel, built for the very rich, into a missionary church for the less privileged.

My long acquaintance with St. Agnes', therefore, taught me an unpleasant truth, and I fear it is a truth, about the denomination in which I was born and brought up. The Episcopal Church, like the Church of England from which it derives, is too often undemocratic, a class church, a door to heaven for the special use of those on top. My father, my mother, and my great-uncle, Bishop Scarborough, did not think of it so. The little parish at Union Hill was not, and is not now, conducted on any such principle, but it is nevertheless true that the major Episcopal churches in New York and in other large cities build chapels some blocks away for the use of the poorer members of their congregation. I don't say that the experience of my grandfather, when the verger put him out of the English church in Glasgow, is repeated in New York City, but I do say that snobbishness is still a strong ingredient in the disposition and the conduct of the Episcopal Church. It gives as yet no great illustration of democracy in religion; in this respect it falls far behind the Methodists and the Catholics.

2

In the early days of its history Trinity Parish had been instrumental in founding and endowing schools for children of its parishioners. At first there was provision for girls as well as boys, but during most of the nineteenth century the girls dropped out, the boys continuing in what was known as Trinity School. In 1806 a corporation was formed, theoretically distinct from Trinity Parish, to carry on this educational work and to expand it when funds should be available. The Trustees of the Protestant Episcopal Public School, as the new corporation was called, continued in fact to be, for the most part, members of the Trinity Vestry and clergy from the Trinity staff. The finances of school and parish have always been kept separate, but otherwise their association has continued very close. When I joined the Trinity Vestry, therefore, it was practically inevitable that I should be elected to the Board of the school.

In 1898 Dean Van Amringe persuaded the School Corporation to resume the education of girls, and under his enthusiastic leadership St. Agatha School began its brilliant career. For headmistress he personally selected Miss Emma G. Sebring, and no choice could have been more farsighted. Miss Sebring herself had remarkable judgment of character and ability, and the teachers whom she engaged were outstanding in their various fields. For more than a quarter of a century St. Agatha held its place among the foremost girls' schools of the country, scoring a high record always in college entrance examinations, and accumulating year by year a large group of alumnae who distinguished themselves in every walk of life.

Because my mother admired Miss Sebring, my sister Rhoda entered St. Agatha while the school was still young, just installed in its new building at Eighty-sixth Street and West End Avenue. Through Rhoda, I became one of Miss Sebring's most ardent supporters in all her educational policies even before I was a member of the school Board. She was a true educator, a remarkable teacher and an equally remarkable administrator, progressive by temperament, preferring to set the pace rather than follow, but thorough and sensible. While she was headmistress the Trustees of the school had an easy time. We went to Board meetings knowing that the soft-spoken lady, whose manners were of an old-fashioned gentleness, would have every detail of the school business well in hand, would report with conciseness and clarity, and would suggest new ideas so reasonable and so carefully thought out that we would adopt them without change.

The headmaster of the boys' school, Trinity, was the Reverend Dr. Lawrence Thomas Cole, formerly President of St. Stephens College, Annandale. Dr. Cole, delightful friend, was a schoolmaster in the English tradition, who managed to get honest work from his boys without severe threats of discipline, and who made the ideals of scholarship coincide easily with practical living and humane culture. Dr. Cole and Miss Sebring were distinct in temperament, he decidedly conservative, she invariably reaching forward to an attractive new idea, but since they both were first-rate educators, they had much in common. Both excelled in gathering fine teachers and in preparing and administering wise budgets. To both of them I am indebted for many ideas about education which I should be glad to think were original with me.

3

I shall speak again of the Trinity Vestry and of my colleagues on the Trustee Board of Trinity School and St. Agatha. Both bodies went through gradual changes during the twenty-five years I knew them, and the change in both cases represented progress toward a modern point of view and a broadening of vision. It is essential to the truth of my story that I should describe the Vestry as I first knew it in rather unflattering terms. Had they conceived of themselves as having religious and humanitarian responsibilities, rather than as custodians of a large property, the record of Trinity Parish might have been one of expanding rather than of narrowing activity.

Yet the gentlemen with outdated ideas whom I here criticize severely were otherwise admirable and important citizens, and I remember them as picturesque characters. The Clerk of the Vestry when I joined it was David B. Ogden, distinguished lawyer, of an old New York family. His

grandfather had been Fenimore Cooper's lawyer, and he was much interested in a letter which I possess from the novelist to the earlier David
Ogden reporting on the successful sale of real estate at Cooperstown.

Mr. Ogden looked like a lawyer in a Dickens novel or a Daumier
drawing. He really had a rich temperament and much quiet humor, but
in his professional moments he concealed these qualities beneath an im-
penetrable surface of studied correctness. When he rose in Vestry meetings to read the minutes or to discuss a proposal, he would lean forward
slightly in continuous readiness to bow to the Court. His heavy watch
chain would dangle below his waist. He would make little gestures with
one hand and with the other he would push back the tail of his coat.
What he said I have forgotten.

In complete contrast to him was Stuyvesant Fish, a massive figure of
heroic proportions, with keen and at times terrifying eyes. I remember
Mr. Fish vividly for his opinions about Prohibition. He did not approve
of it, and since I wrote and spoke against it at every opportunity, he
noticed me as a youngster in whom there were elements of promise. The
last time I saw him was only a few weeks before his death. He was not
looking well, but he came away from the Vestry meeting with me for
the express purpose of passing a few more vigorous judgments on the
Prohibitionists. In his boyhood, he said, he went to church Sunday mornings with the rest of the family, and before the noonday dinner he went
into the garden at his father's request to gather mint for the drinks. He
revered his father's memory and associated mint juleps with churchgoing and other proper Sunday observances. His last remark to me I
recall word for word. "Erskine, I'm damned if I'll go to heaven by an act
of Congress."

Judge Vernon M. Davis, a friend of my father and classmate of my
Uncle Charles, attended St. Agnes' Chapel and was one of the wisest and
most farseeing members of the Board. The monthly meetings were then
held in the Vestry room of Trinity Chapel in Twenty-fifth Street, sometimes in the evening, quite as often in the afternoon. In the latter case
the judge liked to walk up Fifth Avenue for exercise, always stopping at
Maillard's for tea. If the walk took off any weight, I am sure Maillard's
put it back. He had always a fatherly interest in me, and we took the
walk and the tea together. I should describe him as one of the more
liberal-minded members of the Board, with very humane instincts and a
sense of humor, but he preserved a manner quite as professional as Mr.

Ogden's. It was difficult for most people to get at the quality of both men.

William Barclay Parsons, chairman of the Trustee Board of Columbia University, was a dominating personality, an ultraconservative on most questions, a hard-hitting man of action. Whenever our body got into motion, it was probably General Parsons who set it going. Egerton L. Winthrop, Jr., one of Mr. Ogden's successors as Clerk of the Vestry, belonged to the New York in which Edith Wharton grew up. He fascinated me by the richness of his literary culture and by his beautiful old-fashioned manners. I had no occasion to know him well, as I knew General Parsons and Judge Vernon Davis, but I am grateful to him for providing me with a glimpse of old New York at its best.

CHAPTER XXIII

"The Moral Obligation to be Intelligent"

I

I DATE my career as a writer from the early months of 1913. At a Faculty Club lunch table one day I heard some remarks about the difference between modern and old-fashioned virtues, and I asked what the old-fashioned virtues were. Before the discussion drifted to other themes, it prompted in me some further questioning, and that evening at my desk I started to make a list of what I should consider virtues, without pausing to distinguish between old-fashioned and modern. Of course I put down courage and honesty, and well up with them at the head of the list, intelligence. But is intelligence a virtue? I thought it was, and I knew that it was so reckoned in Greek literature and French, but to my dismay I realized that it had a more humble place in Anglo-Saxon ethics. English literature always esteemed strong character as a virtue, but held intelligence in such suspicion that most writers assigned it to bad men, and few readers were shocked to find Lucifer, in *Paradise Lost,* carrying off the intellectual honors, and Iago, in the play *Othello,* saying practically all the wise things which we now care to quote. Further illustrations can be taken from other poets and dramatists and from all the great novelists of English literature. In our tradition, to be intelligent, to be aware of the essential facts of human nature and of the universe in which we live, to train our minds and to use them wisely, has not been a moral obligation. Rather, we find it possible to admire extremely stupid men if only they have pluck or are good to their parents. The heroes of "The Charge of the Light Brigade" can be praised for riding to their death

228

even though they knew that someone had blundered, and the sacrifice was unnecessary.

These ideas so possessed or disturbed me, that in a very few days I had written an essay called "The Moral Obligation to be Intelligent." When I read it to Professor Woodbridge and Professor Keyser, they felt I had scored a point, and when shortly afterward I was invited back to Amherst to make a Phi Beta Kappa address, I expanded and polished my new idea and spread it before my old friends. They too thought well of it, and Dr. Alexander Meiklejohn, the successor to President Harris, told me it fitted into his educational theories. On my return to New York, Professor Keyser suggested that I let him submit the essay to the *Hibbert Journal,* of which he was an associate editor. Dr. L. P. Jacks, the editor-in-chief, liked the piece and published it in October of the same year.

When I say that my writing began with this essay, I mean that for the first time I felt I was saying in a way of my own something that was essential in me, in my thought and character. Perhaps I was impressed also with the kind of attention the essay received. Though the *Hibbert Journal* was not a popular magazine, and though it appeared in England, I began to hear about it from readers on both sides of the Atlantic. It gave occasion to the London *Times* to write an editorial on me which, though it was caustic at my expense, gave me pleasure. The editorial writer had obviously been stimulated by my ideas; in fact, slightly over-stimulated. In his excitement he misquoted me. He was angered by the statement that "Perhaps the Old World has got into a kind of prison, and what is needed is a key to the lock." I wrote to the London *Times* at once, correcting the error. I had said nothing about the Old World; when I wrote the essay and when I read it as a Phi Beta Kappa address, I was speaking not to Englishmen nor to Europeans, but to my fellow countrymen in America, and the mangled sentence actually read, "Perhaps the *modern* world has got into a kind of prison." The London *Times* published my letter on the editorial page, with the simple amend, *Mea culpa.*

In September, 1914, I received a letter from Frederick S. Hoppin, president of Duffield & Company, saying that he had just read my essay in the *Hibbert Journal* of almost a year before, and he wished to ask about the possibility of his publishing it as a book, of course with the addition of some other essays to fill out. This was the first time that any publisher had approached me about any prose writing of my own, and such invitations as I had received to get out a volume of my verse had always carried the implication that I should pay for it. Fred Hoppin still teases me about the letter I wrote him, making plain my reluctance to invest a cent in one of my own books. He brought out the volume under the title of the essay in 1915, slightly enlarged in successive editions. It still is one of the books which win me a friend now and then—or at times a hostile critic.

2

At the Amherst Phi Beta Kappa, Professor B. K. Emerson, the geologist, who presided that evening, applauded my praise of intelligence as a moral obligation. He was supported by Professor Olds, the mathematician, and by Harry deForest Smith, the Professor of Greek, but Professor George Churchill, my former colleague in the English department, a devoted Wordsworthian, expressed the wish that I would now write something "on the other side," in praise of the moral obligation to develop character. He was not alone in being wary of the emphasis on intelligence. My Amherst friends divided on this subject in approximately the proportion of three to one. Most of them, as I said, thought well of my address, but a minority, however polite in their compliments, had some reservations. The fact that President Meiklejohn liked what I said, did not help me. Though he had been at Amherst only a short time, already he and his faculty were feeling out the points in which they disagreed, lining up for the battle royal which terminated a few years later in his resignation.

I met him for the first time on this Phi Beta Kappa occasion, and the impression he made is still a vivid memory. He was a man of great charm; in fact, it's a wonder that a personality so winning should have aroused antagonism on so many occasions. Our acquaintance ripened fast, chiefly through his kind wish to call me back to Amherst, and by his persistence after I had declined his invitation. When he first asked me, I said that since I had only just gone back to Columbia, and since I enjoyed my work there, I had no reason for pulling up stakes again. He found pleasant excuses to revive the question several times, until at the end of the spring term in 1915 he telephoned from Amherst imploring me, at whatever inconvenience, to catch the Springfield train in the next hour, and come to Amherst at once. I replied that if he wanted to talk any more about my returning to Amherst, I wouldn't come. He answered me that he had the problem of the whole English department on his hands, and needed some advice at once. Because of fondness for Amherst, and I suppose because of curiosity to learn what he was up to, I caught the train, reached his house in time for dinner, and after the meal went with him to his study. His first words indicated his good will, also his talent for getting into trouble. In spite of the assurance over the telephone, he began, "Tell me some reasons why you should not return to Amherst."

"Tell me some," I countered, "why I should leave Columbia!"

He had theories about logic and about the proper way to teach it. He liked discourse to proceed by definitions and discussion, and his students acquired the knack of discussing glibly without much information. When he asked for some reasons why I shouldn't accept his offer, I felt as though my mind were being trained, I was irritated at having wasted a day, and I jumped at the chance to implement the discussion with some facts.

"Mr. Meiklejohn, I am happy at Columbia. I know the people there, and they know me. You, on the other hand, really don't know me at all. If you invite me back, it must be because my former colleagues speak well of me."

He protested courteously.

"Mr. Meiklejohn, before you came here, you never heard of me in your life."

He admitted that was so.

"Well," I added, "it's equally true that *I* had never heard of *you*. A college president, particularly at Amherst, has a formidable control over the fortunes of the faculty. This is your first attempt to gather a strong group of scholars and create a new type of college. Wouldn't it be a risk for me to leave Columbia before I know what you can do?"

When I told the incident to Professor Woodbridge next day in New York, he exclaimed, "Thank God it was one Scot insulting another!"

In spite of this passage at arms, Mr. Meiklejohn and I have always had a cordial if bristly friendship. Convinced at last that I intended to stay at Columbia, he asked me to suggest possibilities for his English department, and I named Stuart Sherman. Only a few months earlier Stuart had sent me an invitation, which I had declined, to become administrative head of the English department at the University of Illinois. Now he wrote me for information about the life at Amherst. It is clear now from his published correspondence that he was outgrowing the Illinois post where his reputation was made; he wanted to come East. I had my own plans for getting him to Columbia, but I clung to romantic memories of Amherst, and I thought that perhaps the beautiful Connecticut Valley might prove the setting for the scholarly meditation and the writing which were his ideal.

When he declined, I recommended Stark Young, an old student of Professor Trent's, and George Whicher, one of my first Amherst boys. They both accepted, and Mr. Meiklejohn had his English department off to a good start.

3

On the several visits to Amherst which I made during the years before we entered the war, I noticed a growing difference between the students there and at Columbia. Under Mr. Meiklejohn's training the Amherst boys developed a zest for debate for its own sake, a passion for questioning all statements, particularly those which were soundly based. The medieval art of disputation had come to life again on the Amherst hilltop. There was an undoubted sharpening of wits but not, as it seemed to me, much response to the real difficulties of the world. Though the Amherst boys were acquiring a technique of discussion, I was not sure that they cared deeply for any of the issues which they discussed. It would have been difficult, I thought, to interest them in great imaginative literature, expressing the human heart. They would understand satire more readily than poetry.

At Columbia the boys were not always so nimble witted, but they gave themselves with youthful intensity to grave causes. The war was more clearly foreshadowed in New York than in the Connecticut Valley, and the Morningside campus was full of political clubs, military-minded or pacifist, economic or sociological groups. They met frequently, and there must have been considerable discussion among the members, but the purpose in general was to gather information rather than to advocate a point of view. Men of eminence in public life accepted somewhat readily an invitation from any group of boys to address them; the importance of the younger generation was just then rated high.

One Saturday I was walking from my apartment at 39 Claremont Avenue to my office in Hamilton Hall. I had no classes that day, and expected to use the morning for clearing up my desk, but as I came into

South Court from the west side of the Library, I saw a cab stop directly in front of that building. In those days One Hundred Sixteenth Street had little traffic, and few of us in the neighborhood used cabs. A stoutish man got out and paid the driver. Evidently some eminent statesman about to call on President Butler! I looked more closely. The eminent statesman had indulged intemperately in the pleasures of the table. He was dangerously overweight. He wore a tail coat, with striped pants, and a broad-brimmed hat, and his uncut hair fell toward his shoulders or waved slightly in the breeze. I took him for a Southern senator come to pay his compliments to our University's Republican president. He moved across the Court toward the Alma Mater statue. It was William Jennings Bryan.

But he wasn't calling on President Butler. Not that morning. He turned around the east side of the Library and walked north to the upper floor of the unfinished Gymnasium, where there were several large rooms in which we held our public meetings. I followed him. It was a quiescent interval in Mr. Bryan's political career; he couldn't be campaigning; I doubted if Columbia had asked him to give a lecture on pacifism, his new cause, or on the older issue of free silver. He found his way to a room filled with boys, the undergraduate Politics Club. I followed and took a seat in the back row.

The president of the club was an outstanding youngster, Leon Fraser. He had prepared for college at Trinity School, and he had brought with him to Columbia a reputation for independence of character and intellectual capacity far beyond his years. In my classes I had come to know him as a quiet boy, original and thorough in anything he undertook, invariably illustrating the combination I liked to urge on my students, radical and brave ideas with conservative good manners.

I admired the poise with which Leon Fraser welcomed the famous man, and the diplomatic grace with which he introduced him to the audience. Since the club had for its purpose to study the art or science of politics, and in particular the international political trends of the moment, he, on behalf of the club, had asked Mr. Bryan to share with them some of the wisdom acquired from much experience in this large field.

Here everyone applauded and Mr. Bryan stepped forward. His fine voice was never in better condition. That morning he was the true orator, persuading and compelling by words, but also he was in a witty vein, and it wasn't by mere words that he delighted us. He expressed thanks for the cordial welcome, but regretted that Mr. Fraser had managed to avoid any statement or implication which would betray whether he was a Democrat or a Republican. It is easier to speak on the theme of politics, Mr. Bryan said, if you have some inkling in advance as to where your audience stands.

"Had I the time," he went on, "I could apply to Mr. Fraser an infallible test. I would repeat to him the parable of Dives and Lazarus; I would tell him how the rich man fared sumptuously every day, and how Lazarus, poor beggar, lived on the crumbs which fell from the rich man's table. Of course Mr. Fraser has heard this story before, but I would tell it to him again, hoping he would be sufficiently roused to make an instinctive comment. If he is a Democrat at heart, he would be embarrassed by the picture of the thoughtless rich man, unaware of the misery at his door, and of the poor man picking mere subsistence from the leavings, from the bones and crusts, the pushbacks of the banquet, destined for the garbage pail. But if Mr. Fraser," continued Bryan, "were at heart a Republican, he might exclaim, 'Since there are beggars in this world, and always have been, how fortunate that there are also tables from which crumbs do fall!' "

The effect on the student audience was electric, and so it was on me. Leon Fraser smiled quietly, and after the room settled down, Mr. Bryan went on with his talk, exploding several more bombs, but none so effective as the first.

CHAPTER XXIV

Lafcadio Hearn

I

ON MY return to Columbia in 1909, Professor Trent introduced me to the Authors Club, which then had its fortnightly meetings in the tower of Carnegie Hall. The club had been formed by Mark Twain, William D. Howells, and other well-known writers. These founders, though still living, were no longer in New York City, and the club rooms rarely had a chance to welcome them.

In their place were younger writers and numerous publishers who were not likely to move from New York no matter what their age. There were also several examples of a literary type found only in a large town— the writer who combines creative work with some editorial job in a publishing house, writing for fun and editing for his daily bread. One of these writer-editors at the Authors Club was Frank Moore Colby, essayist and historian, a graduate of Columbia in 1883, Acting Professor of History at Amherst College in 1890, later a teacher of history and economics at Barnard College and at New York University. I knew his reputation as a scholar, I was familiar with two of his books, *Imaginary Obligations,* and *Constrained Attitudes,* and I liked him personally. When we first met at the Authors Club he was editing *The New International Year Book* for Dodd, Mead and Company. One morning I had from him a letter which brought an unexpected opportunity.

March 14, 1913

Professor John Erskine
  Department of Literature
    Columbia University
      New York City
MY DEAR MR. ERSKINE:
  Dodd, Mead & Company have a manuscript here of Lafcadio Hearn's Lectures on Literature, delivered while he was in Japan, together with some essays and fugitive papers, and wish the advice of someone as to its value as
literary material. I have suggested you and I should be very much obliged if
you would let them know whether you are willing to examine the manuscript.
I tried to reach you by telephone just now but you were not in. If you are
willing to look over the manuscript will you please telephone Mr. E. H. Dodd
tomorrow morning and make an appointment with him. If not, will you drop
me a line or 'phone me, mentioning someone at Columbia who might do it?

Yours very truly,

F. M. COLBY

  I telephoned Mr. E. H. Dodd that I would look at the Hearn manuscript. The following letter from Mr. Dodd a day or so later described
the material more fully.

March 17, 1913

Prof. John Erskine
  Columbia University
DEAR SIR:
  I am sending you, by bearer, the Lafcadio Hearn manuscript. May I ask
you to be exceedingly careful of this manuscript as it is the only one in this
country. It is made up of lectures delivered by Lafcadio Hearn at the University of Tokyo and taken down with care by a Japanese pupil. The material
sent you is about 400,000 words, and you will see by the list enclosed that
there is another lot of about 350,000 words to come.
  The main questions which we wish to determine are,
  (1) Whether this is sound and interesting material and whether it approxi-
mates in value the other Hearn books.
  (2) Whether it needs revision and editing. This we believe is true and we
presume that it can be done.
  (3) How should it be presented, as a History of the English Literature and
other volumes of fugitive essays on literary subjects, or in some other form?
  (4) Would it not be advisable, in addition to the revision of the text, to
have it annotated and prefaced by some man of high reputation?
  Doubtless other points will suggest themselves to you, but these seem to be
the principal ones. I hope after your examination that you will be able to talk
the matter over with me.

Yours very truly,

EDW. H. DODD

When what Mr. Dodd called the manuscript arrived, it turned out to be an enormous bundle of typescript, Hearn's lectures on English and European literature which his pupils had taken down word for word, not one pupil but several, and had copied out in their own eccentric typing as a gift for Lafcadio Hearn's widow. Since there were several copies of each lecture, an error in one could usually be corrected from the others. Or if all the students had misunderstood Hearn simultaneously, the muddled passage could be omitted. What remained would be the only existing record of what Hearn told his Japanese students at the University of Tokyo between 1896 and 1902.

He lectured slowly, so that the young men in his class could take down every word. Since he spoke without notes, or at least left no notes after his death, the quality of his teaching had seemed impossible to estimate. But from the typescripts given to Mrs. Hearn by his students it was clear that he had rendered a new service to literature in a series of masterly criticisms. He had tried to explain the occidental mind to the oriental, and in the attempt had interpreted the West to itself. It seemed to me, reading his lectures for the first time, that he equaled the best of English critics, and perhaps surpassed them all.

Mrs. Hearn showed the typescripts to Pay Director Mitchell Mac-Donald, U.S.N., Hearn's literary executor, who brought them to the United States, expecting to get them published as a textbook for schools, for the benefit of Hearn's bereaved family. But the typescripts were queer looking, the copies contained slips of many kinds, all natural enough—words misunderstood, dates not clearly heard. Worst of all, there was no apparent system in the program of lectures, no chronological sequence, no attempt to cover the whole field of English literature. Before Mr. MacDonald showed the bulky material to Dodd, Mead and Company he had given other publishers a glance at it, and all of them had backed away in consternation. Such hope as Mr. Dodd now had was probably inspired by Frank Colby, but not even he was too confident.

Every evening for a week I waded through the material, fascinated, but a little sorry for the editor who might eventually have to straighten out the inaccuracies and see the mended text through the press.

My advice to Mr. Dodd was to abandon all thought of converting Hearn's sensitive criticism into a textbook; rather, to publish the best of the essays in significant groups, choosing those which made the clearest attempt to interpret the West to the East. And I strongly urged the selection of an editor of national reputation. It cost me a pang to say this, since I wanted to do the editing myself.

For some time Mr. Dodd must have searched for a famous editor willing to carry out my ideas; I had almost forgotten about Lafcadio Hearn's lectures when the invitation came to prepare two large volumes of them, *Interpretations of Literature,* 1915. A third volume, *Appreciations of Poetry,* followed the next year, and a fourth, *Life and Literature,* in 1917. Portions of these volumes were reprinted in smaller and less costly format; *Talks to Writers,* 1920, *Books and Habits,* 1921, *Pre-Raphaelite and other Poets,* 1921.

In the course of this editing Pay Director MacDonald lunched or dined with me, usually at the Columbia Club, and we had long talks about Hearn, whose memory he idolized. He was fond of Japan and had invested his savings in a hotel there, thus putting himself in the way of becoming Hearn's friend and benefactor. When Lafcadio arrived in Japan, MacDonald entertained him, partly because he had a highly developed veneration for all literary folk, whether he knew them or not, and partly because Hearn at the moment was out of funds and in the midst of an unnecessary feud with his publisher. For some weeks Mr. MacDonald maintained Hearn, until the mail boat arrived with a letter from the publisher containing a royalty check. Hearn sent it back, explaining to MacDonald that he would have no more relations with such people. The helpful Pay Director used his influence with the postal authorities of the port to rescue Hearn's royalty check from the mail bag, and organize his affairs on a sound basis. Later he encouraged him to undertake the teaching in Japan for which he is still remembered in that country.

2

The editing of Hearn's lectures brought me several unlooked-for benefits. The acquaintance with Pay Director MacDonald was not the least. He was a likeable character, a practical man who by travel in all parts of the globe had acquired a humane and cosmopolitan outlook. He neither exaggerated nor belittled the virtues of the Japanese, just as he neither overlooked nor emphasized Hearn's whimsical frailties. He loved human beings, and he worshiped literary talent more, perhaps, than anyone else I have met. He would have been grateful to heaven, he told me, for the ability to write. His cheerful humor was infectious, and his courtly manner set him apart in all companies. He usually wore an overcoat with a long cape and somehow managed to look like Colonel Newcome, though his comfortably rounded figure permitted the resemblance to be only a suggestion. His loyal eye watched over the Hearn literary properties and the Hearn family until his death in the earthquake of 1923.

A number of Hearn's Japanese students became professors of English in schools or universities, and to perfect themselves in the language they would visit Great Britain, stopping on the way for impressions of the United States. They remembered their teacher with pious loyalty, and since I had edited lectures which they had heard from his lips, they invariably paid me a ceremonial call. They would introduce themselves in advance by letter, and then would come to my home for tea and a good talk. Their command of English was adequate and their knowledge of Western literature amazing, but they were most remarkable, as it seemed to me, for their understanding of human nature. I should have said then that the leading Japanese characteristics were wit, and humaneness, and a sense of justice. When I asked my visitors whether Lafcadio Hearn had portrayed their people correctly, they invariably said he had not. "He had romantic opinion of us." But I failed to get from them their own conception of themselves. Instead, they shared with me their shrewd insights into human nature in general.

I asked one visitor to tell me something about Japanese politics, about the various political parties and how they functioned. He stared for a few moments toward the carpet, as though at a loss. When he looked up I caught the hint of a smile. "Japanese politics perhaps like American." That didn't help me much, but he had not yet said all. After more carpet-study he went on: "Young men have ideals; old men have experience; in between, middle-aged have power."

CHAPTER XXV

World War

I

IN THE summer of 1914 I rented a cottage at Manasquan, New Jersey, where Graham passed most of his time on the beach, digging in the sand or paddling in the water. We expected to enjoy a long and quiet vacation, varied only by visits from my father, my sisters, my brother. I had plenty of writing to do. In the spring the university had decided to celebrate the seven hundredth year of Roger Bacon's birth by staging an elaborate pageant which would dramatize his life, exhibit his influence, and illustrate the age in which he lived. The suggestion of the pageant came from Professor John J. Coss, of the Philosophy department, who planned the scenario and gathered most of the material. I wrote the text, Claggett Wilson, of the department of Fine Arts, Teachers College, designed the costumes and prepared illustrations for the book of the pageant, published by the Columbia University Press in September, 1914. Mr. La Mont A. Warner and Mr. Robert Gray, of Teachers College, designed posters, banners, and stage plans, and Professor Walter Henry Hall selected and arranged incidental music. Through the early part of the summer John Coss came to Manasquan, week ends, to enjoy cool swims and discuss our plans. The performances were to take place in the Gymnasium, with actors from the faculty and the student body, helped out by the University orchestra and chorus. The project was ambitious, but our confidence was great; the Trustees appropriated funds to meet the expense, the text was finished in good time, the book was printed, we were ready to go into rehearsal.

But these cheerful preparations had a strange accompaniment in the newspapers. From Europe came disquieting rumors that Austria would take vengeance for the assassination of Archduke Francis Ferdinand in June, that Kaiser Wilhelm would support Austria, then that Russia would resent a German move. We tried to believe it couldn't happen but when Austria did declare war on Serbia at the end of July, Germany invaded France, Russia invaded Germany, and the war was on, as everyone found out somewhat later. At first there was a fantastic optimism that the fighting would not be serious. Americans traveling in Europe had their vacations spoiled and their return delayed by the outbreak, but when they got home at last they gave reassuring interviews, as though Providence had whispered the future in their ear. Nicholas Murray Butler announced there would be only a short war, since no country could afford a long one. A few people, like my father, who could remember 1870, feared for France. The Germans, he said, would never attack unless they believed that they were ready, and that France was not. We soon knew which prophets were right. The British expeditionary force landed in France, August 16, the Germans bombarded Louvain, August 25, Hindenberg and Ludendorff defeated the Russians at Tannenberg, August 26-31, and the war seemed lost for the Allies until the French made their unforgettable stand at the Marne, September 6-10.

At Columbia the Bacon pageant was quickly forgotten. President Butler called the University Council together, copies of the text which Coss and I had prepared with so much pleasure, were distributed as a mournful souvenir, and we turned our back on the medieval philosopher. For a while all thinking was confused to an extent now hard to realize. Had the United States been invaded, like Belgium and France, or threatened with invasion, like England, we should have been, like them, quick to oppose the aggressor. But the events occurred too fast for the majority of us to understand them, we found it hard to throw overboard our traditional respect and friendship for Germany, and harder still to abandon the faith in diplomacy and arbitration which our intellectuals had for years been planting in us. My instinctive sympathy was with Great Britain, from which my people came, with France, whose culture I adored, and with Belgium, whose neutrality had been cynically violated. Yet I was shocked and puzzled to discover that war haters like President Butler —he had been in Europe that very summer spreading the pure Carnegie doctrine of international arbitration—now wanted us to get into the conflict up to the hilt.

It was still more shocking to find that the war madness had suddenly transformed a few lifelong friends of France and England into unqualified supporters of anything which Germany did or might do. The world had gone insane. My old friend and teacher, Professor Trent, whose weakness as a scholar was that he knew little German, who said in my hearing more than once that he would never set foot in Germany if it weren't to see the great Italian and Spanish paintings in the museums—Professor Trent began to brush up his German grammar and consult his German dictionary so that he could read the news, even Woodrow Wilson's messages and speeches, as translated in the German press of New York City, the original text as given in the *Times* being somehow less authoritative.

We all, I suppose, made sincere attempts to steady down and go on with our work. Major George Haven Putnam, famous publisher and one of the venerated patriarchs of the Authors Club, undertook to bring out the *Cambridge History of American Literature,* in coöperation with the press of the English university, and he asked Professor Trent to take charge of the planning and editing, with associates of his own selection. The Major had no use for Germanophiles, but he was a true friend of Trent's and justly estimated his scholarship; I believe he proposed this task in the hope that it would divert a fine man from the war, restore his balance, and revive his sense of humor.

Professor Trent asked Carl Van Doren and me to join him, and we three agreed quickly on Stuart Sherman as a fourth editor, not only because of the strength he would add to our team, but because he would represent the Midwest. Trent came from the South. We might have added a fifth editor from the Far West, if the Pacific Coast had not been so very far. Even Sherman was at too great a distance. Our collaboration was by mail; in other words, we three at Columbia made the urgent decisions and asked Sherman's opinion afterward.

The two contributors whom I most wanted, we could not have. Because Woodberry's resignation from Columbia had left a tragic scar, and he seemed to be withdrawing from creative or critical work of any kind, I told Professor Trent we must have him in this book at all costs, or it might be thought we left him out at the suggestion of Brander Matthews or President Butler, who had been on the other side of the quarrel. Trent told me to invite Woodberry before anyone else, and let him write his own contract. This I did at once, but Woodberry was reluctant to tie himself down to serious work just then; the war had his complete attention, and he wanted to go abroad, to get into the struggle or at least to get near it. We persuaded him at last to do the chapter on James Russell Lowell, who had befriended him when he was a student in Harvard. "I owe Lowell something," he wrote when he returned the contract, signed. But in the end he backed out, pleading ill health.

I wanted Leon Bazalgette to do the chapter on Whitman, and he signed the contract enthusiastically. He was to write in French, and I was to translate him. But he was called up by the army, though he was not young, and he spent the four war years in the service. When the *Cambridge History* came out in the autumn of 1917, we had to explain, in the last paragraph of the preface, why Woodberry and Bazalgette were absent.

In the course of time I had my own encounter with the war madness. When President Wilson sent home the German ambassador, Dr. Butler called an assembly of the whole University in the Gymnasium, and asked me to be one of three speakers, with Professor Giddings and himself. The invitation came over the telephone, and knowing the mood that Professor Giddings was in, I warned Dr. Butler that I was not a fire-eater. "Say whatever you wish," he replied.

He spoke first, with his usual clarity and dignity, calling on us to play our part in the crisis. Giddings, at that moment only a little more reasonable than a mad bull, urged us to get into the fighting and kill as many Germans as we could; the sooner we annihilated them, the pleasanter the world would be. I spoke last. Ignoring the Giddings war whoops I said I had nothing to add to what had been addressed to us as patriots, but we were not mere patriots—we were scholars, and the scholar's duty in wartime is to preserve the civilization he is defending. I recalled Gaston Paris, who during the Franco-Prussian War put down his musket for a few hours in order to deliver his inaugural lecture at the Collège de France. His subject was *The Song of Roland,* the national epic, and he had the courage to point out for the first time the German origin of the poem. Having honored himself by this service to scholarship, he went back to the trenches.

Half an hour after the meeting when I was hanging up my hat in the Faculty Club, Hans Zinsser, old friend from *Morningside* days, came at me with eyes blazing. "John, you ought to be interned! A speech like that might lose us this war! You should have told the students to hate the Germans, to kill them! Giddings had it right. That nonsense of yours is dangerous!"

2

Between the outbreak of the war in 1914 and the American entry into it in 1917, I managed to do considerable writing, and I launched an educational experiment at Columbia which bore fruit when the war was over. Besides the essays in *The Moral Obligation to be Intelligent*, I wrote a number of poems, most of them published in *The Century Magazine*, the new editor of which, Robert Underwood Johnson, continued Mr. Gilder's hospitality to me. When the war broke out I was busy with ideas for the theatre, only one of which came to anything. Under the influence of the Irish theatre and perhaps of Maeterlinck, I wrote a very short piece, a one-scene rather than a one-act play, called *Hearts Enduring*, which still has performances by amateur actors. I feel ungracious to add that they usually do it very badly.

3

On January 25, 1916, when Graham was five years old, my father died of pneumonia, after a brief illness. For many months he had been in unusual health and spirits, and during the Christmas season of 1915 he and Mother had entertained relatives and old friends with a frequency and a zest which reminded their children of the bright Weehawken years. At one of the last of these parties he was asked to sing, and I played his accompaniments. Though he was in his sixty-sixth year his voice was still well placed, flexible and true. Time must have taken some of its quality, but I persuaded myself, as I listened, that youth was still in it. Afterward we liked to recall that evening—the beloved voice, his tall straight frame, the poise of his massive head, the glow in his face, his snowwhite hair. A fortnight later he came home feeling tired, in no time at all was dangerously ill, within a week was dead.

The shock was terrible. What he counted for in my life I have tried to say. What his death would mean to Mother, we feared to know. Her own health had for some time been failing, and in her despair, tempered by brief and vain hopes, during Father's last hours, she became mentally confused. When Father had lost consciousness and almost ceased to breathe, the doctor sent her from the bedside, to rest in another room.

But as soon as she realized he was gone, she insisted on returning to him, and upheld by our arms, managed to walk with surprisingly firm steps. At sight of him lying majestic and serene, she tore herself free and threw her arms about him with a passionate cry, "Oh, my boy! My dear boy!" Death itself inspired less awe than this lightning flash of the early love which had not grown old.

In my apartment across the hall Pauline kept herself as calm as possible through these unhappy days; she expected a second child, and was near her time. In the night of January 29, the day of Father's burial, she gave birth to my daughter Anna, who brought us happiness, then and always. Mother had sustained the ordeal of the funeral with fortitude, but when she reached home she was on the verge of collapse. My sisters, my brother and I spent the evening trying to cheer or at least to distract her. At ten I went home, but an hour later was back again, with news that the doctor and the nurse had been sent for. The crisis roused all the old war horse in Mother; she took Graham to spend the night with her, she thought of comforts for Pauline, she told Sister what preparations to make, against the chance that the baby might arrive before the doctor or the nurse. This is what almost happened. Everybody arrived together, and delight in her granddaughter restored Mother to sanity.

I had that strange feeling which comes with the loss of a parent, that I had been moved up a generation, into an outpost of some kind; this exposed sensation was complete four years later when Mother died, but it weighed upon me heavily from the moment Father left us.

A few weeks after Father's death the faculty of the College of Physicians and Surgeons invited the University Council, of which I was a member, to visit the medical school and see some of the latest research projects. What interested me most were the experiments which had to do with the heart, that frail wobbly organ on which life depends. For hours I had watched the doctors trying to keep Father's poor overtaxed heart fluttering a little longer, and now as I saw clearly the precarious delicacy of the essential blood pump, I wondered how any of us lasted a single day. From the rooms where the heart experiments were demonstrated we passed to the research in bacteriology, where Hans Zinsser showed us the work on which he was engaged. To reach his laboratory we crossed a bridge above the engine room, over giant dynamos, swift and silent, generating power for the whole plant. I was overwhelmed by the ironic contrast between the apparently loose and eccentric pulsings of the heart and the precise inexorable revolutions of the man-made machines. Yet man cannot make a heart, nor mend one—as I had learned.

In the very next week my boy Graham fell ill of pneumonia, and again I watched the disease approach its climax, repeating in the child step by step the progress toward danger which had been too much for the grown man. But the young heart won through, and Graham came back to us.

4

In the summer of 1916 I taught classes in English composition and gave some public lectures at Chautauqua, New York. Percy Boynton, who directed the Summer School there, had several times before invited me to visit the place, but I had always declined, partly because the camp-meeting reputation of Chautauqua scared me off. Knowing Percy, I wondered what he was doing there, and I agreed to go for three weeks in 1916 only because he told me his service was about to end, and this would be my last chance to see him at work.

But I soon became a warm admirer of the Chautauqua Institution, not precisely as it was but as it might be. Located magnificently on the shore of a large lake, with opportunities in plenty for sports and outdoor life, and with symphonic concerts and solo recitals almost daily, varied with public lectures by famous speakers, Chautauqua overcame my prejudice at once. During the next quarter century its rich offerings were further enriched and enlarged; to the orchestral concerts in the amphitheatre were added a season of opera in Norton Hall, the new theatre, and the music school, directed by Ernest Hutcheson, attracted more and more students of piano, violin and voice. My impression is that the Summer School, apart from music, flourished particularly under Percy Boynton, as music prospered under Arthur Bestor, his successor. The students in my 1916 classes compared favorably with those who attended university summer schools, and the public lectures in the amphitheatre set forth points of view more liberal and progressive than most academic platforms in those days made room for.

Two of the chief lecturers were Earl Barnes, a winning personality who ruffled the placid and cautious by advancing ideals of social justice which now are a little old fashioned; and Scott Nearing, like Barnes an attractive character but resembling Thomas Jefferson, in that he approved of revolutions for their own sake, as symptoms of health and vitality. I doubt if Barnes ever wanted to stir up a row; perhaps Nearing would have been concerned about his waning powers if he didn't start one. Both men were popular in the Chautauqua community, composed though it was chiefly of tradition-lovers.

The camp-meeting atmosphere still hung over the place. Those of us who leaned toward the arts and liberalism, remained on good terms with the local missionaries and saints by ignoring their more aggressive pieties, and they in turn shut their eyes to our errors and frailties and to the fun we got out of them. The Chautauqua of those days was surrounded by a fence, supposedly impassible, and on Sundays the gates were shut; no one could enter paradise or leave it on the Lord's Day. Upon what theological principle or religious insight the rule was based, I never learned, but I can certify that it caused no inconvenience. Pioneering temperaments discovered which pickets in the long fence could be removed and replaced, and the secret was generously shared with those who could make wise use of it.

At the first faculty meeting, held in the open air behind the amphitheatre, the business transacted was even less pressing than is usual in such gatherings; I entirely forget the ostensible point of it. But on this occasion I met Ernest Hutcheson, master pianist and noble gentleman, who with his brilliant wife Irmgart asked me to join their table at Miss Grassy's boarding-house. We were a large and as it proved an exciting family, with Austin Conradi, Arthur Wilson and Eliza Woods, assistants to Ernest in his piano teaching, and the two Hutcheson boys, Arnold and Harold, then extremely young but unwilling to admit it.

CHAPTER XXVI

Propaganda and Pacifism

I

THE reluctance of the United States to enter the war was, as we now see, inevitable. Americans will always be slow to join any European war. Our population has been drawn from too many parts of Europe for us to enter a quarrel there without offending the ancestral pieties of some fellow Americans. Our friendship with Germany was traditional, and though the callous invasion of Belgium and France shocked us, we could not at first see what good would come from joining the fight. Our normal pacifism was increased rather than overcome by British propagandists who rang variations on the theme that by staying out we had lost our souls. The implication was that they, by going in promptly, had saved what souls they had, or had acquired new and superior ones. Most Americans resented the argument. It seemed that the superior souls had still something to learn in manners.

The position of England in the war seemed to us different from that of Belgium and France. Those countries were invaded and fighting for their lives, and so far as we could see they had provoked Germany by no menace or threat. But Britain had long resented the progress of German industry and commerce, and the increasing strength of the German Navy. German-Americans thought their old home had earned its place in the sun, and even Anglo-Americans had difficulty justifying the British disposition to block the natural growth of a strong people. If our detached attitude disappeared later, it was Germany herself who worked the change, by her U-boat attacks.

The French won the lion's share of American sympathy because the victory of the Marne made them the saviors of our civilization, and we recognized a just and primary claim.

We admired the dignity with which, when they needed us desperately, they presented their cause. They assumed that if we all knew their civilization at its best, we should be unwilling to let Germany destroy it. They sent to America their finest scholars, those who because of age were not under arms, and even some who had fought well, and were on leave. Their universities could spare them; the students were at the front. She sent us also some of her great artists, companies of actors, musicians—once more, those whose years excused them from military service. Marshal Joffre and Viviani, that gifted orator, visited Columbia University, and so did King Albert of Belgium and the heroic Cardinal Mercier. Professor Henri Bergson, Professor Gustave Lanson and Professor Fernand Baldensperger gave courses at the University. And always we had with us J. J. Jusserand, France's incomparable ambassador, erudite historian of English literature, who understood Anglo-Saxons and could interpret English and Americans to each other, and both to his own people.

With Lanson we had at Columbia René Galland, then a youthful authority on George Meredith, later a member of the English faculty at Grenoble University, still later at Bordeaux. He became the most intimate of my French friends, one of the best friends I ever had. His fineness of nature was extraordinary and his goodness is unforgettable. His career in scholarship and letters would have been brilliant, had it not been for a weakness of the lungs which sapped his strength even in his youth, and destroyed him in middle life. It was because of the lung threat that he was granted a temporary respite from army service, to interpret his country and its literature on this side the ocean.

He was, like Lanson, trained in the classical tradition, but unlike him he was also a sensitive and discriminating admirer of contemporary writers. From him I learned the importance, for example, of Charles Péguy. Though his home was in Limoges he had made his studies at the University of Lille, for the single reason that Auguste Angellier taught English there. Angellier, poet and critic, must have been a strong personality, with some of the earthy fire of Robert Burns, to whom he devoted an eloquent biography. From René, from his fellow student Hélène Boussinesq, from Emile Gourio and from Emile Legouis, I heard such warm tributes as convinced me that Angellier must have been one of the great teachers of his time. Since I happened to know his poems before René came to Columbia, our friendship began in a common admiration. French critics treat his verse with respect but with little more; they find England in him rather than France. I cannot measure their opinion, but if it is just, perhaps it is the English influence in him which attracts Anglo-Saxon readers.

Next to René Galland, in a less personal way, Professor Lanson made a lasting impression. Short, stocky, bearded, keen-eyed, with a mind as sharp as a razor, he was the ideal illustration of the intellectual giants then produced in numbers by the French university system. His rank as literary historian, by the side of Gaston Paris and Joseph Bedier, is conceded by scholars everywhere, but we who saw him daily in conditions distressing and difficult, had a special opportunity to appreciate his quality as a noble gentleman and a wise diplomat. His feelings about the war were intense. In the first days of it he had lost his only son. He foresaw correctly the troubles which waited for France even if the war were won, and the misery for all of us if it were lost. He must have been tortured by our slowness in taking sides, and the welter of pacifism at Columbia might well have caused him to despair; but his self-command was impeccable, and we never caught sight of him in any but a brave, courteous mood.

We liked to ask him questions about France, and since his patience was inexhaustible, Professor Wendell Bush organized what we called the *Cercle Lanson,* a small group who carried him off once a fortnight to the Brevoort, for dinner and talk. Bush, a gourmet of the first order, always planned the meal for us and at the proper hour collected the *Cercle* in his large car—Lanson, himself, Woodbridge, J. T. Shotwell, James Harvey Robinson and me.

Once when the talk was of various contemporary writers, I had the bad luck and the bad taste to ask Lanson what place he assigned to Romain Rolland, whose *Au-dessus de la mêlée* was anathema to patriotic Frenchmen, particularly to those touched by the war's sorrow. Stupidly I forgot for a moment the dead son.

Lanson answered quietly, with a wry smile. "Romain Rolland's place is in Switzerland."

Though embarrassed by my own maladroitness, I pushed on. "Forgive me, Professor Lanson, but I can't help feeling he played a noble part."

"Monsieur Erskine, will you permit me to feel that he played a part altogether too noble! It is the part which belongs to God Almighty—above the conflict!"

Woodbridge, speaking of the incident the next day, remarked that Rolland's unfortunate title might have been harmless at another season, but to recommend to those caught in the war such greatness of soul as might rise above all conflict, was like going into a hospital ward to lecture the patients on the advantages of good health.

In addition to the *Cercle Lanson,* Professor Bush organized theatre parties to support the visiting French companies, which were necessarily filled out with so many veteran or superannuated actors that only determined Francophiles could support them with enthusiasm. But Bush almost always had Yvette Guilbert in his theatre parties, and the authentic old genius furnished enough delight by the way she listened, to make up for any deficiencies on the stage. She knew by heart the antiquated pieces performed, and she took no pains to conceal her regret that war conditions or a shortsighted policy had made necessary an unrepresentative repertoire.

One evening I was seated next to her. The play was built on a venerable plot. The wealthy young hero had married a girl who brought no dowry but virtue and beauty, which as a matter of fact her husband thought quite enough, but a designing adventuress had her eye on him, and it looked for a while as though he would be pried loose against his will. At the end of the second act the critical scene was reached, the adventuress was about to enter and do her worst, and we knew she would have but a few minutes and must work fast.

In came the siren, fat and forty, not a hint of siren in her appearance! The Devil hadn't a chance, apparently. Yvette was disappointed. Half the house must have heard her exclamation, "O la-la!" But the adventuress was played by a great artist, who made us forget her age and her weight. At the end of the scene Yvette exclaimed with quiet satisfaction, "Not so bad, not so bad. *Pas si mal!*"

She herself was in this country to give her marvelous re-creations of medieval art. At the end of her career in Paris music halls she had become the unique interpreter of the folklore, the poetry and the sculpture of the Middle Ages. I doubt if any other propaganda for France was so immediately effective or so permanently influential.

2

The year René Galland came to us, Henry W. L. Dana joined the English department. Grandson of Longfellow and of Richard Henry Dana, Jr., he inherited and illustrated to an unusual degree the best of New England. Had there been no war, he might have stayed long at Columbia, where he made many friends. In his years of study abroad he had met René, and their acquaintance ripened in New York, to the credit of both, in spite of René's loyalty to France and Harry Dana's convinced but somewhat eccentric pacifism.

One New England trait was left out of his composition; he could not easily make up his mind. He believed—as who did not?—that all war is wrong, and that this one in particular was a tragedy for Western civilization. On the other hand he didn't wish to assist Germany, as he might be doing if he refused to go with the Allies. Beyond his intention, he made himself, or others made him, a symbol of pacifism at Columbia. The professional war-opposers of the moment, some of whom may have been working for Germany, to keep the United States neutral, saw the publicity value of the Dana-Longfellow name, and soon learned how to handle him.

We used to say that if you met him on the street, he going north and you south, you had only to take him affectionately by the arm, and he would turn and go your way, obliging gentleman that he always was. He might protest that his engagements were in the other direction, but if you were firm he would give in.

One afternoon, on some innocuous errand, he met a group bound for Hartford or some other Connecticut town to hold an antiwar rally. Having no reason for going with them and no intention to do so, Harry went. But Hartford didn't want an antiwar crusade, and as soon as a speaker advocated resistance to the draft, the police broke up the meeting. Harry's Columbia colleagues knew he must have been there, when a report came through that a nervous gentleman with Chesterfieldian manners was heard to ask the officers of the law, "Will you have the kindness to tell me whether I am or am not arrested?"

This and other incidents of the kind brought upon Dana the disapproval of the University Trustees. They made a mountain out of a molehill and until some time after the war their relations with the faculty as a whole were somewhat strained. Their patriotic impulses carried them much too far. They overstepped both their authority and their good sense, and in the end they made themselves ridiculous and had to back down. To maintain the purity of the University's allegiance, they dismissed Harry Dana, who made the action easy for them by his lack of decision. If he had fought back, I doubt if any court would have sustained them. They caught a tartar in Professor Cattell, whom they also dismissed, but he waited a few months till the war madness ebbed, and then successfully sued for back salary and pension. They dismissed Leon Fraser from the law faculty, he being an avowed pacifist, but when he was called to the colors he went cheerfully, made a stunning war record, and came out a major, with the Distinguished Service Medal, the French Legion of Honor, the Order of Leopold, Belgium, and other decorations. He was general counsel for the Dawes Plan, and president of the Bank for International Settlements. All this within three years of the day the Columbia Trustees bounced him. It was slightly embarrassing for some of them, who had to deal with him in the strategic posts to which he rapidly advanced. They forgot and forgave; they elected him to the Columbia Board, and he, having a sense of humor, sat down among the ultrapatriots who had, perhaps, kicked him upstairs. But I doubt if his firsthand acquaintance with war and international finance made him less of a pacifist than he had been.

It seemed to me that the Trustees, reacting from their impulsive mistakes, became a cautious, harmless and colorless body, and that the control of the University rested thereafter in the strong hands of President Butler. Yet I can understand why the Trustees lost their heads in excessive patriotism; they took the German threat seriously; every one who could, got into the fighting forces and went to the front; they had sons in Army or Navy, they knew what efforts the enemy was making to trip us up, and they considered all pacifist activity as a stab in the back. It is all plainer now than it was then.

At first I was against our getting into the war. I accepted the theory that the struggle would be brief, and I hoped the United States might play a civilized part by reconciling the combatants, and by binding up the wounds. Later the reports of German atrocities, especially the British report with which the honored and trusted name of Lord Bryce was associated, convinced me there was nothing for it but fighting. Still later, when we knew how much hysteria and propaganda went into these atrocity reports, and when we saw the jockeying of Europe's politicians at the Peace Conference, I lost faith in noble theories which have nothing to support them. Today, after a second world war, I hear the smooth doctrine that international quarrels must be settled either by reason or by force. The suggested choice is far too simple. For the present at least, I am convinced that quarrels can be settled by reason only if reason is backed up by force. I am opposed to scrapping our Army or Navy or Aviation.

The confusion in our thinking about the war is not pleasant to remember. Others were wiser than we. Pacifism is a peacetime theory, but once the war begins, every man must take sides. It is happiest, as it is most natural, to side with your own people, but if you can't side with them, you must fight them. In ordinary life we stand by our folks when they are in trouble, even though we believe they have made mistakes and brought the trouble on themselves. I should be sorry not to behave the same way toward my people in war. The conscientious objector may be morally brave or he may be a coward. I don't pretend to judge him, but for myself, I'd rather take sides. I admire the words of Alan Seeger, who wrote his mother not to think he hated the Kaiser or the German soldiers, but he had lived among the French, and they were his people, and a man must go with his kind.

I admire also the course which many Columbia colleagues were able to take. They went early to the war and played a man's part in it, with no preliminary doubts or self-questioning. Professor Jefferson B. Fletcher was an extraordinary example. The least combative of men, immersed in his studies of medieval literature, he was forty-nine years old when the war broke out, but he went over and enlisted in the French ambulance service, got into the worst of the fighting, transferred to the American Army when we came in, and continued his truly heroic record until the Armistice. Back home, modest as usual, he opened his books and resumed his studies. I never heard him speak of pacifism or patriotism; certainly he never spoke of his exploits or his medals. He simply did what for him was necessary to do.

I remember and admire the point of view expressed by a student, Edwin Korkus, who took his college degree in 1917 and promptly enlisted. When his training was finished and he was about to leave for France, he looked me up in Hamilton Hall, to say goodbye. I can see him now in his trim uniform, with a captain's insignia on his shoulders. He seemed, like the rest of the boys, far too precious to lose.

"Why are you going?" I asked.

"I guess, because I might never be satisfied with my reasons for staying home."

As the war came on, most of the students were pacifists, yet most of them joined up and did well. I wonder now whether there are any confirmed militarists or genuine pacifists. Even deep convictions may alter with circumstances. When Russia became an ally of Germany, our so-called liberals wanted us not to fight the Nazis. When Germany invaded Russia, our liberals wanted the Nazis wiped off the earth. Liberals and pacifists like to choose their wars. Or perhaps it's nearer the truth to say that every man has his favorite war. My favorite was the First World War. I felt, I still can feel, we were defending our own country—and France.

CHAPTER XXVII

Adventure in France

I

AS SOON as the United States entered the war, the country began to pull together. I can remember now little about the vast effort which produced and equipped an Army and a Navy with astounding speed, but I still recall the changes in what was left of civilian life. University activities were readjusted as boys disappeared into the training camps, and teachers were called away to novel duties. Having made up its mind slowly, the country now wanted to get into the fight quickly and have it over.

Even before our troops reached France in large numbers, there was talk of preparations for the upbuilding and the support of Army morale, especially during the period after the war when return transportation might be slow. Self-constituted experts made their guesses as to how long the fighting would last after we got into it, and whether or not England and France would be as eager to bring us back as they were to take us over. Rumor said that our soldiers by the tens of thousands would soon be leaving for France daily. Whatever else our Allies had suffered for three years, at least they had been able at intervals to get home on leave, but when we reached the battle line we might have to stay there a long time.

In all our wars, as I have since learned from much reading, the importance of recreation and morale-building had been recognized, but now the distance of the war quickened the national imagination to the problem. Canadians, Australians and New Zealanders were in the same plight or worse; we could learn from them how to keep the faraway soldier in the right frame of mind for his task. The news broke one day that our soldiers would have special huts or barracks in the camps abroad, even close to the fighting, where they could relax, play games, do some reading, write home. The Army had accepted the offer of Protestant, Catholic, and Jewish welfare organizations, with the Red Cross and the Salvation Army, to equip and furnish these soldier clubs. Volunteer workers were called for—men above the draft age or incapacitated for military service.

This vast morale project, at first vague, was soon sharply defined. In order to avoid confusion or duplication of effort, the Young Men's Christian Association, because of its size and experience, was to have charge of all this work. The other organizations would function through the "Y" rather than alongside it. The volunteer workers, it was hoped, would become Y men for the duration. A single enormous drive for funds would be made, and money would be distributed through the Y. At Columbia, as I remember, the entire faculty contributed at once a day's salary to this war chest.

From some points of view any plan to unify the morale-building work was absurd. Except for the Red Cross and the Salvation Army, the welfare organizations had been built up in peacetime around certain religious convictions, and the sad chance is always strong that religious convictions are accompanied by prejudice. It was more than a little naïve of the Y.M.C.A. and the War Department to expect Catholic and Jewish organizations to see reason or justice in putting the morale work in the hands or under the direction of Protestants. It was still more naïve to suppose that the Y personnel, recruited from all sections of the United States, would invariably possess the tact, the experience, and the philosophic breadth of mind to assume the leadership over men of different faiths without giving offense.

After more than a quarter of a century the bad side of this experiment is easily forgotten, but perhaps the good results of it are forgotten too. Certainly the Y.M.C.A. had an opportunity to which it was not always equal, and it caused some irritations which lingered a while after the war, but in the main its effort was magnificent, in some respects hardly to be improved upon. It learned much, I think, from the Knights of Columbus and the Salvation Army, two organizations which in their dealings with the soldiers showed rare understanding of human nature. The faults sometimes charged against the Y were shortcomings of our

people in general; the very boys who complained of them often illustrated these faults in their own behavior. We were all far from home,
among strange people, and as a nation we had no experience of any
culture but our own. The Y.M.C.A. temperament was often narrow
and insular, but when the war was over the same narrowness, or we
might as well say the same ignorance, made many American soldiers think
more highly of German civilization than of France, the German way of
life having in it more of the conveniences to which the Americans were
accustomed. Beer and sausages, for example. The Americans could appreciate good beer, but at home they had never made the acquaintance
of wine, certainly not of good wine.

The highest tribute to the morale work in the First World War is
this, that the Army realized its immense value, and in the Second World
War took it out of civilian hands and made it part of the military
program. The pattern and the pace of morale building, in both the
European and the Asiatic theatres of this war, were set by the welfare
organizations twenty-five years ago.

2

Late in the autumn of 1917 an earnest-looking gentleman knocked at
my office in Hamilton Hall, sat down by my desk, and with no loss of
time asked if I would go to France. I was wanted, he kindly said, in the
educational work which the Y was planning for the Army with the
Army's approval. Perhaps he said at the Army's request, but I don't
remember. I have forgotten his name, though his call had important
consequences for me. He explained quickly and efficiently what the
Y.M.C.A.-Army educational work would be. Whenever the war ended,
a million or so idle boys in France would be getting into mischief unless
their minds were occupied. Many of them would be worried about their
jobs at home; to some extent they would have dropped behind because
of their war service; they would need to be freshened up, or at least
they would want to go on in their studies or in their profession. A plan
sketched out by Dr. Anson Phelps Stokes, Secretary of Yale University,
perhaps after consultation with John H. Finley, Chancellor of New York
University, had been proposed to the War Department through the
Y.M.C.A., and approved by Mr. Newton Baker and his Assistant Secretary, my old friend Fred Keppel. Until the close of the war this plan

would be developed and perfected through the Y organization, and the educators willing to take part in it would go to France in Y.M.C.A. uniforms. At the close of hostilities the Army would take over whatever educational system the Y by that time should build up. Was I prepared to leave my teaching at Columbia and sail at once for France? Could I give my answer the next day? That very afternoon Dr. Stokes would be at Columbia calling on Professor John Cunliffe, Assistant Director of the School of Journalism. It might be well for me to see Dr. Stokes.

I saw him. Like most professors in the East I had already met the kindly, energetic, and ebullient Secretary of Yale. When I found him in Cunliffe's office, he was urging him to become the Director of the American University Union in London. Professor George Nettleton of Yale would direct the University Union in Paris. These centers for university men in the armed forces had no direct relation to the educational plan. Whether Dr. Stokes had invented them, I don't know, but I think it probable. He could think of more things in a given time than any other man I've ever known—of so many things, in fact, that his plans might have to be carried out by others.

He urged me to join up. He had just returned from France, and was going back in a few days to perfect the educational organization. Dr. Finley would then go over and carry on as permanent educational director for the Army. If I enlisted in the work now, I might be in on the preliminary planning, with the chance of being useful in some way later on.

When I left Cunliffe's office I wrote to Fred Keppel in Washington. It wasn't clear whether the gentleman who had called that morning came only from the Y, or partly at least at his suggestion. But I didn't wait for Fred's answer. On my way home that evening I stopped at Mother's apartment and told her I had been asked to go to France. She was already an invalid, beginning the final chapter of the illness which two years later carried her off.

"Do you think you ought to go?"

"I do, Mother."

"Then you must."

3

The next few weeks were busy. There were arrangements to make with the University, plans for Pauline and the children during my absence, interviews with the recruiting committee of the Y.M.C.A., uniforms and other equipment to try on or assemble.

My little family would stay in New York until the summer. They would then go to New Canaan where by good luck I had already rented a house with an option on it for three years. If the war lasted longer than that, there would be time to plan further. Pauline could give up the New York apartment when the lease ran out and stay in New Canaan.

What troubled me most during these hurried preparations was the thought of leaving the children. Graham had become one close and dear companion, and Anna, still a baby, promised soon to be another. I didn't like to miss even a few months out of her precious early years, and if I stayed away too long she would quite forget me.

There were other aspects of my overseas adventure which I didn't like. By temperament I was not a Y.M.C.A. man, and I feared the Government had made a serious mistake in letting the educational work for the Army get mixed up with the evangelical tendencies of an organization which I had always respected, at a safe distance. My doubts were not disposed of entirely when I met the recruiting commission of the Y.M.C.A. That I was expected to come before them at all, gave me pause. The invitation to take part in work which the Army desired had not carried the implication that I must first be looked over by the Y.M.C.A., nor that that organization would consider itself authorized or qualified to pass judgment on my ability as an educator or on my moral character. A number of other teachers had received an invitation to join this work, and rumors were afloat that the Y.M.C.A. recruiting committee showed a disposition to probe into their religious beliefs, even into their record as church-attenders.

The committee, when I met them at last, proved of course to be a group of courteous gentlemen who asked me no questions which I was unwilling to answer, yet some of the questions were certainly out of place at that time. With the other recruits in every branch of Army morale work, I was enlisting in the service of the country, not of the Y.M.C.A. The men drafted for combat would not be asked whether they were Protestants or Catholics; it would make no particular difference to the Army whether they were regular churchgoers or to what particular parish they belonged. The committee seemed to know in advance where, approximately, I stood in these matters, but they did ask questions, perhaps merely for sociability's sake. When I told them I was an Episcopalian, and admitted, in response to further questions, that I was a vestryman at Old Trinity, the curiosity about my soul's condition came to a sudden end. I was never quite sure whether I had received a high passing mark or had been put on probation.

4

I sailed for France at ten-thirty on the morning of January 10, 1918, on the *Rochambeau* of the French Line, bound for Bordeaux. The *Rochambeau* was a small boat, essentially comfortable and safe, but now in emergency loaded to what seemed a precarious waterline. There were French officers and soldiers on board, returning from a military mission, and Red Cross workers, and French and American civilians on miscellaneous war errands, and a large contingent of Y.M.C.A. recruits, some of them like myself headed for the educational service but all bent on brightening up whatever corner of the Army they should descend upon. We were a surprisingly congenial lot, full of good will, and for a short time able to forget our miscellaneous backgrounds and our somewhat conflicting purposes. Many of the party were professional Y men; some had been supporters of the local Y in their home town, had contributed heavily to the war chest, and were on their way to help spend the money or to see how it was spent; some were entertainers, singers (female and male), actors, sleight-of-hand artists; on a palpably higher level were Winthrop Ames and E. A. Sothern, startlingly out of place in Y uniforms, charged with the organizing of theatrical circuits in the camps and wherever possible behind the front.

Because of the submarine threat, portholes were sealed after dark, and the cabins even at their best would have been suffocating, but from excitement or nervousness or in self-protection French and Americans puffed cigarette after cigarette until you had to lean on the smoke to push your way through. Before we were at sea twenty-four hours we were on each others' nerves, all of us trying to conceal our condition beneath aggressive and somewhat uncalled-for good humor.

I was assigned to a small cabin with three other men, agreeable companions, one of them Daniel Putnam Brinley, the mural painter. Dan came from New Canaan, where I had rented a house; we considered each other at once as neighbors. Since he knew France well, he had signed up for work in the *Foyers* or soldier clubs of the French Army. He was a terrific smoker, but he shared the general reluctance to be

asphyxiated; we spent the daylight hours on deck, often with a group
of Red Cross girls under the leadership of Mrs. Rogers Bacon, whom
Dan and I had known in New York.

The second day out the captain of the ship, genial and hospitable,
announced a get-together party in the dining salon that evening for all
his passengers. By way of preparation the room was thoroughly aired,
and we began at least in an atmosphere of purity. The Y.M.C.A. group
included a number of song-leaders who in a minute or two had organized
the meeting into sections, and drilled us in the performance of rounds
and catches, musical material familiar to many of the group since early
school days.

After the singing came speeches. The Captain welcomed us gracefully
to the ship, paid us many personal tributes which we may have deserved,
but I don't see how he knew—expressed the gratitude of all Frenchmen
for the aid of their Allies—hoped we would all see France many times in
the not too distant future, when she would be herself again—wished us
happiness and success, and called down blessings on our land.

We gave hearty applause and a cheer, and a short man in Y.M.C.A.
uniform rose to express our thanks. He told the Captain he was speaking
as the leader of the Y group. Who appointed him to this responsible
office, I do not know, and I have long ago forgotten his name. No doubt
his merits were numerous, but on this occasion he was tragically miscast.
He came from a small town in the center of the United States where, as
we learned from him later, he was active not only in Y.M.C.A. work but
in the local Chamber of Commerce. He had never seen Europe and
knew France only by name. He was having his first sight of the ocean.
His few days in New York had been his only contact with the eastern
seaboard.

Facing so many new experiences all at once, he kept his balance by
clinging desperately to points of view which had sustained him at home.
Putting on the tone and the manner of a preacher, he exhorted us in various clichés to be brave soldiers and true patriots. By swift transition he
then plunged us into real trouble. It would not be enough, he said, to
help win the war; as Christian men we should seize the opportunity to
reveal to the French people the characteristics of the good life as our
fathers had set them before us. The evil habit of cigarette smoking, he
asserted, had come to us from France. If the health of the French was
not all that it should be, cigarette smoking was responsible. What greater

kindness could we do than to help them give up the bad habit? Some of us, of course, had contracted it, but in order to save France we would, he was sure, reform.

The tenseness in the crowded room was indescribable. I looked across at Mr. Ames and Mr. Sothern, both smoking at the moment, with their eyes fixed on the inspired orator, as he proceeded to the heart of his message. The French people, he said, unlike the best Americans, were addicted to wine drinking. The opportunity would now be ours to set an example as total abstainers. In a happy Christian world there would be no place for tobacco, and none for alcohol unless a doctor prescribed it.

Why the boat didn't sink at this point, I cannot explain. Our host, the Captain, had been amused by the warnings against cigarettes. He was a chain smoker himself. But the expression on his face was something to remember, when the good wines of France were insulted. One member of the Y group got to his feet to announce that he was a tobacco grower, and it was only because last year's crop had been plentiful that he had contributed generously to the Y fund for morale work in France, and had been able to enlist for some of this work himself. In firm phrases he advised the unlucky Y leader not to be a God-awful ass.

After that the meeting broke up. One facet of the American character had been dramatically disclosed to the ship's officers, to the French military men on board, to the amused and astonished stewards listening at the doors of the salon. For the rest of the voyage we all told each other what we thought of the incident, and since even those who agreed had different grounds for their opinion, the debate covered none of us with glory.

None of us, that is, except Mrs. Rogers Bacon. The morning after the get-together party she was seated on deck in the sunshine with the other Red Cross ladies, discussing the Y leader and his speech. Her great sense of humor and her acquaintance with human nature at home as well as abroad enabled her to see fun in what most of us had found only distressing. The Y leader, she said, was probably a good enough sort when not out of his depth. Perhaps he realized too late that his remarks had been less than happy; perhaps he had been kicking himself all night; perhaps at that very moment he was on his knees in the bowels of the ship asking God for better guidance in the future.

While she spoke, the gentleman came along the deck, picking his way among the crowded figures that reclined on bare boards for want of steamer chairs. He didn't look as though he had been praying for guidance. He was happy, even satisfied with himself. When Mrs. Bacon called to him, he stepped over promptly, flattered by her attention. Dan Brinley and I drew nearer, to see and hear.

Mrs. Bacon congratulated the fellow on his speech. He pretended modesty. She said he must have a good deal of practice in addressing large meetings; he admitted that at home his fellow townsmen called upon him frequently. She asked whether cigars and pipes were as noxious as cigarettes. Her tone was disarming; she seemed to be inquiring of an oracle, or at least of an authority higher than any she had met before. He confessed to a little pipe smoking but doubted if much could be said for tobacco in any form. She wondered if the use of the pipe were not an essentially manly habit; he felt that way about it himself.

At this point she was silent a moment, thoughtful, then asked if he would kindly bring her a glass or tumbler. He was delighted to oblige. As he hurried off, she called after him that perhaps two glasses would be better. While he was gone she drew from under her steamer chair a bottle of champagne. Though she had kept it in the shade, it wasn't iced. The Y leader, bringing the two glasses, balked a little at what was waiting for him.

"Perhaps you will open this bottle for me."

He couldn't refuse, of course. She held the tumblers until the warm champagne blew out the cork with a noise heard the length of the ship, and those reclining on the deck saw the advocate of Prohibition pouring iniquity right out in the open, under the eyes of God. Mrs. Bacon had intended the other glass for him, but he declined. Lacking the courage to throw the bottle overboard, and not knowing what else to do with it, he stood there holding it.

5

The service of the French Line between Bordeaux and New York was discontinued after the First World War, to the regret of Americans who like myself knew what a fascinating approach it gave to France. Ships entering the long river harbor had to wait for the tide. At midnight or later they would dock alongside eighteenth-century quays paved with huge cobblestones and backed by a long row of white houses with faded green or blue shutters.

When we left the *Rochambeau* in the morning a squad of soldiers were drawn up on the quay. It was my first sight of the baggy blue over-coats, belted in, of the war helmets, of the bayoneted rifles carried so high on the shoulders that they suggested lances. The quay and the houses along it belonged to the Revolution or to Napoleon, but the guard were what we had been reading about for three years, the *poilus,* boys or middle-aged men, the breed who had stopped the enemy at the Marne and at Verdun.

The train for Paris left about eleven o'clock in bright sunshine, which in that part of France even in winter had a touch of spring in it. I have made the same trip several times since, but the landscape never again seemed so romantic and magical. From the car window we could see the small houses, picturesque with their colored roofs and their garden walls. Women and a few old men were tidying up the wintry fields. The vine-yards were waiting for the turn of the year and the high sun. Tall pop-lars lined the neat roads. Nothing in the landscape spoke of war except the absence of young men. This part of the land, untouched by invasion, seemed to have withdrawn deeper into its colorful past. Montaigne had lived in this region and knew the fields, the forest, and the rivers through which the Paris Express hurried us. Further north we sped through Touraine, and thought of La Fontaine, and Ronsard, and Rabelais, of the ladies and courtiers who had loved and hated each other, and inspired poetry and plots in the lovely chateaux. At this very moment, I recalled, Anatole France lived in retirement near Tours.

But the places which on this journey seemed most attractive impressed me for themselves, not for the great folk who once lived in them. An-goulême and Poitiers, fairly close together, are both located on hilltops between rivers, and to the traveler coming up from the south they seemed like Maxfield Parrish illustrations for a fairy tale. Little white houses with red roofs climb up the hillside to a summit of battlements and tur-rets. Some of the oldest monuments of French history are in these places, and life there, as I knew much later, is uneventful to the point of dull-ness, but history now has a way of bypassing these places. They had their fill of power and adventure long ago. Looking at them on their hillslopes from the car window, I vowed to return many times to explore their little streets. I have not kept this promise to myself; only once have I visited either of them, and then on hasty errands while the war was still on, but I then had the feeling that some of the elder citizens were still more worried about the French Revolution than about the rampagings of the Kaiser. I suspect that today Danton and Robespierre, Louis XVI and Marie Antoinette are personages more convincingly real to Angoulême and Poitiers than the gentlemen whose war record is, as I write, undergoing scrutiny in Nuremberg.

We reached Paris about six o'clock, and Dan and I went to the Hotel Burgundy in the rue Duphot near the Madeleine. Across the street only a few yards away is Prunier's restaurant, where in peacetime the finest of fish dishes were served, as European gourmets knew. Prunier's was closed for the duration, but it shared the vitality and the apparent immortality of all genuine French institutions. It came to life with the peace, as doubtless it is coming to life again at this moment. My affection for the place is based on numerous visits between wars. That evening, as Dan and I unpacked our bags in Room 52 of the Hotel Burgundy, we gave no thought to fish. A zeppelin was dropping bombs on Paris, and the detonations had our complete attention. No bomb fell near us, but shell fragments from antiaircraft guns spattered disagreeably on the sidewalk beneath our window and on the canopy over the hotel door.

PART IV

1917—1919

CHAPTER XXVIII

The Foyer du Soldat

I

I REACHED Paris on January 21. The next ten days were spent very pleasantly finding out why I had come to France, and how I could be useful, now I was there. On the twenty-second I tried to see Mr. Edward C. Carter, head man for all the Y.M.C.A. work in France. An appointment was made for the twenty-third. Mr. Carter, a devoted and charming gentleman, whom I admire for many good reasons and whose friendship I prize, was burdened with an impossible administrative task, and already showed signs, as I thought, of nervous exhaustion. He asked me about myself, my professional career, and the field in which I preferred to work. He went so far as to offer his own opinion that I might at a later date do some educational work in the American Army. He suggested however that I present myself to Mr. Coffin and Mr. Davis, the American representatives in the work of the French Y, the *Foyer du Soldat.*

On the twenty-fourth I called on William Sloane Coffin and Dryden Davis, who proved two of the outstanding men I was to meet in the Y. They knew, having apparently their own sources of information, that I had come to do educational work, but they urged me with flattering warmth to go to the French Army and work in the *foyers* until our troops should need me. When I asked why I had been brought over before I was needed, Will laughed. There would be no need of educators, he said, until there was some educational work. I started to repeat some of the things Dr. Anson Stokes had told me, about the large educational plans, but Will laughed again. Dr. Stokes had returned to Europe, he said, and the educational work would eventually come into existence. Meanwhile the foyers were going concerns, not day dreams or outlines for publicity purposes.

I confess I resented this lighthearted disposal of the program to which I had committed myself, too hastily perhaps, but seriously and sincerely. I wondered if Will were running down the educational work in order to build up these foyers of his, whatever they might be. It was months before I realized how terribly honest he was, with himself and everyone else. He was not selling out Dr. Stokes, who was I believe a cousin of his, and whom he held in affectionate regard. But he knew and thought I should know that though Dr. Stokes had talked with the Army and with the French Government about the great Army-Y educational project, no such project had as yet the slightest existence in fact. Mr. Carter did not refer me at once to his educational chief and put me to work, for the good reason was that there was no such work, and no such chief. Dr. Stokes had concocted the program out of his head, intending later, much later, to find someone acceptable to the Y whom the Army also would gladly put in charge of it.

Late in the afternoon of the twenty-sixth I saw Mr. Carter again, and learned from him that I was to go with the foyer for a month or so, and then come back to the American Army and begin somewhere in the educational work. Meanwhile, until I had the necessary passports for the French Army, I was to lecture daily or nightly in Y huts through the camps nearest Paris.

The arrangement was satisfactory enough. Brinley was headed for the foyer work, and I was glad of his companionship; I was eager to see the French Army; I was personally attracted to Coffin and Davis. So for three more days I waited in Paris, lectured when called upon, submitted to extra inoculations prescribed by the American medical authorities, strolled along the Seine and gathered a few good editions from the old bookstalls, and unconsciously stored up vivid impressions of Paris as I should never again see it.

Our last Sunday afternoon Dan and I spent at Versailles, strolling through the alleys, feasting our eyes on the sycamore trees, on the formal statues, on the stately and haunting vistas. Mild weather had brought out large crowds that day, but in spite of their numbers they remained strangely silent. They sat in the sun wherever they could, or strolled slowly, workmen and their families, soldiers on leave, with their girls. I should have expected more talk, but the war had touched them all. Among the men in uniform were convalescent wounded, using a crutch or a cane. The great fountains on the palace terrace were still. In the sunlight far overhead a zeppelin cruised slowly.

In late afternoon a mist crept over the garden. Dan and I were near the Petit Trianon and hurried our pace to look at the famous stables and cowsheds where the young queen once played at being a mildmaid. The evening was coming on fast and the castle bell began to toll, warning us to leave the grounds before the gates were closed. The enchantment of the place was so strong at that moment that if the queen and her ladies had stepped out of the old building to greet us, it would not have been surprising. The beautiful side of the tragic past was indestructible, more real than the gray zeppelin above us, touched with sunset red.

With the memory of that afternoon I keep the picture of Paris as it was during the war, with its street lamps covered with blue paint and almost extinguished. When the moon was nearly full the Paris of the Middle Ages returned, and the towers of the islands and the Latin Quarter took on a haunting beauty. When the moon was dark, pedestrians liked to carry a cane, less for protection than to tap on the paving stones to warn others. We walked in the middle of the street, using patches of sky and stars for guide, and at all crossings we paused to listen, and to signal our own warnings. My fondness for François Villon grew rapidly in these re-visits to his city as he knew it.

2

On February 1, Dan Brinley and I started together for the French front. His destination was the foyer at Sommedieue, mine was the foyer at Haudainville, but since those villages were close together, we took the same train, at noon. Since railway schedules were practically nonexistent, it was only after many hesitations and delays that we reached Bar-le-duc, where we found a room in an old inn, the architecture of which fascinated Dan. We were less enthusiastic about the inn furniture. Our room contained one bed, hardly wide enough for two people, and too short for me, six feet, one, and Dan, six feet, three or four. We folded ourselves on it somehow, and were debating how to stretch out when one side of the bed gave way, spilling us on the floor. We then put the pillows on the surviving or upper side, and lay across the wreck, with our legs projecting freely.

The next day we spent getting some more passes and visés for the French Army. We had been directed to bring with us at least half a dozen passport photographs, and we now began to understand their use. At each stage of our penetration into the military area, our papers were checked and we received more papers permitting us to go a little further, and every permit had our photograph glued to it.

On Sunday, February 3, we took the 6:00 A.M. train from Bar-le-duc. As we stood up from our sloping bed at five o'clock, the moon was still shining. By twelve o'clock we were inside the war zone, among soldiers, guns, army wagons, sentinels. A man's world. Until we came out of it again, we were not to see a woman or a child.

The small village where we stopped had only two unshattered roofs. One was over the house used by the Army officials as local headquarters. The other roof was over what had been the village inn. The front wall still bore the name, The White Grape, *Le Raisin Blanc*. Dan and I, hungry as bears, wished a meal went with the sign.

Armed with our newest passes, we got on the next train that crawled out of the village, and at dark we reached the railhead. The tracks beyond that point had been broken or twisted by gunfire. Sidings had been improvised for freight cars, but there was no station or other buildings. The traveler must get off and make the rest of his way to the war on foot, unless some Army wagon gave him a lift.

We asked in what direction Haudainville and Sommedieue lay, and an obliging soldier, one of the hundreds who milled around in the mud on no particular business, waved his hand in the dark, wished us luck, and disappeared. We were on our own. The front was five miles away. Overburdened with our equipment, we decided to stop every passing cart until we found one bound for Haudainville and another for Sommedieue. The Sommedieue cart came first and Dan climbed up on it. A few minutes later a Haudainville cart took me along. The tired horses moved slowly. The mud in the roads was deep. After nearly two hours we stopped in pitch darkness and the driver told me to get down—here was my foyer. I sank into mud almost up to my knees. The driver passed me my roll of blankets, my other things. The horses got into motion, the wagon groaned on its way until out of hearing. I looked around for the foyer.

The night was moonless and starless. I could hear the muffled sound of voices. Far stronger than the sound was the mingled odor of coffee and wet wood burning—most characteristic of French smells. Out of the darkness in front of me a doorway was lighted for a sudden instant as a soldier pushed out of the foyer. I walked carefully toward the brief light, found the doorway, stepped inside a large room dimly lighted, filled with two or three hundred soldiers, filled also with tobacco smoke, filled even more subtly with the smell of damp uniforms and sweating human bodies.

The two or three hundred soldiers turned to stare at me. In the rear of the room, behind a sort of counter, two tired-looking men in a special uniform had been serving out hot chocolate. They too stopped to stare at me. They must be my associates in the foyer work. I was not enthusiastic. They recognized me at sight as their new American helper. They were not enthusiastic either. In dead silence I made my way across the room, and we shook hands.

3

The two Frenchmen in charge of the foyer at Haudainville were Octave Martin, journalist in peacetime, and Paul Tisseau, student of philosophy and concocter of utopias. Both were slightly over forty, and Tisseau had such poor eyesight that even with thick lenses he was next to blind.

They did all the work of the foyer—cleaned the place in the morning, brought fresh supplies from the commissary, served coffee and chocolate to the soldiers who came in during afternoon and early evening, and for an hour before taps, or *retraite,* gave them a phonograph concert. By ten o'clock the foyer would be empty, and Martin would prepare a rather remarkable meal for Tisseau and himself—and now for me. In most foyers the directors ate at the officers' mess, but Martin was a great amateur cook, far better than any professional in the regiments then at Haudainville. He drew from the commissary the rations assigned us, and improvised glorious surprises even when the raw materials were not promising. That evening he gave us a dessert of rice flavored with chocolate from the canteen. Every grain of rice was thoroughly cooked yet distinct from every other grain, and the coating of chocolate was evenly distributed, with no superfluous sauce in the bottom of the dish.

On my first evening with these two men, both interesting but for different reasons, Martin said little about any subject but his cooking. His habit was to concentrate. Tisseau was helpful in bringing out dishes and setting the table, but meanwhile he rambled along about the new world which would follow the hoped-for victory. The Allies, he believed, would make an ideal peace, and in every country, particularly France, civilization would take a long jump ahead. I asked for particulars, and he favored me with enough to make my brain whirl. Martin may have heard Tisseau's bright ideas before; perhaps that was why he conversed only about cooking. Actually he was more deeply, and perhaps more sincerely, concerned with philosophical and religious speculations than his colleague. Tisseau had a birdlike mind—chickenlike, rather—which stepped around and picked up kernels with surface alacrity.

He believed there should be a reform in education and in religion. After the war there would be a new kind of university, where nothing of the past would be studied for its own sake, but only to solve the problems of the moment. The curriculum would therefore be always in a fluid condition, shifting the emphasis each season to answer the new questions. As for religion, there would be less emphasis on doctrine and on ceremonies; faith would be expressed outwardly in politics rather than in the old rituals, and religious emotion would be cultivated as the force propelling toward civic virtue. I asked Tisseau if the cathedrals of France would be abandoned or destroyed. He said my question was absurd. When I reminded him that he wanted neither ceremonies nor ritual, he changed the subject, and Martin said it had been a long day and we needed sleep.

Our dormitory was in a building near by, a small stone cottage from which the garret and the roof had been lifted by a bomb. Half the floor of the second story remained. We put on our heaviest coats, wrapped ourselves in all our blankets, and slept on the ground with some canvas bags for mattress, where the floorboards above kept off the rain.

Martin and Tisseau at once fell asleep, but I lay awake thinking over the day and wondering how many sweaters and blankets would really be proof against the dampness. To this question perhaps no one on the French front found the answer. During the months I spent in Haudainville and Sommedieue I never felt cold by day, and never warm at night. Volumes have been written about the trenches in winter, the life in the mud, *la boue,* but the full story can't be told. The mud was under you, around you, over you. It pursued you. I was splashed with it when I arrived at the foyer that first night, and it preserved the dampness in any cloth on which it fell. After a tramp over soft roads your coat would be a mass of heavy clay, and though you dried your clothes before a hot fire until they were baked hard as a brick, yet inside the solid chunks the original dampness and chill lingered. The soldiers came out of the trenches with so many pounds of mud caked on the skirts of their overcoats that often in desperation they cut the skirts off and threw them away. Zero weather soon made them sorry, and the officers tore their hair at this mutilation of the one warm garment the poilu had. His overcoat, when turned upside down, became his blanket at night. Its width was so great that when he wore it as a coat he wrapped it almost twice around him, drawing it in at the middle until he bulged above and below.

The war mud, never thoroughly dried, could not be removed by brushing. Whenever a soldier happened on a brook or a pond, he soaked his coat until the clay melted. The weight of the water, however, made up for anything that had been washed off, and since the water was itself muddy, the clay was usually driven deeper into the fibre of the cloth. When you entered one of the trenches you soon had mud on your hands, and there it stayed until you reached a foyer, or some other rare place where clean hot water might be found. Mud on the hands soon got on the face, then into your food. Normally you had grit on your lips.

Haudainville is near Verdun, so close that after a short walk to the top of the hill behind the foyer we could look down into the cup-shaped depression, at the bottom of which lay what remained of the heroic town. The front line stretched along the rim of the cup, connecting the fortresses which had taken the brunt of the German assaults. Of course the great battle had become history long before February, 1917, but the German and the French armies still faced each other, ready to spring, and even in this sector, technically called "quiet," there were nightly raids and forays from both sides. The regiments took their turns at alternate front line duty and rest, three nights of mud and fighting, three days and nights at Haudainville, making up lost sleep and getting what recreation they could at the foyer. During the phonograph concert the first night after a detachment came out of the trenches, the men's faces showed what they had gone through; their eyes were fixed in an insane gaze. The second night, after a day of solid rest, they began to relax. They had got a shave and cleaned themselves up, their mutilated overcoats were replaced. They looked human. By the third night they were talking pleasantly, joking, even laughing; their recovery was complete. But the next day the poor fellows marched back to the trenches.

4

In the First World War the *Foyer du Soldat* was the symbol and substitute for the hearth the poilu was defending. *Foyer,* hearth, is the French word for home in the ancestral and most intimate sense. "The Bosche destroyed my foyer," men from the invaded district would say; "Now, ten days at my foyer!" would call the happy *permissionnaire,* starting off on leave. Some very real gods of the hearth, pagan gods from the old Roman countryside, were enshrined in the *Foyer du Soldat,* presiding over the religion of the family. There the sturdy, patient men in faded blue found a clean dry floor, a comfortable seat, a cup of hot chocolate or coffee or tea; there they read an *illustré;* there they played cards or more innocent-seeming checkers; there they heard good music, thanks to the phonograph, or drew a book from the circulating library; there, best of all, they found paper, pen and ink, to write letters home.

In the foyer at Haudainville I remember chiefly the letter writing. Certainly the poilus enjoyed the warm drinks, but the enduring impression was less of chocolate and coffee than of stiff brown hands persistently moving the pen over the paper. Hundreds, sometimes thousands of letters were mailed daily from the larger foyers, like that at Sommedieue. Even into the smaller ones, like that at Haudainville, the poilu came with his quiet manner, not as though this were his club, but as though it were a home, his home or yours, and he the host or the guest. But sooner or later he got from the attendants a sheet of paper and an envelope, and settled down at one of the neat blotters on the tables.

The foyers were financed by the American Y.M.C.A. and the direction of each was shared by Frenchmen like Martin and Tisseau, along with an American like me, or sometimes, as at Sommedieue, one Frenchman and one American divided the responsibility. Of course the stronger character always ran the place, but among the directors there was far less friction than in the Y huts of the American Army. I suppose the reason was that no American went to the foyers unless he had a fair knowledge of the French character and of the French language; and the French directors had all at some time served in the Army, and never forgot the enlisted man's point of view.

In appearance, of course, the foyers differed. Those well back from the front might have patronage enough to fill a whole building, as at Sommedieue, where the foyer was installed in an abandoned mill. Or perhaps a single large room, as at Haudainville, was packed nightly with tired but philosophical soldiers, who remained standing without complaint, since the few chairs were needed by the letter writers.

There was one other kind of foyer, a mere cave or dugout in the front trenches, usually in the trench behind the very front. Here there was space for nothing more than one chair, one table, and a furnace to cook the chocolate or coffee. Each of these lonely stations was attended by a soldier, a *planton* or orderly assigned by the officer in charge of the sector. A poilu welcomed the duty since the fire was kept burning during the night and the table could be used as a bed, well out of the mud. Chocolate was served free to the night patrol, whereas in the larger and safer foyers a cup cost a sou. When a squad was far out on a dangerous spot, the officer in command would send one of the men back with a *bon* or order for chocolate for all; when they returned at three or four in the morning, chilled to the bone by the sleet or snow, they would rouse the planton and have their hot drink just when they needed it most.

This service always cost hard work and not a little courage, and sometimes a man's life. The materials—chocolate, water, firewood—had to be carried to the foyers after dark, and near the front the enemy had the range on all approaches. Each front-line trench was visited several times a week by a director from the large foyers, a duty undertaken eagerly and exclusively by Americans, who enjoyed the excitement. They went unarmed, since foyer directors were classed as noncombatants, like ambulance drivers, but the enemy shells were not discriminating, and the gunners let off a few every now and then, on a chance.

My work at Haudainville was light and safe. Tisseau or Martin would take me for a walk daily, almost always in the rain of course; their purpose was to make me acquainted with the roads leading to trenches, and with the location of the other camps behind the line. I visited none of the front-trench foyers, since this part of the work was done by Americans at Sommedieue, a village closer to the front than Haudainville.

These morning walks were grand exercise, and on each of them we met some officers. At the end of my first week at Haudainville my acquaintance had widened amazingly. I had many encounters with the poilus, and the differences in their accent, depending on what part of

France they came from, gave me extra handicaps in my tussle with the language. Until I went to war I should have said that I could speak French. I really could get on fairly well with people who spoke with academic correctness, and slowly, allowing for my inexperience, and on a subject which I knew and could therefore recognize the vocabulary. But it was another thing to be dropped unprepared in the midst of an Army which like our own Army used plenty of slang and were constantly inventing some more. When I dropped off asleep at night I usually had a headache from the effort of listening; and when I woke, it was to the unpleasant realization, not of the war, but of that inescapable language.

Yet the poilus, though their speech was hard for me, almost always said something worth hearing. One morning I was walking alone, and having missed my way I hailed a passing *camion,* or truck, and got a lift back to the foyer. The driver was a farmer from the invaded district, a tall, gaunt man who economized his words like a Vermonter. I tried to draw him out.

"Have you read my President's Fourteen Points?"

He nodded.

"What do you think of them?"

"Thirteen too many."

"Which is the one point you like?"

"Le President did not mention it, but the Germans have my farm."

One of my duties was the conduct of the phonograph concert each evening. The phonograph would be placed on the counter of the canteen with a generous pile of records. I would wind up the machine, then lift a record well into the dim light where I could read the title. From this exercise my pronunciation derived great benefit; every soldier in the room was sincerely eager to help me out. At first when I got the title wrong, the men would repeat it correctly, but in a low tone, by way of tact. After the first evening or two I noticed that the title was always repeated, whether or not I had said it approximately right. The French social genius was showing itself; if they repeated the title when I said it right, my feelings would be protected when they said it right after I had got it wrong.

The discs they liked best were popular songs of a kind we in America never heard in the years before the first war, and very rarely even now. They were not folk songs, still less were they what tourists would hear in Paris cafés. They were sentimental, romantic, often melancholy in theme, and the tunes were simple and undistinguished, except by the same kind of wistfulness suggested in certain moods by the French land-scape. I wrote the favorite titles and composers in my diary at the time. It was a French diary, with the pages ruled in small squares. At the top is printed the date of each day, and the name of the patron saint. After twenty-eight years the pages are discolored and the black ink is turned a pale brown, but the printed lines at the top remain clear, and I see that I landed at Bordeaux on the Feast of St. Agnes, I arrived at Haudainville on Sexagesima Sunday, and I ran off the phonograph concert for the first time on February 6, the Feast of Saint Dorothy. The program consisted of "Quand Madelon"—Robert; "Pimperline et Pimperlin"—Henrion; "Le Soleil"—Borel; "Le Long de Missouri"—Christine; "Marche Lor-raine"—Ganne; "L'Angelus de la Mer"—Goublier; "Les Gars de France" —Daniderff; "Sur les Cimes Neigeuses"—Guidani; "Le Carilloneur"— Daniderff; "La Paimpoulaise"—Borel.

In my visits to neighboring regiments I met many Catholic chaplains, and frequently a Protestant pastor would drop into the foyer for a word with Tisseau and Martin. One afternoon a group of visitors came along, and Tisseau opened up his scheme for overhauling and improving reli-gion as soon as the war should end. Having noticed that the Army, by and large, seemed on excellent terms with the Catholic chaplains, I asked whether anticlerical emotions were disappearing from French politics— whether the war had drawn the people back to the Church.

The answer might have been forthcoming if Martin hadn't sunk down in a corner and bowed his head in his hands. A little startled, I turned to the nearest visitor. "What's wrong?"

Leaning over, he whispered, "Religious discussions remind him of his grief."

"What grief?"

The officer looked at me sharply, surprised that I wasn't informed. "The Catholics murdered a relative of his."

For the rest of that day I wondered that such things could happen in France and be kept from us across the ocean. The next morning, meeting the officer on the road, I expressed my bewilderment. Where had the recent religious trouble occurred?

"Oh," he said, "it isn't recent. A relative of Martin's was killed at the Eve of St. Bartholomew."

5

My few days at Haudainville were a mild induction to more active work elsewhere. On February 10, Martin told me I was to go to the foyer at Sommedieue, where Dan Brinley was stationed. Next morning Dan appeared in person, tall as ever, in a small cart with a very slow horse. He was gathering up some supplies for his foyer—incidentally gathering up me too. Roy Chamberlain, the energetic American director at Sommedieue, wanted someone to help out with the front-line foyers, and I was to come at once. By afternoon Chamberlain had outfitted me with a French helmet and gas mask, and I was following him through French mud from foyer to foyer in a series of introductions to the plantons, with more formal visits to posts of command to be presented to the officers. I was to make the rounds of the front-line foyers three times a week in a stretch of the front almost fifteen miles long.

The central foyer at Sommedieue in the old mill was an ingenius improvisation. Chamberlain had persuaded successive regimental commanders and Generals to rearrange the building for the maximum convenience of the ten or twelve thousand men who rested there for a moment daily on their way to and from the front. The greatest number at one time came of course in the evening, but from the middle of the morning whole companies or battalions would use the place at any moment for a moment's shelter.

What the mill had originally looked like, I don't know, but when I saw it there were three or four large rooms and two small ones used as offices. The supply of tables and letter paper was ample. There was a game room for card and checker playing, and on occasion for boxing and fencing, and of course there was a canteen furnishing chocolate and coffee.

Long ago the windows had lost their panes, but a heavy varnished paper now substituted for glass, and a yellowish light, not unpleasant, filled the rooms by day. Brinley had painted a face card on the paper surface of each window. He was planning to decorate the lanterns which furnished light in the evening, when the face cards were lost behind shutters. The game room was further enlivened by an upright piano, left behind, I suppose, when the inhabitants were driven out by the German advance. I had not thought of the poilus as piano players, but no soldier laid eyes on that instrument without immediately laying fingers on it too.

Behind the mill ran a swift stream which had furnished power in better days. Now it was the Army laundry and bathtub. A hundred yards down the road its waters divided and circled around a small island on which stood, only slightly damaged, the home of the mill owner. Dan and I were lodged here, with Roy Chamberlain, the American director, and others who from time to time were engaged in the foyer work. We cooked our breakfasts—toast and coffee—on a small wood stove salvaged from a junk pile in the village. Lunch and dinner we ate at the French officers' mess, unless we were off on an all-day errand.

My most fascinating duty was now the visiting of front foyers to collect the *bons* for hot chocolate during the night, and to bring back an estimate of the needs for the following week. These visits involved much walking in the deep trench-mud. Between Sommedieue and the actual front line I could always get a lift on some ambulance or other vehicle, but in the trenches I took more exercise than ever before or since. In favorable weather I could cover between twelve and fifteen miles a day. As I write these words I have before me a prewar map of the district, but only one of the places which I used to visit is marked—Bouzée. The other locations of the front-line foyers must have been small villages hardly worth noticing—Ravin, Les Éparges, Autun, Trottoir, Côte des Hures, Mont-sous-les-Côtes. The war, sweeping over them, had left nothing but rubble.

The place most badly shattered was Les Éparges. The front-line trench ran through it, and nothing showed above ground but a few piles of stone and brick, and a sign giving the name of the village. The captain in command when I first visited Les Éparges was named Tilly—very young, a university student when the war interrupted. He had fought continuously since the beginning, and the strain was telling on him. He was to be married as soon as the war ended. Whether he survived the last months of fighting, I don't know. I remember his bright nature, his thoroughly Parisian wit, and the stoical philosophy which the war had taught him.

One day he invited me to stop a moment at his headquarters the next time I came through. His office was a hole in the ground, ten or twelve feet below the trench. A short ladder led down to his door. At eight o'clock, two or three mornings later, I stood at the top of the ladder and called my name to the sentry at the foot. The man turned to announce me, but luckily the Captain, recognizing my voice, bade me come right down. I obeyed, and had just moved away from the lowest step when a small shell fell precisely where I had been standing, and blew the ladder to fragments.

"Oh la-la!" said Tilly, with an instantaneous lifting of his coat collar, as though the cannonade might keep on.

On another day Roy Chamberlain was touring the front foyers with me, and Captain Tilly asked us to stop for lunch. We were to eat in his kitchen, which was an extension of his office, a further excavation below trench level. A large tin pipe, thrust up through the mud, carried the smoke from the stove. As we waited in the Captain's office, our appetites were sharpened by the kitchen odors, tantalizingly delicious. But another small shell came down through the stove pipe, exploded above the stove, and sent that wonderful meal to glory. I can still see Tilly leaping to the kitchen door, and the radiance of his face as he came back. "We have luck! The cook wasn't hit!" He explained that it would be a major calamity if that cook of his were disabled, the most resourceful cook in the Second French Army. I dare say the praise was an understatement. Half an hour later we lunched on a delicious meal of black beans with a mustard sauce, with a salad of dandelion roots dressed with oil and garlic, and three surviving potatoes, fried in oil and divided into four portions. The cook wanted to serve them for three, but Tilly insisted that the man accept his share as a reward for not being killed.

Roy Chamberlain had been pursuing theological studies when we got into the war, and had left for France especially to work in the foyers. He had mastered the language with remarkable speed, and he now could speak precisely and very forcefully. He and Captain Tilly, over our meagre and improvised meal, started a hot debate about French and American ideals of sexual morality. The one point in which they were agreed was that the two countries lived by different systems.

6

Close to the foyer at Sommedieue were the barracks of the ambulance sections which served that portion of the line. Since there was a shortage of French ambulances and drivers, British and American squadrons spelled them out. We would have French ambulances for two weeks; then they would move on, and a squadron of British cars would take their place; after another two weeks an American squadron would come in.

At the foyer we saw a good deal of these Americans and Englishmen in their off-hours. They were grand fellows, the British somewhat bored by the war, in which they had been serving for three years—our men fresh and eager, since we had only recently joined up. Going to the front lines each morning I usually hailed an ambulance and got a ride, and once or twice something occurred which was more than friendly talk. One morning I rode up on a British ambulance just going on duty. At the entrance to the trenches, as I turned to wave to the driver, a French car dashed by with four men in it, a chauffeur and three high-ranking officers.

I had planned a long tour that morning, but at the first foyer I picked up some information that Chamberlain at Sommedieue ought to have at once. I started back. As I came out of the trenches, I met the same British ambulance on which I had come up. There was only one reason why it returned so early. The driver's face was a little set and he puffed at his pipe nervously.

"What happened?"

"You saw that car that passed us? A shell hit it half a mile down the line. I'm taking back the chauffeur."

I glanced through the square window behind the driver's seat in the front of the ambulance. The corpse lay still on the stretcher, but his limp feet swayed with the bouncing of the car over the ruts in the road. His head was nearly blown off. For many a night I could not get those limp boots out of my thought.

On another day I was riding on a French ambulance, driven by a middle-aged man who had been in the thick of it since the late summer of 1914. I ventured the guess that he had gone through severe experiences. He nodded. I asked which incident he recalled as the most terrifying.

He told me of an adventure with a wounded man, a *gravement blessé*. In one of the major battles the stretcher-bearers brought him just one man with the order to drive as quickly as possible to a certain hospital which had a magnet.

"Drive carefully. The slightest jolt, and you will finish him. He has a piece of steel in his heart."

It wasn't easy to navigate the shattered roads without jolting, but the ambulance driver did pretty well until the German batteries began to drop shells in front of him. There was nothing for it but to carry his delicate charge to shelter—if shelter could be found. The road skirted a low hill, and in the hillside, by good luck, as he noticed, there was a grotto or cave.

"Don't worry," he called cheerfully. "I'll get you out of this!"

There was no response. Had the fellow died of fright? He looked back—the car was empty! But in the distance, on the horizon, the critical case—steel splinter and all—was sprinting for his life.

"It was hard to explain his absence," continued the driver. "The Army doctors didn't half believe my story. I never heard of him again."

"How tragic!" I exclaimed. "Just when he thought himself safe, to drop dead."

The ambulance man shook his head. "Not that fellow! He ran till he reached home! Probably started right in having more children. I'm sure he entertains the neighbors boasting of the bullet or the cannon ball he carries in his heart."

There was a lending library at the foyer, a miscellaneous collection of French poetry and fiction. How the books came there, I couldn't learn. Perhaps they had been contributed one by one at intervals by literary-minded poilus who wished to share what they found too heavy to carry. The collection numbered about five-hundred volumes. Chamberlain asked me to catalog and take charge of it, and every evening I was a busy librarian.

The men signed up for the book they wanted, and quite often they returned it before they left the building. Or they carried it off, and sometimes they brought it back. Sometimes also they returned a book which they hadn't taken out. It was neither the right place nor the right moment in history to inaugurate or enforce library discipline, and I thought my duty done when I wrote up the record of books asked for.

Among poets, Victor Hugo was well in the lead. Perhaps the average Frenchman always turns to him in moments of national danger and patriotic exaltation. The favorite prose writer was Balzac. Whether the average Frenchman, farmer or small shopkeeper, reads Balzac in peace-time, I cannot say, but a few years ago when I saw Sacha Guitry's film, *The Story of a Cheat,* I was impressed by the fact that his hero, convalescing from a battle wound, reads the entire output of Balzac, volume after volume. There may here be a disclosure of French psychology, the significance of which I have not yet grasped.

CHAPTER XXIX

Armistice Interval

I

DURING the summer of 1918, as the fighting grew more intense, the atmosphere in Paris became noticeably optimistic. When the Germans made their last push, the city authorities set up a large billboard on the Boulevard des Italiens, and posted each morning a graph showing how near the enemy was to the capital, and what was the speed of his approach. Passers-by stopped for a moment to look, and then went about their business with a smile. When at last General Foch gave the signal to the Allied armies to strike, the billboard was removed. A daily graph could hardly keep up with the German retreat.

From many quarters the warning came that the war was not yet over, but we all believed the end was near. The personnel for the educational work which we had asked the Y in America to recruit, began to arrive in such numbers that we moved our office from 12 rue d'Aguesseau to 10 rue de l'Élysée, a large building which we shared with the American Library Association. No quarters could be pleasanter. Our windows looked on the residence of the French President. The rue de l'Élysée was a quiet street, and our rooms were large, sunny, and peaceful. At least when we first moved in. As additions to our staff arrived, and the work expanded, 10 rue de l'Élysée became even more crowded than the offices we had left at 12 rue d'Aguesseau. My associates urged me to look for more ambitious quarters. But for the moment I found it difficult to make plans. My leave of absence from Columbia had been until the end of September, with the understanding that I might stay longer if the war continued. A letter from the University now asked me what my intentions were. In America too the impression was that the war could last only a few months. But of course the Army hoped for educational aid from the moment the fighting stopped until most of our men came home. Mr. Carter knew, it seemed, as little as I about this postwar program. He told me I was to make such preparations for it as I could, and he conveyed the gratifying news that General Pershing liked what I had accomplished, and wished me to remain in charge.

So, having cabled the University that I couldn't return for a while, I began in earnest to establish contacts with the French and British universities in order to carry out the original proposals of Mr. Stokes, that eligible students from our armies should attend at least one term. Never were any plans more difficult to shape. If the war stopped during the summer, the students might get to the universities for the autumn term. If it continued into the autumn, they might begin their studying in the spring. All this planning and the administration of the plan later was to have been the responsibility of John Finley, but from the moment of his brief appearance at 12 rue d'Aguesseau on his way to his work in Palestine, we had not heard who was to replace him. The whole matter had faded a little from our thoughts.

In August, however, Mr. Stokes sent word from New York to Mr. Carter and to me that he had succeeded at last in persuading some noted educators to serve as a commission in charge of the Army educational work. Just how large a commission he contemplated has never been quite clear, but those who had accepted his invitation were Frank E. Spaulding, Superintendent of Schools in Cleveland, Ohio, and Kenyon Leech Butterfield, President of Massachusetts Agricultural College. Two men of finer qualities could hardly be found.

I immediately handed my resignation to Mr. Carter and cabled President Butler that I would meet my classes on the opening of the autumn term. Of course I was sorry to leave unfinished the work already in motion, and I was conceited enough to feel that I could do some aspects of it better than anyone who was unfamiliar with France and with the French, or who had not enjoyed my recent opportunities to establish relations with them. But since I preferred teaching and writing to administrative work, I adjusted myself quickly to the new situation.

I assumed that Mr. Stokes, operating as educational director of the Y.M.C.A. at home, had consulted with the Army, especially with General

Pershing, who after all was the boss in France. But as a matter of fact Mr. Stokes had been playing a rather lone hand. The Commander-in-Chief had not heard of any educational commission, and when he learned of it from Mr. Carter, he refused to accept a change in the educational setup at so late a date, kindly repeating his wish that I should remain at the head. Mr. Carter told me at once, and simultaneously Fred Keppel cabled from the War Department, that I must stay on the job. Perhaps he communicated with my Columbia colleagues, for they didn't seem surprised when I reversed myself again and said I should be away for another year.

Dr. Spaulding had been designated by Mr. Stokes as chairman of the Educational Commission, but being the man he is, a first-rate sport, he cabled at once that he would gladly work in any arrangement the Army wished. From that moment until we all came home, Spaulding, Butterfield and I constituted the commission in charge. I was chairman, giving my attention particularly to college and university work, and later to the art schools; Spaulding directed the program in division schools and post schools—work of high school and secondary school quality. He organized also a field staff of lecturers and supervisors. Butterfield directed instruction in agriculture, lectured on rural economics and sociology, and supervised the trade schools.

Spaulding reached France first, and with characteristic energy began organizing an office force which promptly swamped the building at 10 rue de l'Élysée. With the public school men who came over with him, he drew up lists of the textbooks needed in various subjects. Professor Daly and my older companions had already listed textbooks in science and the other college subjects. We told the War Department the importance of getting these books quickly, and with the aid of Professor George D. Strayer of Teachers College, who was assisting at the New York headquarters of the Y.M.C.A.—and with the aid also of Fred Keppel— the publishers of educational texts worked out a practical scheme for making cheap reprints of the titles we asked for, and promised early delivery if we would designate a representative to meet with them and iron out one or two minor difficulties. The Army decided to send me back to America on a fast transport, and Dr. Strayer arranged for the publishers to gather in New York as soon as I arrived. I sailed from Havre on September 23.

2

The ship on which I returned brought only a few wounded men and a dozen individuals like myself, each on some special errand. On its crossings to France it carried six or seven thousand troops, but now we had our choice of staterooms, and at mealtimes we ate in unnatural solitude, huddled together at the end of the long table. During the twilights, at dawn and at sunset, the precarious half-hour or so when the submarines liked best to strike, our orders were to put on life belts and stand by the boat to which we had been assigned. A major, hurrying back to the United States on a military errand, constituted with me the entire crew of our lifeboat. Daily we rose when the gong sounded and watched the sun come up. Every evening we met again at the boatside and watched the sunset fade into darkness. During the day we walked the decks resolutely for exercise, or sat around and read. I was taking the opportunity to bring back on this trip the French books I had collected.

Our ship took a course far to the south, I suppose to avoid submarines. The Major and I spent lazy hours watching the flying fish. The nights were hot, and the Major, having a stateroom considerably larger and cooler than mine, invited me to share it, and whenever the heat grew too intense, I accepted the offer, and we would lie in our bunks gossiping till a late hour.

He was a lawyer with a practice in Washington, much of his work being before the Supreme Court. His home was in Chevy Chase, and as the ship sped westward he put the war out of his thoughts and talked much about his young son, whom he was soon to see. We promised each other to meet again in years of peace, and perhaps we shall, some day, but I haven't seen him since the moment we docked in New York on October 4, and he pointed out his wife and his boy, waiting proudly with their welcome.

I went at once to Mother's apartment and found her in better health than letters from my sisters had let me hope. By late afternoon I reached New Canaan and walked in on the children as they were sitting down to supper. Graham was taller and heavier, tanned and healthy; Anna was growing fast—she had already forgotten what I looked like, and I had to prove I was no stranger. A few happy hours restored her confidence.

Next day I began a schedule which continued for almost a month. In the morning I would go to the Y.M.C.A. headquarters in New York at 347 Madison Avenue, and work with Franklin Hoyt and the publishers. I spent many hours selecting recruits for our teaching staff. Our educational plans had been widely publicized, and now that the second and larger phase of the work seemed likely to start, there were many volunteers, some of whom were welcome, but others had to be tactfully rejected. At the close of each crowded day I saw Mother for a moment before I caught the New Canaan train.

The delay in getting back to France troubled me. The Y.M.C.A. was inaugurating a drive for funds to expand its activities in the postwar period, and I was urged to speak at several rallies about the foyers, about the educational work already inaugurated among the troops, and about the plans which kept me busy at the moment. I was glad to help the Y, for which I had accumulated considerable admiration, but it embarrassed me to explain the future educational program as an argument for further contributions to Y work, since it had been understood from the first that when the fighting ended, the Army would take over all that Mr. Stokes had originally planned and all that the rest of us had accomplished.

This uneasiness came to a sharp climax when Fred Keppel sent word that I should come at once to Washington and call on General Robert Irwin Rees of the General Staff, who during the war had been in command of the Student Army Training Corps, thousands of students who were acquiring technical knowledge and skills in the colleges and universities. George Strayer went with me to Washington the next day. We called on General Rees, who told us in a few words that an Armistice might arrive at any moment, and that he had been ordered to France to take command of the educational work. From the questions he asked about it, I was delighted to see that headquarters at Chaumont must have supplied Washington with extremely full and accurate information about what we had done. General Rees ended our interview by saying that General Pershing was now ready to take me and the other educational workers into the Army to serve under General Rees, who would be assigned to the fifth, or training, section of the Staff in France under the command of General Harold B. Fiske. General Pershing thought the graceful way to prepare for the transfer would be for Mr. John R. Mott to write the Commander-in-Chief a letter, reciting the original understanding between the Army and the Y, and offering to give up the work, since the time had evidently arrived for the Army to carry it on. The Commander-in-Chief, replying to this letter would seize the opportunity to thank the Y for its help. Both letters would be published.

Next morning Dr. Strayer and I laid this message before Mr. Mott in the presence of Mr. Stokes and Mr. William Sloane. It was obvious at once that Mr. Mott didn't like the news. Mr. Stokes reminded him that the Army request merely carried out the agreement he had originally made with the War Department. The Y.M.C.A.'s contribution to this particular activity had been made; from that moment forward the Army should assume responsibility for an enterprise too large for any civilian organization to handle.

Mr. Mott listened intently, wrinkling his brow, tapping the desk with his pencil, and showing other symptoms of uncomfortable thought. Then to my amazement he said he was not convinced that the educational work could be carried out better by the Army than by the Y. In fact, he believed it the duty of the Y to hold on to the work in spite of what seemed practically a command from the Army. Furthermore, he concluded, the educational program was one of the strongest arguments the Y had in its new appeal for funds. To give it up now might cost the Y a million dollars in contributions. Mr. Stokes, loyal to the original bargain he had made, told Mr. Mott the work had to be surrendered to the Army, there was no choice, but Mr. Mott shook his head and thought he might hold on to it for a while anyway.

I went home that night thoroughly discouraged. No doubt the Army would eventually take over the work, but if Mr. Mott blocked the transfer, the delay would hold up the arrangements with the French and British universities and the organization of our own schools. That is, of course, just what happened. Some of our best men, like Professor Daly, declined to cool their heels in France while the Y.M.C.A. was balking. They retired from the queer situation and went home. I had counted on them, and their going was a loss.

3

I was lunching with George Hellman one day at the Columbia University Club, when Walter Damrosch happened to pass our table and stopped to speak to George. Dr. Walter, Olympian and suave, was just back from France, where at General Pershing's request he had organized the A.E.F. Bandmasters' School at Chaumont. The Commander-in-Chief had noticed the superiority of French military music, and Walter Damrosch, for the improvement of the American bands, had recommended the addition of wood winds to the brass, and intensive musical training for the bandmasters. With characteristic enthusiasm he told about the course he had installed, with excellent French instructors under the general direction of Albert Stoessel. As he talked I made a resolution to visit this school, just started, and perhaps to include musical instruction in our educational program. Though I had seen Dr. Walter frequently, in concerts of the New York Symphony and the Oratorio Society, this was my first meeting with him. I sat watching his fine face and his magnificent head. It was also the first time I had heard of Albert Stoessel, though his reputation must have been high as virtuoso violinist and as Dr. Walter's assistant conductor.

Having told his story, Dr. Walter went off to keep an engagement, and George turned to me with a gleam in his eye. Did I intend to set up an art school? The idea had not occurred. George expressed sorrow at my oversight, and plunged into a whirlwind argument, or what he would call an argument, but as I've often told him, he can advance a pet idea as though it were an ultimatum. That day he was unusually wrought up, and for an hour or so a stream of insistent eloquence poured through Alfred de Musset's beard. The Army, he said was full of boys who must be eager for instruction in art; there could be no better place for them to study than in France; there were excellent painters and sculptors already in the service, who could teach them; and if I wanted someone to gather the faculty and set the school up—he would leave for France at once.

He rather took my breath away, and I postponed the decision for a few hours. His idea attracted me; I could see extraordinary possibilities, since he had long been an art collector and an art dealer, and presumably knew his way around in the art world abroad as well as at home. I hesitated only because I wasn't at all sure the Army authorities would be enthusiastic about instruction in sculpture and painting. But after a night's thought I told the Y recruiting board that George Hellman was returning to France with me, also Lloyd Warren and Grosvenor Atterbury, distinguished architects, whom he had enlisted to assist him.

The art instruction turned out to be perhaps the most brilliant phase of the educational program, and George by his devoted and skillful direction of the work earned the grateful admiration of the Staff, from General Pershing down. For me, this association with an old friend in what proved for both of us the most dramatic adventure of our lives, was altogether fortunate and happy. George knew well not only his subject but the country in which we were to work. He, with Colonel Charles W. Exton in Paris and later with Major Livingston Watrous at Beaune, constituted my advisory council through the most crowded days of the educational work. Grand men, all of them, good linguists, natural diplomats, warm and loyal friends.

4

On Sunday, November 3, Pauline, the children and I went to morning service at the New Canaan church. I knew I'd be starting to France before the week was out. When Anna grew restless during the sermon, Graham entertained her by drawing pictures. He was already an artist in every nerve, and he used a pencil or a crayon to talk with. On Thursday the seventh, I went to New Canaan in a confused state of mind. During the afternoon New York had gone wild over false reports that an armistice had been signed, and if the war was over, it suddenly became hard to leave the children for another year. The mess between the Army and the Y had something to do with my dejection. The next day I was back in New York, winding up educational business. On the ninth, I said goodbye to Mother and at four o'clock took a taxi to the *Lorraine,* bound for Bordeaux. The parting was difficult. Mother had been failing day by day, these four weeks, and I doubted if I should see her again. But she put on a show of vigor, to cheer me off, and when I looked back at the house, there was her gray head leaning out of the window, one hand clutching her shawl, the other waving to me.

On the *Lorraine* I shared a cabin with Franklin Hoyt, who was in charge of the first large batch of textbooks. On the ship with us were Jo Davidson the sculptor, Lincoln Steffens, Owen Johnson the novelist, André Tardieu, Louis Aubert of the Tardieu mission, and several military men of high rank, notably Colonel Réquin of Foch's Staff. All the French who had been in Washington were going home. The war was over.

The news of the true Armistice, flashed to us Monday the eleventh, made us thoughtful and silent. The military men knew what the war had cost in blood and agony, and they had no strong hope of a lasting peace. After dinner Steffens, Davidson, Colonel Réquin and I sat talking in the smoking room till nearly morning. I had had no previous acquaintance with any of the three, but before breakfast the next day I had learned something about the Colonel and Jo. In another twenty-four hours I began to know Lincoln Steffens.

Jo looked a little taller than he does today, perhaps because he still had something of his youthful slenderness. His magnificent statesmanlike beard, suggesting Lord Salisbury, had not yet turned gray. His deep voice and his masterful eyes were as they are now. It was at the beginning of a memorable chapter in his busy career. Since most of the great soldiers and the heads of governments would be at the Peace Conference, he planned to make busts of them for historical record. His extraordinary genius for portraiture may have been known before, but this work established his reputation once for all.

Lincoln Steffens had not, then, quite so many lines in his face as his later portraits show, but he was known the world over as super-reporter and investigator. He was going now to watch the Peace Conference. He was of medium height, slightly taller than Jo but not much. He parted his hair but it tended to fall in a bang. He wore a slight mustache, and on the very end of his chin the tuft of a beard. The expression of his face was kind, with a touch of Mephistopheles in it. He considered himself a disillusioned realist, and was rather proud of his ability to take a large view of events and individuals, but he was full of contradictions. Along with clear-eyed realism he had almost an oversupply of sentimentality. He knew it himself. In one of our talks in France he confessed a boyish love of revolutions, at least at their start, a fondness for romantic situations, and a lifelong capacity to lose his heart in unexpected directions. He was marvelous in intimate talk, stimulating himself as well as his hearer, so that sometimes, if I'm not mistaken, he remembered as things said, things which he had only imagined in passing. Shortly after I had published the *Private Life of Helen of Troy* I happened to meet him in the Pennsylvania Station, and he spoke about the book. "I recognize what we talked about in Paris," he said—"your opinions of women." But that wasn't what we talked about in Paris.

5

Before the train left Bordeaux I heard a report that the Army would go home with unexpected speed, and no educational work would be attempted. On the train I met one of our itinerant teachers who asked whether the Army would after all take the work over from the Y. I reached my room in the rue de Verneuil feeling discouraged and uncertain. But next morning at the office in the rue de l'Élysée, I felt better. From squads of new Y.M.C.A. secretaries, Spaulding had appropriated for our work several women of unusual executive or office experience who were willing to serve, temporarily at least, as stenographers. One of them, Caroline M. McCullagh, was to keep the minutes of the Educational Commission. President Butterfield and General Rees might arrive any day. Of course Spaulding was disappointed that we had not yet been transferred to the Army, but somehow or other the educational plans would be carried out, he was sure. To give us the additional room we needed he had persuaded Mr. Carter to rent the large house at 76 rue du Faubourg Saint-Honoré. This building, formerly a magnificent private home, stood at the end of the rue de l'Élysée. We started at once to move into it, and when General Rees and Butterfield arrived, it became at once the scene of our Commission meetings, often with General Rees present to advise. There we planned, and from there carried out, the organization of the work in French and British universities, the division and post schools throughout our armies in France and in occupied territory, and from our discussions in those pleasant rooms evolved the idea of our own American University at Beaune.

CHAPTER XXX

76 rue du Faubourg Saint-Honoré

I

MY COLLEAGUES in the Commission were dissimilar in temperament, but both extremely easy to work with. Dr. Spaulding, an Amherst graduate, had studied much in Europe and was at home in any scholarly or cultural environment, but he had made school administration his life work, and he represented American ideals of administrative efficiency in that field. He knew personally all the strong men in the school systems of the various States, and he had himself trained many of them. When it was known that he was to look after this type of education in the Army program, his ablest friends volunteered in great number. Recalling our work together, I think of his alertness of mind, his steadiness of nerve and his sense of humor—and of the devoted disciples who backed him up. He handled for the Commission all of our difficult business negotiations with the Y, which was unable or reluctant to supply transportation or funds for our expanding program. When the Army finally took us over, it was Dr. Spaulding who skillfully and tactfully adjusted old or unfinished contracts and negotiated new ones with the teaching personnel or with the French. He set up high school courses in divisions, and courses of less advanced grade in isolated regiments. He gave me invaluable advice in the negotiations with French and British universities and in the organization of our own university at Beaune. I did not have his experience with school trustees and boards of regents, with city councils and State legislatures. Public education is involved in politics, but so is any enterprise in which we have to persuade our fellow man to go our way. Now we were dealing simultaneously with the Y.M.C.A., the Army, and the university authorities in France and in England. However cordial the general good will, there were snags in plenty. If our enterprise survived, it was only by grace of patience and tact and constant re-statement of our point of view until we got it in a form the other fellow could approve. I don't know what we should have done without Frank Spaulding.

Kenyon Butterfield I had known by sight at Amherst when he was President of the Massachusetts Agricultural College. Professor Olds had spoken often of his sensitive and idealistic spirit. Like Dr. Spaulding he was an experienced administrator, and he brought to France with him some of the best agricultural experts in the United States. The importance of agriculture for our country would, I knew, be set before the Army competently and convincingly. But Dr. Butterfield was a poet and a dreamer, and he had joined our Commission in the hope of accomplishing even more than the encouragement of agriculture and the improvement of farm conditions at home. He foresaw then, and repeatedly urged upon us, the necessity of international organization to avoid world famine. I confess I thought he was worrying himself over nothing. Like most people then, I could not believe the United States or England or France or Germany would ever be short of food. Dr. Butterfield admitted the crisis was still distant, but when it came at last, he said, it would stay for a long time. It didn't really need to come if Europe and America planned together well in advance.

He was a melancholy man, intense in all his emotions. Like most idealists he had strong prejudices. I don't know that he was an out-and-out pacifist, but his dislike of war induced in him a dread of all military organizations. It remains a puzzle to me that he would join the Army Educational Commission, even though it was to function only a short time. Dr. Spaulding and I never could bring him to our point of view about compulsory national training. He was sure it would mean Prussianism. He denied that a general rounding up of youth might provide a check on disease and ignorance, or that national training might include any opportunities for truly democratic education. When we began discussing an improvised American University at Beaune, he opposed the project warmly, on the ground that a single large school might tempt our military commanders to dictate the program and slip into it some Prussian ideas.

With the Army officers personally he was always on excellent terms. In spite of his fear of what he called the Prussian temperament, he controlled the work in his own department with an iron hand. Dr. Spaulding and I, in whom he suspected terrible tendencies toward dictatorship, were soft and easygoing in comparison. ·

We three were fortunate to be under the direct command of General Rees. He had the temperament of a diplomat and the tastes of a scholar. In youth, before entering the Army, he had studied law, and his work as director of the Student Army Training Corps had brought him in contact with educators all over the United States. About college presidents or professors he had nothing more to learn.

He was a handsome man, fairly tall, with an alert and friendly face. The keenness of his dark eyes was balanced by the kindness of his smile. I was attracted on our first meeting in Washington by the quality of his voice and the way he used it. Perhaps because of his law training, his judicial faculties were highly developed, and in talk they modified to some extent his natural promptness of decision. Just when you knew he had made up his mind, he would hesitate for a second, as though considering conscientiously one final argument for the other side. He had a strong sense of humor and a love of all beautiful things. He always backed George Hellman's art work, and in gratitude George would take him on tours of inspection through the life classes. We teased the General about the amount of inspection the models needed. He always laughed at us benignly, and he always accepted George's invitation.

2

As soon as the Armistice was signed, the French and the English both made agreeable plans for helping the Allies to understand each other. At the University of London and at the Sorbonne, lectures were arranged to be given chiefly by Americans, though at the French university some British scholars were included. The lectures at the University of London were given at Bedford College on successive Fridays from October 18 to December 13. The speakers were George Santayana, E. Price Bell, editor of the *Chicago Daily News,* Professor John W. Cunliffe, Dr. George E. MacLean, ex-president of the University of Iowa, Mrs. Bowlker, president of the Women's Municipal League of Boston, Major R. M. Johnston, Professor of History at Harvard, myself, and Vice-Admiral

William S. Simms. I was to speak on "American Character," on December 6. There was a different person in the chair each lecture, and I was supposed to be presided over by the Duchess of Marlborough, but on December 6 her place was taken by Major Leonard Darwin, fourth son of the great scientist, a most courteous and sympathetic chairman.

The Sorbonne lectures, given on an endowment called the *Conférences Louis Liard,* were planned at the same time but were not given until April and May. The speakers were Dr. Joseph A. Blake, head of the American Hospital at Neuilly and Professor of Surgery at Columbia; Charles H. Haskins of Harvard; George H. Nettleton of Yale; Charles Vibbert of the University of Michigan; Yvon Eccles of Balliol College, Oxford; James T. Shotwell of Columbia; W. P. Ker of the University of London, and myself. I spoke on April 3. When I told Professor Legouis, who conveyed the invitation to me, that my subject would be Shakspere's *Tempest,* he smiled, and without relaxing his Norman dignity, commented as if to himself—"Ah, an allegory of the war! Caliban of course will be the Kaiser. Is it too much to hope that Miranda is the new France? Undoubtedly Ferdinand is the United States."

"But who is Prospero?" I asked.

He shook his head over my stupidity. "What a question, dear Erskine! President Wilson, of course."

The hurried trip to London gave me an opportunity to see Cunliffe at the London branch of the American University Union 16 Pall Mall East. With him was associated Dr. MacLean. Together they prepared the way for the sending of American troops to British schools, and what they told me about the postwar situation in English and Scottish universities helped enormously. I met also Edwin W. Pahlow, who had been teaching history at Lawrenceville School and after the war taught the same subject at Ohio State University. Pahlow was working with American troops in England as one of our educational force, and in due time he came into our Army with the Educational Commission. He was a sensitive, cultured fellow, with sound knowledge of English history, and with his own special love of the English character. Knowing our plans for educational work in France, he took me one day to Hornchurch, just outside of London, where the New Zealanders had established for the diversion and instruction of convalescent soldiers, a school or college or university which surpassed in some respects anything we later accomplished. It was a small institution, but it gave instruction in any subject the students wanted—in the crafts, the trades, the fine and applied arts, the usual branches of book learning.

When I started for London, my friend Mr. Theron C. Crawford asked me to call on his daughter, Mrs. Lovat Fraser. The address was 11 Tregunter Road, and on the afternoon of December 10 in the densest of fogs I persuaded an unwilling taxi-driver to take me to that street and number. Why the driver was surly when I asked him to go so far, I didn't know until he found the place, and I said he might drive me back in fifteen or twenty minutes. He got down from the wheel and offered to fight me. "Don't you go in that direction, anyway?" I asked. "I thought you might like to have me again as a fare. But don't worry—I withdraw the suggestion if it spoils your temper." He took his fare and his tip, touched his cap, and apologized. "I've had nothing to eat since breakfast," he said. "There aren't cars enough to go round."

From the fog and the war-weary mood of this encounter, I stepped through Lovat Fraser's door into an extraordinary home painted like his stage costumes and scenery, and his book decorations. The walls in the hall were yellow, the balustrade of the stair was red, the treads, if I am not mistaken, were ebony black for the visitor's aid in finding them in the general blaze.

Lovat Fraser was upstairs playing with a child. His wife was doing an errand somewhere, but would soon return. I conveyed Mr. Crawford's messages; we talked about Paris and the war, in which he had been badly gassed; I had just referred to his unusual taste in decoration, when his wife came in.

"Every time the weather changes, if the fog is thicker or thinner, Lovat gets out his paints, the kind that come in pails with big brushes, and does the house over to match the weather. Once I stopped him just in time when he had the idea of a white floor and a black ceiling. I was glad to notice as I came in just now that he has done nothing to the grand piano while I was out, and I refuse to let him make the bathtub more cheerful."

I left that merry home against my will, but I had a dinner engagement. Lovat Fraser, I now knew, created brilliant scenic decorations by expressing the joy of his own heart. Not long after our meeting his war injuries took him to his grave. As we talked that day he probably knew, as I certainly did not guess, that his lungs were done for, and his time was short.

3

In one of my meetings with Pahlow, I made the acquaintance of an extremely tall young man from Tennessee, a Rhodes scholar named John J. Tigert. During the war he had been working with the British Navy in the North Sea, but now he wanted to get into the educational work of the Army, and we hadn't exchanged many words before he suggested going back with me to France. He was a graduate of Vanderbilt University, with the founding of which his family had much to do. He had and has a gorgeous Southern accent, suggesting Tennessee or Kentucky of some other mountainous region. What attracted me to him, however, was his earnestness and his persistence. When he fastened his teeth into an idea, he just couldn't be shaken loose. Education was his master passion, as it naturally would be, after an ancestry thick with preachers, professors and college presidents. At Oxford he had made the acquaintance of a kind of education not to be come at easily in the United States, certainly not in the South. When I first met him he was fired with the dream of raising standards in our schools and colleges. Since immediateness is the essence of his temperament, he wanted to begin at once.

Such a man would not easily be stopped by any obstacles. I took him to France. Since we had a calm crossing on a starry night, we spent the hours on deck or leaning on the rail, Tigert holding forth in an unbroken rhapsody about the American character and the American mind as they would be after a proper amount of plowing, hoeing, raking and planting. I can't remember that I went to bed at all that night. When we landed at Havre my head was slightly confused, I suppose from lack of sleep. Next morning Tigert and I walked around the town until time for the Paris train to leave. If our Beaune University had then been in existence I should have kept him for one of the faculty, but he wished to work with troops in occupied territory, so I sent him there. He made a fine record. After his return to the United States he served as professor of Philosophy in several colleges and as president of another; from 1921 to 1928 he was U.S. Commissioner of Education; since 1928 he has been President of the University of Florida. When I saw him a few months ago we were reminded of that Channel crossing in December, 1918, when he spent the night telling me how he'd like to educate the whole United States.

CHAPTER XXXI

French and British Universities

I

AS SOON as I got back to the office at 76 rue du Faubourg Saint-Honoré, the meetings of the educational commission commenced in earnest. General Rees came to Paris from Chaumont at least once a week, and with him we planned Spaulding's schools throughout the army, and lecture circuits for Butterfield's agricultural experts. We gave our attention first to those activities which could be begun at once.

Next we took up the plans for entering qualified soldiers in the French and British universities. Here unfortunately there was no great hurry, since the war had ended too late for us to connect with the autumn term, and the spring term would not begin until 1919. Meanwhile of course our connection with the Y.M.C.A. would have to be terminated, but General Rees, experienced lawyer that he was, rather thought the natural sequence of events would force a carrying out of the original understanding with the Army.

The correct move for us, said the General, was to complete all the arrangements with the French and British educational authorities, and set up a military organization to execute the plan. Then when the spring term arrived, the Y.M.C.A. would find itself in a ridiculous position, since it had no authority over the soldiers, no right to dispose of their time, and apparently no adequate funds to pay for their board and lodging, nor for their tuition. The Army certainly would not permit the boys to accept as a gift a term of residence at Oxford or Cambridge or the

Sorbonne; all expenses must be met, and the boys must be provided with the money.

Since all this was my part of the work, almost every detail is still burned into my memory, but even if I forgot, I could recover the facts from the extraordinary minutes of the Commission meetings kept by our secretary, Miss McCullagh. She was too much interested in our discussions, she said, to organize the minutes while the meeting was in progress; she preferred to take down every word and extract the minutes afterward. When the educational work came to an end and we were sailing for home, she gave me a complete file of the records, with the exact words spoken by each of us, the name of the speaker beside the speech, as in the script of a play.

From the first of our discussions about the university work, it was evident that more boys would want to go to college than the French and British universities could find room for. We know today, harassed GI's know quite too well, that after a war there's a rush of returning veterans back to their interrupted studies, and there's also a new generation of students. The same situation existed though not to the extent and not in such numbers among the French and British universities after the First World War. We ought not to forget the generosity of both countries in reserving at least half the places in their finest schools during the spring of 1919 for the American boys waiting for a ship home.

General Rees and I were sure, both of us, that we'd have to organize somewhere an American university for those who couldn't be admitted to the French or British. We wanted to make sure that the privilege of temporary residence in a foreign school went only to those who were unusually well qualified in mental ability and in character. That is why we built up so carefully a system of military commanders to watch the whole experiment.

2

General Pershing had an exceptional acquaintance with educational conditions in the United States, and understood thoroughly our opportunity in France. As a soldier he saw also that the proposed schools and lectures through the Army would help to preserve law and order during the post-Armistice reaction from battle strain. In a talk at Chaumont, soon after General Rees came to France, the Commander-in-Chief remarked that of course he could try to maintain discipline by drilling the soldiers a number of hours each day, and by giving them artificial tasks, but he doubted that American boys would put up with such treatment. The buck privates as well as their officers knew the war was over, they had done the job the country asked of them, and that was that. They were eager to get home, not only to see their families and friends, but to reassure themselves that they hadn't lost their place in the economic procession. "They are worrying about new developments in business and in society, and though they haven't been over here long, some of them fear they have lost touch.

"We can reassure them. I count on the Educational Commission to provide opportunities for any kind of study the men want. Teach them Greek if they ask for it, though I dare say they won't. If a man has been a house-painter and intends to go on with that work, send him home a better painter than he was when he enlisted. They have all sacrificed something; let's see to it, if we can, that they gain something too."

General Pershing was a great soldier, but as he spoke that morning at Chaumont he seemed a good deal of a statesman, and you couldn't come near his headquarters without knowing he was an unusual executive. Order, precision, neatness, marked his appearance, his manner, his speech. The soldiers liked to emphasize his hard-driving, tough qualities, but they meant to pay him a tribute, as in the nickname for him, "Black Jack." He was the kind of leader men want in a fight, but he was another kind of leader too, and I had the privilege to see this side of him. If he thought you were equal to a task, he gave it to you, and from then on he backed you up. He never interfered, but you had the feeling that something terrible would happen if you failed. Though he didn't try to run his Army single-handed, he kept a remarkably close eye on what his subordinates were doing. During the Armistice, as long as we remained in France, he traveled constantly from one end of the country to the other, wherever there were American troops, and in the educational work we soon grew accustomed to his sudden visits. He knew his inspections gave our program importance in the eyes of the whole Army —also in the eyes of French educators, who expressed amazement that a general in the field should take such an interest in culture.

Though I did not meet General Pershing in France as often as I should have liked, not more than half a dozen times, I came to admire him greatly, and for qualities not always ascribed to him. He had several kinds of ability which are of value in peace as well as war. He could judge character, and he could recognize in young men what they were likely to be as they grew older. Many of our top generals in the Second World War were his young hopefuls in the first. Whenever he appeared we learned to look for Colonel George C. Marshall in the neighborhood. Pershing's interest in education came not only from his early service as military instructor in land-grant colleges, but from his deep conviction that the problems of human society should be solved, if possible, by training of the mind and the character, rather than by police discipline and penalties.

Speaking of the soldiers just after the Armistice, he said to me, "They are relaxed—let down—inclined to run wild—but all they need is something to occupy their minds. Keep their minds busy, or they'll concentrate on girls and cognac. Then there'll be street fights, and France will want to throw us all out."

When Columbia University gave him an honorary degree in 1920, Dean Woodbridge, sitting next to him at the Commencement banquet, was astounded by his interest in new social movements, and by his accurate knowledge of them. "How can he be a soldier, with such a heart and such a mind?"

The exclamation may have been natural for a university officer meeting the General for the first time on an academic campus, but Woodbridge would not have been surprised had he seen Pershing looking after his Army in France.

The Educational Commission was under the command of Brigadier General Rees, and through him, under the command of Brigadier General Harold B. Fiske, chief of the fifth section of the Staff, the training section. The soldiers who called Pershing a martinet had no word left to describe General Fiske. He was a drill master. Not quite so tall as Pershing, and less impressive in appearance and manner, he was always spick and span. He made me think of those headmasters who maintain unnatural correctness of speech and deportment because their life job is to set a good example to school boys. General Pershing, in spite of his immaculate appearance, seemed always at ease with himself; General Fiske had his stiff moments and his easy ones.

To me he was courteous and friendly and he gave our educational work loyal support, but I assumed that he did so because it was Pershing's wish. I can't imagine that by himself he would have found a place for civilian or cultural forms of education in his training program.

3

General Pershing, General Fiske, and General Rees had under them a number of officers in charge of Army students in France and England. Since the largest contingent would attend classes at the Sorbonne and other institutions in Paris, it was decided to place there the officer responsible for all the university groups in France. General Rees, I suppose after consultation with General Fiske, selected for this post Colonel Charles W. Exton, a West Point graduate, who had served in Cuba during the Spanish American War, afterward for three years in the Philippines, and for another three in the Hawaiian Islands. For four years he gave instruction at West Point, and during the two and a half years before our entry into the First World War he served as military attaché in Switzerland. In competence, in appearance, and in his beautiful manners, he was the ideal West Pointer. He spoke French, and his years in Switzerland had given him in many respects a European point of view.

He was the first appointment General Rees made to the military organization of our educational work. Colonel Exton came at once to Paris and set up his office with the Commission at 76 rue du Faubourg Saint-Honoré. When we moved our headquarters to Beaune a few months later, he transferred his desk to the Paris office of the Training Section at 53 Avenue Montaigne. So long as we were all in Paris I used to lunch with him almost daily. He enjoyed, as I did, the civilized continental way of keeping business separated from food, and at a number of moderately priced restaurants we used to find an excellent lunch and a table in the corner, where we could exchange opinions about the state of the world. Exton's opinions were worth listening to.

When General Rees was in town he would join us, and so would Spaulding and Butterfield on rare occasions. But my two Commission colleagues had the American habit of pushing without pause from breakfast to dinner. More than a sandwich at noon was for them riotous debauchery, and to save time they liked to have the sandwich brought in.

Colonel Exton was assisted by Major Julian Lowell Coolidge, Professor of Mathematics at Harvard, and by Stephen Hayes Bush, of the Army Educational Corps, Professor of Romance Languages at Iowa University. During the war Major Coolidge had served as liaison officer attached to the French General Staff, and after the Armistice he continued as liaison officer for the educational work. He had absolute command of the

French language, he was well known among his mathematical colleagues at the Sorbonne, his war experience had brought him in contact with all the important officials in Paris.

I first met him when he came one day to my office in the rue de l'Élysée looking for light on some educational question which an American officer had put up to him, probably an officer who had studied at Harvard and thought with good reason that Professor Coolidge could more probably answer hard questions than the Y-Army outfit, at that time just getting under way. The question happened to be one that the Major couldn't answer, and neither could I, but we worked out a solution together, and in the process became firm friends. He and Colonel Exton with their quite different backgrounds made a strong team, the Major knowing the French university system from the inside, and the Colonel having at his fingertips Army traditions and regulations which would apply to the students, or which could be interpreted to serve their needs. When the spring term at last began and a large number of our soldiers were registered at the Sorbonne side by side with the French students, the University invited Professor Coolidge to give a course in mathematics. He gave it in French, becoming a visiting professor for the term.

It was easy to foresee that for the Army students in Paris a dean would be needed, someone to give the boys whatever educational advice they needed, to see that they got into the right courses, to keep an eye on their progress, to mediate or interpret between them and their instructors when difficulty arose from the difference between French and American customs. Professor Bush was the Paris dean.

This setup, military and educational, was repeated in the detachments which went to the other universities. Since the number of students would not be so large outside of Paris, the other detachment had only one officer in command, but with him was always associated a dean, a professional educator.

I should like to say much more about Coolidge and Bush, for both of whom I retain affectionate regard. Major Coolidge was short of stature, in appearance very alert and somewhat whimsical. He was the type of professor which the American campus prizes, an original, a "character." At my first glimpse of him as he came into the office at the rue de l'Élysée, his military costume made a weird impression. I had never seen anything like it. As a matter of fact, it was simply the regulation uniform of an

American officer as worn by Professor Coolidge, for his own comfort and in unconscious expression of his own character. Instead of the long over-coat he had a jacket heavily trimmed with fur. I believe this warm garment is common in Alaska, and that morning Paris was cold. The major carried his officer's cap in his hand, or rather in both his hands, flattening out the cloth head-covering and rolling it up as he talked. He laughed easily in a nervous, friendly way, and he had a singularly sweet smile. Both the French and the American officers admired him as com-rade and fellow campaigner, and they stood in awe of his scientific eminence.

Stephen Bush was large, energetic, generous in physique and tempera-ment, a gusty character. His scholarship in the field of romance lan-guages and the history of French culture was considerable, but he was so irrevocably an American type that no amount of studious application would ever enable him to pass for a Frenchman. He was just the man to deal with our soldier-students, and perhaps the French authorities, knowing him well, found it easier to understand the boys.

4

Our organization for the British universities was simpler since there was no language problem. The officer in command was Colonel Francis F. Longley, who had his headquarters in London at 47 Russell Square. Colonel Longley, like Colonel Exton, was a West Pointer, and perhaps it was Exton who nominated him to command our soldier-students across the Channel, but Longley's record in the war had been so brilliant, and his personality was so widely known and liked, that his appointment was almost a foregone conclusion.

He was slightly taller than Colonel Exton, a handsome man with a warm personality, the charm of which would have been hard to resist, if anyone had tried. He was widely read; I remember that on the evening when we first met in Paris, he disclosed unusual ability to quote great poems from memory. Colonel Exton prodded him into this performance, offering to wager that his former West Point comrade knew more good poetry by heart than I did. I didn't take him up.

To assist him in England, we tried to find young men with commis-sions who had once been Rhodes scholars. I dare say that Longley's staff represented a volume and an altitude of scholarship and culture rarely if ever attained by any military group of the same number.

5

In perfecting the organization to look after our students in French universities, I made some elementary blunders and acquired some elementary information about Army rules and regulations. I had assured the *recteurs* that the soldiers who wished to study would enter at the beginning of the term, and would remain till the end. The term was for four months. In my talks with General Rees I had assumed carelessly that the boys might be sent on leave. Eventually I woke up to the fact that leave is not granted for so long a period as four months, and that a soldier gets no extra pay. Only the officers could afford tuition, board and lodging at a university.

After discussion with General Fiske, General Rees heard from the Commander-in-Chief that properly qualified students would be sent to the universities on special military duty. They would have a generous supplement to their pay—what was called "commutation of board and lodging," some four or five dollars daily. As the tuition fee for the term was moderate, the extra pay enabled a buck-private, if he qualified scholastically, to sign up for study. We decided to send eight privates for every officer, but when soldiers are sent on a military errand, they have a military commander, a medical officer, perhaps a quartermaster, certainly the usual supply of sergeants to keep them in order, and other kinds of personnel not found in college halls. I began to have bad dreams of a detachment two-hundred strong marching into the University of Poitiers or the University of Grenoble, headed by some tough character from the Regular Army, more respected for his swearing than for his spelling. How could we ensure that the officers in charge of the student detachments should be gentlemen and scholars, such as the university faculties would be happy to welcome?

When I asked General Rees if I could appoint the detachment commanders, he laughed, and said that Pershing would probably like to retain his command of the Army, but some good results might be reached another way. Who were the men I'd like to nominate? I gave him the names, selected from the registration cards of the American University

Union, and these officers were ordered down to Paris for a talk one Sunday morning with General Rees and me.

They were all university graduates who had seen active service in France. As far as possible we assigned them each to a French university where he would be for some special reason much at home. It was our intention to provide each with an experienced educator to serve as his dean, but we couldn't find at the moment enough men of the type we were looking for. Several universities had to go deanless. In those cases the commanders managed to get along somehow.

The total number of students at French Universities was 6,040. At each university the local citizens, encouraged by the central Government at Paris, formed committees to arrange comfortable quarters for Army students, as far as possible in private homes. The success of this hospitable plan was quite remarkable. The boys had been warned that any incorrectness of behavior would cause them to be sent back at once to their regiment. In the whole spring term there was need for disciplinary action for only two students out of the six thousand. Each detachment developed the college spirit which they were accustomed to at home. They organized athletic teams, glee clubs and dramatic societies, and they published a school paper, some papers of course more ambitious than others.

6

For Great Britain, Colonel Longley appointed Edwin Pahlow as Dean or chief educational adviser, Captain C. L. Moore, Adjutant; Captain A. M. Jackson, personnel Adjutant, and Captain N. S. Cox, Supply Officer. The students were distributed over so large a number of institutions in the whole United Kingdom that it was impossible to duplicate the organization we had for the French universities. The senior officer present at each institution was the detachment commander at that place.

The total number of students in Great Britain was 2,023. A single paper, the *American Soldier-Student,* was published for all the detachments in Great Britain. It can hardly be called a student publication, for although journalistic-minded soldiers attending London institutions did a good deal of the work, Colonel Longley was editor-in-chief and Mr. Pahlow was associate editor.

In Great Britain as in France the Americans pursued their usual undergraduate habits and practiced their national sports. The first number of the *American Soldier-Student*, May 14, 1919, reported a baseball game between the Cambridge and the Manchester teams, the first game of baseball ever played on the historic St. John's cricket grounds, with fully five thousand interested spectators lining both sides of the field.

It would be difficult to say whether the American students in the French schools or those in the British enjoyed themselves more. Certainly the kindness extended to us in both countries was extraordinary. I wondered what my grandfather would have said about it could his ghost have spoken. Some of the distinguished British scholars thought up charming courtesies with which to say goodbye when at last we started for home. Dr. Arthur G. Shipley, Vice-Chancellor of Cambridge, addressed to each of his American students the following letter of farewell:

> CHRIST'S COLLEGE LODGE,
> CAMBRIDGE
> 12th June, 1919

DEAR SIR,

I had hoped to say a personal word of good-bye to the American Soldier-Students on the 11th, when the American Ambassador intended to be here. He was, however, detained in Paris, and the opportunity did not occur. May I, however, write you a word of thanks and of farewell? I am thankful to the American students for coming and living a few months amongst us. I want every American Soldier-Student to feel he has a second home in England; that he has a share in an ancient college in one of the oldest of the British Universities; and I want him to keep in touch with it.

If the United States and Great Britain can keep together in peace as they have done in war, nothing else matters.

> Oh ye who in eternal youth
> Speak with a living and creative blood
> This universal English, and do stand
> Its breathing book; live worthy of that grand
> Heroic utterance—Parted, yet a whole,
> Far, yet unsever'd,—Children brave and free
> Of the great Mother-tongue, and ye shall be
> Lords of an Empire wide as Shakespeare's soul,
> Sublime as Milton's immemorial theme,
> And rich as Chaucer's speech, and fair as
> Spenser's dream.

> Yours very cordially,
> A. G. SHIPLEY
> Vice-Chancellor.

CHAPTER XXXII

Beaune

I

THE transfer of the educational work to the Army was announced in General Orders No. 62, dated April 8, 1919. Our students in British institutions entered at the beginning of the summer term, in April. The corresponding term for French universities ran from March to June. Toward the end of January the French authorities began to be nervous, having had no word from the Army about the number who would attend, or when they would arrive, though all other details had been agreed on.

Toward the end of January, René Galland and I called on Louis Aubert and offered our opinion that some public gesture from the French Government might set our plans in motion. In a few days Mr. Tardieu, in the name of his Government, made to General Pershing a formal offer of the French universities for the service of the American troops. General Pershing then appointed General Rees and me to accept the offer and arrange for the carrying out of the work. As he knew, the arrangements had already been made. There was no further delay.

2

Even before our Army students were safely in the French and British universities, we were planning a large American school or cluster of schools to take care of those for whom the crowded foreign institutions had no room. On January 21, 1919, the Educational Commission, meeting with General Rees at 76 rue du Faubourg Saint-Honoré, decided that the Army must set up a university of its own, with a faculty drawn from scholars and scientists already serving in the armed forces. The next three days General Rees and I spent in his car, looking for an American hospital in the central part of France, which might be converted into classrooms and dormitories. Any large field hospital would already have some kind of chemical laboratory, and the rest could be added. We drove to Chartres, to Tours, westward as far as Nevers, without finding what we wanted.

The hospital at Mars, near Nevers, was suitable for our purposes, but the use of it could not be obtained, and General Rees returned to headquarters at Chaumont, to consult with other members of the Staff. On February 5, Colonel Ira L. Reeves, commanding the One Hundred Thirty-seventh Infantry at Sampigny, was ordered to report to headquarters, and there was directed to inspect the hospitals at Allerey and at Beaune as possible sites for the University. Two days later the Colonel recommended Beaune, with Allerey for Dr. Butterfield's use as an agricultural school. On February 8, Beaune was definitely chosen as the site of the A.E.F. University, and Colonel Reeves was appointed its military commander. No better location could have been found, and no abler officer to transform the vast hospital into a practical though unconventional equipment for the various schools of a modern university.

Colonel Reeves had risen from the ranks in the Regular Army. I believe he enlisted at the earliest possible age. He was a born soldier and a born leader. After service in Cuba and in the Philippines, he was retired because of severe wounds, and for a few years taught military science in various western universities. Later he was President of Norwich University. He came to France therefore with distinction both in education and in soldiering. He won new honors, leading his men at the front, and was just recovering from severe gassing when General Rees asked for him as University commander. He was a loyal and inspiring associate, an inexhaustible reservoir of good humor, good sense and novel ideas. That he recognized at once the unique qualities of Beaune, is proof of his taste and insight.

Beaune, in Roman times Belna, is a small, walled town with about thirteen thousand inhabitants. It lies south of Dijon on the line to Lyons. Above and below it are small villages whose names read like a wine card —Gevrey, Vougeot, Meursault, Puligny—Montrachet, Nuits-St.-Georges.

Beaune, the center of the Burgundy wine district, has been celebrated for its product since the fourth century.

Of the ancient wall nothing is now left except two round towers and sections of a deep moat, but the original town is clearly marked by the architecture of its houses and by the pattern of its narrow streets. Its famous hospital, the *Hospice de Beaune,* was founded in 1443, and its buildings have been in continuous use since before the discovery of America. The modern suburbs, outside the walls, contain several interesting buildings, especially the Hôtel de la Poste, which in a less modern form entertained Washington Irving, and before him Thomas Jefferson.

The American hospital, which we were to turn into a university, had been built on a piece of land one mile square, east of the town. The hospital buildings had been put up by American labor battalions with material brought from America. Hundreds of barracklike concrete buildings constituted the wards. They had been built to contain about forty-thousand beds, only a small proportion of which were in use when the war ended. From the hospital grounds there was a fine view of the Burgundy landscape in every direction. To the west we could see the town with the spires of the church and the Hospice; along the edge of the western horizon stretched the famous *Côte d'Or,* the golden hillside which exposes the minerals in its soil to just the right angle of the sun's rays to produce the great wines. Allerey, where we were to have our farm school, was five or six miles south of Beaune.

3

On February 11, I started for Beaune with Spaulding, Butterfield, George Hellman, and Grosvenor Atterbury. Colonel Reeves was waiting at the hospital, where we met him for the first time. He was entirely recovered, it seemed, from the gassing, and we were all impressed by the athletic energy which seemed pent up in his tall, straight body, and by the alertness of his unusual mind. He described to us the resources of the hospital, showed us over the place, asked what we wanted done.

That afternoon and evening he and I dictated to a field clerk a list of materials to be requisitioned—microscopes for laboratories, brushes, paints and canvas for the art school, typewriters, additional barracks of wood for extra classrooms or for the University Library, chairs literally by the thousands. It hardly seemed possible as we thought up the various items that the Army could produce them all, but everything came through on time. The request for art materials, for example, was a boon to some quartermaster, who was glad to get rid of what the camouflage department had left on his doorstep. We got a carload of paint, brushes, and canvas, another carload of miscroscopes. Colonel Reeves asked for two hangars and any number of machines and engines of all sorts for the workshops of the engineering school. Later, when the material arrived, he put the hangars together, end to end, ran a railroad track down the center of this enormous room, and let the incoming freight cars unload machines and engines right and left, until he had a laboratory on a most imposing scale.

Between us we thought of practically everything, but in one essential I slipped up badly. A day or so before the trains brought in our ten thousand students, I went to his office in something of a panic to confess I had omitted to requisition paper and pencils. He was bothered for slightly more than half a minute. "A friend of mine at Nevers," he said, "has several tons of paper. He mentioned it a minute ago over the telephone. He probably has pencils too. I'll get in touch with him."

The Colonel had his own way of getting in touch. That afternoon two large trucks started for Nevers and the Colonel rode with the driver on one of them. At five in the morning the trucks were back with all the paper and pencils we needed. The Colonel was at breakfast, bright eyed and lively as though he hadn't missed a wink of sleep. "I might have telephoned about that paper," he said, "but in the Army, if anyone knows you're asking for anything, he may get the idea he wants it too. It's better to take it first and then put in a regular requisition for it, as I'm going to do now as soon as I reach my office."

George Hellman and I shared a room at the Hôtel de la Poste. General Rees arrived from Chaumont on the twelfth, and the Commission spent the day with him deciding on what teachers we needed. After hours of educational planning, we all dined at the Hôtel de la Poste. George and I retired in the happiest mood I had been in since my first arrival in France the year before.

The hospital grounds which would be the University campus, were cut into blocks by long, broad avenues or boulevards and by narrower cross streets. There were some open squares and several large spaces, the central one large enough for a parade ground or athletic field. Instead of getting some needed sleep, George and I lay awake naming the avenues and streets, the squares and the fields. To the avenues we gave the names of the great universities of the world—Oxford, Cambridge, Sorbonne, Harvard, Johns Hopkins, etc. To the cross streets we assigned the names of the best-known American colleges—Swarthmore, Haverford, Amherst, Williams, etc. The large spaces were named for Allied Generals—Pershing, Foch, etc. Of course one thoroughfare was Norwich University, in honor of the Colonel. He had signs painted quickly and posts put up at street corners bearing the names. The Municipal Council of Beaune proudly gathered in all these signs when the University disbanded to go home. I have seen them in the little city library and museum, where no doubt they still are.

Regular classwork began at the University on March 15, 1919. At that time the faculty numbered 309, and the students, 5,000. In the British and French universities the Americans who registered for courses stayed until the term was completed. This out of appreciation of the hospitality which had reserved places for the Americans. At Beaune, any student, if he wished, could leave for America with his regiment whenever it was sent home. At the beginning of the term the registration went up from five thousand to almost ten, but at the midterm it was down again to 5,685. Final classes were held May 29, final examinations June 2 and 3. Final reports from all classes were received by the Registrar on or before June 5, and all colleges were officially closed June 7.

The University published a catalog in two volumes, the only university catalog, so far as I know, ever printed by an Army in the field. The second volume contained the names and home addresses of all the students. Throughout the term 9,571 had registered. The second volume contained also the names of the educational and the military staff with their professional positions in civilian life. The faculty totalled 797. Copies of the catalog were sent to the registrar of every recognized university and college in the United States. When a student left Beaune, whether at the end of his courses or earlier with his military outfit, he received a certificate showing what courses he had taken, for how long a time, what grade he had earned in each, and with what instructors he had studied. This certificate was signed by the teachers, by me as educational director of the University, and by the Colonel as commander. The student could then present the certificate for credit at any institution in the United States. with the catalog giving a description of the courses and identifying the teacher; the local institution could assign whatever credit it thought proper.

The University was composed of twelve schools under the following Deans:

Agriculture	Harry Hayward, Professor, Delaware College
Arts, Fine and Applied	George Hellman
Business Administration	William Henry Lough, President, Business Training Corp., New York City
Correspondence	J. Foster Hill, Principal, Hill Vocational Institute, Scranton, Pa.
Education	Joseph M. Gwinn, Superintendent of Schools, New Orleans, La.
Engineering	Louis E. Reber, Dean, Extension Division, University of Wisconsin
Journalism	Miller Moore Fogg, Professor of Rhetoric, University of Nebraska
Law	Capt. Warren Abner Seavey, Professor of Law, University of Indiana
Letters	Maj. William Hammond Parker, Professor of Political and Social Sciences, University of Cincinnati
Medical Science	Col. Joseph Herbert Ford, C.O., Base Hospital 26
Music	Franklin Whitman Robinson, Institute of Musical Art, New York City
Science	Lt. Col. William Freeman Snow, Professor, Hygiene and Public Health, Leland Stanford Junior University

Dr. Richard Watson Cooper, Secretary of the Association of American Colleges and former President of Upper Iowa University, served as Registrar at Beaune with Captain Rubey J. Hamilton, head of Science department, Kewanee High School, Kewanee, Illinois, assisting him at Allerey.

Such an improvisation as this university of ours, could not have functioned without great imagination and resourcefulness on the part of almost everybody concerned. Two illustrations stick fast in my memory. Among the books I had asked for on my pre-Armistice trip to New York were no law books. At that time I had not supposed I should ever be organizing a law school. When the prospective students arrived at Beaune, however, over a hundred of them asked to study law. Because I knew that Captain Seavey taught the subject at Indiana, but especially because I liked his looks, I told him the situation and asked what to do. There probably wasn't a textbook in English this side of the Channel. "Oh, yes, there is," he said. "It has been some time since the Armistice and the boys that are really interested in law have probably picked up a secondhand textbook here and there. Let me meet the whole group."

He met them and found among the hundred, seven or eight different textbooks on different phases of the law. He also found in the camp a duplicating machine and appropriated it when nobody was looking. Then helping himself to some of the paper which Colonel Reeves had brought home on his truck, the Captain set some willing law students at making copies of the textbook. "There you are," he reported, "you have the text for seven different law texts—not the text that I would select but we have no choice. What else can I do for you?"

"You can be Dean of the Law School," said I. "I know nothing about this and you seem to know everything."

Helping himself to wood from the University lumberyard, he soon had a group of law students, those who were not grinding at the copying machine, busy making desks and seats for his law classes. He found the teachers he wanted and in a week the Law School was functioning with moot court and all the usual embellishments. He had the power of inspiring his students. Only the boys in the art school approached our Beaune lawyers in zeal and industry.

In a different way I felt embarrassed about the instruction in physics. We had textbooks but no apparatus. I didn't want to see physics taught simply by lectures and recitation as though we were still in the Middle Ages. I spoke to one of the physics teachers about it—if I remember correctly to Dr. George Stradling, head of the Science department, Northeast High School, Philadelphia. "There'll be no trouble," he said. "We'll use the machine shop and draw on the lumberyard. We'll make the apparatus as we go along."

I remember visiting his classrooms a few weeks later. The hour was little more than half over but on the table in the middle of the room was a sparking machine which the class had made that morning. "The machine sparks," said Dr. Stradling. "The experiment therefore was complete and I dismissed them for the day."

Since a labor battalion was assigned to Beaune to keep the roads and the buildings in order, we established a post school with courses of high school grade and the members of the labor battalion were invited to choose their subject like the other students at the University. A few of them had small choice; they were illiterates. We taught them to read and write. At one moment the range of our curricula at Beaune was from the ABC's to Oriental Languages and the kind of mathematics that Professor Einstein knows a lot about.

4

George Hellman had a large Art School at Beaune, and the work in painting and sculpture was surprisingly good. There was an exhibition at the end of each week, at which the whole University took a good look and gave its individual opinion. But George also had a more advanced Art School in the large and attractive building near Paris, at Bellevue, Seine-et-Oise. At the end of our work the Army published a special report of this school with attractive illustrations. The lovely book is now a collector's item. Lloyd Warren was the Dean of this school and he had with him Ernest Peixotto, then a Captain of Engineers, and Solon Borglum of our Educational Corps, Captain Leslie Cauldwell and other well-known artists.

George intended the Bellevue School to represent the art work at its best and no doubt the three hundred fifty students were in every way a credit to us. But at Beaune, as it seemed to me, George assembled an equally remarkable faculty and managed to develop a school spirit which could well stand comparison with Bellevue. I particularly admired Lorado Taft, the sculptor, who finding himself in the Burgundy landscape, the home of Rude and his great predecessor Claus Sluter, exuded a most contagious enthusiasm for the art of sculpture and for the movable archeological remains which surrounded us wherever we chose to walk on a fine afternoon.

George Hellman had his difficulties in the painting and sculpture classes where the instructors demanded models so that their students might learn to draw the figure. George asked Colonel Reeves what would happen to us if we brought down some professional models from Paris. For a moment the Colonel put a searching eye on us. "Hellman, you mean nude women?" "Colonel, that's what I mean." "Well," said the Colonel, being the man he was, "I suppose the models are part of this art business and naturally the Army ought to have the best of the real thing. I'll rely on you, of course, to see that nothing happens on this reservation that shouldn't. Aside from that, do what you think right, and consider that you have my approval."

George brought down two girls from Paris and saw that they were so well chaperoned that they went back after two days. Their posing in the life classes was most satisfactory but they gave it as their unvarnished opinion that provincial towns like Beaune are dull places. In the evening a hard-working girl had nothing to do but talk to herself or read a book.

The Medical School, of course, could give only pre-Medical instruction since we had no wish after so much battle gore to teach dissection, and a supply of cadavers would have been difficult to arrange. Our young M.D.'s went in for chemistry, the study of Medicine, and the other book learning.

5

My University office was in a concrete building, long, low and narrow. Beaverboard partitions marked off a few rooms on one side, leaving a corridor on the other. My office was at the end. To get at me, visitors had to pass my Assistant Educational Directors, Captain Gaunt and Lieutenant Stretcher, and run the gantlet of my secretarial force, who liked to leave the door of their rooms open so that they could see who was coming in or going. My office had a concrete floor without rugs. My desk was a rough affair put together by a carpenter in our lumberyard. There was also a rough table and three chairs, one for myself and two for visitors. When more than two called, they sat on the table.

My assistants were able men. John Leonard Gaunt, Captain of Infantry, had been Superintendent of Schools at Tyrone, Pennsylvania. Everett Thomas Stretcher, First Lieutenant Infantry, had been in civil life Educational Secretary of the Portland, Oregon, Public Schools. Though slightly less aggressive in manner than Captain Gaunt, he was equally quick at diagnosing visitors and making the right disposition of them. People of all sorts, rendered curious by this American school, would come uninvited just to see the place, or to ask some favor.

My chief secretary was Caroline May McCullagh. Before she enlisted for Army service, she had been head of the office force in the Wells-Fargo National Bank, San Francisco. She and Captain Gaunt between them knew everything that was happening in the University. Thanks to them

I was on guard when straws were blowing the wrong way against the wind.

Caroline McCullagh had as her assistant Miss Frances Peirce, secretary to the Superintendent of Schools, Westfield New Jersey. Though she had no such business training as Miss McCullagh, she knew the high school and college world as Miss McCullagh did not. Eliane Monteanu helped out with the typing of letters in English, but I prized especially her splendid command of French. Not only did she know the language, but she was fairly acquainted with the French personalities we were dealing with. She never failed to remind me of some point of etiquette in which I was not quite meeting French standards. When we approached the end of our term, she reminded me that the French teachers and the educational authorities in Paris, as well as the town officials in Beaune, would appreciate a farewell letter of thanks from General Pershing, General Rees, Colonel Reeves, and myself. The total number of letters would be large, but after a brief consultation as to what should go into them, she typed them all herself, beginning weeks in advance; we then sent copies to Chaumont, for General Pershing and General Rees to sign; and a few days before we left, we mailed out the whole bundle from Beaune. Our reputation for ceremonial politeness went up.

I realize with wonder how hard my office staff worked—Captain Gaunt, Lieutenant Stretcher, and the three secretaries—when I recall my daily schedule—every day in the week. The couriers brought the mail, large sacks of it, early each morning. By eight o'clock the Captain, the Lieutenant, and the three secretaries had sorted it out, and I spent half an hour telling Miss McCullagh what to do with it. Much of the mail was routine business on Army forms, requiring only the approval or disapproval of the Educational Director, or the briefest line of advice or explanation. There were letters from the detachments in England and from the commanders or deans at the French universities, but after reading them, I had only to say, "Answer so-and-so," and Miss McCullagh would dictate to the other secretaries a reply so much in my own style that when it came time to sign it I couldn't be sure I hadn't chosen the words myself. Of course the Army is the best place to learn how to say all you have on your mind in the fewest number of words.

At eight-thirty, I would telephone to Colonel Reeves to find out if he too, had cleared his desk. If so, we gave an hour and a half to visiting the classrooms, inspecting kitchens and mess rooms, calling on the boys who might be laid up in the hospital, and discussing additions to our equipment. If a new class had been formed in any subject, another classroom was probably needed, at an hour when all available space was occupied. The Colonel would make a note of it, we'd decide where to put the additional room, and that afternoon the labor battalion would run up some wooden barracks.

Our campus was large and the classrooms were widely scattered. We had to walk fast to cover the ground in an hour and a half. Then from ten to eleven, I was in my office to keep appointments which Gaunt and Stretcher had made for me. From eleven to twelve-thirty, I put my signature on letters and papers and answered the second morning mail, which had arrived while the Colonel and I were inspecting the campus. After an hour for lunch, I was back at the office at one-thirty to hold a council of war with Gaunt and Stretcher. From two to two-thirty, I kept additional appointments which they had made for me. From two-thirty to three, I signed more outgoing mail and dictated more letters. At three, I met with the Colonel and the deans at committee or faculty meetings. By five the day was nearly over. When the Colonel and I had made another tour of inspection, he went off to see the boys parading for Colors. Then we had a few minutes to rest and wash up for supper. Then I usually went back to my office for the first quiet moment of the day.

6

These days were not merely crowded. I was surrounded with friends, new and old, and fantastic or ridiculous incidents seemed to invent themselves for our amusement. I saw George Hellman constantly, and by a coincidence William Aspinwall Bradley was in the Hygiene department of the Medical Service, and was ordered to Beaune to look after our welfare. Major George Norton Northrop, who had been teaching at the University of Minnesota, and of whom I had heard much, was a member of our English department. Having spent years at Oxford, he knew many British writers, most of them serving at the moment in the British Army. He thought he could persuade Lord Dunsany to get leave and come to Beaune on an inter-Allied lecture tour. It was a great idea and Dunsany said he'd come but for quite a while he didn't. I forgot the whole matter in the press of other things.

Not the least of my distractions came from the French department.

Bec and Bourgogne had entire charge of the French teaching at Beaune, with the assistance of such American professors as we could find. But the demand for French instruction was appalling. The elementary class numbered over fifteen hundred. We appealed to the French Government for aid. They ordered down a company of some forty or fifty young French officers, a few of them trained teachers, a few of the remainder promising young writers, all the rest charming boys who bore famous names and were a delight to meet. The arrival of this group drove Bourgogne to tears; he was too conventional and too well disciplined to like this kind of help. Bec, however, made the best of it. He saw what was probably in his Government's mind—the hope that acquaintance with these young men would improve American relations with France, and since the young officers were highly intelligent, Bec after days of intense labor in an improvised normal class, made them competent in Gourio's direct method of teaching the language.

Bec and Bourgogne immediately found themselves under fire from two directions, neither of which I had foreseen. In the French educational system there were language teachers who used other systems than Gourio's, and they resented the opportunity which Bec and Bourgogne had at Beaune. Most American language teachers resented any direct method of teaching French. In the United States today, fortunately, we usually teach modern languages to be spoken, but in 1919 many of our French and German professors couldn't use the language they professed. In the Army, of course, were many college teachers, and I had asked for all the French professors who could be spared from other duties. My thought was that if they assisted Bec and Bourgogne, they could learn the Gourio direct method and bring it home with them. But on the whole these gentlemen were not pleased to work under the direction of the two Frenchmen. They had been accustomed to teach French as a dead language, and they blamed me, quite correctly, for getting them into what they considered a silly and discreditable position.

One of them, an infantry captain, who in peace had held a professorship in a Western university, directed a long letter to headquarters exposing what he considered the foolishness of the French teaching at Beaune, and the incompetence of me personally to direct the education of hundreds of soldiers. I had selected the wrong teachers, he said; he himself was better qualified to take charge of the French department than Bec and Bourgogne, and he would be glad to do so if they were removed, and if he could then reorganize the department without interference from me. Further, he said, it was useless to ask the soldiers how they would prefer to be taught. Naturally they got some ill-considered pleasure from walking out of the French class into the town of Beaune and chatting with the natives in atrocious American French. Naturally the natives would be flattered into saying that the Americans were making progress, but in a few weeks we'd all be home in Massachusetts or Kansas or Idaho, with no French people to practice the language on. Before the end of the year what little command of the language had been gained from Bec and Bourgogne would vanish like melted snow. On the other hand, if the students could take his course on Racine and Corneille as he gave it to sophomores when he was home, they would learn from him, not to speak French, but to appreciate those famous authors, a benefit which would be theirs for life.

The writer of the letter had mastered imperfectly the Army system of communication "through channels." Letters on military business are supposed to go to the officer next superior to yourself, and from him to his superior, and so on till they reached the top, if they are intended to go so far. Somewhere in this chain the complaining letter reached an officer who recalled that I was at the head of the educational work, so he sent it back to me, perhaps with some impish pleasure in letting me see what my reputation was among some of my associates. I showed the letter to Colonel Reeves, who had little interest in methods of language teaching, but who became suddenly and violently angry at what he called an attempt to double-cross or stab in the back. "If he has a Captain's commission, he knows better. Say the word, and I'll put him on Kitchen Police. He can peel potatoes for a week or two!"

I reminded the Colonel that sooner or later I'd return to the United States, and the letter writer and I would want to resume normal relations in the academic world. "I'll get rid of him," I promised, "when the opportunity comes."

Within two days I had my chance. One of the Army detachments in a French university wrote in for an extra dean or some parallel officer to assist in the oversight of the students and in the consultations with the French faculty. I sent for my critic-captain, showed him the letter, and asked if he would come to my rescue by accepting a transfer. "They want this aid in a hurry," said I, "and since there is no one else with quite your qualifications, you're elected, unless you prefer to stay at Beaune. If

I may send word you're coming at once, I'll consider myself in your debt."

Of course he never suspected I had seen his letter. As a favor to me he consented to cut short the happiness which he had found in working with me at Beaune. We shook hands, both grinning like Cheshire cats, and I never laid eyes on him again.

One day the French military authorities at Dijon telephoned Colonel Reeves that General Marillier was driving south in his car with the intention of paying the University a brief visit. We might expect him about 3:00 P.M.

The Colonel asked me if I knew anything about General Marillier. "Nothing at all." "Never heard of him before?" "Never." "They told me it was the University he is visiting. What do you suppose he wants?" I couldn't guess. "Well, he's a French General anyway, and we'll receive him with the proper honors if we can find out what the proper honors are. Better to overdo it than seem uncordial."

So the Colonel gave orders to march the entire student body past the mysterious French general in a swank review. All leaves were cancelled for the late afternoon, and our students got themselves in order, wondering who was about to inspect them. They rather thought it might be Pershing himself. General Marillier arrived, a short, stocky gentleman, slightly pompous, but for the moment at least aggressively ingratiating. With him came a tall, serious young man dressed in black and wearing a derby hat. After the preliminary greetings, we showed the University equipment to the General and his civilian companion. We then started to the review stand, the University band bagan its tooting, the students got in motion, and the long parade saluted past the General, who complimented the Colonel on our fine appearance. Then we took the visitors to supper, still ignorant of the purpose which brought them. After supper they sat for a while in the sheltered spot outside the headquarters mess, which we called the garden though it contained few flowers. Comfortably seated with a cigarette, the General asked the Colonel by what method we taught French. The Colonel invited me to explain. The General gave a little exclamation of contempt, and said that the Gourio method was very bad. His young friend, Monsieur So-and-So, had a much better one. I replied with speed that the Minister of Public Instruction had recommended to us the Gourio method, had also recommended

Bec and Bourgogne, who were present in the camp, and that we were entirely satisfied.

The old nuisance looked at me for a moment with fatherly pity. His Government, he assured me, quite frequently did not know what it was doing. If the Ministry of Public Instruction was weak in anything, it was in the teaching of the French language. For that reason, and wishing to save his brave comrades, the Americans, from further imposture, he had brought down with him a young protégé of his, Monsieur So-and-So, who was prepared to reorganize our French teaching for us.

When I mentioned Bec and Bourgogne, the young protégé, who seemed a gentemanly fellow, begged the General to say no more about it, but to get out his car and drive on; he would not have come if he had understood that we already had a teaching staff which was satisfactory. But the General was a stubborn ass; he told his protégé a brave man never retreats, least of all when the going becomes difficult. The young teacher protested that the General had put him in a false position with Bec and Bourgogne and the Minister of Public Instruction would mis-interpret. The General retorted that he was acquainted with neither Bec nor Bourgogne, but he did know the Minister of Public Instruction, and didn't care a fig for his interpretations or misinterpretations.

Colonel Reeves, Major Watrous, George Hellman, and a number of us sat listening to the altercation, which promised to be endless. Colonel Exton, down from Paris for a few days, preserved the appearance of diplomatic attention, just managing to hide his amusement. We arranged at last that Bec and Bourgogne should dismiss their eight o'clock class the next morning, and that the General and his protégé should use that hour to expound to us all the advantages of the new method. The General didn't see why the presence of Bec and Bourgogne was necessary, and the protégé was reluctant to expound his method, but since I was firm, the eight o'clock meeting was held, and I managed to have a word in advance with Bec and Bourgogne, explaining what the fracas was about, and appealing to their sense of humor. They were annoyed, but they blamed the General and not us. The General bubbled over; his protégé looked unhappy. Bec, Bourgogne, the Colonel and I listened in silence. At the end I asked the protégé a few questions about his method, just to show I had been listening. At the end of the hour the General called for his car and drove off.

A few days later I wrote him that after thoughtful consideration we would continue the method of language teaching which the Minister of Public Instruction had advised. The General's protégé, in a day or two, wrote me his handsome apology for having invaded us, against his will. For almost a week Bec and Bourgogne looked glum and hurt, but gradually their smiles returned, and before we all left Beaune they were as ready as the Colonel and I to joke about General Marillier and the review we gave him.

7

The students had opportunities, of course, to practice their French in the Beaune shops and in the homes of the citizens, who entertained the Americans constantly and more than generously. But the boys had a special opportunity in one of the oldest buildings inside the ancient walls, the fourteenth century country home of the dukes of Burgundy. After the University had been operating for three or four weeks, the Mayor of the town, Monsieur Vincent, walked down to the campus one afternoon and told Colonel Reeves and me that the Beaune citizens, observing the value which Americans set on clubs—Y.M.C.A. Clubs, Red Cross Clubs, Knights of Columbus Clubs—thought we ought to have a Beaune Club, a place to amuse ourselves in the heart of the old town. The municipal authorities, therefore, with the advice and collaboration of distinguished ladies in the countryside, were putting in shape one of their most highly prized buildings, and as soon as the floors were scraped and electric lights had been installed, they would ask us to accept the house for our recreation as long as the University functioned. The repairs, he thought, would be completed the following Thursday; he hoped we could attend a ceremony of dedication at five o'clock, to be followed by tea and dancing. Next Thursday we saw, for the first time, the inside of the famous home of the dukes of Burgundy. The entire building, five or six hundred years old, had been put in beautiful condition. In a graceful and moving speech Monsieur Vincent hoped that the American students would drop in, any afternoon in the week at their convenience, for conversation or dancing. A large phonograph was installed, and the ladies of Beaune and the surrounding country had promised in various groups to be present to dance with the boys.

Colonel Reeves could rise magnificently to such a moment; without waiting to find the words in French, he told the Mayor in plain English that such a museum piece as that building would never be considered by us a mere clubhouse in which to pass an occasional hour; as soon as he returned to the University he would issue an order to the effect that no student could enter this building unless he was studying French and promised to speak the language while he was there (immense applause from everybody in the crowded little room); furthermore, the Colonel said, while we remained at Beaune, he would display the American flag, with the Mayor's permission, over this ancient Burgundian home, and a sentinel would protect the property day and night (more applause and louder).

The faculty and the military staff had their own good times as soon as the work was running smoothly—or even before. Colonel Reeves got us all together the first nights of the term and introduced the Commission, the various deans, and the rest of the faculty, one by one. Of course he had at that time only a brief acquaintance with any of us but his introductions were apt and unforgettable. After presenting to his staff Spaulding, Butterfield and me, he came to George Hellman, who was seated toward the center of the large but crowded room. "There's one man among these educators who has already made a hit with the students. They talk about him behind his back. That's always a good sign; it shows the boys have noticed their professors. This afternoon I heard one soldier say to another, 'Glory-be, have you seen that teacher with a beard —the one who looks like Jesus Christ?' Mr. Hellman, will you stand up and be presented!" George, with extraordinary composure, rose and turned slowly around so that everyone could see the famous beard. The laughter continued, wave after wave. George from that moment was one of the best-known figures in Burgundy. Before next morning citizens of Beaune had heard about the beard and kept an eye open for it. In another day there were rumors of it as far north as Dijon.

George Northrop, George Hellman, Livingston Watrous, the executive officer of the University, and I, with the Colonel, spent most of our free moments together, moments more deeply savored because they were so few. We sat at the same table or near each other at mess; at least once a week, usually on Saturday or Sunday, we dined at the Hôtel de la Poste. Once or twice the Colonel was persuaded to come with us but he was a teetotaler, and if there is a place on earth where a teetotaler would feel in the wrong pew, it is the Hôtel de la Poste at Beaune.

The first evening I dined there with Hellman, Northrop and Watrous, the venerable proprietor, Monsieur Chevillot, came into the dining room to ask if we were getting what we wanted. We had just given our order. He hoped we would permit him to be of service to us at any time and in any way. "Mr. Chevillot," said I, "we hope to be here often. During my stay in Beaune, will you be my professeur de vin and tell me what wine to order." He laughed. "Willingly. Any time." "Mr. Chevillot, why not begin now?" He laughed again. "What have you ordered?" When we told him, he threw up his hands in despair. "Messieurs, le Bon Dieu Himself couldn't choose a wine for such a meal as that! You begin with an acid, you end with a sweet, and all the way through you go from acid to sweet and back again. You leave yourself no palate at all."

8

When we went to Beaune the last of winter was lingering on the countryside. The grounds of the University were muddy, our barracks were damp and windy. In our quarters, a narrow building next to the mess, the Colonel, Livingston Watrous and I had three rooms in a row, all opening on the corridor but with doors also into each other. Much of the faculty business of the day, the provision of extra chairs for a certain classroom, or the putting up of another blackboard, was arranged while we three were shaving in the morning, calling to each other. The Colonel was an early riser and he went to bed early, but he would read awhile before sleeping. Watrous and I had some fine long-range conversations with him, all three in our beds pretending to read but interrupting each other.

When six weeks had slipped by, we began to notice that our dormitories were less damp, the mud had disappeared from the roads, the trees were green, there were even some buds on the occasional lonely bush left over from the days before the building of the hospital. We had been too busy to notice the spring until it arrived. What had occupied our minds, was the immense task of getting the schools of the University into motion. Now that the preliminary work was finished, we were in the mood to settle down for a long academic term. This University which we had created, was still only an improvisation, but given the years, we could make it a marvelous institution. I say "years" deliberately. I was not the only one who yielded to the illusion that we were building something permanent. Yet no sooner had our planting taken root, when orders began coming through from headquarters at Chaumont to get ready to pull it all up and pack our bags for home. I still feel the shock of the first warning, yet we had known from the beginning that the educational program was only a stopgap. Immediately after the war the shortage of transports had seemed very great, but now the number of available boats was apparently increasing, and no soldier wanted to stay away from his family longer than necessary. Yet it would have been easier to accept the home-going orders in the late autumn, when the rain and the mud were beginning. In the Burgundian May, when the landscape was colored with the bloom of orchards and vineyards, and the air was heavy with the scent of innumerable fruit trees, to leave Beaune seemed a fantastic absurdity.

I remember our University episode as consisting of a beginning, and an end, with little between. First there was the titanic labor of constructing and launching the enterprise; then there was a series of goodbyes and farewell parties beginning at Beaune, following us back to Paris, continuing to the ship waiting for us at Brest. At the time it was a dreamlike experience; it seems altogether a dream now.

Shortly before May 29 we were notified that on that day a special train would bring from Paris a delegation from the War Department representing the French War Department, the Tardieu Mission, and the Ministry of Public Instruction. Since we could guess, of course, that the mission had some other object than merely to look over our improvised University, we learned the names of those who were coming and prepared to welcome them.

The train arrived at two o'clock. M. Lafferre, Minister of Public Instruction, got off, followed by M. Du Courtois, representing the Minister of Public Works; my friend Louis Aubert, representing M. Tardieu; Colonel Reboul, and Colonel Roux, representing the French General Staff; M. Chantrin, representing the Department of Agriculture, M. Firmin Roz, head of the American section of the French Propaganda Office; Professor Levi-Bruhl, of the Sorbonne, Professor Abel Franc of the Collège de France; Major Coolidge and perhaps a dozen others. First we took the party to the office of Colonel Reeves at the University headquarters; then we inspected classrooms, library, laboratories; then we moved over to Pershing Field where there was a review of the entire student body, followed by the bestowal of French decorations.

In awarding their national honors, the French make fine distinctions, not always clear to the foreigner. General Rees, Colonel Reeves and I had the ribbon of Chevalier of the Legion of Honor. Major Watrous, the Executive Officer of the University, Dr. Spaulding and Dr. Butterfield had the ribbon of Officier de l'Instruction Publique. All the deans had the ribbon of Officier d'Academie.

In the course of the ceremony I made a *faux pas* which delighted the French visitors and our student body. I had seen French decorations bestowed but had failed to observe the etiquette in detail, never expecting to be mixed up in it. M. Lafferre pinned the medal on General Rees and Colonel Reeves, but General Robert Duplessis, Commander of the military region about Dijon, decorated me. He was an elderly gentleman of unusual culture and erudition, an archaeologist as well as a professional soldier. In his prime he had made army maps of North Africa, charting the desert at night by the stars; in the daytime he had excavated ancient Roman and Carthaginian remains. We met often during the term at Beaune, and I think he liked me almost as much as I liked him. If I am not mistaken, it was he who suggested that M. Lafferre, the civilian educator, should decorate the General and the Colonel, and he, the man of war, should decorate the university professor. When he gave me the traditional accolade of the kiss on both cheeks, I forgot what I was supposed to do next, and returned the kisses.

For the evening we took over the Hôtel de la Poste, and sat down to a true Burgundy banquet. Since the Army naturally provided no funds for private hospitality, the visitors were the guests of our deans, our faculty, and our military staff. We invited also, of course, the Mayor and other officials of Beaune, and members of the Town Council. There were speeches by M. Lafferre, General Duplessis, General Rees, Colonel Reeves, and myself. To our surprise, and somewhat to our amusement, there were several unscheduled speeches during the afternoon and just before we sat down to dinner. Those of the visiting party who held Cabinet posts or otherwise stood high in French political life had all prepared speeches which they had given to the press before leaving Paris that morning. As soon as they realized that we had arranged no opportunities for them to get rid of all this oratory, they began to make their own arrangements. They couldn't tolerate the idea that the Paris evening papers would be printing words of theirs which hadn't been spoken.

During the afternoon, when our tour of the University brought us to the camp theatre, in which a boxing match was taking place, Colonel Reeves interrupted the match between rounds to introduce the visitors.

The cordial applause suggested to one Frenchman a happy thought; he pulled from his inner pocket a fairly thick manuscript, and began reading at a terrified speed, as though he feared someone might stop him before he got through. His fellows copied the method whenever the tour came to a momentary pause. By dinner time we thought all the addresses must have been delivered, but we were wrong.

I presided at the dinner, and as I was helping the chief guests to find their place cards at the head table, two of them got into a friendly altercation. "You first, my dear So-and-So." "No, I insist—after you." I thought some question of precedence had been overlooked in our arrangement of the chairs, but suddenly another manuscript was pulled from a pocket, and another eloquent address inundated us. The subject was road building or agriculture, I forget which, but whatever it was, the other subject was dealt with immediately afterward, and we applauded them both.

On May 30 we held the usual American ceremonies for Decoration Day. Just outside the wall of the Beaune cemetery there were several hundred graves of boys who had been brought to the American hospital at Beaune, and had there died. The French citizens decided to pay a joint tribute to our dead as well as their own. General Duplessis came from Dijon with a troop of cavalry. The Mayor and the Town Council were present. I was to speak in English for the Americans, and Mr. Dubois, Principal of the local high school, or lycée, was to give the French address for the youths who had gone out from Beaune and had not returned.

Everyone in the University, staff, faculty and students, marched to the American graves, and after I had spoken and flowers and flags had been placed, and a salute fired, and taps sounded, we proceeded to the old cemetery and listened to M. Dubois. One dramatic incident made the day unique. The bugler sounded taps with more than usual impressiveness. Behind the graves lay the ancient cemetery. Behind that, the old town, and behind the town rose the hillside, the massive Côte d'Or. It was easy in that lovely scene to pray that our dead would rest in peace and light, yet it was a strange fate which had bidden these soldiers of ours to rest so far from home.

The bugle had ceased, we were following our quiet reflections, when some thirty or forty trumpeters among General Duplessis's dragoon sounded in unison, not taps but a triumphant peal. The cavalry were lined up behind the reviewing stand, we had not seen the men raise the trumpets to their lips; the glorious sound caught us by surprise. I remembered how Roland, in the song which the French regard as their national epic, blew his horn for aid, and how Charlemagne, miles away at the other end of the pass at Roncevaux, commanded all the trumpets in the army to answer.

We enjoyed M. Dubois's speech when we came to it, but the French trumpet call was the climax of the day, for me the climax of my war experiences in France; and as I then believed, and still do, it was an emotional symbol of the resurgence and long triumph of the French soul.

For a few days, after so much kindness and so much celebrating, the University settled down to a final stretch of quiet and hard work. The students were taking their examinations. The deans and the Educational Commission were writing their reports, which I was gathering up, and putting into a unified statement for Colonel Reeves to pass on to General Pershing. I had already written for the Commander-in-Chief a plan for a system of national training based on our experience at Beaune. When I first thought of the idea, I talked it over with General Rees, Colonel Reeves, Colonel Exton, Major Coolidge, and any others who would listen. In spite of many distractions, this plan took possession of me. Before I wrote it out, General Rees got for me the opportunity to discuss it with General Fiske and with the Commander himself, who gave me permission to publish it in the *Review of Reviews,* October, 1919.

Meanwhile, as I worked on the larger account of our adventure, I dreamed of the far-reaching educational results it might have. That was twenty-seven years ago. I had not yet learned how quickly a war is forgotten, how determined our country is to get rid as completely as possible of any wisdom forced upon us by a war—until there is another war. Nothing came of my hope for combined military and civilian training to be carried on in peace at home, as we had instituted it in Burgundy. But at the end of the Second World War, I had the satisfaction of knowing there were army schools in Germany, Italy, France and England, modeled on our University at Beaune, and planned from Washington by a group which included Colonel Francis Trow Spaulding, Dean of the Harvard School of Education, and son of Frank Ellsworth Spaulding, my fellow Commissioner in the other war. And with Spaulding's son in Washington was our old friend Major—now Colonel—Livingston Watrous, Executive Officer at Beaune.

9

On June 5, General Rees, Colonel Reeves and I were invited to meet the *Conseil Municipal* in the office of the Major in the Hôtel de Ville. There in a dignified ritual, obviously of long tradition, we were created honorary citizens of Beaune. My diploma contains in its rhetoric so much of all provincial France, and in particular so much of the men who bestowed this honor, that for my pleasure I quote the second-half of the text, omitting the complimentary preamble:

Under the *"Presidence de M. Jacque Vincent, Maire de Beaune, le Conseil Municipal, fidèle interprète de la pensée et des sentiments de la population tout entière, à l'unanimité, confère à Monsieur le Docteur John Erskine, Directeur de l'Education à l'Université Americaine, pour lui et ses descendants, le titre de Citoyen de Beaune."*

Need I add that a banquet followed at the Hôtel de la Poste? Several of the *Conseil Municipal* were winegrowers, and all of them were connoisseurs. In special honor of the occasion each brought to the feast a rare bottle. The names of the wines and the years were listed on the menu, and I copy them here for the envy of posterity:

> Meursault, 1908
> Chablis-Grenouille, 1911
> Beaune-Hospices, 1906
> Pommard-Hospices, 1904
> Corton, 1907
> Corton Clos-du-Roi, 1904
> Chambertin, 1907
> Richebourg, 1904
> Mousseux rose
> Marc de Corton de Grancey, 1898

To sample these great wines we were supplied with small glasses, such as winetasters use. But even a seasoned winetaster would hesitate to swallow in succession even very limited quantities of such noble liquor. General Rees was on the Mayor's right hand, I on his left, and kind Jacques Vincent, whose years were many, took the opportunity to warn me against Prohibition, which at that moment, as all the world knew, threatened the United States. "Now you can tell your people, M. Erskine, how innocent is good wine, the wine of Burgundy. It gives health, it inspires good humor. When enjoyed, as tonight, in the company of good men, it sharpens the wits and increases wisdom. In brief, it is the gift of heaven, wholesome as mother's milk." M. Jacques Vincent always spoke in the relaxed voice of age, but now his words gradually trailed off into silence. His head slumped forward on his chest. He was sound asleep. In a sense he had proved his point—mother's milk had operated as nature intends.

I turned to my neighbor on the left, and General Rees devoted himself to the man on his right, both doing our best to ignore the fact that the Mayor was, so to speak, under the table. Then a sudden apparition at the door of the room made me fear that I too was not quite myself; the door pushed slowly in, and a face appeared above it, a friendly face wearing a broad grin, obviously belonging to someone who either was a giant or at the moment was standing on a chair. An exclamation from those at the dinner table who faced the door, made the others turn around. The door opened further, and Lord Dunsany stepped from behind it, Captain Dunsany, as he was known in the British Army. Northrop's friend had reached Beaune a little late, after we had forgotten his promise to come and lecture to us.

He had arrived on a night train, he didn't say from where. He had walked up from the station and he had no luggage, but he didn't seem to care whether he had or not. When we asked if we should drive to the station and pick up his bag, he answered casually that he had lost it and doubted if it could be found before daylight. Since it was bedtime for us all, we took him back to the campus and found a bed for him at the headquarters' barracks. Never have I seen such an easy campaigner. As soon as he saw the bed he flung himself on it, then sat up, took off his shoes and his leggins, removed his coat, loosened his belt and the neck of his shirt, declined the offer of pajamas, relaxed in a long stretch which shot his legs out far beyond the mattress, and was asleep before we had got out of his room.

For two days he entertained us with readings from his works and with amazingly good talk. Like every true Irishman, he could talk. George Hellman and George Northrop took charge of him part of the time, showed him the interesting sights of the old town and the countryside, and saw to it that he showed up at the mess on time, approximately for dinner. Meanwhile, we found his baggage in a ditch, where he had dropped it when it got heavy. The camp breakfast hour was six-thirty, but he got off that bed of his about ten. Though I bribed the cook to

get him some coffee and eggs, there must have been protests, for Colonel
Reeves asked me to "tell that poet this is an Army camp, not a hotel."
When I parted with Dunsany that night, I reminded him as gently as I
could that our breakfast hour was six-thirty. "Righto!" he called cheerfully, and in half a minute he was sound asleep. Next morning he showed
up at eleven.

He wanted to visit the American Army of Occupation, and the Educational Directors at Coblentz were glad to have some lectures, so we
put him into a fast car with two drivers and an extra can of gasoline.
He was a grand fellow, but he left us marvelling that the British Army
had been able to function during the war.

I turned my attention to a lecture of my own on Walt Whitman, which
was scheduled for June 10 at the University of Dijon. With Luther L.
Dickerson, the University librarian, I made arrangements with the Mayor
of Beaune to present the town library with several thousand of our books
dealing with American history. The collection was installed in the Hôtel
de Ville, and is still consulted by students in the town, and by visitors
from Dijon and neighboring places. Each book contains this inscription:

> The gift of the people of the United
> States to their army in France through the
> American Library Association.
> Part of the library of the American
> Expeditionary Force University, Beaune,
> Côte d'Or.
> Presented to the City of Beaune by
> the University and the American Library
> Association, Memorial Day, 30 May, 1919.

On June 11 Dr. Butterfield held his inter-Allied conference on agriculture, with delegates from the American and British armies, the French
and the Belgian. The conference came so late and I was so busy closing
my office and packing, that my attendance at this important meeting
consisted of merely sticking my head in the room several times that day.
The talk I heard was startling and depressing. The experts agreed that
in several parts of the world the soil was neglected or worn out, and the
food supply sooner or later would come to an end. If the conference had
an immediate remedy to suggest, I can't remember what it was, but I
believe they addressed a memorandum on the subject to the League of
Nations, if and when the League should come into being.

On June 12, with Miss McCullagh and Miss Monteaunu I went to Paris to finish the assembling of my report. Colonel Exton made a place for us in his office at 53 Avenue Montaigne. Madame Monteaunu, Eliane's mother, found me a room in a pension kept by Madame Regert-Monod at 195 rue de l'Université.

10

Spaulding, Butterfield, and George Hellman sailed for New York at once. When George arrived in New York he called on my mother immediately and gave her a good report of me. For this thoughtfulness I shall thank him as long as I live. Mother was growing feeble, and George's call brought back for a while some of her strength and courage. She asked me later what he had done in our work. "Didn't he tell you, Mother?" "No, he talked of no one but you." I've told George I regard this as his greatest sacrifice to friendship.

On Friday, June 20, I was ordered to report at General Pershing's Paris headquarters, 73 rue de Varenne, where he decorated me with the Distinguished Service Medal. On the Fourth of July there was a gala performance at the Opéra for Marshal Foch and General Pershing. Representatives from the two armies made up the audience. I doubt if *Faust* was ever performed before or since in a crowded house with no ladies in it. At the performance I had an opportunity to talk between the acts with General Pershing, General Fiske, Colonel George Marshall, and Major Coolidge. The opera company had not got back to peacetime form, and the performance, to tell the truth, was distinguished chiefly by good intentions. The military audience were all extremely cordial to each other, but seemed self-conscious to be caught in an opera house. I walked home with Major Coolidge afterward and his sensible talk brought me back from the somewhat fantastic evening to the work we had still to do.

On June 21, at the *Cercle Interallié,* the Americans who had engaged in the educational work gave a lunch to distinguished French educators who had helped us. Since the weather was warm, the table was set in the garden. At my right was Joseph-Léon Bonnat, the famous portrait painter, who in his long life had painted Victor Hugo, Theophile Gautier, Alexandre Dumas, Gustav Doré, Pasteur. He was eighty-six years old, as he told me with marked satisfaction. Hugo, he said, always brought Madame Drouet with him, when he came for a sitting. Bonnat did more than one portrait of Hugo, but apparently he remembered with most pleasure Gustav Doré, who, he said, was a merry comrade, a funmaker, a veritable gamin.

As he talked, one of the other guests came up and suggested that he put on his hat to avoid catching cold. "I shall not catch cold!" exclaimed Bonnat. "These memories keep me warm."

On July 5, I sailed from Brest on the *Aquitania,* which was bringing home personnel from all sections of the General Staff. General Fiske and General Rees, Colonel Longley and Major Coolidge were on the ship, and General Denis Nolan of the Intelligence section, whom I had met at Chaumont but came to know and admire during the voyage home.

I was bringing gifts for my children, a large doll for Anna from the Nain-Bleu, a full regiment of leaden French soldiers for Graham. Major Coolidge helped me carry these bulky presents ashore. By a quirk of memory, this kindness remains with me as the last event in my war experience.

PART V

1919 — 1937

CHAPTER XXXIII

Reading in Great Books

I

MY MEMORIES of the final days in Beaune and in Paris are
crowded and rather thin, as my memories were of the end of my
trip to Europe in 1907. The reason in both cases is, I think, the same:
my mind was saturated with new impressions, until I could hold no
more. But perhaps experience becomes ours in other ways than through
clear impressions. I came home intending to take up my life again at
the point where the war had interrupted, and to pursue unchanged my
former ambitions. For a while I believed I was doing so, but perhaps
my character had been modified more than I realized; perhaps I could
not even recall my old purposes and plans exactly as they were.

Beginning with the autumn of 1919 I received three invitations to become president of a college or university. I suppose it was natural for
friends to think that after Beaune I would continue in the organizing
or administrative side of education. These invitations pleased me, but I
declined them promptly. I was more eager than ever to be a teacher and
a writer. At Beaune I had envied the teachers who could meet the men
daily in the classroom while I sat in my office and saw to it that they
had a classroom, with students in it.

Now that I was meeting my own students again, my two passions for
poetry and music, both of which had been somewhat undernourished
during the war, took hold of me more strongly than ever. I gave a course
for college students in writing, fiction as well as poetry. I urged the boys
to create, to produce. In private I began to practice the piano, which for

many years I had left untouched. What was the use of studying poetic masterpieces unless we found our own relation to art by practicing it? How can an art really be practiced without an audience? I arranged for a public reading of undergraduate poems, an event which was repeated annually, and the University came to know as poets Irwin Edman, Clifton Fadiman, Mortimer Adler, and others who have since made a name for themselves, though not primarily in verse-writing.

In the Graduate School the English department needed an additional course for M.A. students, and when my colleagues invited me to give it, I decided to lecture on as many of the world masterpieces in poetry as I could crowd into two hours a week from October to June. The title of the course was "The Materials of Poetry." My scheme was to show how actual events and actual people had been transmuted into myth or fable by popular imagination and by the genius of great and perhaps long-forgotten artists. I wanted to show that the materials of poetry are always found in life, but changed, according to psychological laws, by memory or by imagination.

Gathering the substance which went into these lectures, I reviewed all my former reading and became acquainted with much that I had neglected. The first two or three winters after the war were the most industrious period of my life, and perhaps the most profitable. The course in "Materials of Poetry" attracted so many students that in the eyes of my colleagues it became something of a scandal. No one could possibly have got more out of the course than I did. I had found a new way of interpreting literature, as a function of life, as life itself.

In the College I took up again the plan for reading great books which I had been advocating when the war broke. Most of my colleagues were still hostile to the idea, and they tried to protect the students—and themselves—from it by decreeing that my course should be open only to the specially qualified, who would take it as an extra, or as they liked to say, as "honors." The registration the first year was not large. We divided the class into small sections so that discussion might be easier. All the sections met at the same time, on Wednesday evenings, and over each section two of my younger colleagues presided. From the beginning it was the young teachers who made the course possible. We read a book a week, and spent all Wednesday evening talking about it. How often was I told by angry colleagues that a great book couldn't be read in a week, not intelligently! And how often have I retorted, with my own degree of heat, that when the great books were first published, they were popular, which was the first step toward their permanent fame, and the public who first liked them read them quickly, perhaps overnight, without waiting to hear scholarly lectures about them. I wanted the boys to read great books, the best sellers of ancient times, as spontaneously and humanly as they would read current best sellers, and having read the books, I wanted them to form their opinions at once in a free-for-all discussion. It would take two years of Wednesday evenings to discuss all the books on my list. Even by the end of the first year all the boys in the class would have in common a remarkable store of information, ideas about literature and life, and perhaps an equal wealth of esthetic emotions, which they shared in common. Here would be, I believed, the true scholarly and cultural basis for human understanding and communication. Compared with this result, what a waste of time it seemed to spend a term or a year mastering one book or one author in detail, and acquiring the mastery by yourself, as it were, in solitude.

This course of mine in reading great books has been adopted in many colleges, but not always as I intended it. Many teachers have turned it into a course on philosophy, on some specific philosophy, and others have tried to expand it into an educational method for teaching all subjects. With these aberrations I have no sympathy whatever. Science, I think, should be studied in the laboratory, not in the literary gropings toward science before laboratories existed; and to confound all the racial and personal variations of history in one philosophy is, I think, to abandon that training of the mind which enables us to observe accurately and make distinctions. I was concerned with no philosophy and no method for a total education; I hoped merely to teach how to read.

2

During the first year the reading list was modified from month to month. It was Raymond Weaver, as I remember, who urged that if we were to read Dante, we should first know something about the Scholastics, especially about St. Thomas Aquinas. The point was obviously valid. St. Thomas Aquinas would be read immediately before Dante. But how much of his immense work, and what parts of it? We went for advice to Father Cornelius Clifford, then giving a course on St. Thomas in the Philosophy department. He smiled at our ambition, but he named passages in the *Summa* which might not be altogether too much for us. When the evening approached we asked him to preside over the discussion. All sections of the class would be gathered in one room. He came and gave us an illuminating evening, leading the discussion so adroitly that the boys surpassed themselves.

One of them provided unexpected excitement. He told Father Clifford that he found Thomas Aquinas disappointing as a logician. Father Clifford nearly fell off his chair. "My dear sir, if St. Thomas is not a logician, he certainly has enjoyed a reputation which he doesn't deserve." We laughed, but the student stood by his guns. "Father, take that argument of his to prove the existence of God; it doesn't convince *me*." "Son," replied Father Clifford, "he wasn't trying to convince you. He wrote for believers like himself. He was trying to give logical and intellectual form to a faith which he and his hearers—or his readers—already had. Since the instrument he used was logic, you have the right to point out any flaw in his argument. What is the trouble with his proof of the existence of God? At what point does he begin?" The student answered correctly and cheerfully, even conceded that the next point Thomas Aquinas made was admissible. He was granting essential premises without realizing that he threw away his case. When in a minute or two he saw his position, his face turned white. I remember no other instance in my experience of such a physical effect from an idea. "Father," he said, "I apologize. He *is* logical. All the same, I am not convinced of the existence of God."

The room applauded, and the discussion took other directions. But the student at once elected Father Clifford's philosophy course in order to improve himself in logic. Mortimer Adler, one of my poets, who was a member of the class in Great Books, had his life changed, I believe, by this incident. At least, from then on, he took courses with Father Clifford rather than with me.

In the early years after the war I gave much time and energy to the Poetry Society of America which then held its monthly meetings at the National Arts Club, and indulged in frightful debates, quarrels, or feuds over the proper way to rhyme a sonnet, or turn a triolet. In the membership of the Society were some charming and highly intelligent people— Corinne Roosevelt Robinson, Leonora Speyer, Florence Lamont, and other lovers and practicers of verse writing. But except for the friendships which came incidentally through these meetings, they were a prodigious waste of time. All literary societies are. Every writer needs an audience, but his audience should not be a private corporation, with admission rules and dues.

Much more wisely spent was the time I gave to the newly formed Council of American Learned Societies. I was a delegate from the Modern Language Association, along with Professor Edward Armstrong of Princeton, who had served as dean for the soldier students at the University of Bordeaux. Professor Charles Haskins of Harvard presided over the Council and directed it toward great usefulness to American scholarship and culture. Since I was Secretary and Treasurer of the Council, I came quickly to know Charles Haskins somewhat well. In heart and mind he was a giant. Under his leadership the Council brought about the publication of the *Dictionary of American Biography,* a work of national importance. I never conceal my satisfaction that my name appears at the beginning of the Introduction to Volume I. I cherish this honor as I prize my citizenship in Beaune.

CHAPTER XXXIV

Chamber Music

I

MY SISTER Rhoda was giving serious attention to her piano. I
think she felt the need of music after Mother's death in June,
1920. Her playing always had an intimate, personal quality, and now
when she was at the piano she seemed to be searching for a language
subtle enough for her thoughts. She and my other sisters, Anna and
Helen, continued to live at 609 West One Hundred Fifteenth Street.
Early in the war my brother had married Marguerite Wiese. When the
war ended he lived for a while in New York, then established his home
permanently in Scarsdale. I moved my household to 39 Claremont Avenue, and to give the children a summer home I bought an abandoned
farm at Wilton, Connecticut, and began to repair and develop it. When
I visited Bob I heard music; he and his wife both played; when I dropped
in on my sisters, Rhoda would be playing to herself or practicing; and
if I stayed home, Graham would be working at his finger exercises or
his pieces, getting ready for his weekly lesson.

Whether I was influenced by environment, or whether the urge would
have come on me anyway, I wanted to play again. I began to practice
systematically, to the extreme annoyance of my wife Pauline. I dare say
piano pounding can break up any home, if you pound hard enough. The
purpose of so much practicing, I didn't know and couldn't explain,
though the question was put to me more than once. I had my teaching,
and in the back of my head the hope persisted that I might write; why
clutter my life with another art? But often I caught myself, in the midst

of a classroom exercise, asking whether to leave well enough alone, or whether to begin part of my life again, get back the technique I had in youth, and proceed to some real skill. I knew I was deluding myself when I dreamt of professional competence after neglecting my music for twenty years. But on the other hand, I expected to find no pianos in the next life; if I wanted to play, I must do my best here and now.

I might as well tell the whole truth, as far as I can; my love of music was a love of performance. Perhaps love of performance is the essence of my nature. If I hadn't gone in belatedly for performance in music, I doubt if I should have discovered the kind of performance natural for me in literature. Having once crashed through the barriers to expression in music, I found myself free to write what I wished, as I wished.

After my fingers were limbered up, I joined a group of colleagues at the University who enjoyed perpetrating chamber music. Our performances at first were execrable, and the improvement which followed much practice was small, but on the whole we enjoyed our own noise. At first we consisted of Professor Robert L. Schuler, Professor of History, who long ago had played a violin in the performances of *The Governor's Vrouw;* and Harold Sproul, graduate student in English. We three gave our attention to the trios of Beethoven and Brahms. In time we were supplemented and improved by Herbert Dittler, violinist and member of the Music department; by Frederick Charles Hicks, Law Librarian and an excellent flute player; and by Burnet C. Tuthill, a recent Columbia graduate, who played the clarinet like a professional.

At first we kept our performances more or less to ourselves, but when we had enough repertoire to fill an hour and a half, we began to perform publicly, in the University parlors, for the benefit of small audiences brought there by friendship or curiosity.

In January or February of 1924 I happened to meet Walter Henry Hall, the University organist and choirmaster, who during the summer session gave symphonic concerts in the gymnasium, with players from the New York Philharmonic. "I hear you're taking up your music again." Indeed he must have heard! He lived only one floor beneath me. "Why don't you play a concerto with me—say the first Wednesday in August?" I could have offered many good reasons for not playing a concerto, but I knew I was not likely to be asked again by anybody. "What concerto would you suggest, Professor Hall?" "Why not good old Schumann?"

That summer I played the Schumann five or six hours a day. Meanwhile

Professor Hall, kind soul that he was, began to wonder how well I played. He had never heard me. He prompted Arthur Newstead, who lived next door, to offer—quite casually—a second piano accompaniment, in case I wanted to practice in style. With Newstead's help I trained intensively, and just managed to get through. The only thing I can say for my audacity is this, that the playing of the concerto without breaking down, put me ahead five years. At least so many years of nervousness had been concentrated in one day, and overcome by one desperate effort.

After the summer of 1916, when I lectured for Percy Boynton at Chautauqua, I did not see Ernest Hutcheson, the pianist, until the war was over, and he, like everyone else, made a new start in an interrupted career. He played frequently in New York, but though I missed few of his concerts, and sometimes waited with other admirers to say a word of thanks, our acquaintance made no advance until one afternoon I met him and his wife Irmgart on the upper deck of a Fifth Avenue bus. In those days the upper deck had neither roof nor sides, nor other protection against the wind. Ernest and Irmgart were warmly dressed, and apparently had chosen exposed seats to enjoy the cold. They were talking happily and laughing, like children on a skating party or a sleigh ride. We exchanged a few greetings, from which I had the impression which he always gave, of a singularly warm and loyal nature—also the suspicion that he had forgotten my name, and was trying to recall where we had met.

The chance meeting set me thinking about a few lessons with him, to brush up technique and overhaul my dilapidated repertoire. In the spring of 1924, just before Professor Hall invited me to try a concerto, I wrote Ernest for an appointment; I had heard him play, I said, now perhaps he would listen to me. If he thought me worth teaching, I'd like to study, but if he decided that his third or fourth assistant was good enough for me, I'd put music out of my thoughts.

The appointment was made, and he heard me play several things, none of them in a way to earn his approval. I was in bad condition, he said at last; he could tell what hope there was for me if I'd spend the summer on Czerny exercises and Bach Inventions. I went off, determined to limit myself faithfully to this austere diet, but in a few weeks I was practicing the concerto.

I didn't tell him what I was up to, and since he was out of town during the summer, he missed the news. I wrote him the day after. "I didn't tell you," I explained, "for fear you'd call out the police." His reply was brief. "Beautiful music, isn't it! Bring it down in the autumn, and I'll show you how to play it."

He was one of the remarkable piano teachers of our time, and when I began to study with him he was at his best. Since I had done some teaching myself, I admired the sureness with which he diagnosed the needs of each student, and the methods by which he brought about the desired progress or reform. Though he had his individualistic way of playing, he did not wish to be imitated; he wanted his pupils also to be individuals. For that reason he tried to impart principles rather than solutions of isolated difficulties.

During a lesson he would stand by his piano, probably leaning over the music, which he spread on the top rather than on the rack. He remained standing until I had done my playing. I suppose he knew that if the keyboard were before him, it would be difficult not to play a passage for me whenever my performance was less than adequate. He preferred to tell me what was wrong and how to correct it; if I failed again, he would repeat his analysis of the difficulty and explain once more the solution. If by chance I stumbled on a slightly different solution, he would say, "For you perhaps that is better." He never lost track of the interpretation you were aiming at, and after matters of technique had been attended to, he would either tell why he didn't like your misunderstanding of the piece, or he would sit down at last and show you his interpretation, or other possibilities—ending perhaps with the formula his students waited in hope to hear, "However, you have found your own way of playing it, and it sounds like you. Don't change it. Let it change itself, as time goes on."

An artist must have practice in facing an audience. Music lessons in private can take the pupil only part of the way; to cure nervousness, there must also be frequent encounters with some sort of public, the more critical the better. Great music teachers have always, I suppose, made their pupils play for each other. The advantages are more than the cure of nervousness; the pupils become familiar with music which they are not yet studying, and they hear criticisms of the playing done by their fellows. They also hear, or should hear, occasional comments on the music itself, spontaneous appreciation of the composer's art.

Ernest Hutcheson used to bring together all his pupils at his home every Wednesday evening. A different group was scheduled to perform each week, but anyone might be called upon without warning. His most advanced pupils, like Oscar Wagner and Gordon Stanley, were themselves excellent teachers, and their pupils always were present and took their turns performing.

On these occasions Ernest occupied an armchair at the end of the room, and listened like a sort of recording angel. He must have known it was terrifying to play before him with all the other pupils watching for a slip. After you had finished your piece he criticized firmly, even severely, centering on your interpretation. Discussions of technique were for private lessons. The chief value of the evening lay in the severity with which Ernest and his pupils judged you. I soon learned that whatever I could play before those keen youngsters, I could play before anyone. As if the weekly audience were not hurdle enough, there were usually two of three visitors, professionals. You might go to the Hutcheson home shattered in advance by the prospect of playing a Chopin scherzo before pupils who could play it better, and when you entered the living room Josef Hofmann might be waiting for you, or Harold Bauer, or Harold Samuels.

On Wednesday evenings there would be concertos as well as recital numbers, and it was an education in itself to hear Ernest play the orchestral accompaniment on the second piano, often suggesting with incredible skill the quality of various instruments.

2

In these years, from the end of the war until 1937, I was closely associated with Ernest, and in several ways he contributed much to my life. He is an Englishman, profoundly English. Though born in Australia, and after his early boyhood educated in Germany, he spoke, thought, and felt about England as though every hour of his life had been spent in the mother country. His affection for English habits and customs was perhaps greater than he realized. He had much too fine a nature and too remarkable a mind not to be cosmopolitan. His travels and concert tours in Europe, Russia, and America, gave him an international approach to the modern world, and his attitude to countries not Anglo-Saxon, to France, Spain, and Italy, for example, was as sympathetic as deliberate good will could make it, but he had always a special response to the land and the traditions of his own people. With this one exception—that his integrity prevented him from admiring second-rate music in England or anywhere else.

His integrity was perhaps his most remarkable trait. He had both an honest mind and an honest heart. He could not pretend, least of all could he deceive himself. Being first of all a superb gentleman, he preferred to keep silence when an honest opinion would have been adverse. I do not here refer to his opinion of a pupil's performance. The courtesy of his manners acted as a tonic on the behavior of those who studied with him. In the Wednesday evening meetings, and during the pleasant refreshment period which followed, he gave his pupils, without intending to do so, lessons in hospitality and social deportment.

He was of medium height and frail in appearance. His pupils spoke of him as "Hutchie," with a protective tenderness in their tone, but he was sturdier than he looked, and he had unusual capacity for sustained work in one direction at a time. Continuity was necessary for his happiness. He had a prodigious memory, and his habits were orderly in the extreme, yet on occasion he could be as absent-minded as any professor or artist. His powers of memory were as remarkable in the fields of literature and history as in music. I once asked him how many pieces, short or long, preludes and fugues or modern concertos, he could get ready for performance on short notice. Instead of making a rough guess, he promised to look up the precise figure. Throughout his career as a concert artist he had kept a record of the places where he had played and the music he had played there; the purpose being to guard against repetition if he played there a second time. Apparently he never forgot any music he had once known well. Next day he told me his practical repertoire, the numbers from which he could choose a program and get into concert condition with three or four days of hard practice, came to over three thousand.

He was the first pianist to give a continuous series of piano recitals on the radio. The series ran for two winters weekly, and I listened to almost all the programs. Each week he played a concerto, or part of one. At the end of the two years he had repeated no concerto, and apparently he could have gone on indefinitely.

In literature I sometimes tried him out in areas which he might not have explored with care. Once I mentioned to him a favorite story of mine from the *Arabian Nights,* giving enough of the plot to start his memory. At once he named the character to whom Scheherazade attributed that particular story, and he went on to discuss three or four stories which I had forgotten.

The First World War hurt him deeply. England was his mother land, and Germany was the country in which he had found his musical career and had met the brilliant woman who became his wife. That England and Germany had to go different ways, was for him a personal tragedy. He hoped music might bring them together. Indeed, he looked to music to reëstablish peace and kindness among all nations. Musicians, he thought, should conceive of their profession in austere and high-minded terms, setting for themselves only the highest ethical standards. As a matter of conscience, he avoided the freakish idiosyncrasies which artists permit themselves; he didn't think the artistic temperament should develop in ways to embarrass the neighbors. Yet his own absent-mindedness could, on occasion, get him into a jam. Once when I was traveling with him, we changed cars at a junction, and just as the train approached to take us on our way, Ernest recalled a magazine he wished to look at. Suddenly and stubbornly, deaf to warning, he ran off to look for a newsstand. Unfortunately he found one, and not only the publication he was looking for, but others still more interesting. We missed the train by a wide margin. Perhaps his best performance in absent-mindedness occurred at a street corner, where our taxicab set us down. Ernest carried a briefcase. When the taxicab drove off, he followed on a hard run. "Driver! Stop! My briefcase!" He thought he had left it in the cab. He might have run faster if the weight of the briefcase hadn't handicapped him.

Irmgart Hutcheson had musical talent. She and Ernest met in extreme youth, when he was her piano teacher. But her real gift was for all forms of healing. She was a born physician, and should have studied for that profession. When I began taking lessons with Ernest, I saw the amount of time and thought she gave to the physical and mental condition of the young folks who came to him. If their health seemed less than it should be, if they were undernourished, if there were something on their mind, Irmgart got at the trouble and managed to cure it. She was interested in psychology and mental healing, and if a pupil suffered from nervousness or lack of confidence, took the case in hand and promptly worked miracles.

At the end of each Wednesday evening, having, as one might think, worn herself out preparing the refreshments which the party lingered to enjoy, she liked to gather a few pupils and visitors in one corner of the room for a little talk, which might seem impromptu, but which she planned and controlled. Perhaps she was making an occasion to study more carefully some young person about whom she was worried. At these moments Ernest would light his pipe and relax, his part of the day being over; now it was Irmgart's turn.

CHAPTER XXXV

Helen of Troy

I

IN 1921, Will D. Howe invited me to contribute a volume to a series of textbooks he was editing for Bobbs-Merrill Company. I had
met Will a few years earlier when he was Professor of English at the
University of Indiana. Each book in the series was to deal with a different author, in what was supposed to be a stimulating combination of
biography and anthology. The life of the author was to be told at length,
with the narrative interrupted every now and then by quotations from his
works chronologically selected. It was a compliment to be reckoned
among the galaxy of professors who had joined the enterprise, but after I
signed the contract and began to look the Milton over to see how to cut
him up, I wondered who was making the bigger mistake, Will or I. The
other contributors found the anthology-biography sandwich as difficult as
I did; the series from the start was not a success, and the rumor spread
that Bobbs-Merrill would abandon it.

Meanwhile, I was reading widely in search of fresh legends for my
graduate course on "Materials of Poetry." Each year I expounded the
same principles of evolution, from actual events to the great stories which
imagination made out of them, but I needed fresh illustrations to keep
from falling into a rut.

In 1923, I was reading the first volume of George Grote's *History of
Greece,* the chapters in which he discusses the legends of gods and god-
desses, of heroes and heroines. The fifteenth chapter, dealing with the
legend of Troy, reminded me of several stories which might brighten up

my lecture course, but at first I did not see the possibilities of Helen, until a footnote toward the end of the chapter made her suddenly interesting. The note is brief enough to give here: "It is curious to read, in Bayle's article Hélène, his critical discussion of the adventures ascribed to her—as if they were genuine matter of history more or less correctly reported."

I wanted to see this article on Helen, since Grote found it conspicuously realistic or lifelike; his own scholarly discussions of the legend were safe from any such charge. And what were these other adventures which he talked about?

Pierre Bayle published in 1697 an ambitious encyclopedia in four large volumes. He called the work *Dictionaire historique et critique*. It had great influence on the encyclopedists of the eighteenth century, but I dare say it had still more influence on me. When a man writes such a work singlehanded, doing all the articles himself, the result is likely to be spotty. Pierre Bayle would have showed up badly under the letter "H" if it hadn't been for Helen of Troy, about whom his information was prodigious. He could not be expected to foresee the result of modern excavations at Troy, but he was acquainted with every literary reference to Helen. These references he dealt with in copious notes, hitched on to the text of his article. Rather, the article is appended to the notes, they being ten times as long and a hundred times as informative.

I first consulted Bayle in the University Library, but before long I ran down a copy for myself. The four precious volumes out of which I have ladled considerable profit of various kinds are before my eyes as I write. I was fascinated by that period in Helen's career of which Homer gives one tantalizing glimpse in the Odyssey; after Troy, Menelaus took her back to Sparta, and for the rest of their lives they lived—how? In the Odyssey we are told that Telemachus, the son of Odysseus, visited the home of Helen and Menelaus, and found them on very fair domestic terms. The expedition for Troy, remember, had been for the purpose of punishing Helen. When the city fell, her husband went looking for her with a sword; not having seen her for some time, he had forgotten how beautiful she was. On my library wall hangs a drawing from an old vase, depicting the scene. Helen stands waiting to be killed; Menelaus is dropping his sword behind him, as though sorry he brought it along; a little Cupid in the air is scattering roses and olive branches. The war is over. Nothing to do now, but go home and meet each other daily at the breakfast table, like any other husband and wife.

What did they talk about? I began to imagine conversations in which Menelaus, having overstrained himself in the effort to forget the past, suddenly remembers it and picks on Helen; calm, controlled and as though her conscience were clear, she answers sweetly and reasonably, and in no time at all argues him off his feet. These scenes I invented as I walked from class to class, and wrote them down when I reached home. They soon grew to a modest book.

I was to have a half-year leave from the autumn of 1925 to the spring term of 1926, and I planned to give my children their first glimpse of Europe. Having wrestled with a foreign language in the war, I resolved that my son and daughter should learn to speak French and Italian early. We would go to France first, entering by Bordeaux; we would then cross to the Riviera; from there to Italy; after a stay in the chief cities, we would cross the Alps to the north of France; last of all we'd see Paris.

But wishing to go away with a quiet mind, I asked the Bobbs-Merrill Company whether they still needed that Milton book. They replied that they wouldn't insist on Milton, since the "How to Know the Author" series had been dropped, but a book of some kind they thought they should have, out of respect for the contract. I asked whether they'd like *The Argument of Helen*. They were reasonably cautious, but after I had revised and shortened and polished the thing, I sent it on, and they telegraphed that they liked it.

At the Faculty Club from time to time, when someone asked what I was working on, I would say, *The Argument of Helen*. They would ask, "What is that?" I fell into the habit of replying, "It's the private life of Helen of Troy." The effect was invariably so gratifying that I told Bobbs-Merrill to substitute *The Private Life* for the first title, *The Argument of Helen*. The publisher sent back a nervous question whether the new title might not be considered frivolous. Admitting the possibility, I reminded him that it was Helen's public life which was scandalous; in private she was as I had represented her, a conventional woman, differing from her sisters only in looks and in brains. The brains were my gift to her. In Homer and the Greek dramatists Helen is inspiring to look at but not to listen to.

The book was finished and in type, a few weeks before I took my family to Europe. I doubt if I should have written it, and I am certain I never should have published it, if I had not acquired some extra courage in the process of taking up my music. I needed courage to publish Helen. I had interpreted the lady in a way which scholars might not approve, and I had endowed her with a philosophy of life which might shock American readers. As I sent off the final proof I wondered whether I was God's masterpiece in fools. So far my life had been fortunate and happy; by luck and hard work I had made friends and a more than respectable name; would this little book spoil it all?

Looking myself squarely in the eye, I knew the book gave me more satisfaction than anything else I had ever done. I had been happy writing it, and now that it was written I loved it. There was more of myself in it than in all my previous writing put together. If playing the Schumann Concerto set me ahead five years, writing the *Private Life of Helen of Troy,* set me ahead twenty.

2

The voyage from New York to Bordeaux in September was particularly happy because it was the children's first ocean crossing, and the life on the ship kept them in continuous excitement. Our boat, the *Chicago,* was small, but there was more than enough room on it, since few travelers in peacetime were as fond of the Bordeaux route as I was. I don't know whether all children are quick at picking up words in a foreign language, but Graham and Anna taught themselves a surprising amount of French before we landed. Any word or phrase that caught their ear, had to be explained, and as soon as they knew what it meant, they tried it on the stewards, who were endlessly patient.

At Bordeaux I hoped to see René Galland, who was teaching English at the University there, but he hadn't returned from his vacation. We went on to Arles, where we stayed a while, and from there to St. Tropez, where we made another stop, and from there to Villefranche.

On whatever travels I had made before, I had always been preoccupied with my own impressions, but this time I was watching the children's state of mind. Graham was fourteen, Anna nine. Though she refused to concede any superiority in her big brother, his influence on her was great. As soon as he saw the Mediterranean and the red-roofed houses along its coast, he got out his box of water colors. Immediately Anna had to have water colors too. I cherish a number of Graham's sketches and several of Anna's, salvaged from the wastebasket, where they both were disposed to consign their work. It pleased me that they turned to art naturally, without exaggerating the importance of their talent, but talent they both had, and Graham's interest in drawing and painting grew and deepened. At Arles he was fascinated by the Roman monuments, and at his request I got permission for him to sketch in the museum.

Florence and Rome in their different ways gave us the emotions that every traveler who knows history must take from them, but the Fascists under Mussolini were then beginning their ruthless career, and the city of Dante and Michelangelo, and the ancient capital of Italy, were already shadowed by the new tyranny. We found many residents in both places ready to praise Benito and his Black Shirts for putting a little order and discipline into the population, but the illustrations they gave did not seem undiluted benefits. The economic and industrial life of Italy, we were told, had been in process of disintegration; when you got on a street-car you couldn't be sure it would proceed to its destination; at any block the conductor and motorman might announce they had decided to go no further that morning, and the passengers might as well get out and walk. With the dawn of the magnificent era, there was an end to all anarchy. If the motorman and the car conductor staged a private strike, Benito's boys descended on them with clubs and castor oil.

More than once, when I went out to buy a paper, I found the newsstand entirely bare, with a litter of ashes and half-burnt scraps on the sidewalk. Some Black Shirts had stopped to read the headlines, and, annoyed at the news, had put a match to all the papers.

When we reached Florence the town was excited over a double murder. A leading citizen had shot an officer of the Fascist outfit, and the friends of the officer had blown the leading citizen to pieces. The papers played up the incident as political news; the leading citizen had fired the first shot because he belonged to the old régime and hated all reformers. The Fascist officer had a magnificent funeral. Every house in the city, literally without exception, hung out a flag with appropriate drapes of mourning. It did look as though the grief were unanimous, but Anna had been wakened early by strange noises in the street, and had called our attention to trucks full of armed Fascists stopping at every door where the flags and the mourning hadn't yet been displayed, and waiting with their rifles until the error was corrected. Only later, and in whispers, were we told by some of our friends that the leading citizen had been incited to murder by finding his wife in bed with the Fascist hero.

In spite of the trouble in the air, our visit to Florence was happy. We stayed at the Pensione Ravasso near the Cascine, at 1 Via Curtatoni, a small but most efficient hostelry which had been recommended by a painter friend. The Pensione Ravasso was owned, managed, governed, and directed by a formidable lady who might have been the mother of the Gracchi. It was she who kept the institution solvent, and better than solvent. It was her husband who made it attractive. In his youth he mastered in France the art and science of cooking, and he wore the ribbon of the Legion of Honor as testimony to his skill. The cuisine of the Pensione Ravasso was a dream. I never saw Signor Ravasso in his white apron and his tall cook's cap; when it was time to serve the meal, he bathed and dressed himself in beautiful linen, and put on a smart semi-formal suit, such as an ambassador might wear. In this striking attire the Signor stood by the windowshelf through which each dish was passed from the workers in the kitchen to the waiters in the dining room. The Signor lifted his eyeglasses, gave the food a final inspection, then permitted the waiter to serve it.

Crowded though Florence is with memories of great Italians, yet like other travelers I wondered at the extent to which England had occupied Italy in the nineteenth century—in controvertible proof of her peculiar gift for colonizing. Florence in 1925 was still, as during the preceding century, a cultural and economic refuge for English men and women and for their anglo-minded imitators from America, who thought better of themselves for retreating from their native land, to hobnob with the ghosts of the Brownings, and maintain a Baedeker acquaintance with the Medici, with Savonarola, with Machiavelli. One afternoon returning from a visit to Mrs. Browning's grave, Anna asked, "Why did so many English come to Italy to die?" I explained as well as I could why dying in Italy had once been the fashion, and why the fashion was changing.

My remarks had a convenient illustration in the amiable retired banker who at the moment was staying at the Ravasso. His home was near Oxford, he told me, but Americans like to rent it, and he enjoyed translating dollars into liras. Also, he added, his wife and daughter enjoyed their annual brush-up on Italian art. During the day the two ladies plodded through the galleries, book in hand, training themselves to approve of the right canvases for the right reason.

Crossing the Alps, we reached Dijon in midwinter, in the kind of frost which leaves the ground white each morning for creaking cartwheels to cut up with black tracks. Every man we passed in the street had his muffler around his neck, and whether or not he wore gloves, from habit he rubbed his hands to keep warm. Our intention was to go on at once to Beaune, but we met my old friend, General Duplessis, retired from military life and occupying himself with the Historical Society of Burgundy, and with the chairmanship of a committee to look after foreign students at the University of Dijon. For the pleasure of talks with him we stayed at Dijon several days, but twice we took the train down to Beaune. M. DuBois, who in the days of the University had been Principal of the Lycée, was now Mayor of the town. The University buildings, all except the Colonel's headquarters and my office, had been torn down or carried away. A farmer had converted my office into a home, and was living in it with his family. Our first visit to Beaune was unannounced, and Mr. DuBois happened to be out of town. He telephoned to me at Dijon, scolded me affectionately for taking him so unawares, and urged me to return the following day.

We went, of course, and for over an hour he entertained us in his office, telling my children what an important man their father was, and reminding them that they too were citizens of Beaune, since they were descendants of a citizen. It was their duty, he said, to return annually for a glimpse of their honorary ancestral home. All very kind, but I had my eye on the clock, remembering the irregular train schedule. When at last I rose to say goodbye, M. DuBois smiled, took me firmly by the arm, and led me toward the door of an inner room, the large chamber in which General Rees, Colonel Reeves and I had received our citizenship. Now the room was crowded; the Mayor had assembled the *Conseil Municipal* and some thirty or forty citizens who had known us during the University days. A large table in the middle of the room held wine bottles and glasses, and a good supply of cakes. The Mayor was offering us the very French tribute of a *vin d'honneur*.

Everybody drank everybody else's health. Every toast called for a speech. The Mayor let me send his office boy to the florist's, to buy a wreath for the monument to the boys from Beaune who had fallen during the war. We had contributed to this memorial before the University disbanded. When the wreath arrived, the *vin d'honneur* turned itself into a procession; we marched to the crossroads where the marble stands, on the way to Dijon; Anna leaned the wreath up against it; then, our hearts

being warm, we made more speeches, shook hands all around, marched
back to the Hôtel de Ville, and shook hands again.

I got my tired family to Dijon shortly before midnight.

3

In Paris old friends were waiting. Will Bradley, happily married, had
established himself as an international literary agent. Horatio Krans
was permanent director of the University Union, now in the building of
the Carnegie Foundation, at 173 Boulevard St. Germain. Maurice Bec
was teaching English again at the Collège Chaptal, and amusing his fellow professors with kind exaggerations of the ability he had found among
his pupils at Beaune.

For a week I went down to Bordeaux, to see René Galland. He was
married, had several children, and seemed likely to have more. Together
we explored the history-crowded country around Bordeaux, spending a
warm winter afternoon at Labrède, having a look at Montesquieu's cha-
teau, the large room he built for his library, the study with a large fireplace, where he wrote *L'Esprit des Lois.*

In Paris again, I found at Brentano's, on the Avenue de l'Opèra, half a
dozen copies of my *Helen of Troy,* and bought them all for my French
friends. In the distraction of travel I had forgotten about the book, and
as yet I had no word how it had been received. Bec loved it, and elected
himself its French translator.

And Graham wished to study at Julien's, having discovered the well-
known but old-fashioned *atelier* in the rue du Dragon. For the rest of our
stay he worked there every day. When it was time for us to pack up for
the return voyage, I promised he might have his freshman year at the
Sorbonne, with all his spare time at Julien's, on condition that he passed
the Columbia entrance examinations with high marks. When I made the
promise, I forgot he would be ready for college in two years.

CHAPTER XXXVI

Lecture Tour

I

URING these months of travel I wrote a few pages each day, and
brought home the first draft of *Galahad,* published in 1926. While
writing my first novel I had planned two others on the same theme,
domestic relations in the United States; after *Galahad* was to come *Adam
and Eve,* published as a serial in *Collier's* in 1927, and in book form later
that year.

Meanwhile I began writing critical articles for Mrs. William Brown
Meloney, then in charge of *The Delineator,* and short stories for Ray
Long, the editor of *Cosmopolitan.* Obviously I was doing too much, but
the urge to write, like the impulse toward musical performance, had
found an outlet; and the love of teaching was stronger than ever. For
ten years I practiced several professions at once, grateful to fate for so full
a life, until my nervous system crashed, in 1936.

Daily my piano claimed from two to four hours. Almost every summer I spent a week at Chautauqua, where Ernest Hutcheson taught and
Albert Stoessel conducted symphony concerts. They let me try out piano
concertos before the large amphitheatre audience, and each summer I
practiced chamber music with the Musical Art Quartet, neighbors of
mine in Wilton. Sascha Jacobson, the first violin, and Marie Rosanoff, the
'cellist, gave an annual benefit concert for the Wilton Library, in the
attractive little reading room, and I played their accompaniments, or
joined them in trios.

At the University in the postwar years I had some brilliant students who could have been teachers if they hadn't preferred to write. I think especially of Henry Morton Robinson and Clifton Paul Fadiman. In the College, I continued my course in writing, in Elizabethan literature and in Great Books, and in the Graduate School my lectures on "Materials of Poetry."

On March 2, 1927, I signed a contract with Louis J. Alber, lecture agent, to make a coast-to-coast tour the following year, from February 6 to April 14. During this period of slightly more than two months I was to talk my way to the Pacific through the Southern states, then along the western seaboard from San Diego to Seattle, then back to New York across the Northern states. Going and coming, I was to make dashes into the central part of the country. The schedule was heavy, seven lectures a week and constant travel, but I enjoyed making the acquaintance of my country, and by keeping close check on timetables I finished the tour without missing a lecture. Once I nearly came to grief. My agent had scheduled me to speak in Richmond in the afternoon and at Norfolk in the evening. The places are about ninety miles apart, and he assumed there was train service between them at just the right hour, but there wasn't. Richmond friends found for me a fast automobile, had it waiting at the door of the lecture hall, and I ran for it the moment the lecture was over. By breaking all speed regulations and records I reached the Norfolk hall five minutes before lecturetime, supperless but with time enough to get into a dinner coat, for platform etiquette.

In the autumn of 1927, eight months after I agreed to make this tour, I was elected to the Board of the Juilliard Graduate School of Music, and my colleagues promptly made me chairman of the Administration Committee, the other members being John M. Perry and Paul Warburg. For the tour, therefore, I had to ask leave of absence from both the University and the Juilliard School, and since it was known through the country that I was chairman of the committee which operated the school, and therefore had a voice, presumably, in the allocation of its funds, I was warmly cultivated everywhere by music enthusiasts and patrons, who drew my attention to local projects of theirs, which could use a little additional endowment. And in other ways the tour acquired a musical tinge. Though the lectures were on literary topics, one audience gave me an urgent request, at the close of the talk, to play something for them. Since there was a good piano on the stage, I complied—which was a mistake. Succeeding audiences pretended to feel cheated if they too didn't get a recital after the lecture.

2

Most of the places on my itinerary have become familiar to me through later visits. It isn't easy in every case to remember now the first impression. A few remain distinct, either for some great beauty or for some other unusual experience. New Orleans and San Antonio, Pasadena, and places on the Pacific Coast, startled or overwhelmed me with various kinds of loveliness. The Missions of San Antonio gave me my first glimpse of the Spanish influence in North America, and New Orleans, of course, fascinated with its reminders of Old France. Texas, in spite of its thriving cities, Austin, Dallas, Fort Worth, and the towns on the Gulf, seemed remarkable chiefly for its size. I had not known there was so much space in the United States. My schedule, zigzagging back and forth from one engagement to the next, no doubt made the State seem larger than it is, but after nearly two weeks of waking up in the morning and finding myself still in Texas, I became persuaded that the map was incorrectly drawn. The immense stretches of the landscape, the endless ranches, the horizon-wide fields, which at that moment submitted to the spring plowing and harrowing, were more like the ocean than anything I had ever seen on land.

Once while watching a tractor draw a flock of plows after it toward the skyline, I asked a man near me, a Texan, how many acres that field contained. He named so many thousands that I hesitate to give the incredible figure. "When will the tractor come back on its next furrow—group of furrows?" "It's late afternoon, Mister. He'll probably be back tomorrow."

The blue flower in the Texas landscape is very lovely, and Texas sunsets have a peculiar magnificence, but the glory of the State, I decided, especially in the western part, is the kind of man it produces. Never before had I thought my own sex much to boast of for good looks, but the tall figures, muscular and trim, the quiet, deep voices, the clear, steady eyes, seemed the marks of a heroic race, the sort of men, fighters, riders of horses, whom Phidias carved in his temple-marbles. The western part of Texas and Wyoming are regions where men not long ago invariably carried guns. I would not imply that pistols have become obsolete, I merely call attention to a habit formed over a long period. In western

Texas or in Wyoming, when a man talks to you, he doesn't blink; he keeps his eyes wide open. In older and more sensitive days, gentlemen couldn't be sure what might come up in conversation, and in a hot argument there might be no time to wink; some hands were "mortal quick."

I confess to some regret that I had come to Texas so late in history, when the wild, dangerous conversations had disappeared into a legend, to be traced only in a wide-eyed stare. But my schedule brought me at last to a university in an oil town, a new place. The university had ivy on some of its buildings, and the ten thousand students sang college songs about their Alma Mater, "Dear old So-and-So." Anywhere in America a student who has completed three out of his four years of residence, loses all sense of history and thinks of his college as venerable. The Dean of this institution was white haired, but he was a well-known scholar, brought from some older institution.

The morning after my lecture the Dean entertained me while I waited for my train. We walked through the town. He showed me the fine new buildings in the business district. We stopped for a moment in the lovely city park. Almost the first building the oil pioneers had erected, was a small but substantial jail, which in their haste they set squarely in the middle of the site which nature had reserved for the park. There would soon be a new jail somewhere else, the Dean explained, but I was in time to see the children playing on the smooth lawn around the grim little building, while the incarcerated drunks watched cheerfully through the bars.

"What I admire in Texas," I said, "are the men, so tall, so straight, so clear eyed. For example, that young fellow in the business office next to my hotel."

"Oh, Ned," said the Dean. "Poor Ned!" His tone was melancholy.

"What's the matter with him?"

"We don't like to speak of it, but he shot a man a few weeks ago."

"Good heavens! He didn't look like it, when I saw him this morning. Do you let murderers out on bail?"

"Oh, he's had his trial," said the Dean quietly. "We all went down to see he got justice. The University closed for the day."

"He was acquitted?"

"Certainly."

I had to know the story.

"It concerns a woman, his mother. That's why we're all sorry for him.

She's a lady, but she's pretty old, even a bit senile. She fell in love with a boy younger than Ned, and though we tried to persuade her not to, she married him. The difference in age was bad enough, but the fellow wasn't a gentleman." The Dean lowered his voice. "He drank!"

Something terrible was indicated, far beyond the normal satisfaction of Texan thirst.

"The night they came back from their honeymoon he celebrated with a quart of liquor, and hit her over the head at her own dinner table! Hit her with a loaf of bread! Then, if you'll believe it, the next morning the damned fool walked right past Ned's office door."

I laughed.

"On what ground was he acquitted?"

The Dean made a little gesture with his hand, brushing off a silly question. "There was some lawyer's talk of self-defense, but the fellow was a skunk, and the general feeling was that someone should stop him. We were grateful to Ned."

I looked at my watch. "Mr. Dean, I'd like to meet Ned. Will you introduce me?" I got my bag at the hotel and stopped at the office next door. Ned extremely tall, extremely slender, extremely blue eyed, a gentleman, with emphasis on the "gentle." That man wouldn't hurt a fly. On the station platform I asked one final question.

"Mr. Dean, has he given up carrying a gun? I looked him over carefully; his jacket was fitted close and buttoned tight; there was no bulge under his arm. Would he be carrying it up his sleeve?"

The Dean smiled. "Mr. Erskine, I've lived in Texas all my life, and I have *never* seen a gun—till it was needed."

I shall go to my grave convinced that the Dean carried a gun at that moment.

3

The most enjoyable part of the tour was the time I spent lecturing in and near Los Angeles. William de Mille invited me to stay at his home on Monteel Road, a comfortable house perched on the hillside, with a view of the city and the ocean. For a week he put his car and his driver at my service, and sometimes I would leave early in the afternoon and drive a hundred or even two hundred miles to my engagement. Back again at one in the morning, I would find William waiting for me in his dressing gown, and we'd go out on the stone terrace for a long talk, and a long drink, and a long view of the city lamps and the distant lights on Catalina Island. Having talked till dawn, we slept till noon, or until I started out for another distant lecture.

When the talks were scheduled in Los Angeles, as several of them were, I reached William's terrace a little earlier, or he would have a group of friends for dinner. Once I left for my lecture, as it were between courses, and got back for the rest of the evening.

A lifelong friendship can rest firmly on the companionship of a few days. My fondness for William in early years, grew out of our work together in *The Gouvernor's Vrouw*. After the week in Hollywood in the spring of 1928, William and I had a new friendship. Each thought correctly that the other had changed, and we both understood why, or flattered ourselves that we did. To reach San Diego I took the day train down and came back on the sleeper. William came with me. That *was* a satisfactory talk! Half a day, and half a night.

4

I reached Butte, Montana, before breakfast. On the platform a reception committee waited for me. They were mine managers, strong characters, who had planned the warmest and most thorough hospitality which boyish hearts could invent and much practice could carry through. Having asked whether I preferred a he-man's day or a quiet session with the Ladies' Sewing Circle, they took me for breakfast to an uninhibited restaurant, where the first course was a highball. From breakfast we went to the mines, all of them, not to slight a single manager among my hosts. In rubber coats we dropped down the shafts, to regions of high temperature, losing five pounds in each sweatbox. Coming to the surface, we drank a highball to restore the essential moisture. After a morning of this give-and-take we got into dry clothes and lunched at a pleasant club, where there was a continuance of moderate drinking. I felt rather balmy, but my mind was still clear, and I could articulate. I knew, because I made the experiment.

After lunch a call on the wife of each manager was in order, and by way of greeting the lady and the children, healths all around had to be drunk in strong cocktails. Precisely at four o'clock I found myself trying to play one piano with two other gentlemen, who invariably wanted to use the same black or white keys that I did. A sobering thought occurred;

I had come to Butte to give a lecture! Convinced at last that I really wanted to find my hotel, the hospitable managers took me there, and in five minutes I was in the bath tub. Slightly hazy whether a hot bath was called for, or a cold one, I alternated, until in the course of an hour I came out of the fog. At dinner my hosts made personal remarks about the inability of professors to stand the pace, but for the sake of my audience I refused to touch another drop.

My lecture at Butte had been arranged by the Literary Society of the town, a group of ladies who probably were accustomed to the ways of their men-folk. Throughout the day the members of the program committee had been receiving bulletins of my progress, and when I appeared at the lecture hall they showed—as it seemed to me—signs of relief. They knew I would be there, but they hadn't been sure in what condition. So far as I could see, they were satisfied, or even pleased, by my platform performance. Beyond question the audience was hugely entertained, not necessarily by what I said, but by the coöperation I had from my loyal hosts, the mine managers. If accidentally I lifted an eye or an eyebrow, they took it as a signal that I had said something witty, and a laugh should be forthcoming. After each rousing guffaw I found myself making a hasty attempt at something funny, so that the hilarity might have an excuse, even if belated.

At the end of the evening they escorted me to the train and cheered me off. They were an amazing group, apparently with unlimited reserves of endurance, but as soon as the train drew out, I crawled into my berth and fell asleep.

When I arrived at Butte that morning I had a cold. When I left I had none.

CHAPTER XXXVII

Juilliard School

I

BY THE will of Augustus D. Juilliard, who died in 1919, the Juilliard Foundation was established for the encouragement of music in the United States. The Trustees named in the will selected as Secretary of the Foundation, Dr. Eugene A. Noble, who organized the Juilliard Graduate School of Music in its first form, which to nobody gave entire satisfaction. The term "Graduate School" was never explained; the instruction provided did not presuppose necessarily any training in a degree-giving institution, and the standards by which pupils were admitted were not clearly defined.

In 1927 the Trustees of the Foundation made a fresh start, setting up under a State charter a board of nine directors to take charge of the school. I was one of the original nine. At the same time the Foundation took over the Institute of Musical Art, the school founded by Frank Damrosch in 1905. The new Board of Directors had the double task of making the Juilliard Graduate School function effectively, and of amalgamating with it the excellent Institute, over which Dr. Frank Damrosch would continue to preside as dean.

For the remainder of 1927 and most of 1928 I had the supervision of both schools as Chairman of the Administration Committee. Before I went on the lecture tour and after my return, I was kept busy with office hours at the Graduate School, then located at 49 East Fifty-second Street, and with frequent calls on Dr. Damrosch at Claremont Avenue and One Hundred Twenty-second Street. I also did some traveling for the Board in vain attempts to persuade well-known educators to accept the presidency of the reorganized school. Men of experience and ability shied away from a task which certainly was complex and might prove thankless.

In the summer of 1928, Allen Wardwell, chairman of our Board, conveyed an invitation from our colleagues to take the presidency myself. I was hoping that we might find a president before October, when Graham would be going to France for his year at the Sorbonne; I wanted to go with him and see that he was comfortably settled and well started on his work.

What attracted me in Allen Wardwell's invitation were the relations which might be developed between a powerful music school and the whole American educational system. Undoubtedly there was much to be done for the art of music by itself; there I could have the guidance of great musicians. But I knew how weak our universities and our public schools were in the study of the fine arts. If music was someday to become a well recognized subject in general education, the Juilliard Foundation and the Juilliard School ought to supply leadership in that direction.

Perhaps some such ideas had occurred to my colleagues on the Board. I know now that one of them, Mr. Paul Cravath, had been corresponding with General Pershing about my work at Beaune, and I am sure I was selected for the presidency not for musical ability, but for experience in American education.

I accepted on condition that the Board permit me to carry out my plans for Graham. It was agreed that I should take him abroad and visit him from time to time during the year. In return for this privilege during the first six months of my administration, I accepted only half the year's salary.

So far as Graham was concerned, the plan worked out beautifully. I took an apartment at 8 rue de Val-de-Grace, where his mother kept house for him and Anna. During the winter I crossed the ocean a number of times, was delighted with his progress, and renewed French friendships. Exactly ten years after the *Conseil Municipal* of Beaune had made me and my descendants honorary citizens, I took my descendants to Beaune, and at the Hôtel de la Poste gave a dinner to the surviving members of the *Conseil,* the very same dinner, according to Mr. Chevillot's records, that the *Conseil* had given me, though with not the same wines. This time the wives of the City Council were present, and the widows of those who had died. Since both my descendants could talk French, I sat back proudly and reflected how rich my life was in the kind of blessings I liked.

2

Perhaps it was just as well that during my first year as president of the Juilliard School I was absent much of the time; had I been continuously on the ground, I might have moved too fast in the changes which had to be made; but whenever I had completed a number of weeks at the School and was in somewhat of a ferment over its problems, the trip abroad gave me an interval to reflect and to reëxamine my plans.

The problem of amalgamating the two schools was formidable, to say the least. I was soon convinced that nothing could be done while they were located so far apart. I persuaded the Trustees that a new building should be put up directly north of the Institute, and the Institute building should be remodeled to fit into the total plan. The architects, Shreve, Lamb and Harmon, were engaged, and at once began suggesting the form the composite Juilliard School ought to take. At once I found myself in a conflict which called for diplomacy. Dr. Frank Damrosch was glad to see his School developed by Mr. Juilliard's money, but he would have liked to spend the money himself without suggestions or supervision. Three of the nine Directors on our new Juilliard School Board, Paul Warburg, Paul Cravath, and John L. Wilkie, had been Trustees of the Institute, but Dr. Frank had a sort of resentment against them for bringing about the merger with the Graduate School, even though the arrangement gave him immediately increased funds for the work of the Institute, and for himself a much larger salary and a guaranteed pension.

Ernest Hutcheson, one of the piano faculty at the Graduate School, enjoyed, because of his professional ability and his personal character, the confidence of the other teachers. He was by taste and preference a teacher, but against his will I secured my Board's approval of his appointment as Dean of the Graduate School. I chose him not as an administrator, but as a moral force badly needed to improve the School's spirit. But Ernest was always a sensitive person, and he knew Frank Damrosch's hostility to the merger. Having himself taught at the Institute in former years, his friendship for Frank, D, as for his brother Walter, was warm. Rather than plunge into an angry or irritated atmosphere, Ernest wanted to abandon the idea of a single school building, and let the Graduate School stay downtown.

I wasn't sorry that it took about two years for the Graduate School, the Institute and the architects to get together on the plans. By the time we began to build, the two schools had argued with each other so much that they began to be as close as many a human family, intimate but on edge, imperfectly reserving their opinion about each other. The new building at 120-130 Claremont Avenue had its formal opening in the autumn of 1931.

In the first phase of the Juilliard Graduate School, Dr. Noble, who by temperament was a discriminating art collector, had assembled a faculty much as he would have gathered a collection for a museum. He engaged only great artists and famous teachers. A museum doesn't worry too much if its treasures happen to belong more to one period than to another. Granted that the seventeenth century is better represented than the thirteenth, that the French Renaissance throws Italian primitives into the shade; the balance can be restored with time, and there is no particular hurry. Dr. Noble was not a pianist, but since pianists happened to be plentiful, he engaged a remarkable collection of pianists. He had Alexander Siloti, Carl Friedberg, Ernest Hutcheson, Mr. and Mrs. Josef Lhevinne, Olga Samaroff, and several who remained only a short time—Ernest Schelling, for example, and Yolanda Irion. He told me he did his best to secure Harold Bauer.

His violin department was also notable—and top heavy, Leopold Auer was its head with Paul Kochanski, Hans Letz, and Louis Persinger. The voice department included Marcella Sembrich, her pupil Florence Kimball, Anna Schoen-René, Paul Reimers, and Francis Rogers. Felix Salmond taught the 'cello, and Rubin Goldmark taught composition.

Obviously the art-collector way of gathering a faculty paid no attention to the probable number of pupils, nor to their needs. If only applicants of first-rate ability should be admitted, the chances were overwhelming that the remarkable piano faculty would prove far too large. If the School were in healthy condition, there ought to be more good voice material than four teachers could take care of, and certainly one teacher of composition, no matter how eminent, might be overtaxed to care for the entire School.

The result, as I observed it, was that the Graduate School, until the Institute was amalgamated with it, contained some outstanding talent and much that was mediocre. All the teachers in the piano department, for example, had plenty of pupils, but not all of the same quality. This phenomenon may have been new in music teaching, but it was no novelty in general education. Johns Hopkins University was started as a graduate school exclusively, but in the course of time a college was inserted under it. The Institute of Musical Art, if inserted under the Graduate School, might help the advanced instruction to be more consistent and efficient. In the early days of the Juilliard, if a candidate had any talent at all, or had talent without proper preparation, he or she was accepted in the hope of later improvement. After the schools were joined, such a candidate could be assigned to the Institute until he or she qualified for promotion.

Though I did not intend to interfere with the individual teaching, so long as the results were good, I had one or two convictions about musical education in general. The new building on Claremont Avenue was to contain a concert hall, in which not only recitals but symphony concerts and opera performances could be given. So far as I knew, no music school in the world contained adequate facilities for public performance by students. How could we tell whether our pupils were properly taught, unless we heard them perform—heard them frequently—and unless the public were invited to hear them too? If music critics could be persuaded to come, so much the better. In general I wanted music teaching to come out of the mysterious privacy in which, at least in the United States, it had a tendency to shroud itself. I wanted the Juilliard School constantly to show its hand, and to face any legitimate criticism. Since we live in a world which is difficult for all artists, I could see no reason why musicians, like some painters and some poets, should claim special cotton-batting protection from public opinion.

Finally, I hoped that the School, in the spirit of Mr. Juilliard's legacy, would serve not New York alone, but the whole country. I did not at first see how we could reach out, but I was resolved sooner or later to create a method. In time, I hoped, talent would come to us from all sections of the land, and having profited by what the School gave, would return to the section that produced it. I knew from the record of general education that the influence of cultural centers is as it were to skim or loot the landscape, to remove its intellectual topsoil, and create spiritual dust-bowls. Talent gravitates to the large cities, and is unwilling to be blasted out of them. Yet since talent is the lifeblood of the nation, it ought to flow freely through the whole arterial system.

3

The complete account of my years at the Juilliard would need a separate volume. The School Directors were asked by the Foundation to pass on the innumerable appeals for aid which came to them, and the Directors expected me to do the sifting, with the aid of my colleagues. The Carnegie Corporation, of which Fred Keppel was president, likewise received requests for aid, often in the field of civic or communal music, and Fred K asked me to form a committee to advise him in making grants. I assembled a group from our faculty, with the addition of Harold Bauer, whose acquaintance with the music needs of the country was remarkable, and whose understanding of the social function of music I admired. Over my desk came a large proportion of the dilemmas or projects which occupied American music lovers from 1928 to 1937. Since I had no wish to monopolize for the Juilliard Trustees the privilege of wrestling with these problems, I made a point of asking Josef Hofmann, then directing the Curtis School, to join us in enterprises which affected the country as a whole, especially in advising Fred Keppel about the Carnegie grants. But Mr. Hofmann replied that the business of a music school, as he understood it, is to train performing artists, not to worry about the needs of the general public. Our points of view were diametrically opposed. I too wanted to train artists, but not to send them out to starve; I thought the school that trains artists has some responsibility to prepare an audience for them; and audiences as well as performers need training.

CHAPTER XXXVIII

Opera Librettos

I

SLIGHTLY more than a year before the School moved uptown to its new building, Albert Stoessel told me that Louis Gruenberg had in mind an opera, which he would compose as soon as he could free himself from some routine work. Albert knew that Ernest Hutcheson and I admired Gruenberg's talent, and he probably thought I would persuade the Foundation to make the composer a special grant, as we had already done in the case of Deems Taylor. But after a talk with Gruenberg, I hit on a different plan.

He wanted to compose music for a fantastic, whimsical story; in effect, he was thinking of a fairy-tale opera. As soon as he had time, he would write the libretto himself, basing it on Barrie's *Peter Pan.* I told him that three friends of the School would be glad to provide an income for a year, in monthly payments, if he could devote himself to the opera, and if the School might have the privilege of making the first presentation of the work, provided it were within the ability of our students. He agreed, and the contract, signed that day, went into effect at once. He did not ask who were the three friends of the School. They were Paul Warburg, Ernest Hutcheson, and myself.

After some weeks had elapsed, he appeared one day at my office in Fifty-second Street, much worried.

"How can I write an opera if I have no libretto?"

"Didn't you intend to use *Peter Pan?*"

"When I ask Barrie, he won't give me permission."

375

"You mean to say, you hadn't already secured permission when we first talked of your plan?"

I began to be worried too. My friends had joined me in subsidizing Louis's masterpiece, and nothing was happening. Suddenly Louis had an idea. His face brightened.

"Why don't you write me a libretto yourself?"

I felt I was doing enough for that opera, and I had a novel half finished; but to salvage the plan in which I had involved Warburg and Hutcheson, I wrote the text of *Jack and the Beanstalk*. Gruenberg set my text to delightful music, and the School presented the opera with considerable success on November 20, 21, and 22, 1931, when the new building was dedicated. *Jack* later had a splendid performance by a professional company at the Chicago Opera House, and in a slightly shortened form it has been given many times before high school audiences.

Immediately after the presentation on Claremont Avenue, we engaged the Forty-Fourth Street Theatre and gave *Jack* there for two weeks. Ernest Hutcheson and Albert Stoessel wanted the alternating casts to have the experience of playing before Broadway audiences. Whatever the benefit of this experience may have been, the cost was terrific. We never repeated the experiment.

2

A few years later I received a letter from George Antheil, then in Europe. He said he was meditating a new opera, and would like the privilege of using for a libretto *The Private Life of Helen of Troy*. He went on to say that he wanted to do an intimate opera, of Mozartean quality, scored for a small orchestra and a small cast. He added the hope that I might not be one of those who held his *Ballet Méchanique* against him; he believed he had sowed his musical wild oats, and could now go on to serious composition.

The letter contained so much of George's personal charm that I took a long chance and wrote him that I had a sequel to *Helen of Troy* which, if he wished, I would send in the form of a libretto. George, on his part, took a long chance and accepted my offer. I wrote the text of *Helen Retires* and sent it to Europe, without having the slightest idea what his music would be like in its second, or reformed, style, nor what kind of text he was looking for.

He had some notion that Leopold Stokowski would produce the opera at Philadelphia, but if Stokowski ever intended to do so, he changed his mind. There was also a plan to produce it in the summer opera season at Chautauqua, New York; to assist this project the Juilliard School paid for the copying of the chorus parts by the Universal Edition in Germany.

Antheil came to America at last, bringing his music with him, part of it still in his head. There seemed to be no likelihood of a production. Stokowski came up to the School one day and heard George play his opera and explain it. Ernest Hutcheson, Albert Stoessel, and others of the Juilliard staff studied the score, and listened to the protests which it aroused from the vocal faculty. Madame Sembrich and Madame Schoen-René agreed that the music would be very wearing on young voices, and hoped their students would never be asked to attempt it. But Hutcheson, Stoessel and I felt strongly that in spite of many absurdities and extravagances, Antheil's composition had so much vitality, and in many experimental ways was so provocative that it would be an error not to produce it. The School presented *Helen Retires* on March 1, 2, and 3, 1934. The sets and costumes were designed with extreme originality by Frederick Kiesler, a friend of George's who has continued to design scenery and costumes for Juilliard operas, and in conjunction with the Architectural department of Columbia University has given at the School a valuable class in stage design.

The production of the Antheil opera was from many points of view the most brilliant event at the Juilliard School during my presidency. I consider the performances more exciting than anything else I ever saw or heard in the theatre. George's music richly deserved the applause as well as the protests which it received; it was beautiful, and to an equal degree baffling, irritating. My libretto had grave faults. The text was occupied with ideas rather than with physical movement which could be followed by the eye. Frederick Kiesler's settings to a degree made up for this defect; with the exception of a few scenes, the opera was fascinating to watch. But the excitement I mentioned as characterizing the performances, came from the vitality of George's music. I consider him one of the most extraordinary talents of my time. If he had been less of an improviser and more of a conscientious craftsman, he could have gone far; but it was his nature to dash from one field of art to another and to glitter brilliantly for a while in each, always kindling, by his indescribable personal charm, more faith in his future than he was concerned to justify.

His high spirits and his characteristic oddities made our brief collaboration a fantastic experience. One afternoon before the opera went into rehearsal, Leopold Stokowski came to the School to hear a piano version of the score. Ernest Hutcheson, Oscar Wagner, Albert Stoessel and I gathered in my study to see how he would take it. George sat at the piano with his orchestral score, not the final copy but an early pencil version. From the illegible pages he drew sufficient hints and reminders to give a consecutive rendering of his intentions. As he played, Stokowski leaned over his shoulder. George had pianistic ability, and could talk volubly as he stormed through his music. Stokowski got a running commentary on the notes he was trying to hear, George raising his voice to lift the comments clear of piano sounds, and thumping harder and harder to lift the piano over his voice. At the climax of the din he glanced up at Stokowski and shouted, "In the orchestration, this passage is *pianissimo!*"

I can imagine nothing more arduous than the composing and slow perfecting of an opera. No wonder that most musicians would rather write concertos or symphonies. The born operatic composer is willing to pay the laborious price of perfection. After the performances of *Helen Retires,* George came to me with an offer from a small European opera house to put on the work at once.

"Do you think we could improve the thing?"

"In many ways," said he. "I'll write new music for some spots, and mend the others."

"The libretto," said I, "needs more than mending. If you're game, I'll rewrite most of the text."

Apparently he was enchanted, and we agreed to meet in a day or two for exchange of new ideas. But he was soon called off on some other project. I heard nothing more about the European opera house that yearned to perform our masterpiece. George went to Hollywood, and began writing articles on endocrinology.

3

In 1938 Beryl Rubinstein, pianist-composer and Director of the Cleveland Institute of Music, asked permission to use for a libretto my short story, *The Sleeping Beauty.* After a number of discussions I agreed to recast the plot in libretto form. The opera was to be presented by Rodzinski and the Cleveland Orchestra. By the time the work was completed, I was no longer President of the Juilliard, but Ernest Hutcheson, who succeeded me, arranged with Rubinstein to give the first performances at the School, and to use the same cast at the Cleveland performances. Rubinstein's music was charming, and Fred Kiesler created ingenious and beautiful sets for the School performances. For Cleveland, on a far larger stage, the opera needed different scenery, which was skillfully designed by Richard Rychtarik.

It was a pleasure and something of an education to have a hand in these three operas. The experience convinced me of several things; first, that I can't write a good libretto; second, that American composers in the academic tradition—or at least those who have entirely missed the salutary training of tin-pan alley—are not good song writers; and third, that unless the composer knows how to write songs, he isn't likely to write a good opera. Song is the essential language of opera, lyrical song rather than the musical chatter which is called dramatic singing. In other words, collaboration in these three operas taught me to appreciate the masterly qualities of *Porgy and Bess* and of *Showboat,* as yet the only first-rate American operas. George Gershwin and Jerome Kern were song writers. Gruenberg, Antheil, and Rubinstein began their musical career as pianists, and it remained an instinct with them to compose for instruments rather than for the voice.

CHAPTER XXXIX

Municipal Art Commission

I

THE economic depression in the second half of President Hoover's administration brought distress to artists in every field, particularly to musicians. In most of the plans or schemes to meet this crisis, I was involved, since appeals for funds usually came to the Juilliard. The Musicians' Emergency Aid began to function at this time, and other organizations did what they could for the rescue of worthy artists who suddenly found themselves unemployed, with small hope of recovering their former degree of prosperity.

But the depression affected others besides musicians, and because of my experience with the University at Beaune, I became, to my surprise, chairman of the so-called "Adjustment Service," which furnished free advice to adults displaced by the depression. The Adjustment Service was sponsored by the American Association for Adult Education, and financed by a gift of $100,000 from the Carnegie Corporation. The Director of it was Jerome H. Bentley, then Activities Secretary of the New York Y.M.C.A., now business manager of Wells College, Aurora, New York. The other members of the Executive Committee, in addition to myself as chairman, were Morse H. Cartwright, Director of the American Association for Adult Education; E. K. Fretwell, Professor of Education at Teachers College; William J. Donovan, attorney, "Colonel Bill" in the First World War and General Donovan during the Second; Spencer Miller, Jr., Secretary of the Workers' Education Bureau of America; Walter W. Pettit, Assistant Director, New York School of Social Work;

Morris E. Siegel, Board of Education; and Robert I. Rees, my old friend and commanding officer General Rees, now Assistant Vice-President, American Telephone and Telegraph Company.

The Adjustment Service functioned from February, 1933, to May 31, 1934, on the thirteenth floor of the National City Bank building at Madison Avenue and Forty-second Street. This space was donated by the bank. Most of our furniture was lent us by the Y.M.C.A. and by Henry L. Doherty and Company. Over twelve thousand men and women availed themselves of the Service. The procedure was simple. Anyone who needed advice, either in finding new work or in getting on better in their present job, could make an appointment for an interview with an adviser. The advisers were trained by a group of psychologists and psychiatrists, who generously put their wisdom at our disposal. At the end of the first interview the adviser would have the answer to essential questions about the person interviewed. The psychologists and psychiatrists would study these answers, diagnose each case, and tell the adviser what to do next.

After the organization was running smoothly under Jerome Bentley's direction, my job as chairman was light indeed. I went down to the Adjustment Service once a day to see what was going on, spending always as much time as I could in the counsel room where the experts studied the reports of the advisers and recommended the course to be taken in each case. I had never seen a cross section of society under this kind of microscope. Obviously the distress of the moment had existed or had been latent before the economic crisis forced it into the open. In modern society only a minority have found their proper niche or know what they'd like to do if they could, or have any equipment for their jobs. In so-called good times an almost terrifying number secure work beyond their powers. In a sense they are the victims of the good nature or the poor judgment of their employers. During a stretch of prosperity, business and the various professions manage somehow to stagger along under the weight of excess baggage, but in bad times, when the struggle for survival becomes desperate, the tendency is to throw overboard the unserviceable and the untrained. The conclusion is hard to escape, that education, even the avowedly cultural kind, should accept responsibility for fitting each generation for its part in the economic world. Some of the cases which came to us had enjoyed excellent training, but had been in jobs where that training could not be used. These were cases of maladjustment, comparatively easy to straighten out for such people who found the proper work, and so far as I know they were happy. But most of the unemployed had training in no field whatever.

I stress this point because it reappears uncomfortably in my memories of two projects for the relief of artists during the depression, and for the future advancement of the arts.

2

Toward the end of 1933 a small group of us had a plan which we thought the new President, Franklin D. Roosevelt, might approve. Indeed, we believed we had assurances of his approval. Members of the group, or friends of theirs, had talked with him about the plight of artists and about this particular scheme to enrich the art opportunities of the whole country.

As we all know, the larger cities of the nation, and only those cities, constitute the beaten path on which musical or theatrical entertainments do their touring. Smaller places, cities of only one hundred thousand inhabitants, rarely see the best shows or the best art exhibitions, or hear the best music. Our group believed that in each of these neglected places there probably was at least one large hall, perhaps an armory, which the town might be willing to turn over to us. We would undertake to assemble, probably in New York, theatrical companies, musical groups, and art exhibitions which would travel toward the center of the land. A troup of actors thrown out of employment by the crisis, could be rehearsed in a show and started off on their long tour. Behind them would come, perhaps, a small orchestra, well rehearsed in good programs. The orchestra might be followed by an exhibition of contemporary paintings, selected from the work of good artists, who at the moment could find no market for their work. Our purpose was to provide audiences for the most expert in each art. The gravest danger to the country, if artists should temporarily have no career, would be the loss of skills which could not be recovered for decades.

Admission to all these forms of entertainment would be twenty-five cents. Such a price would enable a play, an art exhibition, or a good concert, to compete with a motion picture. In every case the artists would take the gate receipts. Assuming that several performances were given in each place, and that the places were close together, the intake for the artists might come to a respectable amount. The committees which organized the troupes on each coast and started them on their way, would donate their services. But there would be one big expense which only the Federal Government, we thought, should or could assume; capable men and women would have to be sent out from Washington to sell the idea to the various towns, to secure the donation of a large hall or armory, and to keep an eye on the venture after it got started.

The group who evolved this idea, appointed themselves a committee to go to Washington and lay it before President Roosevelt. I am afraid I must admit that I was chairman, though the idea did not originate with me. Others on the committee were, Ernest Hutcheson, Ernest Schelling, musicians; Jonas Lie, DeWitt Lockman, and Ernest Peixotto, painters; Joseph H. Freedlander, architect. Professor James T. Shotwell, my Columbia colleague, took a warm interest in our quixotic idea, and frequently sat in at our meetings.

I was then living at 471 Park Avenue, in an apartment house of the older fashion which favored large rooms. Because I had the space, the preliminary meetings were held at my home. One evening we met there for dinner, a French peasant meal of the casserole type which those artists would remember from their student days. A few bottles of Beaune wine helped out immensely. My guests wished to retaliate; we agreed that all should give a dinner in turn, and only when the cycle was complete should we call on the President.

Eventually we got to Washington. To save Mr. Roosevelt's time I had written out our plan as briefly as possible. I read it to him for what immediate comment he cared to make, and we left it with him for study. In principle he endorsed the idea. He agreed that the Government should bear the expense of organizing the halls or armories, and he thought we might be right in estimating the cost of this fieldwork at something around $250,000. He could find the money, he said; he asked us to give no publicity to our plan nor to his acceptance of it. He wished to make all announcements himself.

Jonas Lie had reserved the privilege of giving the committee a dinner in Washington after our visit to the President. It was a cheerful feast. We had no doubt of Mr. Roosevelt's ability to make our idea succeed. We believed that the arts in America were entering a happy chapter.

We never heard of our plan again. Perhaps the W.P.A. projects were somehow related to it in Mr. Roosevelt's mind. But the W.P.A. did little to preserve veteran skills. In politics majorities count, and the youthful and untrained will always outnumber the mature and competent. All my life I wanted youth to have its opportunity, an opportunity to acquire training—not merely a chance at work which untrained talent cannot handle. Yet we can at least be grateful to the W.P.A. for the State guide-books; the cost of producing them with untrained workers was ghastly, but the value of the books, in spite of the errors they contain, has been proved. In successive printings errors will probably be eliminated, and by the use of these guides we are coming to know the American land-scape—if not American art.

3

The plight of American painters and musicians was aggravated in the late twenties and early thirties by an influx of artists from Europe. Not even the depression had destroyed the legend of American wealth. Though England, France, Italy, and all the other European countries had rigorous restrictions on the entry of American actors or musicians, we had no tariffs of that kind. Only with the greatest difficulty could American musicians give concerts abroad, but any European could come over to us if he had the fare.

The solution which American musicians proposed was a high tariff or embargo against all foreign artists. The argument was that we had too many musicians in the United States already; only for exceptional reasons should we let in another.

I was called upon frequently to discuss this problem at large music conventions; both factions in the debate wanted the Juilliard influence on their side. I got into the quarrel with a good deal of energy and en-thusiasm, since I believe in no tariffs of any kind, least of all in tariffs on art. My argument was that practically everything good in our land has been brought to us by the talents, often unsuspected, of immigrants. If Europe wanted to strip itself of genius and send it all over here, I thought we might as well let European culture continue this form of slow suicide.

The movement in favor of legislation against the entry of more mu-sicians was blocked. The problem for American musicians, however, re-mained, and the members of the committee which had called on Mr. Roosevelt, re-assembled and got in touch with many others, to explore the possibility of a department of Fine Arts in our national Government.

In the late spring of 1934 we addressed to President Roosevelt a letter on the subject, signed by fifty well-known musicians, writers, architects, sculptors, and painters. The letter outlined the problem which the arts were facing, and the various ways in which we believed a department of Fine Arts could help.

From this letter there was as little result as from the one which we had handed to Mr. Roosevelt in person. Now I am glad nothing came of our plea for a department of Fine Arts. In our letter we said, what we all thoroughly realized, that a Fine Arts department, to be useful, must be kept free from politics. In Mr. Roosevelt's first term I was impressed by his idealism. I went so far as to believe that he would want to keep a Fine Arts department clear of political influence, and that he would be able to do so.

4

On July 29, 1935, Mayor Fiorello LaGuardia appointed me a lay member of the Municipal Art Commission, a post which I retained for two years.

The Municipal Art Commission in New York serves chiefly to keep bad art out of town. The Commission can inaugurate no civic enterprises, but every change affecting municipal buildings, monuments, parks, etc., must have its approval. When I joined the board the chairman was Mr. I. N. Phelps Stokes. The other members besides myself were Ernest Peixotto, A. Paul Jennewein, Jonas Lie, Edward C. Lamb, Louis V. Ledoux, and R. T. H. Halsey. We met at least once a month in a poorly ventilated room on the top floor of the City Hall, and gave our blessing to the vigorous improvements which Bob Moses was making in the city, or we argued at length about ghastly sketches for murals submitted to us by workers in the W.P.A. arts projects. In those days artists on the W.P.A. payroll seemed to have the first and only chance at decorating city buildings. Naturally Mayor LaGuardia wanted us to coöperate, if we could, with whatever effort the Federal Government was making to relieve the plight of the artists. We on the Commission were willing enough, but we had, as it were, a front seat at the tragedy which the W.P.A. projects were enacting. The artists whose sketches were submitted for our approval may have had some talent for painting, but it was untrained talent, and it probably was destined to perpetrate easel canvases rather than murals.

Ernest Peixotto, during his term on the Committee, solved the problem for us from month to month with the magnificence which made his character unforgettable. Invariably he would propose that the committee postpone a verdict on the sketch submitted until he had a month or two to work with the young painter. He himself, world famous for his murals, was too eminent an artist to be employed during that crazy period. By giving free lessons to the W.P.A.'s egregious protégés, he licked their work into passable shape, and by his generous pleading softened us up to a point where we could vote for the thing.

I have mentioned here some matters which may seem to be unrelated, but are not. My experience on the Art Commission, like my experience with the Adjustment Service, drove into me the sad truth that we Americans set small value on training or competence. England used to be the country that took a humorous pride in "muddling through." I began to think that perhaps "muddling through" may be a form of competence, and perhaps in order to muddle successfully, you have to be trained.

CHAPTER XL

Metropolitan Opera

I

DURING the First World War the Metropolitan Opera Association had its share of hardships. The attendance naturally fell off, some of the leading artists were absent, and German opera had to be omitted.

With peace, the opera company expected the return of its old prosperity, but changes had occurred in the public taste and in the wishes of American musicians. There was a marked increase in the popularity of Wagnerian opera. There were also uneasy questions about the neglect of American singers and American composers. The Metropolitan Opera Association had never been an American institution, except in the sense that American patrons and American audiences supported it. Mr. Gatti-Casazza, the General Manager, conducted the house as though it were Italian; Italian artists and Italian operas were favored; as far as possible the employees on the Thirty-ninth Street premises were Italian; Italian was the language used in conducting the Operas's affairs. The Board of Trustees were Americans, but Gatti-Casazza preferred not to speak English to them. Mr. Paul Cravath, when President of the Metropolitan Opera Association, told me his interviews with Gatti had to be in French, since his Italian wasn't fluent.

A few American singers had managed to get on the Metropolitan stage, but only if they had previous training in Europe. Gatti once said that the Metropolitan was not, and should not be, a training school for young singers. In Europe, at the Scala and at other great opera houses, exceptional voices had always been allowed to get stage experience in small parts, but this system as followed in Europe involved work on the part of the management. Mr. Gatti evolved a star system which eliminated the training of inexperienced talent, and even the artistic responsibility of making new productions. He liked to engage top-flight artists with wide experience in their rôles—perhaps they had sung together on European stages. For a New York performance they had only to do what they had learned to do abroad, and their superb singing carried the day. Metropolitan audiences saw beautiful acting if Scotti or Chaliapin or Bori happened to be in the cast, but they learned to be content if only they heard a beautiful voice. The stream of beautiful voices fell away after the First World War. Neither Italy nor Germany continued to supply the Metropolitan with experienced artists. The Norwegian, Flagstad, engaged by Gatti at the close of his administration, was practically the only great singer from postwar Europe.

The President of the Metropolitan Opera Association had long been Mr. Otto Kahn, princely benefactor of music and other arts. In Gatti-Casazza's prosperous years Mr. Kahn had paid many deficits, small or large, from his own pocket, and the impression prevailed that the Opera Association had strong financial reserves. But in the seasons 1928-1929 and 1929-1930 the Metropolitan began to be in difficulties, for which the recent war and the depression were blamed. Through a series of years the public was informed that subscriptions and attendance had fallen off, that the Association faced a huge deficit, and that there could not be another season unless a generous fund were raised. The Opera was saved by what became an annual effort. It was obvious that the institution would be wiped out unless it were put on some secure and permanent basis.

One or two uninformed music critics began to attack the Juilliard Foundation for not handing over its endowment to the Metropolitan. Some of them went so far as to say in print that Mr. Juilliard had intended his money for this purpose, and that the funds had been diverted to the music school by his executors. There was no truth in this charge. Mr. Juilliard, in his will, left the executors free to use the money as they thought best for American music, merely suggesting, as purposes which would give him pleasure, collaboration with the Metropolitan Opera Company, and the founding of a first-rate music school.

Before the executors decided on a program, Dr. Noble, their Secretary, called on Mr. Gatti-Casazza to inquire whether aid from the Juilliard fund would be acceptable. Since the Opera was not yet in trouble, Gatti backed away from the offer for the same reason that Dr. Frank Damrosch declined the suggestion that the Foundation should take over the Institute of Musical Art. Dr. Damrosch wished to administer entirely in his own way the school which he had build up; Mr. Gatti knew that if he accepted Juilliard money he would be expected to do something for American talent, in which Mr. Juilliard had expressed an interest.

When Mr. Gatti declined any aid for his main season, Dr. Noble suggested a brief supplementary season, to be paid for by the Juilliard, in which works should be presented which were not in the Metropolitan repertoire. The offer was declined.

Mr. Edward Ziegler, who was Gatti's assistant, has told me that he never heard of this Juilliard offer. Gatti never mentioned it to him, and therefore he doubted that the episode occurred.

But I have reasons for believing it did. Having seen the complete report, going back as far as possible, which the auditors made for the harassed Board, I am sure Mr. Gatti did not tell Mr. Ziegler all that went on at the Metropolitan. I have heard Dr. Noble refer to the episode in the presence of Mr. Juilliard's executors. The matter did not seem to be news to them.

Among the Directors of the Juilliard School were several members of the Metropolitan Board. Naturally the Trustees of the Foundation were invited to contribute large sums to the Opera, and the Trustees asked my advice. I was in position to hear the gossip among musicians about Mr. Gatti's management of the Metropolitan. The artistic results had been superb, but according to general opinion in the musical profession, the financial record was bizarre. The money raised each season to save the Opera had melted like snow. I advised the Foundation that any large gift from us would follow these other sums down the drain. I became the target of Gatti admirers, particularly of those music critics who believed that the Juilliard money had been intended for the Opera's use.

When one of these critics, Olin Downes, repeated his charge in print, I challenged him for his authority. He admitted that Mr. Juilliard's will did not support him, but he said that Mr. Otto Kahn had the information directly from Mr. Juilliard himself in his last days. I wrote to Mr. Kahn at once, asking for light. Mr. Kahn wrote back that he had never made such a statement to anybody, nor had Mr. Juilliard ever said anything of the kind to him. I sent a copy of this letter to the accusing critic, suggesting that an apology to the Juilliard Trustees was in order. Olin did not feel that it was.

2

Metropolitan affairs went from bad to worse, and the decline was accelerated after the death of Mr. Kahn on November 29, 1934. Mr. Paul Cravath succeeded him as President of the Metropolitan Opera Association, and with Mr. Cornelius Bliss, Chairman of the Board, made heroic efforts to save the day, but it was too late. Something was radically wrong. An incident shortly occurred which I know only at second hand, since I was not then on the Board. At the end of the season, Mr. Gatti reported the usual terrifying deficit. He read the figures from a small piece of paper which he held in his hand. A new member of the Board, Mr. David Sarnoff, asked to look at the paper, then asked for a breakdown of the figures, then when no breakdown was available, asked to see the auditor's report. Mr. Gatti was offended by the request. There had never been an audit in all the years of his administration; he felt that an audit would be a reflection upon him. Mr. Sarnoff disavowed any reflection upon anybody, but audits were a normal thing in American business, and he didn't care to stay on a Board which didn't have an audit of its affairs.

The audit was ordered, and Mr. Gatti announced his intention of retiring. He was persuaded to continue for at least another year. In general the audit showed that during the difficult postwar period, when the income was sinking from year to year, the budget had been increased at the same pace, especially the salaries of the artists, especially of the Italian artists. Also the General Manager's salary. For the year just ending, with a formidable deficit, the cost of a fairly short season in New York had been slightly over three million dollars. Top-flight Italian singers received three thousand dollars a performance. It should be remembered that the union wages of orchestra, stagehands and other essential contingents, were in those days lower than they are today.

Another drive had to be put on for the next season. Shortly before Christmas, when the season had run only a few weeks, Allen Wardwell, Chairman of the Juilliard School Board, and active in Metropolitan affairs, asked me over the telephone to join him at the Century Club, where he said we could have a strong cocktail and brace ourselves for some bad news. I hurried down. The bad news was the decision of the Metropolitan Board to throw up the sponge. As Allen put it, "They want to leave their baby on the Juilliard doorstep. You criticized the Opera management; by implication you said that with different management opera might succeed. Can you tell us now what kind of management to set up?"

I agreed to draw up a plan and have it in his hands the next morning. That evening I consulted a number of professional musicians. After midnight I typed out the plan which the Metropolitan and the Juilliard Trustees accepted. In spite of much difficult going, the plan has been in successful operation ever since. I still prize the carbon copy of my amateurish typing.

Herbert Witherspoon was chosen General Manager to succeed Mr. Gatti-Casazza. Edward Johnson was chosen as Assistant Manager, with the idea that he might be Witherspoon's eventual successor. When Herbert fell dead of a heart failure on May 10, 1935, Edward took up the work and carried on. The Juilliard Foundation contributed some money for immediate needs, and without making public promises, held itself in reserve to see Witherspoon and Johnson through. Allen Wardwell, Ernest Hutcheson, Felix Warburg, and I were put on the Metropolitan Board. For the first few years I was Chairman of the Administration Committee. Whether there would be a deficit at the end of Edward Johnson's first year, neither he nor I could foretell, but when the season was half through we thought we couldn't possibly be in the red for more than thirty thousand dollars. By careful watching of expenditures at the Juilliard School, and by paring the School budget here and there, I saved this amount against a possible Opera loss, but the deficit showed in the audit as only fifteen hundred dollars.

3

Edward Johnson gave American operatic talent its chance, and under his leadership the Opera Association reached the country at large over the radio, and through long and steadily lengthening spring tours. Probably Mr. Gatti himself, were he here now, would be grateful to young American singers, however they might fall below his memory of great stars. Now that the old Europe is gone, opera throughout the world literally depends, at this moment of writing, on some of these young

Americans whom the Metropolitan has trained. They are invited to fill out the casts of South American opera houses which formerly, like the Metropolitan, drew on Europe for their singers. Incredible though it seems, some of them are now wanted in European opera houses, which are trying to stage a comeback.

What form opera will eventually take in America, none of us knows. The operatic star no longer receives a princely salary, but the players in the orchestra, who are artists quite as much as the singers, are better paid than they used to be, and other salaries have gone up in the spirit of the times. Also, in the spirit of the times, the price of tickets has gone down. Opera, like every other enterprise, is deeply involved in the current warfare between price ceilings and wage floors. Our one comfort is that if there is a solution for manufacturers and for storekeepers, there will probably be also a solution for grand opera.

With this difference, that workmen don't necessarily crave an audience, and artists do. As soon as young singers make a name for themselves at the Metropolitan, they will be enticed away by the radio and motion pictures. Even if the Opera Association could pay as much as Caruso received for every performance, radio can pay more, and pictures can outbid radio. The lure is not the money, but the size of the audience. Unless the opera is broadcast, the modern singer feels that it's almost a private performance.

CHAPTER XLI

Lausanne Conference

I

IN THE summer of 1931, I attended the Second Anglo-American Music Education Conference, at Lausanne, Switzerland, sailing from New York on the *Paris,* July 18. The conference was in session a week, from July 31 to August 7. Hurrying back to France, I started for home the next afternoon on the *Aquitania.*

Twenty-eight days, four exciting weeks, crowded with glimpses of old friends and meetings with new ones.

The conference was the idea of Percy A. Scholes, English educator, who devoted his tireless energies to the spread of culture and good will among Anglo-Saxons. He was not only a trained musician but an optimist. The 1931 Conference, as its name showed, was the second he had organized, and when we all scattered at the end of the week, he was talking about a third. So far as I know, the first produced no ripple of influence upon anyone, the benefits of the second were social rather than musical, and the third conference never came off.

Scholes had for fellow optimist, collaborator or accomplice in his conference-planning my friend Paul J. Weaver, Professor of Music at Cornell University. Paul and his wife seemed to believe, with Scholes, that if strangers can be brought together from places sufficiently distant, cultural enlightenment and international good will must result from natural frictions and combustions. At Lausanne I saw a number of fine artists falling in love with each other at sight, and an equal number falling into hot argument. With no excuse, I should say, in either case.

The choice of a meeting place was difficult. The British favored Lausanne because they had been there before. The Americans agreed because they had never seen the town, and thought they might as well. For the British, Switzerland was conveniently near, for the Americans it was expensively far. The British attendance was large, and the Americans, conscious of the effort by which they had got there at all, resented comments on the feeble support which the art of music receives in the United States.

I was invited to attend the first Conference, but couldn't. It was Paul Weaver who persuaded me to attend the second. He and Scholes wanted two chairmen, an Englishman and an American, to preside alternately. Sir William Henry Hadow, editor of the *Oxford History of Music,* was one chairman; I was the other.

I saw no reason for limiting the conference to British and Americans. Neither country could claim a first rank in music. Why cut out Germany and Italy, which had almost monopolized the art? Why pass over France and Russia, which had made priceless contributions? It was decided, after much correspondence, that musicians from all European countries, if they wished, should be admitted, for this one week, to the society of Anglo-Saxondom. Apparently they didn't wish. Few non-Anglo-Saxons showed up, and they only after being hand-picked, through special invitations. I had won a technical victory, but the British had their way. "Union now" had not yet become a slogan, but we Americans felt we had been gathered together for the greater prestige, not of music, but of English music.

2

When I boarded the *Paris,* I expected to find few acquaintances; in fact, I welcomed the prospect of a restful trip, with drowsy hours in the deck chair, and a chance to read several books. When a pleasant gentleman whom I knew slightly, stopped in front of my chair and asked if I played chess, I recognised no threat to my leisure. Yes, I knew the game, but was out of practice. For the rest of the week I had practice enough, of a kind.

My friend was Edward H. Blanc, well known in New York, a man of considerable culture and charm. He went to his rest long ago, and if his ghost does any eavesdropping, he already knows my good opinion of him, in spite of our chess games. He knew all the moves, the standard openings and defenses, but he talked his strategy over with himself as he pushed the pieces around. "Let me see, what next? Yes, that's it—king's bishop there—or is it the queen's bishop?" If he regretted a move, he changed it, first asking permission. I never saw much difference between his right moves and his wrong ones. He was quick to detect an error on my side. "Take it back, my dear fellow. *Please* take it back! I always do. . . . If you won't correct your mistake, I can't correct mine! Really, you are destroying my game!"

He was rather neat in his dress, but he usually wore a battered soft hat, which, as he thought, brought him luck. In the First World War he was torpedoed in the middle of the Atlantic by a submarine. At the moment he was wearing the soft hat. When the explosion threw him into the water, a wave lifted the hat from his head. A second wave washed him back to the deck of the sinking ship. A third wave, obligingly, handed him his hat.

I didn't know then the strength of his superstition. Only a few years later it caused his death. A breeze took off the famous hat while he was waiting for a train. The picturesque headgear fell in front of the engine wheels; he made an impulsive dash to save it, and was struck.

When Raoul Pugnet, commanding the *Paris,* gave the usual Captain's dinner, I was one of his guests—to represent American literature, he said. The others at the table were actors and actresses returning from Hollywood. I was seated next to Madame Françoise Rosay, one of the remarkable artists of our time. Her fame outside of France began with the film *Kermesse Héroïque,* in which she played the Mayor's wife. But at the Captain's dinner I knew nothing of her genius in the theatre or on the film; I merely found out for myself that she was a very French personality, of an admirable type, full of good sense and practical wisdom, not to be misled by illusions about human nature. We had several dances together, and she talked freely of her children, of their careers, of all her domestic interests. To this day, whenever I see her in a French motion picture, no matter what rôle her versatility interprets, I remember the character revealed that evening on the ship—herself, entirely apart from her profession.

Toward the end of the trip, one morning just before noon, a steward interrupted Mr. Blanc and me in our chess game. Captain Pugnet graciously desired my company for lunch in his cabin. I pushed back my chair, to desert the half-finished game.

"What's the matter?" said Blanc.

"I must dress up a bit."

"Nonsense! You're not going into society."

"Suppose there should be ladies?"

"They wouldn't be critical, not on shipboard."

I finished the game, to please him, and reached the cabin a minute late. There *were* ladies, four of them, to be entertained by Captain Pugnet and me. Two American women were going to Paris to write newspaper columns about the fashions; one of them was Helen Worden of the *World Telegram*. There was also a Belgian girl, with her chaperoning mother, on their way home from an American beauty contest. The girl had previously taken first prize in continental beauty shows, and had gone to the United States with the title of "Miss Belgium." She was a handsome creature, with a full figure and an empty face. During the meal she hardly said two words, but she must have had enough brain to know that her mother was chagrined by the failure to carry off a prize in the American contest, or to pick up a permanent husband, or even a temporary lover. Here she was, like a calf brought home from the fair because no one just then was in the market for calf.

Mother was voluble about the tragic situation, forgetting that Americans sometimes understand French. Her chatter did not please Captain Pugnet. At the earliest appropriate moment he proposed that we have some music. He was a violinist of considerable agility, and he played on an instrument of his own manufacture. His cabin contained a small upright piano, also made by himself, or at least he had picked up the various parts over a period of years as he cruised from port to port, and had assembled them with his own hands. In our honor he had fresh-tuned the contraption that morning. Using these available instruments, he and I got even with the haranguing Belgian mother by performing César Franck's *Sonata*.

Later that day Helen Worden and her friend met me on the sun deck, where cocktails were served by Marcel, whom hundreds of travelers remember inseparably from the old *Paris*. Fortified and at our ease, we took to pieces the character of the prize beauty and her maternal press agent.

On the train from Paris to Lausanne I found George Northrop and his wife, bound for a Swiss holiday. They had seats in the car ahead of me, but I transferred myself to their compartment and talked briefly with

George about our days at Beaune, and much more with Catharine about life at the moment, our own lives and the lives of several other people. The music conference continued to seem remote.

3

But at the end of my journey it became a sudden and very pleasant reality. The lovely town on the hilly shore of the lake, closed in by the Alpine skyline, overflowed with musicians. Most of the Americans stayed at the Lausanne-Palace-Beau-Site Hotel, where I found myself among old friends, Paul Weaver, Russell V. Morgan, of Cleveland, President of the National Music Supervisors Conference, Mrs. W. L. McFarland, Director of the Music Division of the National Association of Settlements, Harold Vincent Milligan, President of the National Association of Organists. At the Palace Hotel I met John P. Marshall, Professor of Music at Boston University. His friendship remained one of the precious things I took from the conference. A short distance down the lake, at Montreux, Beryl Rubinstein, pianist-composer and Director of the Cleveland Conservatory, had a cottage for the summer, within reach of the conference meetings.

The British musicians were a large and distinguished group. Percy Scholes seemed to spend his days with Paul Weaver, ironing out some awkward wrinkle in the program; W. G. Whittaker, of Glasgow, alternated with Bruce Carey of Philadelphia in demonstrating the art of choral conducting, members of the conference serving as choristers; Ernest MacMillan of Toronto University, Principal of the Toronto Conservatory, held panel discussions with other teachers of Composition on the proper ways of presenting their subject; and Stanley Roper, organist of the Royal Chapel, Windsor, planned with John Marshall a series of evening concerts which delighted all of us, or almost all; Ethel Bartlett and Rae Robertson, two-piano team, gave brilliant programs in the ball room of the hotel, as did Yves Tinayre, Beryl Rubinstein and the Prague String Quartet; Charles Faller, organist of Lausanne Cathedral, Ernest Bullock, organist and choirmaster of Westminster Abbey, and Harold Milligan, organist and choirmaster of the Riverside Church, gave recitals at Lausanne Cathedral. One afternoon Jacques Dalcroze brought a dozen of his pupils from Geneva to expound and illustrate his method of acquiring habits of relaxation and grace.

Sir Henry Hadow and his wife, both elderly but young in spirit, gave the conference a quality it could not have had without them. Sir Henry and I had met after the Armistice, when I went to London to lecture at Bedford College. He was charged with providing educational opportunities for English soldiers not yet demobilized, and I remember his courteous questions about our plans for the A.E.F. University. He was too busy to visit Beaune, but he knew what we accomplished there, and our encounter at Lausanne was a sort of reunion.

He was a fastidious gentleman, of an old fashion, astute and quiet humored, delightfully convinced that the country in which he was born and the Europe of his youth had been good enough to satisfy any reasonable person. Only in music was he intolerant. The modern composers were too much for him, and he never gave them a hearing if he could help it. When the Prague String Quartet, in tribute to English music, played a work by Arnold Bax, Sir Henry clutched his umbrella firmly in the middle and stalked out of the room. I couldn't hide a grin.

"As you please, my dear fellow, but I cahn't endure the nonsense—I really cahn't!"

4

When the American delegates returned to America, several reported the accomplishment of the conference in letters to music journals, saying for the most part nothing but complimentary things—complimentary and not particularly illuminating. One of the English delegates wrote for the *Nottingham Guardian* of October 7, two months after his return, a different account, honest and thought provoking. "Though the results of the Conference were by no means unfruitful, they would probably be of little public interest. My object is rather to give some of the impressions I formed of the condition of music in America and of American musicians themselves."

The writer then made some entirely fair points: the educational systems of the two countries are very different; each speaks a different language, especially in the field of music education; Americans are badly off, compared with the English, in the special field of Church music, whereas secular music means more to the average man in the street in America than in England.

In conclusion, the writer felt the benefit of the conference was human rather than musical; we came together, each group bringing its prejudices and misunderstandings, some of which we dropped in a few days.

This article from the *Nottingham Guardian* is pasted in my scrapbook, where I read it over whenever I'm discouraged about Leagues and Unions of Nations. Conferences serve this purpose at least, that by meeting face to face we learn something of the truth about each other, and in the process, whether or not the truth is agreeable, we get used to the idea that in this world we must be companions, and may even become friends.

Perhaps Switzerland will always suggest itself as the natural meeting place for European peoples, since so many great Europeans have left the memory of themselves to enrich that inspiring landscape. But we forget that most of these immortal visitors were exiles or refugees, more interested in escaping from their fellows than in uniting with them. And what irony there must be in the attempts of artists to form societies and academies and aim discourses at each other. In his creative mood the artist needs nothing so much as solitude. When his work is finished, he wants an audience which will look or listen—and not talk back.

CHAPTER XLII

Accident

I

THE year 1935 opened with great promise. The School was prosperous, the Opera was looking forward to a new chapter, I had plans for much writing, and my piano playing was at its best. On February 19, I played the Second MacDowell Concerto with Ossip Gabrilowitsch in Detroit, and five days later the Schumann Concerto with Eugene Ormandy in Minneapolis. On May 11, I played the Schumann Concerto again with Frederick Stock at Cornell College, Mt. Vernon, Iowa. On the afternoon of the tenth, when I reached the college, Jacques Jolas offered to play the second piano if I wished to run through the Concerto to limber up after the long train trip. I never had any illusions about my technique, but when I dressed for dinner that evening I knew I was playing better than ever before. Frederick Stock, Jolas, and several others were dining at President Burgstahler's house. When I came downstairs to join the party, Dr. Burgstahler handed me a telegram—announcing that Herbert Witherspoon had dropped dead that afternoon.

Telegrams began to pour from New York, and continued through the evening, the latest arriving about three in the morning, and answers were needed for them all. I couldn't sleep. At breakfast I found myself a nervous wreck. Since the concert program would not begin until two-thirty, I went to bed again, slept until one, had a shower and a cup of coffee, and reached the hall three minutes before I was to play. I hadn't tried the piano and the Concerto had not been rehearsed, but thanks to Frederick Stock's genius and to the abnormal condition of my nerves, the performance was far beyond any abilities of mine. The experience was a mystical one, significant to me because of what happened later in the year. That it took a good deal out of me, I knew even before I learned from the bathroom scales that I had lost five pounds.

That summer I played much chamber music—on August 11 at Music Mountain the Schumann Quintet, with Jacques Gordon's string Quartet, and the same piece on September 16 on the radio with the Musical Art Quartet.

2

On the evening of November 5, I lectured in Lansing, Michigan, intending to speak the next afternoon in Detroit. After the Lansing lecture some of the audience asked me to play, and since there was a concert grand on the stage, I said I would if the instrument was in tune. It was, and I enjoyed myself for thirty or forty-five minutes, going afterward to the home of Mr. and Mrs. Edgar H. Clark to play some more, until past midnight. Since Lansing is near Detroit, the train can make the distance between the two places in two hours. There was a two o'clock train which would get me to Detroit at four. The hour worried kind Mr. Clark.

"Why don't you have a good night's sleep; I'll drive you over in the morning."

His offer was more than welcome; I enjoyed a sound rest, the Clarks breakfasted with me at the hotel, and somewhere around eleven o'clock we were rolling toward Detroit in a comfortable car over a fine road. Mr. Clark drove, his wife was on the seat directly behind him, I sat beside her, with my bag in front. There were no cars ahead of us. A steady stream of vehicles passed us going toward Lansing.

Suddenly Mr. Clark jammed on the brakes. We were approaching a curve in the road, and around that curve, heading toward us at high speed, came a heavy truck. It was only a few seconds before we struck. Afterwards I was glad to remember the idea that came to me in the brief interval—that I had enjoyed this world, and life owed me nothing.

When the truck smashed into our engine, I shot over the back of the front seat and through the non-shatterable glass of the windshield, cracking my skull, breaking my nose, damaging my right knee and ankle, and splintering the small bones in my right hand. I must have broken my skull before I broke my nose; temporarily I enjoyed the very practical anesthetic. Mr. Clark, behind the driver's wheel, was badly hurt, and his wife had a sprained wrist and shattered nerves.

The crash occurred near Brighton, Michigan, where a private hospital took us in until the ambulance came from the Henry Ford Hospital in Detroit, which was to be my residence for a month. The doctors at the Ford put me under some real anesthetic, and my first clear memory was seeing Helen Worden hurry into the room, and shortly afterward my son, Graham. They had come the moment they heard of the accident; they stayed with me till I could travel; they brought me home.

At the hospital I was chiefly under the care of two remarkable doctors, remembered now as the kindest of friends. One was George Kreutz, the nose and throat specialist; the other was Daniel P. Foster, the heart specialist. Having discovered that my heart was almost the only sound part of me, he might have washed his hands of my case, but he stopped at my door several times a day, brought me a portable radio and some books, and kept me in a cheerful mood for Kreutz to work on.

3

After a long convalescence at home, under the care of my own doctor, Harold Keyes, I recovered most of my health. The broken nose didn't quite seem to be mine, something missing from my right knee occasioned the suggestion of a limp, and the knuckle of the little finger on my right hand was crushed beyond repair, so that smooth and fast piano runs would be impossible. But these were minor damages, and the rest in the hospital and at home made me believe I was better than I was. For a long time I had been overworking, and my nervous system was ready to break. The temporary rest merely postponed the catastrophe. I resumed my full program at the School, I gave many hours to the Metropolitan Opera, I practiced the piano more than ever in an effort to surmount the handicap which the accident had given me, and I began to write short stories and serials for *Liberty Magazine,* then edited by Fulton Oursler, old friend and companion in literary mischief.

Looking back now I can recognize the warnings which at the time I ignored. On January 11, 1937, the "Bohemians" of New York, the musicians club, of which Ernest Hutcheson was then president, gave a program of American music, at which I played a group of pieces by MacDowell, Howard Brockway, and John Alden Carpenter. I intended to play also Beryl Rubinstein's "Arabesque," which he had dedicated to me, but I had learned it only in recent months, and suddenly my memory refused to work. Even the MacDowell pieces were in danger of slipping away.

On January 31 the Players Club held a Pipe Night, at which Theodore Steinway presided, and the theme of all the speeches was music. I improvised a talk on opera, perhaps because several operatic tenors were present. Since we were all in a genial mood, my head wasn't turned when Frank Mason asked me to write out those astounding remarks of mine. I promised Frank a copy, but even as I spoke I was terrified to realize that I couldn't remember a thing I had said, nor even what my subject had been.

Eight days from that evening I suffered a stroke. My head had been bothering me, I found it hard to think. Suddenly, shortly after noon, my whole right side went to sleep. I had reason enough to think my work was done, and no gallant idea occurred to me, as when I had seen the truck approaching on the Brighton road.

The prospect of encumbering the earth, a loglike paralytic, is as severe a test of faith and will power as a man can face. That I ever got on my feet again, I owe primarily to Helen Worden, and to a great neurologist, Dr. E. Livingston Hunt. Harold Keyes brought in Dr. Hunt at once. I don't remember his salutary treatments in detail, but some incidents of his first and second call I could never forget.

The first day, after telling my nurse the things I could or could not eat, he glanced over at me.

"What do you usually drink?"

Supposing the question a joke, I answered, "Doctor, anything I can get!"

"No, what would you drink tonight if you were well and dining alone?"

"Oh—I used to begin with an old-fashioned."

He nodded to the nurse. "An old-fashioned with his supper."

"But Doctor, I thought alcohol would be ruinous for one in my state."

"I'm not worrying about your health," he said. "I'm prescribing for your self-respect."

When the nurse that evening brought in a weak old-fashioned on a neat tray, I decided that perhaps I might consent to live.

Next day he took me many steps further. "Were you writing anything when this happened to you?"

I told him I was halfway through a story for Fulton Oursler.

"Well, finish it. This is Wednesday; have it finished by the end of the week."

I laughed. "How can I, with a dead right arm and lifeless fingers?"

"The nurse will put the typewriter on the bed beside you, or on your lap, whichever is comfortable. You must use both your hands. If you can't do more, lift your right hand, and let it fall on the spacer. I can tell you this, if you don't type out the rest of that story by your own effort, you'll never be able to type again.

"Another thing—when the night nurse comes, before the day nurse leaves, you must walk six times around this room. Don't laugh—lean on their shoulders and drag your leg anyway you can, but get around the room six times. If you haven't the will power for that, you'll be bedridden all your days. But if your will *is* strong, you'll be walking around the block, with the help of a cane, inside a fortnight."

Having finished the story, which was a chapter in *The Brief Hour of François Villon,* I completed the novel without further interruption. Within less than a fortnight—in little more than eight days—I took my first walk around the block, helping myself with a cane, under the eye of my nurse. From then on I have been building up a life that seemed shattered. I even practice my piano playing again, very modestly and strictly for my own pleasure.

I may say something more, later, in the proper place, about the cures and remedies which helped my nerves, but it is convenient to end this chapter in the mood with which I gave up the presidency of the Juilliard School, on July 1, 1937. I thought then that my active life was ended, and that the remaining years would be spent in writing and reading, and thinking it all over.

PART VI

1937—1946

CHAPTER XLIII

South America

I

EARLY in 1940 the postman brought me an envelope from the Department of State, containing this letter:

MY DEAR MR. ERSKINE:

I shall be in New York City on December 16 and 17 and hope I may have the opportunity of talking with you concerning the program of the Department of State to encourage the visits to South America of a small number of scholars and writers from the United States. The Department is in a position to make available from funds provided by the Congress, grants to cover travel expenses for a trip of approximately two to three months.

I trust you may find it possible to consider acceptance of one of these grants.

Will you let me know what hour Monday afternoon or Tuesday morning or afternoon it would be convenient for you to see me?

Sincerely yours,

CHARLES A. THOMSON.
Chief
Division of Cultural Relations.

When Mr. Thomson came to New York, we lunched at the Century, and I learned the pleasant circumstances to which I owed this invitation. South American diplomats in Washington had complained of the type of North American who races through a country, spending a day or two in each city, then shoots through another country, then through a third and a fourth—and before reaching home collects his frantic notes in a volume called perhaps *The Inner Soul of South America*. Would it not be possible, the diplomats asked, for the Department of State to sponsor the visits of some northern writers, chosen for their sympathy with South American culture, who would be free to write or to lecture, as they pleased, but who would stay for a month or so in the country to which the Department sent them.

Just when this idea was presented by the diplomats, I don't know; I believe it came out of informal and perhaps unpremeditated conversations. But the Department of State responded wisely, after much thought, or so we at least think, who were finally chosen. A list of names was drawn up, and Argentina asked for me. Since Montevideo is only an overnight journey from Buenos Aires, the Department suggested that I consider Uruguay part of my assigned territory.

In a letter dated December 30, 1940, Mr. Cordell Hull conveyed the formal invitation to make the trip, on the travel provisions authorized by Government regulations—a per diem of five dollars aboard ship, and a per diem of six dollars during the stay abroad.

Much more inspiring were the paragraphs describing my duties, and the purpose for which Mr. Hull courteously hoped I would undertake the errand:

During your trip you may wish to consider giving a number of lectures dealing with the literary and musical life of the United States. I believe that these lectures and the personal relationships which may be established should do much to develop deeper comprehension of this country among the intellectual and cultural leaders of the nations visited. . . . I shall be gratified if you find it possible to accept this invitation for I believe the interchange of distinguished leaders among the American republics may prove a vital factor in assuring that community of interest which is essential to the safety and well-being of this hemisphere.

2

I should have preferred to go south in July, for the subtropical winter season, but the Department of State wanted its cultural ambassadors to get started as quickly as possible. Germany and Italy were busy in South America spreading distrust of England and the United States, which in our case was not difficult, since we had given cause for resentment, in Colombia and Panama and elsewhere; but now the moment approached when we could no longer afford to be unpopular. How bad the situation must have been, is indicated by the importance attached to the visits, at the last moment, of a few writers and scholars.

I wished to go later, partly because the opera and the theatres would then be at their height, but also because I needed time to recruit my finances. My long illness had been very costly, the financial crash and the depression of 1929 and the years following had long ago wiped out what wealth I had accumulated, and after my resignation from the Juilliard I depended entirely on royalties from books and earnings from magazine articles and stories. This income was sufficient if I wrote steadily, but it would cease when I started on my southern trip. I didn't like the idea of turning myself into a foreign correspondent; I wanted to meet people without creating the suspicion that I intended to write them up. And if I were asked to lecture, the question of a fee could not be raised; a representative of the Department of State must preserve his amateur status. Had I gone in July, it would have been easier for me, but as the international situation changed, July would have been too late.

I went to Washington, was introduced by Mr. Thomson to the Ambassador from Argentina and the Ambassador from Uruguay, and sailed from New York, May 9, 1941, on the *Brazil,* of the Moore-McCormack Lines.

There are few finer ocean trips than the three-week voyage from New York to Buenos Aires. Whatever strength my nervous system still needed, the salt air supplied; I could exercise my lame knee all day in the healing sunlight, or if I wished to be quiet, I could study Spanish, or talk with some extremely interesting fellow passengers. For example, there were a group of bankers and businessmen, bound for Montevideo; several of them were Yale graduates, with a broad-minded attitude toward professors, and they included me in their jolly parties, which occurred at least once a day.

There were two delightful ladies from Buenos Aires or its suburbs, Mrs. Doris L. Sneath, an Englishwoman whose husband was associated with one of the American businessmen; and Madame Jeanne Froment, of the central part of Buenos Aires, as French as Mrs. Sneath was English. They shared a table in the dining room, and furnished glamor to the parties of the businessmen. The Sneaths lived at Hurlingham, near the famous club.

Among the Brazilian and Argentine passengers, were many I should have been glad to know, but they held themselves aloof, with one welcome exception, Enrique de Gandía, historian and secretary of the National Academy of History. Learning that I was on board, he looked me

up, and for the remainder of the voyage, and during all my stay in
Argentina, he did more than any other of his compatriots to help me
understand his country and his people. Before the voyage was over, he
explained to me Argentine politics, and social traditions, and the merits
or defects of the various newspapers; he told me the best places to eat, to
buy books, the avenues on which conservative Argentina could be seen,
and those on which the younger generation displayed modern fashions
and practiced modern manners. His English was far better than my
Spanish, but usually we talked French. It was some time before I discovered his really outstanding quality, his devastating sense of the ridiculous. Under impeccable courtesy lurked a yearning to laugh at human
antics, and an uncanny instinct for uncovering whatever deserves to be
laughed at.

At Barbados I went ashore for a glimpse of the little island, picturesque
and poverty stricken. Afterward I grudged the waste of time. I had
brought with me on the boat a manuscript to finish, a short biography of
Mendelssohn which was to appear that autumn under the title *Song
Without Words*. At Rio, having feasted my eyes on the incomparable
harbor, I decided to stay on board and write while the ship was lying
still, but Gandía looked me up and rebuked my insanity, not to give Rio
at least a casual inspection on my first visit. We took a long walk and a
trolley ride, and perhaps I disappointed my friend by feeling that the
city, fine though it is, may always be an anticlimax after the fantastic
harbor, where nature outdoes Hollywood at its own game.

Gandía proposed some coffee, and we sat for a while at a sidewalk table
on the Rio Branca, famous avenue. Two remarks of Gandía's remain
with me; he said there were many excellent writers in Buenos Aires, but
two in particular I must surely meet, Enrique Larreta, and Eduardo
Mallea. Larreta he described as the dean of Argentine letters, a novelist,
critic, historian, who had served in diplomatic posts, and who represented
the older generation, well acquainted with Paris and Madrid and steeped
in French as well as Spanish culture. Mallea was much younger, still in
his thirties, but his cultural roots, like Larreta's, were in France and
Spain. He wrote novels and criticism, and he was literary editor of *La
Nación,* one of the two large papers in Buenos Aires.

When I asked if Mallea belonged to a more liberal group than Larreta,
he answered, "Simply in the sense that he is younger. A good artist of

any age is liberal." From which I concluded that Gandía was a conservative.

But I was struck by the evident fact that until the recent disturbances in Europe, South Americans, even in Brazil, had taken much of their training, certainly their literary culture, from Paris, since the output of France in all the arts had been more vigorous than that of Spain. But there must be many young people in Buenos Aires who had never seen the older and happier Paris. Intellectually, did they resemble the boys and girls of their own age in the United States?

The other remark of Gandía's which taught me much, was that North Americans and South Americans would always fail somewhat in mutual understanding unless each learned the other's history. "I have liked the United States ever since I began to read your history. If you will take the trouble to learn by what steps we have reached the point where we now are, and through what crises we have come, you will like us."

In the Buenos Aires Customs an attractive, friendly man was waiting for me, and with him a number of newspaper reporters and photographers. The man was Enrique Ewing, representative in Argentina of Henry Snyder, exporter of American books to South America. Ewing had therefore been for some time my literary agent in Argentina, and having learned of my coming, either from Snyder or from the Embassy, he constituted himself my guide, counsellor, and genuine benefactor. His name was Henry, of course, but he changed it to Enrique for the convenience of Spanish-speaking tongues. I remember him with Gandía for the unselfish thought they both gave to my happiness while I was in Argentina.

Ewing began by persuading the reporters and cameramen to go easy with me until I was settled in the Hotel Continental. Then he piloted me through the Customs and took me and my bags to the hotel, where our Embassy had not, as I hoped, reserved a room, but since Ewing was on cordial terms with the management, I soon had the accommodations I wanted. The rest of the morning and all the afternoon was occupied with interviews, no great mental strain, all the interviewers asking the same question, what errand brought me to Argentina, and my reply being invariably that I came to learn. Having been ignorant long enough, I now hoped to meet the people and see something of the country. They liked the answer, which fortunately was true, and in their newspapers they expanded and embroidered my words until I sounded like a benign and venerable sage.

At half-past nine I dined in a restaurant on the Avenida de Mayo, a handsome boulevard which suggests Paris—the same newspaper kiosks, the same cafés, the same old women selling papers or flowers, and the same damp coffee smell, particularly at night, when the mist is heavy. My dinner, with a pint of native wine, cost four and a half pesos, about $1.12. Gandía had told me to ask for a *lomo,* the tenderloin cut of beef which South Americans esteem more highly than a filet, and I applaud their judgment. The *lomo* I had that evening and at other times, whether at restaurants or hotels, was a cut three inches high, three wide, and four or five inches long—quite enough for a family, but as my waiter said, if they didn't serve the meat in large quantities, what could they do with it?

I must not get started on this subject! Argentina would have a higher opinion of our intelligence if we didn't build a tariff wall against the finest meat in the world, and pretend in excuse that it is of inferior quality. In Argentina a whole steer can be bought for the price we pay for a steak in New York. Today a *lomo,* of the size I have described, is bought in Buenos Aires eating places for a *peso,* slightly more or less as the market changes. The *peso* is worth about a quarter.

Good weather started me off on my Argentine visit—good weather and kind friends and a *lomo.*

3

Next day I lunched at the residence of the American Ambassador on the Avenida Alvear, a gorgeous palace, the kind in which Hollywood makes all rich Americans live, even to the monumental staircase. Mr. and Mrs. Norman Armour, most thoughtful of hosts, had asked a group of prominent literary folk to meet me—the President of the Argentine Authors' Society, several novelists, critics, editors—Victoria Ocampo, the moving spirit in the more conservative writing circles, a woman of culture and wealth—her friend María Rosa Oliver, perhaps more adventurous in her thinking, a brilliant talker. She spoke of the world situation at the moment, asked what part the United States would play in the war, and the question on all minds, what was to be the future relation between the United States and the other republics of the hemisphere.

I had some good talk with Eduardo Mallea, the novelist of whom Gandía had spoken, the literary editor of *La Nación,* and a collaborator with Victoria Ocampo in several literary reviews. He was a quiet man, thoughtful and somewhat reserved. Had I been able to speak Spanish I should have learned much from him. Enrique Larreta, whom Gandía had mentioned as the elder statesman of Argentina letters, was absent from the country, and did not return before I came home; it was the only disappointment of my visit, that I did not meet him.

After the lunch I drove back to the Hotel Continental with Harold Callender, correspondent for the New York *Times,* who the year before had reported from New Zealand, Australia and the East Indies, who at the moment was covering South America, and who after our entry into the war sent notable dispatches from North Africa and from Paris. Having watched his thorough methods of investigation and study, I couldn't be surprised at the name he has won in his profession.

The next day I went to the Chancellery and was introduced by Mr. Armour to James Gantlebein, the secretary who would explain what was expected of me as a cultural visitor. I had interpreted too literally the casual observation and leisurely meditation in one place, which the Department of State had stressed. Already a stream of lectures had been arranged for me in Buenos Aires, and another series in Montevideo. For some reason which I now forget, I was to visit Montevideo at once. On my return to Argentina, I was scheduled for a busy trip to Córdoba, for more lecturing at the venerable university. When I finished with Córdoba I should be free to give full attention to Buenos Aires, and if in transit I could touch any other places, I was welcome to do so.

The lectures were to deal with fiction, poetry, drama and music in the United States. Since my Spanish was inadequate, I was to speak in French, unless some English-speaking groups asked to hear me in a language I really knew. During my stay in Argentina and Urguay I spoke five or six times a week, with additional impromptu talks at hospitable dinners and lunches. I called on noted scholars, university officials, authors and musicians. Once I yielded to a request for some oratory at an exhibition of modern art, a subject I like to talk about, but the artists rarely care for what I say. In Buenos Aires I visited the motion picture studios, where Hollywood traditions seemed to be followed conscientiously; and in Montevideo I rose at six one morning to see the cattle raisers drive their herds to the open air market, where buyers from the packing houses ride around among the steers, look them over, and bid for them on the spot, a herd at a time.

4

From a much overcrowded schedule, certain incidents and persons stand out.

One morning in Buenos Aires I received a note from Miss Mary Cannon, who was doing some research in Argentina for the Women's Bureau of our Department of Labor. She wrote that a group of Argentine writers and journalists wanted to meet me, and she believed I would be interested to know them, since they were young, keen, and in the current of life. A few afternoons later she took me to a cocktail party given by one of them, Josefina Marpons, novelist. The others were Manuel Palacin, a novelist in politics; Fiorencio Escardo, a witty young doctor, baby specialist, also a novelist; Luis Rienadi of *Gráficas Noticias,* radical in his temperament, very attractive; Leon Bouché, editor of the important magazine *El Hogar,* to which most of the group contributed. Here was the younger generation I had wanted to meet, to balance the established and conservative writers I had met at Mr. Armour's. We talked till ten o'clock, then adjourned to a simple and excellent restaurant that recalled the Left Bank and the Latin Quarter. After good food and more good talk we drove along the River Plata, and I reached the hotel shortly before three o'clock. In an early issue of *El Hogar* I was astonished to see my portrait sketched in charcoal, with a clever write-up of the evening by Josefina Marpons.

Most of the group I saw again. They represent the true Argentina, open minded, creative and constructive in their thinking, fond of their traditions, but fettered by none of them.

In Montevideo I remember with special appreciation Mr. Eugene Millington Drake, British Minister to Uruguay, and Señor Alberto Guani, Uruguayan Minister of Foreign Affairs. Millington Drake made a point of attending my lectures, and in other ways giving my visit special emphasis and endorsement. He is remembered in Montevideo as a loyal and wise friend of our country at a difficult moment. When his lifelong friend Alejandro Shaw gave a reception for him in Buenos Aires, he had Mr. Shaw include me among the guests, so that I might know the Argentine Shaw, international financier and art connoisseur, and distant relative of George Bernard.

Señor Guani, at various times Minister of his country to Austria, to Belgium, to France and to Great Britain, and repeatedly delegate to the

League of Nations, is a ripe citizen of the world, if ever I met one. Our Embassy presented me to him in the usual etiquette; he came to one of my lectures at the University, and then suggested to the Embassy that he'd like a private talk with me.

There would be no point in trying to conceal the pleasure I had from this diplomatic compliment, nor the vividness with which I remember what Señor Guani said to me in his office in the old *Cabildo* or City Hall, on the Plaza Constitución, opposite the ancient Cathedral and quite near my hotel, the *Nogaro*. The Minister of Foreign Affairs was in his youth professor of literature at the University, and being quite a tease he put me through an oral examination on the books I had bought and read since coming to Montevideo. I had bought a dozen or more and had read them all, but my new professor told me they were without exception the wrong ones, popular at the moment but of small importance; of course I asked which were the right books, and he gave me a few titles, about which I now have some doubts. The bookseller who advised my original purchases wasn't so far wrong.

Then Señor Guani turned serious, and said that we all should study geography. Soon every country would be dealing with every other country, and it would be silly to think the map of the world was shrinking unless we knew what was on the map. Ignorance, he remarked, with Spanish sententiousness, is the worst form of distance. Then with a slow smile, "Admit that you have always thought the United States nearer to Europe than Uruguay. But Uruguay was present in the League of Nations, and the United States was not." Perhaps he was still teasing; certainly he was not strictly logical on this and other themes, but I felt I was listening to a great man, perhaps to one literary man pleading with another for more human understanding in a world which would have rough sledding before it came to a smooth road.

The day before I left Montevideo, I was asked what thing, of all I had not had time to see, I most had wished to see. My questioner was Dr. José Pedro Segundo, former Director of Secondary Education, one of the leaders in all cultural movements. The answer was easy; I wanted at least a glance inside the Teatro Solis, the famous house in which Patti had appeared, and many other immortals of music or the stage. During my brief stay the auditorium had been closed in preparation for an exhibition of paintings by Juan Manuel Blanés, whose portraits of Uruguayan notables and whose pictures of gaucho life had made him almost a national hero. Dr. Segundo thought he could arrange a peek inside the building, in spite of carpenters and picture-hangers, if I would meet him at the front door next morning, at ten o'clock. I was there on time, and so was Dr. Segundo, and so was Dr. Montero Bustamente, president of the *Comisión Nacional de Bellas Artes,* of which Dr. Segundo was a member. All the other members of the Commission were there too, and the workmen stopped their hammering and furniture-moving for an hour, so that these kindest of friends could show me Blanés paintings, important for themselves and for the history they record—could show me also every part of the delicious little theatre, an architectural gem.

.

5

Córdoba made me keenly aware of the South American contrast between carefully guarded tradition and extreme up-to-dateness. The Rector of the University asked me to lecture before faculty and students on the subject of "Music in American Schools"; he and his colleagues had heard of our school orchestras and bands and choruses, and he hoped to get the facts from me, without exaggeration. As I assembled facts and figures and typed out my speech, I wondered how I could convince my hearers that I wasn't stretching the truth. I told how many high schools we have, how many orchestras, how many symphonic concerts the students give, how many performances of oratorio, cantata or even opera; how the students are taught to play the instruments, what instruction is given in theory, music history and appreciation; what entrance credit is given for music in colleges and universities.

I lectured in one of the original classrooms; the ancient University has modern buildings and a fine equipment for its School of Medicine and its other branches of science, but I was speaking in an austere little hall where instruction had been given decades before Harvard College had been thought of. In the midst of my discourse I felt panicky; why should anyone in that audience understand or believe what I was saying? When I stopped, the applause was courteous and several professors shook my hand, but nobody gave an opinion of what I had said. The Rector walked with me to the street door, we said good afternoon to each other, and I started for my hotel.

Before I had gone far I heard my name, and turned to face three young men, students of the University, who had heard the lecture and wanted my advice about a music club they had organized. In my discouraged mood I felt I had had enough for one day, but I asked them to call on me next afternoon, which they did. Their club met weekly, wherever they could find a room large enough. The membership was over one hundred, and their dues paid for a phonograph and a considerable number of records. At their meetings they played a symphony or some other important work, one of their number first giving its history and explaining its significance.

I attended the meeting that week. The attendance was larger than usual, the interest in the program extraordinary, and the unaided effort of the young people, pathetic. None of them had serious training in music. Because the death of Paderewski had been reported the day before, the phonograph played his "Minuet" and his rendering of a Chopin mazurka, these pieces happening to be in the club library. The chairman then asked me to say something about Paderewski as pianist and composer, and since I had met him and could describe him personally, my remarks were well received.

At the end of my Córdoba visit I paid a farewell call on the Rector of the University. Not a syllable had I heard from him since my lecture, but I didn't care to leave without saying goodbye. To my surprise, he was delighted to see me. His office was full of men who no doubt had appointments with him, but he put them out and seated me beside him. "Ever since your lecture, the professors and I have been talking about music education. Since I am by profession an engineer, I know nothing of the subject, but you made us realize its importance. Let me ask you one question—is it not very expensive?" I told him it was, but in the United States our school budgets had become used to the burden gradually over a number of years.

"We must act quickly," he said. "There is much to do. I have already put into my annual report to the Government at Buenos Aires a request for a department of Music here at the University, with the necessary equipment."

I told him of the music club I had attended, and he spoke sympathetically of these and other students for whom opportunities in music were not yet provided in school or university. We parted in the best of spirits, I with the hope that my lecture hadn't been a total failure.

6

Rupert Sneath brought to me in Buenos Aires an invitation to speak at the Hurlingham Club one evening at a get-together party for English and Americans. The famous club, from which so many splendid polo teams come north or visit Europe to trounce all competitors, is distinguished by the best of English traits, good sense. Polo, golf, cricket, and tennis are expensive games, needing beautiful grounds superbly kept up; the clubhouse at Hurlingham is simplicity incarnate, all the money going into the essentials, the playing fields. On the night of the party the house was crowded, there was a plain supper with cafeteria self-service, and the guests gathered in a large room for my speech. Mr. Horace Hale, a grand Englishman, very English, an Oxford blue, introduced me. At the end of my talk I stepped off the low, improvised platform, forgetting that my right leg would be stiff from standing so long. By good luck I didn't fall, but a pleasant-faced man in the audience came up and asked, in a quiet voice, "How did you hurt your shoulder?" I said my leg had suffered in an automobile accident, but my shoulder was all right. He pulled a card from his pocketbook.

"I've enjoyed the talk— Let me thank you by fixing the shoulder. That's my name and address."

Before I left the clubhouse I learned that he was Martin Sherwood, who specialized in mending or adjusting the bones of polo players after a fall from their horse. When I went to his office he showed me without delay that in the Michigan automobile accident I must have jammed a bone in my right shoulder so that it pressed down on some arteries and nerves. After he had manipulated the bone with an electric massage, and lifted it back into correct position, the circulation to the base of the brain was somewhat restored, and I had better control of the damaged right arm and leg. He told me to walk back to the hotel, a mile away, and to return next day. I walked with more freedom than had been possible since the accident. His treatments started me on the way to recovery; when I returned to New York, or some little time later, I found that Harold J. Reilly in his Health Service had the knowledge and all the equipment for treating similar cases in Martin Sherwood's way. That I can now walk long distances, or dance, or play the piano again, I owe to these two men. Perhaps the greatest profit I had from my South American trip was the correct diagnosis of my shoulder which Sherwood's quick eye made at the Hurlingham Club.

7

When I went to Buenos Aires Norman Armour, the Ambassador, welcomed me as I have told, but he was soon called back to the United States on some business, and I was left in the kind hands, more than kind, of Pinkney Tuck, Edward Maffitt, and James Gantlebein. Mr. and Mrs. Tuck, delightful cosmopolitans, gave me many happy hours. Edward Maffitt, who after my return to Buenos Aires from Montevideo shouldered the responsibility of looking after me, was married to a girl who had his own youthful spirit and—he would wish me to say it—even better looks. At their home I met interesting people whom otherwise I might have missed. Maffitt advised me, always wisely, in the smallest details, and when he and his wife, with the Gantlebeins and the Tucks, came on the *Brazil* for a farewell drinking of healths just before I sailed for home, I wondered how many travelers appreciate the unselfish devotion of our consular and diplomatic service. I realized it first in Buenos Aires and Montevideo.

In the latter city, Selden Chapin, First Secretary of the Embassy, was Chargé d'Affaires. He was a remarkably accomplished and well-trained young man, having started his career at Annapolis, intending some day to be an admiral. Even before he transferred to the diplomatic service he must have had a remarkable education, not only in books and sciences but in human nature. His wife had a social genius which supplemented in a happy way his strong qualities.

His second in command was Reginald Bragonier, my special guardian. Bragonier, like Maffitt, was a Yale graduate, in spite of his youth a man of rich culture. He must have had always a gift for friendship and for human understanding. Through him I met Dr. Segundo. He went with me on my last morning in Montevideo to look at the Solis Theatre. Through him also I met Dr. Zamora, noted physician, and particularly fascinating to me because he had much of the psychological genius, even of the personal appearance, of my old friend and colleague Carl Friedberg, the pianist.

On the homeward voyage I had for ship companion Barnett Miller, Professor of History at Wellesley College. In our years of graduate study we had been fellow students in Professor Trent's seminar. But I had become used to meeting myself and my yesterdays in Argentina. It had been a joy to meet again Stanley Alchin, the President of the American Chamber of Commerce, but really more deserving of fame as one of the boys in the first freshman class I ever taught at Amherst, in 1903.

At the Hurlingham Club, I met Manuel Alonso, international tennis player, engineer by profession. Mr. and Mrs. Alonso returned on the *Brazil* with me. I count them now among my dear friends, and we never meet without talking of the relations between our country and Argentina, and what can be done to bring the two republics closer.

CHAPTER XLIV

The University of Miami

I

IN THE spring of 1939, Walter Scott Mason, Director of the Winter Institute of Literature at the University of Miami, invited me to lecture for a week. The so-called Institute was an extension of the University's activities into the public lecture field. The other speakers that year were Philip Wylie, John B. Kennedy, Leonard Liebling, Dorothy Canfield Fisher, and Charles Francis Coe.

Two lecturers gave the program each week, my teammate being Philip Wylie. I spoke Monday afternoon, Tuesday evening, Wednesday evening, Thursday afternoon, and Friday evening.

The following year, in the spring of 1940, the invitation was repeated, and I spoke again for a week. My fellow lecturers were Carleton Smith, Henry Seidel Canby, Audrey Wurdermann, and Joseph Auslander. On this visit to the University I saw a good deal of Bowman Foster Ashe, the President, who evidently was in doubt whether the Winter Institute was rendering all the service it could. I had my own opinion, and when he asked me for it, I answered with considerable enthusiasm. This was before my visit to South America, but I told Dr. Ashe that the location of his university at one of the gateways between North and South America made it essential, I thought, that the public lectures of the Institute, as well as certain of the other courses, should offer something which Northerners going south, or South Americans coming north, would be glad to hear. I had enjoyed taking part in the Institute, but I couldn't believe that popular lectures should be all the University offered to the Institute audience.

In the summer of 1944, Hervey Allen, one of the Trustees of the University of Miami, wrote me that the Winter Institute would now have a new title and expanded scope. It was to be the Institute of Arts and Sciences. He hoped it would present a program suitable both to University students and to thoughtful people in general. It was to be administered by a committee, himself, Professor Virgil Barker, and Professor Charles Doren Tharp. The Committee invited me to become what he called Resident Director of the Institute. I was to preside over all its public meetings; more important, I was to secure the speakers, and I was to take such part as I chose in planning and giving supplementary or related courses for undergraduate students.

I spent two happy spring seasons at Miami trying to formulate and to carry out an educational project which would be an answer to a remarkable opportunity. The University, after an almost fatal financial setback at the beginning of its career, had struggled desperately to survive, and was at last headed toward prosperity when the war broke and set it back again. But war or no war, in the spring of 1945 it showed plenty of vitality, and under Dr. Ashe's courageous leadership I had no doubt it would develop into a great institution. I wanted it to be an inter-American university.

Its handicaps were serious enough. Though it had plenty of land, it had little money. Though Dr. Ashe had cajoled a rather unusual faculty to work with him at Coral Gables for large hopes and small salaries, the war called many of them away. There had always been a tendency, which I think he should have discouraged, to waste his best scholars in administrative jobs. The University had, and has, no library to speak of, and until proper buildings at last go up, no place for more books even if they were given. Classrooms and residence halls, adequate scientific equipment, were all lacking, yet the spirit of the place was so courageous and cheerful, and in one or two departments such astounding results had been attained, that I had faith in the place. The University orchestra, organized and trained originally by one of the best musicians in the country, Arnold Volpe, had already reached such a point of excellence when I first visited the University, that it was considered the premier musical organization of greater Miami, and supplied the city with all its symphonic programs.

For the two seasons of my directorship I secured the speakers after consulting with my colleagues at Coral Gables. For the season of 1945 the visiting lecturers were Clarence Stein, architect and city planner, who lectured to the public and talked to the students about "The Form of Future Cities"; Harlow Shapley, Director of Harvard College Observatory, whose subject was "The Expanding Universe"; Warder Clyde Allee, zoologist and biologist of Chicago University, whose subject was "Man— Animal and Human Being"; and Carlos Davila, journalist and ex-President of Chile, who spoke on "The New Era in a Post-War World."

The students who attended the public lectures and the smaller discussion groups were required to do special reading and to write papers, which I corrected and discussed with them.

At the Winter Institute of 1946 the lecturers were Edward C. Carter, Secretary-General of the Institute of Pacific Relations, who spoke on "The United States, the U.S.S.R., and the Pacific Area"; Samuel K. Allison, of Chicago University, who spoke on "Nuclear Energy in War and Peace"; and Robert Moses, whose subject was "Faith Without Works: Footnotes on Municipal Planning."

Since the University has no adequate lecture hall, the large meetings of the Institute were held in the auditorium of Miami High School, where the acoustics are abominable and the seats uncomfortable. In spite of these handicaps, the attendance was fairly good. In the smaller discussion groups the registration increased steadily from the first year to the second, and throughout the spring season of the second. But I was disappointed that we could make no progress toward an offering which would attract South Americans or would educate North Americans to a better understanding of Central America and South America. To tell the truth, Miami University wanted to be as provincial and as insular as any other small school. Perhaps it wanted to grow in physical size but not in its ideas. It had a fine orchestra, less fine since Mr. Volpe's death but still very good; it had a notably fine football team. I began to fear that only the best of the faculty wanted anything more, and they of course could get more, in the overcrowded condition just now of all colleges and universities, by leaving Miami for a post elsewhere at a higher salary.

Before I came away, after the 1946 Institute, I told my friends I felt it useless to return unless the Institute could be developed, which would be impossible without a proper hall for the large lecture audiences, an adequate library, and a place to keep the books in. I knew that a building program of some sort was contemplated, and in time, no doubt, it will be achieved. If I am still alive, I shall give three cheers. But I reserve the right to keep on regretting that I hadn't the ability to commit the University to an educational program above the mediocre.

Perhaps any university in southern Florida would be handicapped by the enervating climate, and by the presence in the neighborhood of so many wealthy people enjoying their vacations. The atmosphere is far from intellectual.

During the Winter Institute of 1946 neither the President nor any of the Trustees except Virgil Barker, member of the Institute committee, attended a single lecture by our distinguished visitors, or met them in private. They were all too busy. The University was about to confer an honorary degree on Winston Churchill, who was vacationing in the neighborhood. The ceremonies were held on the football field. The oratory was diffused by loud speakers. The faculty were colorful in caps and gowns, the student audience and their friends numbered somewhat over twenty thousand. The weather was ideal. After the ceremony the Trustees entertained Mr. Churchill and several hundred other guests at the Surf Club. Such window dressing the University had not had before; whether it will try to put on such a show again, who knows? For the rest of the term the institution was flat on its back. I was reminded of the legendary Mississippi steamboat which had so large a whistle and so small a boiler that when the whistle blew the engine stopped.

Early in 1946, Hervey Allen told me that because of other responsibilities, he had severed all connection with the Institute. In June, Virgil Barker wrote me that because of changed circumstances affecting the Winter Institute, Dr. Ashe had asked Dr. Tharp and himself to plan and conduct the one to be held in 1947. Since I probably had some plans or ideas for the next Institute, Dr. Barker suggested that I pass them on to him and Tharp.

All of which is quite normal in human relations. I do not doubt that the new manipulators of the Institute program will provide something acceptable to their clients. I enjoyed having a part in bringing to the Institute some men who loom large in our day, scholars, scientists, and public servants. I should rather have had Winston Churchill as one of the Institute lecturers than as the recipient of an honorary degree.

2

After the Winter Institute of 1945 I gave a lecture at the University of Florida, Gainesville, and the next season a week of lectures. The President of this State university is John J. Tigert, my well-remembered associate in Army education after the First World War. Now as then, Dr. Tigert is primarily an educator, and something of his own dynamic convictions has got into the atmosphere of his really remarkable institution. Though Gainesville is far from the southern coast and might feel out of touch with South America, the State University has established courses which attract South Americans, and other courses which seem to me well de-signed to give Northerners a sympathetic understanding of the peoples across the Caribbean. Strange that such training should be offered inland, at the northern end of the state, rather than at the southern gateway, but the main thing is that the opportunities should exist at all, and that we should know where they are.

CHAPTER XLV

Another War

I

AFTER my return from South America in 1941, I went to Hollywood on a lecturing and writing errand. On Sunday, December 7, I was listening to the broadcast of the "Metropolitan Opera Auditions," when the program was interrupted by the news that the Japanese had attacked Pearl Harbor. I was too old for this war, and not in good enough physical shape; my son Graham went. I wrote much, chiefly pleas for France, when some of her friends despaired of her.

In the other war I had been spared the debates which went on at home. Nearer the front the issues are clearer, and in spite of the battles there is more peace. Now when I wasn't worrying about my boy in Italy, I was reading in the papers or hearing over the radio the well-intended absurdities of people in public office, prophesying or pontificating about the course of the war and the future after the war. From what mystic springs was so much wisdom drawn? I listened humbly to the tirades addressed to me and all citizens by hitherto obscure persons now in the employ of some Government bureau, who scolded us, the common folk, for not taking the war seriously.

They weren't talking about the war, not really; they were rallying us to the support of Franklin D. Roosevelt, now that some of us were not sure just where Mr. Roosevelt was leading, and feared he wasn't sure either. For two terms I had given him an almost sentimental admiration. I still think his place in history will rest upon those years, when he articulated for his countrymen principles of liberalism which the majority were hungry to hear. That is reason enough for his fame; much of what followed can be forgotten and forgiven. But after Pearl Harbor, when Winston Churchill told our Congress that the real war was in Europe, and we should not be diverted prematurely to a war against Japan, I began to lose faith in our President. Mr. Churchill seemed to tell the American people that their duty was first to help England win her European war, and afterward England would show us how to polish off the Japs. So far as I could see, Mr. Roosevelt did not protest. I wondered if by some strange shift the liberal temper, the youthful courage, had surrendered the leadership to conservative prudence. I could but notice that some clauses in the Atlantic Charter, like "with due respect for existing obligations," seemed to guarantee a *status quo* in the postwar world. Mr. Churchill was reporting to a conservative constituency, Mr. Roosevelt to an extremely liberal one. How could they really agree. Where would we end if we took orders, and stopped thinking for ourselves?

2

Wendell Willkie was a friend of mine, a true patriot, a sincere democrat, a lover of his kind. He was no politician, as his enemies were happy to observe; the childlike directness of his nature was for some of us at least a temporary ray of hope at the moment when an overendowment of political shrewdness was bartering away the Democratic Party and lowering the tone of political morals. It was Wendell Willkie, not Franklin Roosevelt, who won men everywhere to the ideal of a world democracy; the dream, coming from his honest lips, sounded possible.

During the campaign, Wendell dined at my home one evening to meet a group of men, prominent and influential, who were not sure whether they would vote for him. I thought if they met him, they would. It would be difficult to put a man in a more awkward position, but his frankness and naturalness were amazing. Obviously his faith in the democratic ideal, as American democracy used to define itself, was complete; he believed it his duty, as a candidate, to show himself exactly as he was. When asked what he thought should be done in certain circumstances, he gave the answer if he had it, or he admitted his mind on that point was not yet made up. But somehow he gave the impression that if he had the opportunity, he would grow into the stature of any necessary leadership; difficulties would give him strength. That evening, and on other occasions, I was impressed by what was undeveloped in him; even his boyishness of manner, which at times seemed to indicate immaturity, was a sign also of character reserves as yet untapped. When he returned from his world travels, just before the end, I thought that all he had seen, and all the people he had met, had contributed to an astounding growth.

After his defeat in the election, he went away for a short vacation, and the first evening on his return to New York he dined with me again. Some of the guests had been present at the earlier dinner, and two or three took him to task for the strategy of his campaign. Roy Howard was angry with him for having told the reporters that afternoon that he would give his support to President Roosevelt till the end of the war, at every point where he and the President had the same democratic ideals. Roy protested that such a policy would never build up a strong opposition, and an opposition was what this country needed. Wendell said he was not interested in building up opposition; he wanted to do what he could to spread a few ideals which all of us must follow if the world is to get out of the bog in which civilization is mired.

I am afraid some of his hearers gave him up, then and there, as a possible David to overthrow the Goliath of the extreme liberalism which they discerned on the horizon.

3

It happened that during the war years I traveled much through the United States, necessary travel, all of it, and usually in hard conditions, on overcrowded trains where it was luxury to find even a seat in the day coach, and sometimes a dreary part of the night would be spent standing up. Soldiers and sailors had the right of way, and they filled the cars to overflowing, but never once did I see on their part any irritation or lack of good humor. Some few of them must have been at some time out of temper, but they didn't show it; in fact, their high spirits often cheered the civilian traveler and set an example of courtesy. I don't mean that I remember the armed services as wearing wings; they were much like the boys I had known in the other war—perhaps with higher animal spirits and a capacity for more subtle forms of mischief. But I shall always think of them in this Second World War as having the qualities any country could wish in its men. Like many another citizen, I looked forward to the end of the struggle when the demobilized soldiers and sailors would take a hand in the peacetime duties of citizenship; if their impulses then were as they had been on many a hot train ride, quite a number of bad political blots might be cleaned up.

4

Usually when a group of boys traveled together they played cards or they sang. If a woman in the car had a crying baby, they usually borrowed it, to see what mass entertainment could do. Perhaps the fondness of soldiers and sailors for babies is a phenomenon in all wars, but I gathered from what I saw in this one that our population would shortly increase by leaps and bounds.

Because I am fond of music I should be glad to testify, if I could, that the singing I heard in trains was excellent. It was not. It had no other merit than energy and good will. On one train a sailor enthralled us by a shrill, continuous solo on a mouth organ. I enjoyed it as much as the rest of the audience, but like them, for other than musical reasons. A number of wrist watches were timing him, and bets were made on how long he could keep it up.

If a soldier or sailor traveled alone, in a surprising number of cases he read a book. I got the impression that most of the armed services carried in their luggage at least one book, sometimes a work of fiction, but more often a textbook of science, or a history of some country not our own. One boy, a sailor, told me he never read a book for pleasure and of his own volition until he had to spend monotonous days on a warship in the Pacific, and the ship's library, as he said, kept him from going nuts.

The book he was reading dealt with the correct methods of bookkeeping and accounting. I asked if he intended to be an accountant.

"Hell, no! Not if what it says here is true."

Then why was he studying the book?

"I just got started out of curiosity—hearing so much about that business. But I don't think it's for me."

I asked how soon he would be going back to his ship.

"In another week now."

For a moment I had been worrying about the ship's library, but I don't believe the sailor kept the manual of accounting as a souvenir.

CHAPTER XLVI

A New Life

I

WHEN I began this story of many years and many friendships, I thought I should recognize the end when I came to it, but now as I write these words, life for me, as for others, is beginning again. In spite of the troubles which harass the world, I feel more hope, more vision, all around me than ever before. The miseries of mankind are appalling, but one advantage, or one penalty, of having read much in the long and doubtful record of mankind, is the resulting conviction that such miseries were always present, though never before did they touch so many consciences.

My reading suggests cheerful thoughts about the enormous burdens which still press and will continue to fall upon us in the United States. We must set our own house in order, we must see to it that the children of all of us have a fair chance, and we must pay our bills, some hundreds of billions, incurred for the general good, not simply for our own. The nations who were our allies, as well as those which were our enemies, are all more or less in the condition which in private life is called bankruptcy. They turn to us to stake them. Americans respond with different emotions to these wholesale invitations to hand over a few billions more. Some of us complain that we have become the target of international panhandling; others point out that the wounded pride of those who ask help turns quickly to bitterness against us, to sharp envy that the luck is all on the American side. But no matter what our comment, we do give the aid so far as we can. I think the other nations are right in envying us our luck. We in the United States are just now the luckiest people in the world. We have the privilege of underwriting an entire civilization.

For decency's sake, to save the other nations from at least some embarrassment, what aid we have given and must still give is called lease-lend, or a loan, or whatever compliments the borrower with the implication that of course when he is on his feet again he will pay us back. But few thoughtful people expect such incredible sums to be repaid in cash. If they could be, I believe we Americans should not want them to be. For us there is a better kind of repayment—repayment in power. Our Yankee philosopher, Emerson, who in his day was rated by English critics as a superficial thinker, even a charlatan, once said that all debts are paid. The inexorable law of compensation permits no debtor to escape. He who borrows and cannot repay in cash, repays in loss of credit and loss of self-esteem; and the lender is repaid in the respect of his fellows, respect whether they love him or not, in his influence in the community, and in an increase of his own faith and courage. If our country can stake all the others simultaneously and not blow up in the effort, then our republic will be the most powerful on earth, all the more powerful if no one repays us a cent, and if we remain solvent, like our fathers before us, only by plain hard work.

It is good to watch the returning G.I.'s crowding the schools and colleges along with the still younger Americans who did not have to fight. In the war effort the country has become aware of undeveloped privileges and powers. I believe we are on the way to train ourselves for a wise and skillful use of a unique opportunity. We can afford to put up with any amount of carping and criticism, since we know what overtaxed nerves and what natural envy inspires it.

Happy in the condition of my country, I am happy in my own life as my years rapidly increase. My boy is safe home after a strenuous and honorable service; my daughter, Anna, now Mrs. Russel Crouse, becomes a good writer, to my delight. Her main business, however, is building her home and adoring her husband, who is one of my admirations too. On July 3, 1945, Helen Worden and I were married in Albuquerque, New Mexico. Since we both are fond of the West, we talk of spending much time there—also in Mexico and in South America. I am not ready to settle down yet. But in my stationary moments I enjoy my small book-filled apartment in New York, where I made the best of lonely years. Helen's books, added to mine, would make me feel that I was living in a library if Helen didn't give me reason to feel still more that I live now in a delicious home.

For ten weeks during the last two autumns some optimistic friends have gathered in the book-lined living room to hear me lecture on current publications dealing with international understanding or misunderstanding, or on great literary masterpieces which acquire fresh meaning in the crises of our days. Florence Kimball and Marie Doro thought of the idea one Sunday afternoon in Hollywood. They imparted it to Mrs. Charles Mitchell and Mrs. Anne Benkard. These four assembled the others of the class—a class, I must say, of an astounding I.Q.

From time to time Helen and I greet in our home a small but precious circle of friends who for years have contributed to our happiness, and whom I must list here, among the persons I shall always remember— Howard and Dorothy Cole, Manuel and Ginetta Alonso, Bob Holt, Hattie Bell Johnston, Walter and Margaret Damrosch, Ernest Hutcheson, Leon and Ethel Freeman, Carlos Davila, Olga Samaroff, Judge Philip McCook, Fannie Hurst, the Felix Gouléds, Leonebel Jacobs, Mabel Comstock, Roy and Peg Howard, Bill and Margaret Hawkins, Oliver Gogarty, Edward Johnson, Florence and Schuyler Smith, Theodore and Ruth Steinway, Julia Steinway, Kurt and Helen Wolff, George and Irene Hellman, Charles and Elizabeth Mitchell, André and Simone Maurois, George and Arlene Bye, Edward Waterman, Melville and Florence Cane.

Helen and I love to write, and the clatter of our machines is for us a kind of music. My damaged fingers are now well enough for me to play the piano again, as from time to time I do, since Helen likes that music also. As authors we can feel no rivalry since our methods differ, she being, as I think, a genius at reporting, and I being compelled by temperament now as always to get at the facts of life through my loves and prejudices.

I don't like to put an end to this book. Writing it has been great fun, and there is much more I want to say. I'd like to speak about my career as an educator, in more detail than I have found room for here. I could add many pages to what I have suggested of my experience in music, and of my adventures as a writer, and if I live another year I won't promise not to begin all over again.

Index